# P.S.

The Autobiography of Paul Simon

# P.S.

The Autobiography of Paul Simon

**Bonus Books, Inc.**
Chicago, Illinois

**Library of Congress Cataloguing in Publication Data**

Simon, Paul, 1928–
    P.S.: The autobiography of Paul Simon / Paul Simon. 1st ed.

ISBN 1-56625-112-5


Bonus Books, Inc.
160 East Illinois Street
Chicago, IL  60611

*First Edition*

*Printed in the United States of America*

# Contents

*Dedicated to*
*Reilly, CJ, Brennan, and Nick*

*Our Grandchildren*

# *Introduction*

Modesty is not a virtue of those of us who hold — or have held — public office. Modesty is not a virtue of those who write autobiographies. This book then is a product of immodesty compounded.

When Aaron Cohodes, my publisher, asked me some years ago to do this I declined. But when he renewed his offer after my retirement from public office I accepted, because I have had the chance to deal with a great variety of issues over my lifetime, and as a student of history I know that we can learn from the experiences of others.

I am grateful to many for reviewing this manuscript, including my wife Jeanne, our children Sheila and Martin, and my brother Art. Marilyn Lingle had to struggle with my typing and scribbled notes to produce the copy for the publisher. Others who have helped either by reviewing the manuscript or helping in some other way include Jeletta Brant, Gene Callahan, Kevin Coleman, Karen Drickamer, James Fox, Terra Golembiewski, Nicole Hayes, James Holloway, Mike Lawrence, Charles Nicodemus, Brian Rutzen, Cheryl Schnirring, Robert Shireman, Jerry Sinclair, Judy Wagner, and Steve Zidek.

Any mistakes are mine, not theirs.

No one in life succeeds by himself or herself. What is true of life is true of a book. For the many not mentioned who have enriched my life and indirectly enriched this book, I am grateful.

— Paul Simon

# Chapter 1

# *The Early Years*

Perhaps being born the year before the Great Depression of 1929 made me fiscally conservative, and the misery faced by so many people made me socially liberal.

I was born November 19, 1928, in Eugene, Oregon. My parents had just returned from being Lutheran missionaries in China. Years later I would tell Chinese-American audiences that I was "made in China" and also that no other member of the United States Senate grew up playing mah-jongg, a Chinese game. My parents returned to the United States after a mini-theological controversy in the midst of the civil war there. My father accepted what Lutherans refer to as "a call" from Grace Lutheran Church in Eugene to serve as its pastor. The theory of the call is that the voting members of the congregation assembled (then only men), after prayer and deliberation, issue an invitation to serve that has a combination of human and divine factors. Then the person receiving that invitation prayerfully determines whether or not to accept the call.

My father grew up on a dairy farm in Wisconsin, near Bonduel, about thirty-five miles west of Green Bay. His parents would probably be characterized today as lower middle class economically. My Grandfather Traugott (meaning "trust God") Simon, like most Americans in the latter part of the nineteenth century had agricultural roots, and he married a Lutheran parochial school teacher, Eleanor Elbert. Early photos show a man with almost movie star good looks and an attractive young woman. Eleanor knew tragedy early. Born in Courtland, Minnesota, in 1871, a few years after the Civil War, her mother's first fiancé died of smallpox, and a sister of my grandmother lived only three months. Large families were common, and death visited them frequently in the days of primitive medicine. Like many others in this Germanic community, the Elberts spoke German and English. The family moved every few years, to Milwaukee, then to Budsin, near Crystal Lake in Wisconsin, on to Salters in Jackson township. At Salters the Lutheran congregation offered the teacher housing, five acres to farm, and $350 a year. Before they left Salters the Elbert family had ten living children. Eleanor's brother Paul graduated from college and took a teaching position at a parochial school in Bonduel, Wisconsin. The school needed a teacher for the primary grades and in 1896 Eleanor accepted her brother's invitation to become that instructor. She had sixty pupils in her class that first year! Most teachers then did not graduate from nor even attend college. An indication of the future social conscience of the family was a letter Eleanor wrote to her family about the mother of two of her pupils who died eight days after giving birth. The new mother had purchased material to make a dress for each of the two older girls, and my grandmother sewed the dresses for them. A small thing, but a portent of a sensitivity that she would transfer to her own family later.

In a letter to her home my grandmother describes Bonduel, but could be describing almost any small Wisconsin town of that period: "There is a public school, and a cheese factory where they make good brick and cheddar cheese. A man by the name of Bachmann manages the factory. A shoe, boot and rubber store is run by A. Boettcher. Theodore Meyer owns the Bonduel Roller Mills. He saws lumber, shingles, and such things. Then there is the hotel called the Midland House, owned by H. C. Zuehlke. There is a blacksmith, harness maker, and milliner, two hardware stores, saloons and other places. I forgot the dry goods store. It is owned by Christ Bonnin. . . . He sells furniture, coffins and other articles besides groceries. . . . When farmers want to sell cows or pigs, they have to load them on a lumber wagon or drive them on foot to Seymour, Cecil, or another town. If the day is hot, animals sometimes die on the way or soon after."[1]

Then she added an important note: She met Traugott Simon in the church choir, the native son of one of the settlers of Bonduel. Soon she wrote to her family: "Traugott took me home again last night. . . . You must have guessed it by now, Traugott and I DO love each other. He walks all the way from his farm near Zachow, which is six miles, to come and see me." His father bought him 200 acres of timbered land which he gradually cleared and seeded. His father also gave him one cow. A year-and-a-half older than Eleanor, he married her in July 1899 in Melrose Park, Illinois, where Eleanor's family now lived.

My grandparents kept careful records of their earnings and expenditures. In January 1902 they had income of $50.05; from churning butter (75¢), sale of sheep ($10.70), potatoes ($15.79), beef ($12.65), and clover seed ($10.16). Their expenses that month were $6.67 more than their income, but that included a tax bill of $23.80. The items purchased included two books, a magazine, and a newspaper, presumably subscriptions to the last two. Two months later, however, they had income of $121.77 and expenses of only $10. Income included $84 from the sale of logs, $11.95 from raccoon pelts, and 49¢ from the sale of butter and eggs. For the year 1902 — three years after their marriage — they had income of $532.14 and expenses of $504.84. That did not allow luxurious living, but eggs sold for twelve cents a dozen, for example, and my grandparents did not want for essentials. Much of the food they ate grew on their farm. They spent less than five dollars a month for groceries.

The year of my father's birth, 1903, they bought two geese for one dollar each and a horse, because of the death of another horse, for twenty-five dollars. The hide from the horse that died sold for two dollars.

My grandfather was a good farmer but not an outstanding farmer. His greatest skills were working with wood. To build a new barn, he cut down the trees, sawed them into logs, and erected the barn with the help of friends and neighbors. I have a creative wooden lock which he made to put on that barn, a well-designed and well-crafted piece of work.

Holding the family together fell to the lot of my grandmother. Theirs was a partnership marriage when such things generally did not prevail. Running the farm and seeing that the family had food and shelter fell into his domain, but decisions about rearing and religion became hers, though both shared each responsibility. When my grandfather sometimes charged items purchased at the hardware store, it upset my grandmother, the more frugal of the two.

My grandparents were largely of German extraction, though family historians point out that some of the territory in which my ancestors lived crossed over into Denmark and Poland, as borders changed from time to time. But they lived in predominantly Germanic communities in the United States, and even though they were one or more generations from their European roots, they adapted to the language of their community. Services at the Lutheran church they attended were conducted in German and English, with more people worshiping at the German service. At that point in our nation's history we had a much higher percentage of citizens with a mother

tongue other than English than is the case today, though you would
hardly guess it from some of the alarmist literature that now is distributed.

My grandparents' second child, Martin, my father, arrived on
February 16, 1903. They paid the midwife two dollars. My grandparents wanted him to become a Lutheran pastor and that meshed with
his wishes from early childhood on.

My grandparents had nine children. The oldest, Gertrude, later
became a medical missionary in China, and then Hong Kong. A
dynamic person who worked particularly among tubercular patients,
she had a large high school in Hong Kong named for her following
her death. The other eight children contributed significantly in various ways, three of the boys becoming ministers. The youngest,
Henry, became a district president of our branch of the Lutheran
church, the equivalent of a bishop in the larger branch of
Lutherandom or the same title in the Roman Catholic Church or the
Methodist Church. Probably because he was the youngest, ten years
older than I am and nearer to my age, I felt closer to him than to my
other aunts and uncles of my father's family. To accommodate nine
children the small house my grandfather built had to be replaced by a
much larger ten-room home.

When my father had barely reached the age of two, my grandmother's younger sister died in childbirth, a none-too-rare occurrence
in the period.

My grandfather gradually shifted more and more of his agricultural emphasis to dairy cows, and the family helped with milking. All
the children knew how to milk before attending school. Their childhood involved work on the farm, and long walks to school in a rural
community almost totally free of crime, though my grandfather's
brother, William Simon, did place a classified ad in the *Bonduel Times*:
"Whoever took my four fine hams out of the smoke house, please
bring them back so I can finish smoking them." There is no record of
a response.

At the age of eleven my father wrote a letter to his Elbert grandparents and noted: "Our storekeeper's wife, Mrs. Bramschreiber,
encourages Mamma to charge her groceries, but Mamma won't. She
says they have to be paid sometime anyhow." My grandmother made
dresses for the young girls in the family out of larger dresses given her
by relatives. And though the family struggled financially, there are no
oral or recorded recollections of anyone ever going without a meal, an
advantage of living on a farm. Canning fruits and beets and cucum-
bers when they ripened also helped during the winter months.

My father's sister Clara recalled: "In winter we rode the sleigh to church every Sunday. On Saturday afternoons Pappa and the older children lifted the large wooden, topless box onto the sleigh and laid the boards across for us to sit on. When it was colder than usual, we sat on horse blankets or quilts. Then Mother would heat the bricks and flat irons to help keep our feet warm. We had a beautiful team of grey and white mottled work horses. When everyone was dressed in their church clothes, Pappa hitched the harnessed horses to the wagon. . . . Off we went, gliding over the snow. This was especially thrilling on Christmas Eve when the stars were out and everything was covered with snow."

I visited my grandparents at their Wisconsin farm at the age of three, and I can remember nothing about them or the visit, other than the porch that circled their large house on which I enjoyed running. When my brother and I were nine and eleven my grandparents visited our Oregon home, a gift from their children for a fortieth wedding anniversary. I recall it as a warm, marvelous visit. The sense of humor of my grandfather impressed us, perhaps exhibited more to grandchildren than others. My father's youngest brother, Henry, does not remember that great sense of humor. Years later I picked up the *St. Louis Post-Dispatch* and saw an Associated Press picture of my grandmother, then in her late seventies or early eighties, translating books into braille, a voluntary effort on her part. After leaving college I visited my grandparents a few times, but they were getting feeble. My grandfather enjoyed playing his fiddle but his memory had faded. We have a picture of them with my daughter as an infant, their oldest great-grandchild. As a boy I would correspond occasionally with my grandmother, and even though I did not see that much of either grandparent, they were an important presence in my life.

The branch of the Lutheran Church called the Missouri Synod had prep schools covering the high school years for those who wished to enter the ministry. At the age of thirteen my father left home for Concordia in Milwaukee for that purpose. During his third year there, almost half the family income went to pay for his education. The combination of education and religion was a high priority for my grandparents.

After finishing at the Milwaukee school, he attended Concordia Seminary in St. Louis. I do not recall my father ever telling me anything particularly eventful about his academic studies, though from conversations with others it is clear he had above average abilities.

My five-foot four-inch father played on his high school basketball team but could not make the seminary team. However, he attended games and at one he attended on January 22, 1926, he met Ruth Troemel, who attended the game with one of her friends, Alice Schoenhoss. My father took Ruth and Alice home — Ruth first — and then he asked Alice for Ruth's telephone number. The next day, a Saturday, he called and asked her to attend a concert with him that evening. Sunday, he visited at her home, and six months later they became engaged. A graduate of a two-year high school program, my mother worked for Ralston-Purina in St. Louis, eventually keeping track of time cards of employees in the building in which she worked. Though she worked there only a short time, they promoted her quickly.

My mother's childhood did not have the same idyllic caste that my father's had. Born in the vicinity of Fort Dodge, Iowa, she is listed as having the family name of Ainsworth (presumably English by background) but shortly after birth went to a Lutheran orphanage, and a Lutheran pastor there took her, and probably other children, to St. Louis for adoption. Herman Julius Tolzman, an accountant who became known by his middle name, and his wife Sophia adopted my mother. Sophia became seriously ill and died when my mother was three. During the latter part of her illness, she asked her sister Amelia Troemel and her husband Gustav to take care of my mother. The only memory my mother has of Sophia, the mother who adopted her, is of the funeral. Two years later Sophia's husband Julius died. "I was seriously ill with whooping cough," my mother relates. "My father would come to visit me every day. He suddenly stopped coming and I was told he had died." Years later she learned he committed suicide. At the age of five my mother had lost both parents. The Troemels had six older children, and suddenly having a seventh and much younger child did not bring great joy to the parents, particularly Amelia. Gustav ran a small bakery on the south side of St. Louis, and spent long hours there. Amelia repeatedly let my mother know that she "didn't belong to us" and that she was unwanted — several times a week as my mother recalls — and while Gustav cared for her, the older children in the family who also treated her with kindness had either left home by that time or soon would. All of this resulted in an unhappy childhood for my mother that left its emotional scars.

The relatives of my mother to whom we were closest — emotionally and geographically — were her step-sister (never called that) Emma, her husband Rudy and their children and our cousins Vicky, Leah, and Carlos. They lived in Oregon City, about 100 miles from Eugene. The nearest Simon relatives — Ernest and Irene (Simon) Andres, and my cousins Dorothy, Eldon, and Arnold — lived near Woodburn, Oregon, where they farmed. We visited them frequently.

One thing that still bothers my mother, who is ninety-one as I write this, is that she first learned of her adoption from my father, just prior to their marriage. The home in which she grew up did not mention it, probably out of the best of motivations. The jolt she felt when my father told her lives with her yet. My father discovered it going through the legal papers necessary for marriage and assumed she knew.

The engagement of my parents coincided with my father's graduation from the seminary. On September 8, 1926, they married. Three days later they boarded a train for San Francisco, had a brief honeymoon there, and then boarded a freighter that took a limited number of passengers, and spent the next twenty-three days on the sea voyage to China where my father had "accepted the call" to do missionary work. They landed in Shanghai and took a river boat up the Yangtze River — more than 1,200 miles, a scenic but slow venture. On New Year's Day of 1927 my father wrote from Wanhsien, Szechwan, China, to his family in Wisconsin: "The past year has been by far the most eventful in our young lives. Last year I was studying Greek — this year, Chinese. Then conveniences — now few, anywhere we go. Then I only casually considered going to a foreign country. Then I did not even have a steady girlfriend — now I am married. . . . Then I was a carefree individual — now I am four-fold happier." Then he added on a more serious note: "I still do not pray nearly as often and as earnestly as I ought to and would like to. . . . We are really in the midst of wars and rumors of wars. . . . All China seems to be full of soldiers, but a person becomes accustomed to them as he does to the dogs that bark at you from most houses. Yang Sen [apparently in charge of this part of China] sent Ruth and me a Christmas greeting. He is a fine General." However, my father looked with less than complete favor on the general's having five wives.

About a year and three months after arriving, my father preached his first sermon in Chinese. But as he progressed in his knowledge of the language and the culture, the civil war in China heated up, and my father became engaged in a controversy within the missionary community known as "the term question" — what Chinese word should be used to refer to God. The Lutheran missionaries in China voted 11-2, siding with my father in favor of a distinctive Chinese word for God that differed from a more generic term that people used for a variety of forms of worship. But a senior missionary who differed with the majority appealed to the mission board in the United States, and that board agreed with him and issued an order that missionaries in China had to use the generic term which the large majority opposed. The issue inflamed passions and caused people of conscience on both sides to write lengthy discourses. My father felt crushed by what today appears to be an arbitrary decision by a board thousands of miles away that did not understand the issue. Years later my father told me that he still believed that he held the correct position, but that he could have been more diplomatic in handling the matter.

The combination of the doctrinal dispute over the Chinese term to use, and the civil war, caused my parents to return to the United States. Probably also a factor: They soon would become parents. Missionaries with small children or who soon would have them received priority in leaving, even though both sides in the civil war generally respected the fact that people from other nations were non-participants. My parents came back with the expectation that they soon would return to China.

My father filled a temporary pastoral vacancy at Grace Lutheran Church in Eugene, Oregon. About a month after my parents moved there, on November 29, 1928, my mother gave birth to me. Two years later the only other member of the family, my brother Arthur, arrived.

It gradually became clear that my parents would not be able to return to China because of the unsettled situation there, and my father accepted the permanent pastorate of the church. Prior to my parents coming to Eugene, a small band of twenty-five Lutherans purchased the building from the Church of the Brethren, an edifice with a beautiful all-wood interior. The church had a tall tower, so tall that when there were strong winds the building shook. A member in those days, Ken Brauner, recalls that during evening services he and other young people would sit in the balcony and when storms hit "the whole balcony would pitch and sway, creak and groan, as though it would come crashing down at any moment." In a 100-mile-an-hour windstorm in 1962, it did.[2] When we had cool weather, my father got up at five on Sunday mornings and started the wood furnace in the church. Men volunteered with their shovels to dig a basement under the church, and how beautiful that basement looked to me when finished. I remember the church as being huge, and to a child it was, but since then I have seen pictures of it and I realize that when my parents came home after a Sunday service attended by more than 100 people, that excited them — and filled the church. Our lives revolved around the church and its activities.

Our closest friends were church members: the Sullivans, the Libkes, the Zinikers, and others. And when we bought groceries, we bought from Mr. Gieseke. (First names were used much less frequently then even by reasonably close friends.) His cash-and-carry store offered the advantage that it was neither cash nor carry. We charged our grocery bill, as most people had to, and Mr. Gieseke often delivered to our door, sometimes selling cosmetic Rawleigh products in the process (Rawleigh being a somewhat primitive predecessor of today's Avon products). I also recall the Metropolitan Life Insurance salesman who stopped at our home once a month to collect twenty-five cents on an insurance policy my parents had.

Behind the church on Ferry Street in Eugene stood the parsonage, where we lived. The frame building had six small rooms for living and a large kitchen, all above a ground-level dirt-floor basement. The basement held jars of fruit and vegetables my mother canned, and sizable quantities of wood that we used for both the kitchen cooking stove, which also heated that room, and a stove in the middle of the house that served as our main source of warmth. The wooden floors had linoleum covering that showed considerable wear. I vividly remember years later in another home when we had our first rug, which seemed an almost unbelievable luxury to me.

These were depression years. My father earned $62.50 a month as pastor, and during the fruits and vegetable harvest my mother worked at the local cannery, the Eugene Fruitgrowers Association. They paid her on the basis of food processed, not hours. My mother, always nimble with her fingers, whether typing or working in the cannery, helped our family finances considerably. My parents made a good team. My father had a good business sense — or he could not have been successful in his later publishing venture — but he sometimes would be inclined to be more idealistic and more generous than our family finances warranted. My mother had a slightly more pragmatic streak on some of these things, helping to preserve our family's economic integrity in difficult times.

Our family was more fortunate than many, but out-of-work relatives stayed with us frequently, and in those days homeless men referred to as "tramps" or "bums" would come around asking for food, and we always provided some. My mother thought they had some type of mark on our house, letting others know that they could get free food from us. (Years later, the senior Mayor Richard Daley of

Chicago told me his mother said the same thing and his family also always helped.)

My parents did well enough financially that my father could study part-time at the University of Oregon in Eugene, completing work for a doctorate.

We lived in a very different culture then. No television, but listening to the radio stretched our creative juices and we could clearly visualize the people in the Lone Ranger or Gang Busters. By the time I entered high school I listened every Saturday night to the *Lucky Strike Hit Parade* to discover the ten most popular tunes in the nation that week. Small stores had hard round balls of gum called jawbreakers that we bought for a penny. All stores had Blackjack gum. Candy bars sold for either a penny or a nickel and gasoline cost 18 cents a gallon. If *Parents Magazine* said a movie was fit for children, my parents allowed us to attend on a Saturday afternoon — once a month until we reached the age of ten and then once every two weeks. Laurel and Hardy and Tom Mix had great appeal, and the State theater in Eugene had a hole in the screen where an irate viewer had thrown an obstacle at a villain. Without my parents' permission, I saw an aging former boxing champion, Joe Louis, spar a few demonstration rounds.

Kindergarten did not exist in Eugene or most of the nation. My first four years of education were at Washington Grade School — and the local public library which I haunted. I shall always be grateful to those who made that library possible.

More difficult economic circumstances than some students faced did not present problems for me. Several students in grade school dressed better than I did, but it did not seem to bother me — though I remember it, so I guess it did bother me a little. I also remember things that most young people in our country have not experienced, like my mother putting socks over a small wooden device to patch holes with carefully crafted thread work. Every sliver of soap had to be saved and then placed in a small metal device that my mother would shake in a pan of water to make suds for washing dishes. It still bothers me to walk away from a motel or hotel room and leave a fairly large piece of soap. Art and I had baths every Saturday night. We slept in a double bed with metal spokes at the head, the important middle spoke dividing our territory. If either of us crossed into the other's territory during the night we became vocal about it.

On a rare special day we would stop at Christensen's Dairy Store and get an ice cream cone. And visiting my uncle and aunt, Rudy and Emma Messerli, in Oregon City, I ate strawberry shortcake for the first time, an exotic taste that lingers with me yet.

Many church members farmed. We visited farms frequently, and in the pre-Rural Electric Administration about half of them did not have electricity. Every farm had a few cows and after milking we turned a crank on a separator to divide the cream from the milk. It took two of us children to haul a milk can to the edge of the road where the "creamery" truck — for some reason never referred to as a dairy — picked up the can or cans. No refrigeration. I have often wondered how many people got sick on that milk. We then referred to undulant fever, a rarity today but common then and known as "milk fever." Life on a farm today is dramatically different and better — and safer for those of us who consume food.

My brother Art and I learned to work from early childhood on, for which I am grateful to my parents. We had certain duties in the house, like drying the dishes, but no allowance. However, every year my father planted a garden in our back yard, and for each can we filled with stones and glass from the garden, we received one penny. Starting in about the fifth grade we also worked for farms in the area, jobs we could then legally get from the Employment Service. I picked string beans and cherries, weeded rows of beets and carrots (hard on your back!), all of it paid by the pounds of beans or cherries, or the number of rows weeded. We did not earn much, but we learned the value of money and hard work. Later my father started printing religious material with equipment we had in a converted garage in back of our home. Art and I put in one hour a day there, and three hours on Saturday, as part of our responsibility to the family. For any hours we worked more than that we received fifteen cents an hour.

During his earlier years, Art had health problems, none of a major nature but sometimes he did not appear to be as robust as he should have been. He had a particularly bad case of whooping cough (still a major killer of children in the developing world), and a form of typhoid fever, as well as other minor ailments. At one point our family physician incorrectly thought he had leukemia, the impact of which I did not understand other than that that diagnosis upset my mother. But he gradually outgrew his health problems, and when he became the star pitcher on our grade school softball team I took special pleasure in cheering him on.

Neither of us had great skills athletically, but we enjoyed playing. My father built a backboard against the side of our garage and we played basketball between ourselves and with friends. Both Art and I wore glasses from the early grades on, and that primitive basketball court accounted for several occasions when we broke them, not a source of pleasure to our parents. I also vividly remember when an older high school student, Ernie Danner, was playing softball with Art and me and two of our friends. One of his classmates rode by on a bicycle and shouted to Ernie, "What are you doing, playing with those little kids?" Ernie Danner responded with words that gave us great pride, "These kids can play better than you can." Art and I followed athletic scores and the sports pages faithfully, particularly anything to do with the University of Oregon. Besides encouraging my reading skills and giving me good exercise, following sports later played a role in getting me my first newspaper job.

My father had a creative streak, and would do things most parish pastors did not. Periodically he would have an African American minister from California, Rev. Marmaduke Carter, speak in our church. He stayed in our home when he came, probably in part because our church could barely pay his train fare to Eugene, and not any hotel bill. He slept in the double bed my brother and I ordinarily slept in, and we would fight for the honor to sleep with him — an honor I am sure he would have appreciated not having! But we learned lessons of race relations from our earliest childhood days.

My father also started branch Sunday Schools, including two in mill towns more accustomed to hearing religious terms in profanity than in worship.

When he tried to get some children's religious literature which the church could give to those attending Sunday School, he discovered none existed, and so he started writing and publishing a little four-page paper printed on newsprint called *The Children's Hour*. Russell Evans, a Christian Scientist, assisted him in this endeavor by providing a low printing price. I remember particularly vividly that Russell Evans's Valley Printing Company had as its neighbor the Rose Bud Bakery, the aroma of which tantalized me. Occasionally my brother and I would persuade our parents to buy something at the bakery, making a trip to what seemed to us like a dull printing plant worth the effort. My father started this publication for his own church but interest spread, and when he had a circulation of 11,500 he decided to leave the parish ministry and devote himself full time to his publication. I should have made that word plural, publication*s*. He also started a monthly magazine for parents called *The Christian Parent*. That had reached a circulation of 2,500.

My parents bought a home on West 26th Street, two blocks outside of the city limits of Eugene, which had a population of 23,000. They put an addition on the garage, put a concrete floor in part of it, purchased printing equipment with a loan, and my father became a full-time publisher and editor. My mother took care of the book work and Art and I learned to operate the printing equipment.

The new house seemed large, though pictures show it to be anything but that. But Art and I now had space for separate beds in our bedroom. I remember little else about the room except that I had a picture of General Douglas MacArthur and his corn-cob pipe hanging over my bed during the years of World War II. The house had shingle siding and a steep roof on a fairly narrow lot, but my father bought four adjacent lots for ten dollars each. That gave the two of us and our friends plenty of room to play.

The move to 26$^{th}$ Street brought other momentous changes in our lives. We got an oil heating stove, so that we no longer had to pile the wood in the basement, and bring it up frequently for a stove that seemed to burn mountains of wood. Not only was it cleaner and less work, the oil stove could be set to provide a constant level of heat. What an incredible improvement! I felt we were living in luxury. To add even further to our new standard of living, the old kitchen stove, which had a seemingly insatiable appetite for wood that Art and I had to chop, had as a replacement a smaller, cleaner modern marvel: an electric stove.

But moving outside the city limits meant that Art and I would have to attend a rural school. We protested vigorously. We called the Dunn School we were slated to attend the Dumb School. It had several grades to a room and we assumed that would stunt our intellectual growth immeasurably. But our protestations went for naught when my father checked and found that we would have to pay steep tuition to attend the city schools. Walking a mile and a quarter to school did not please us either. However, once we started, much to our surprise, academically this rural school was ahead of the city school we had attended. Within a few days we made friends and settled in comfortably.

Two of my years there I had a remarkably fine teacher, Mrs. John Rodgers. She made learning fun and exciting. One of the great advantages of such a rural school came when as a fourth grader I had finished my work; I could listen to her instruct the fifth graders and the sixth graders in the same room. One day she sent a note to my parents saying that if they liked the idea, I could move from the fourth grade to the fifth grade, which I did. She stretched us. In 1940 she had us debate before the PTA, "Should Franklin Roosevelt Be Elected to a Third Term?" I am pleased that she lived long enough so that I could tell her how much her teaching meant to me.

One of those in my grade at Dunn School became a friend for life,

Donald Schmieding. Don's father operated the Midgley Planing Mill in Eugene that Don eventually took over. A businessman with an unusually sensitive social conscience, he has quietly contributed much to the Eugene area over the years. And when I first ran for the Senate in 1984, Don and his wife Sylvia donated three months to come to Illinois and campaign for me — no small contribution!

One of the families who lived about a mile-and-a-half from us, and sent their children to the same grade school, was the Wayne Morse family. He became dean of the law school and later a United States Senator, a genuine maverick who served in the Senate as a Republican, then an independent, and later a Democrat. In the third grade his daughter Nancy had a crush on Art, to Art's embarrassment. At that age his interest in girls had not developed. I occasionally saw Wayne Morse after I entered politics, and then my wife Jeanne and I had a chance to visit with his widow a few times. I did not serve with him in Congress and did not get to know him well. But years later when I received the Wayne Morse Award for Courage in Government, it had special significance for me.

Around the time we moved, our family finances improved enough so that we started taking family vacations, piling blankets and clothes into the old 1929 Model A Ford, driving through the wooded hills about ninety miles to Munsel Lake, near Florence, Oregon. Munsel Lake's position about two miles inland from the Pacific Ocean meant less strong wind and a great place for a small family. The word "motel" had not entered our lexicon, and we stayed in a cabin at the isolated lake and enjoyed swimming, boating, climbing on sand dunes, and paying a daily visit to the mighty ocean, sometimes fishing. We prepared all our own meals; I don't remember ever going to a restaurant there.

The least pleasant time of my early years were the first three years of high school. As I mentioned in telling of my father, Missouri Synod Lutherans had a system of pre-seminary high schools. My parents wanted my brother and me to become ministers, and so when I graduated from eighth grade at Dunn School the family assumed I would go to Concordia in Portland, a residential high school designed for those with ministerial ambitions.

Concordia had only twenty-two students, all male. Because of my November 29 birthday, and because I had skipped a grade, I started high school at the age of twelve. Those who were juniors and seniors could inflict hazing on freshmen and sophomores, everything from being hit by a paddle as many times as an upperclassman wanted to running errands to the nearby grocery and drug store. Some of the freshmen had upperclassmen as roommates, who seemed to get great pleasure in paddling and inflicting rather painful requirements on the freshmen. I resolved that when I became a junior I would never do that, and I didn't, my non-participation causing some resentment on the part of a few of the other juniors and seniors.

Academically the school excelled. I had Latin, Greek, German, and a high school curriculum exposure superior to that given most secondary school students. The four-person faculty afforded me an opportunity to grow intellectually, for which I am grateful. Because the school enrolled so few students, I managed to be on the basketball and baseball teams, though even with such a small enrollment I barely made them. I served as the sixth man on the basketball team, the first substitute, and managed to get enough time to earn a letter; and in baseball I played second base, where I fielded reasonably well but had a breathtaking batting average of .115. I enjoyed sports, but no college scholarships came my way!

Of the twenty-two at the school, some intended to become ministers and a few were assigned there by the courts as an alternative to going to the state reformatory. Distinguishing between the two types of students sometimes did not come easily. I recall one student, who became a pastor, who slipped down to the local burlesque show every Saturday. At that point in my life I found that more revolting than I do today, having now seen more of life and the deficiencies of all human beings, including myself.

*Life* magazine in that period would have a picture or two of a semi-nude woman about every third week, and the Concordia principal would take ink and cover the picture. We would hold the page up to the light to catch the details, and if that didn't work, there would be a mass exodus to the drug store two blocks away, where we could look up the picture in the stand that contained magazines for sale. At that point our culture did not tolerate magazines like *Playboy* or *Penthouse*.

The language of the students, in terms of profanity and telling "dirty jokes," was much like the language of my Army basic training unit years later. I regret to say I took on all of these bad habits, wanting to be part of the crowd. That continued until my junior year, when a student named Don Brandon transferred from a public high school and did not use profanity and tell off-color jokes. Don later became a professor at the University of San Francisco. His conduct so impressed me that I quit the bad speech habits then and have never gone back to them. It makes me no more virtuous than anyone else, but it illustrates the power of example. Years later political columnist

Robert Novak asked me whether I ever swear, and I told him, "Only when I read your column."

I am sure I tried the patience of the small faculty. My report cards indicate deportment was not a strong suit for me, at one point noting that another student and I played football outside without our shirts on, a violation of campus rules. Deportment problems in high schools today are a little more serious!

In those days young people hitchhiked in relative safety. I frequently hitchhiked on weekends between Portland and Eugene — about 120 miles — something that amazes me now since I started at the school at the age of twelve and my parents exercised caution about so many things. During my college years and during my Army time, I did the same. In all those years, only twice do I recall being picked up by drivers who had too much to drink, but otherwise I never had a problem. Hitchhiking provided cheap transportation and a chance to meet interesting people.

Most weekends I went home, but one Saturday and Sunday sandwiched between Thanksgiving and Christmas vacations I stayed in Portland, and I remember it because of what happened that Sunday. I attended services at Trinity Lutheran Church, perhaps one mile from the school. As two friends and I walked back to Concordia, we noted excitement among people along the way. We asked what had happened, and they told us that the Japanese had bombed Pearl Harbor. I had no idea about the location of Pearl Harbor, but I knew from the conversation that it was a U. S. base, and that meant war. My friends and I went to the home of the principal, F. W. J. Sylwester, and my classmate Bob Sylwester, for Sunday dinner and the silent group listened to the radio — no television then — getting much of the initial information from an eloquent national radio preacher, Dr. Walter A. Maier, who totally changed his Sunday sermon because of Pearl Harbor. After the initial shock, most Americans felt that it would take only a short time to respond to the attack and defeat Japan. The war monopolized conversation and resulted in an immediate and overwhelming sense of coming together as a nation, but few people I knew or listened to had any idea how long and costly the war would be.

Not just at this school, but generally, people had nicknames attached to themselves more frequently than today. When I read the obituaries in my local newspaper in southern Illinois where I now live, it is much more common for older people — men particularly — to have nicknames than the younger people who die. But sometimes the nicknames were cruel. One student at Concordia with a long nose and a receding chin had the nickname "Mole". Some were worse. Why I did not become more sensitive to that at the time I cannot explain.

After three years of that boarding school I knew I did not want to become a minister. My guess is that if I had not gone to this pre-seminary school, I might have entered the ministry. But I persuaded my parents to let me return to school in Eugene, where I graduated from Eugene High School. There I had two outstanding teachers, Juliette Gibson, who taught journalism and served as adviser to the school paper on which I served as sports editor, and Golda Wickham, an English teacher. Both took a real interest in students. Miss Gibson, as we always called her, had the bark of an army sergeant, and would not have won any personality contests, but she demanded quality in our work, and we learned, whether we wanted to or not. Mrs. Wickham had a more outgoing personality but did not hesitate to give us sizable assignments, and made everything from Chaucer to Shakespeare come alive. She later became Dean of Women at the University of Oregon.

We had some uncommonly fine student leaders at Eugene High School. Warren Webster, our student body president, followed his father into becoming a Baptist minister, and James Luckey, head of the men's student organization, eventually headed a museum in Hawaii. That relatively small high school in a few years graduated Neal Goldschmidt, who became Governor of Oregon and the Secretary of Transportation for the nation; Cecil Andrus, later Governor of Idaho and U. S. Secretary of the Interior; and this future U. S. Senator.

We attended high school in a different era. I think I knew what went on there, but I never heard of anyone using drugs. When a few male students really wanted to have "a wild time," we would sneak into the woods somewhere and drink a little beer, the taste of which I have always hated. But I drank a little on one occasion when I was in high school, a sort of testing of emerging manhood. (Years later, while serving in the Army in Germany, when German families automatically placed a stein of beer in front of me I drank a little to be polite. A distorted sense of taste that makes people like beer or green peppers is beyond my comprehension.)

When I reached the grand old age of fifteen in 1944, I served as a substitute mail carrier for the Eugene Post Office. It faced serious personnel shortages. World War II drew men away from civilian jobs, and in those days not only were women not used as mail carriers, I never heard anyone even mention the possibility in all the discussion of shortages. I did learn that a substitute carrier gets the hilliest route, where the more economically fortunate live, who subscribe to heavy magazines and various book clubs. When I regularly finished my mail route ahead of others, two of the older carriers pulled me aside and urged me to take more time on my route, pointing out that I would make more money, since they paid me by the hour. The unspoken but obvious other part of their consideration was that I made them look bad coming in earlier from a tougher route. I sympathized with the fact that they did not have the eagerness of a fifteen-year-old, and if I had been carrying mail for as long as they had, I might be doing it more slowly also. I managed to find some things to do in the morning before sorting my mail, helping clean up the post office, and leaving for my deliveries a little later, and then getting back a little later.

One small thing happened while I delivered mail. I occasionally saw a beautiful grey, bushy cat in making my rounds, and one day I saw the cat pounce on a robin, and walk away with the squealing robin in its mouth. That bothered me for several days, and is still vivid in my mind. Life is not always as you would like it to be.

The summer before my post office job I worked as a stock boy at J. C. Penney's, my first job outside of working on fruits and vegetables on area farms. My first job with a regular pay check!

After graduation from high school I had the good fortune to land a part-time job writing sports for the *Eugene Register-Guard* under the tutelage of a genuinely fine journalist, Dick Strite, the sports editor. He assigned me to make up the sports page or pages each day, pull the copy off the wire and determine what stories should run, write headings, and cover minor events that occurred in the area, including the circus of Saturday night wrestling, which we treated as genuine, even though we knew it was more show than athletic event. Occasionally Dick let me write a sports column, and I would earn a few dollars now and then serving as a "stringer," phoning in sports news to L. H. Gregory at the *Oregonian* in Portland. Dick Strite wrote good stories, and expected the same of me. He also had the affliction of most journalists in that day, a love of whiskey and smoking. His top right-hand drawer had a fifth of whiskey in it, which he made clear I should not touch. Years after I left the *Register-Guard* I stopped back there to see Dick. He had survived a heart attack and I asked him whether he planned to follow his physician's orders. "Hell no," he said, showing me a package of cigarettes.

William Tugman, editor of the paper and father of a boyhood

friend of mine, Tom Tugman, occasionally assigned non-sports feature stories to me. Those stories would not win any journalistic prize,
but they helped to teach me writing. The only way to learn how to
play tennis is to play tennis, and the only way to learn how to write is
to write! Bill Tugman later played a key role in getting Wayne Morse
elected to the United States Senate. After retiring as editor of the
*Register-Guard* he moved to Reedsport, Oregon, and took over a
weekly newspaper.

My job writing sports gave me an excuse to buy a used car, and
used it was. A 1934 Ford, it showed every sign of wear, but despite the
torn upholstery and substantial oil consumption, it gave me transportation. A University of Oregon star halfback, Jake Leicht, made it
to the East-West Shrine game in San Francisco, then perhaps the
biggest football end-of-the-season event outside of the Rose Bowl. I
got a press pass and a few dollars from the *Register-Guard* to cover it,
and started for San Francisco with Art and my classmate Don
Schmieding. We still had gas rationing, and good tires were rare. We
had enough coupons to get there on gas, and had to buy one miserable used tire. Forty miles south of Eugene we ran into a flood and
after going through high water our brakes did not work for a short
period. Crossing the Golden Gate Bridge we heard something rat-
tling and cars passing us — which most of them did — pointed to the
bottom of our car. But we couldn't stop on the bridge. We discovered
nothing more serious than a dangling tailpipe. We made it both ways,
a great adventure.

I sensed that my destiny would be in journalism, and though my
experience involved sports coverage, I had an interest in politics from
my early years. My father took me at the age of eight to hear Eleanor
Roosevelt speak. I listened with fascination to the radio broadcast of
the Republican convention that nominated Alf Landon in 1936. My
father's political roots were in Wisconsin with the LaFollette
Progressives. He met "Old Bob" LaFollette once, and to his dying day
believed that the two greatest Americans who ever lived were
Abraham Lincoln and "Old Bob" LaFollette. Because the LaFollettes
eventually became Republicans, my father considered himself one
also. Oregon Republicans have a progressive streak (Charles McNary
served in the Senate from Oregon then, with Wayne Morse, Robert
Packwood, and Mark Hatfield later representing the same tradition).
But despite considering himself a Republican, I can remember the

Roosevelt sticker on our Model A Ford. And Dad took an interest in issues, occasionally writing letters to the editor that stirred mini-controversies, such as his letter to the editor defending the right of retail clerks to strike. Race relations interested my parents — today it would be called civil rights — and probably because of their concerns, I went through the most moving book I ever read, *Black Boy* by Richard Wright. An autobiographical story, it did not reach the recognition of another of his books, *Native Son*, but it hit me at the right time and moved me deeply.

When we moved outside the city limits, only a few homes lined the street on which we lived, but building stopped at our place. From there we had open fields in which we could run, have neighborhood softball games, and occasionally see pheasants take off. Pheasants in a field usually do not move until a person comes right up to them, and when we roamed through the fields the sudden flapping and take-off of the big birds frightened us. About a city block from our home, across an open field, the only local radio station, KORE, had its facilities. My father gave guest sermons on the station occasionally and one caused a controversy. In February 1942, President Franklin Roosevelt ordered 120,000 Japanese Americans living in California, Oregon and Washington, none of whom had committed a crime, from their homes. They had from one to three days to sell all of their property and put all their possessions into one suitcase before the federal government sent them to camps in Idaho and other inland states. This happened two months after the start of World War II and the Japanese bombing of Pearl Harbor. Patriotic fervor gripped all of us. My father, who usually avoided any political references in his sermons, somehow worked in an objection to how our government treated the Japanese Americans. My mother believes that he also sent a letter to the editor on this, but I do not remember that. I recall a few hate phone calls and hostile comments from friends. I remember standing in front of a cutter in the printshop in back of our house while my father explained to Art and me why what the President did was wrong. But my father's actions embarrassed me. Thirteen at the time, I did not appreciate the pointed remarks, half-joking and half-serious, from my friends. I wished he had not done it. But it taught me an important lesson I have never forgotten: If you believe something, stand up, regardless of the opposition. In retrospect, I wonder where were those who should have stood firmly for the rights of their fellow Americans? Where was the American Bar Association? Where were the other members of the clergy? The State of Washington branch of the American Civil Liberties Union immediately objected, but the national ACLU moved more slowly. One of the ironies of the situation is that one of the few public officials to protest the action, while the President had it under consideration, was J. Edgar Hoover, head of the Federal Bureau of Investigation, whose later record showed considerably less sensitivity to civil liberties. While the action of our government cannot be compared to Hitler's Holocaust, it is illustrative of the reality that the passion of a nation can be aroused against a minority if leadership is irresponsible. My father's actions are a source of pride to me today, but the situation that developed then is a reminder of how badly public officials can go astray in an emotional situation. There need to be restraining voices defending the rights of minorities or those expressing unpopular views.

---

[1] Clara Simon Stuewer, "Lorchen," 1979 — a manuscript by my aunt about my grandmother. Several of the quotations and other information in this chapter are from the same source. My uncle, Henry Simon, also supplied helpful material.

[2] From anniversary booklet of the church, November 1955.

# Chapter 2

# *The College Years*

My father's publishing endeavors grew, and mailing the printed materials from the west coast to all parts of the nation meant that sometimes they arrived late for Sunday Schools, or for parents who used the daily devotions in the magazine. Although our family loved Oregon, my parents decided to move to the Midwest. After a look at many locations, they settled on Highland, Illinois, then a community of 5,000, thirty-five miles east of St. Louis. My father signed a contract to build a small brick plant across the street from an old brewery in Highland.

Getting the family from Oregon to Illinois presented a problem. Our seventeen-year-old Model A Ford (a source of embarrassment to me on dates) did not have the life remaining in it to make a trek across the mountains to the Midwest. During World War II manufacturers made no new cars, and local dealers had long lists of people who wanted them when they became available after the war. We had our name on a list but we remained near the bottom. Our neighbors and close friends across the street, Norman and Beryl Pohll, had a new 1946 Plymouth, the envy of the neighborhood. When they learned of our plight, they offered to sell us their Plymouth at cost, take our old Model A, and then take our spot on the waiting list. At that point people paid sizable sums to get a car from someone higher on the lists, but the Pohlls refused to take an extra dime. Their act of generosity I shall never forget.

Because of my birthday, and skipping one year of grade school, I started college at the age of sixteen, my initial year being at the University of Oregon. Since I worked thirty to thirty-five hours a week at the *Register-Guard*, my plunge into college had limited impact on me, with the exception that I had as my faculty advisor a small, quiet, shy man, the dean of the school of journalism, George Turnbull. He took an interest in me, encouraged my writing, and his gentle admonitions meant a great deal.

But because of my work schedule I took part in no extra-curricular activities at the University of Oregon, and my educational enrichment was not as great as my later college years would be. Partly because of my experience, I have always favored enough aid for students in the form of grants and loans so that if they want to go to school full-time they can, and are not forced into the work/school combination that may diminish their college experience. "I worked my way through college" has a good ring to it, but is not necessarily a good thing.

When my parents told Art and me about the move, I first decided to stay in Oregon and finish my college years there, but the tug of the family and the excitement of moving to a new area prevailed. I transferred to Dana College in Blair, Nebraska, a small liberal arts college of Lutheran and Danish background. Unlike my first-year college experience, I did not work (except for a few hours each week in the college canteen and for the summer months) and found my years at Dana more exhilarating in every way. I had some outstanding teachers, particularly Elmer Rasmussen, who taught psychology; Paul Nyholm, religion; and Marie Tucker. Miss Tucker taught zoology, which I took to fill out my science requirements. My interests in the scientific field were minimal. I took her zoology course intending to get my credits but not expend any great effort. However, Miss Tucker made us work, and much to my surprise I not only learned, but I enjoyed it, a tribute to what a superior teacher can do.

Because of the location of the University of Oregon in Eugene, I commuted from my home. That, and my newspaper job, relieved my parents of financing my first year of college. But at Dana I stayed in a dormitory, and found the daily bull sessions enriching. The ethnic (with one exception) and geographical diversity of the student body I found stimulating. The Lutheran and Danish and Nebraska-Iowa presence were matched by people like Ben Limjoco from the Philippines; Sam "Socko" Kachichian from Racine, Wisconsin; Norman Bansen from California; Lloyd Neve from Minnesota, and others. We had lengthy discussions well into the morning hours, primarily focused on politics, religion, and women. The idea of male and female students staying in the same dormitory had reached no campus in the nation during my years at Dana, 1946–1948.

A day or two after arriving I had a date with Eunice Petersen, the only date I had with her but it became significant for my college and cultural life because she persuaded me I should try out for the Dana College Choir. I did and I made it. I loved it. As a boy I took three years of piano lessons, under duress. My mother had hopes that Art and I could become at least musically superior. Our cousins—Carlos, Leah, and Victoria Messerli—displayed exceptional musical talent, and she expected at least the same from us. But in vain! I can still remember that piano teacher hitting my knuckles with a pencil when I struck the wrong notes. Art and I finally persuaded my father that taking more lessons did not make sense, and he gently worked on my mother. However, she did take us to concerts frequently, and as boys we heard Jose Iturbi, Fritz Kreisler, Lanny Ross, Gladys Swarthout, Nelson Eddy, the Don Cossack Choir, the Hall Johnson Choir, and other artists whose names mean nothing to most people today, but in an earlier day excited listeners. The Dana College Choir, under the direction of Paul Neve, gave me much more appreciation for music, particularly the choral variety. Years later when *Life* magazine asked if I had a favorite musical group, while my younger Senate colleagues mentioned rock bands and other popular entities, I said the Dana College Choir.

Informal singing sessions in the college canteen, or outside under a large tree in favorable weather, added another cultural dimension.

I became a member of the school paper staff, and the assistant editor of the yearbook. The library was not in the category of one of the world's greatest, but it gave me a chance to read and devour so much that I found fascinating. Years later I read the autobiography of Kansas journalist William Allen White in which he said he got more from the University of Kansas library than from the University of Kansas classroom. That held true for me too at Dana.

My friends the Johnsen brothers, Paul and Ray, organized an intramural basketball team, for which we had numbers attached to our uniforms like 3/8 and 1/12. We won few games but we enjoyed ourselves.

My parents saved my letters from college. I obviously did not have history in mind when I wrote them. They show a little more interest in journalism and politics and religion than most students might show, but generally are typical. Art always seemed to owe me a letter; I frequently asked for stamps; and I wrote frequently about money. "Last night was a polio benefit game here. Cost me one dollar which sent my pocketbook well down into the red," I wrote, obviously hinting. In one letter I note that my suit had worn out but I bought one from a fellow student who had gained weight. He paid $35 for the suit and I got it for $15 but I needed some money to get the pants adjusted. I also bought a pair of gabardine Army surplus pants for $10 and assured my parents it was a good deal. I spent $3.43 for a new white shirt. Some days I kept a meticulous account of my spending, but other days I did not. My spending included $1.50 for a corsage for my date at the major spring social event at the college. Another entry simply says: Date, $1.00. I am sure I impressed her! On a postcard I sent to my parents I wrote: "This is Saturday night. I have exactly six cents in my pocket so another fellow and I (he's also broke) are taking our girls walking."[1]

Involved in the usual senseless but harmless college pranks, I helped assemble one of the student's beds in the main room of the library with the help of another student who had a key to the library, startling Sena Bertelsen, the librarian, when she walked in the next morning. We took the Model T Ford of Art Sorensen and Jim Hansen, not a heavy car, up the wide front steps of the Old Main building and parked it there. But we also did constructive things on a voluntary basis for the college and the community.

As I finished my sophomore year I ran for student body president, overcoming two popular and respected opponents. I headed a move to have a large hall rented in Omaha for a Dana College Choir concert, my assumption being that if you have a large hall and put posters around Omaha the hall would be filled. It was a disaster. We had a huge hall and fifty or seventy-five people bought tickets, the few present in the audience almost outnumbered by the choir. The auditorium, which seated perhaps 2,500 people, looked ominously barren. No one cited it as the high point of my service as student body president.

More meaningful, no African Americans had ever enrolled in the college, not unusual for liberal arts colleges in the year 1947-48, but not good. I headed a successful effort to make it the clear policy of the college not to discriminate, and to welcome African Americans. A member of the Board of Regents from Colorado who read about my activities in the college paper wrote to the Dana president to ask if I was a Communist. That shook the president up; he talked to me about it.

Because I held membership in the National Association for the Advancement of Colored People, which at that time many considered to be a radical group, I took the liberty of inviting the head of the NAACP, Walter White, to visit our campus. He could not make it, but agreed that his assistant, Roy Wilkins, later the leader of the national group, could speak. When the president of the college, R. E. Morton, a good but cautious man, already uneasy after the trustee's reaction to my move toward integrating the campus, learned that Roy Wilkins would speak at Dana, he promptly disinvited him. I learned about it too late to reverse the action.

Two years later Dana had its first black student, and since that time the college has been solid in this area. When I later served on the Board of Regents, Dana had a higher percentage of African American students than any private college in the state.

As the newly elected student body president I attended the first convention of the National Student Association at the University of Wisconsin in Madison, with perhaps 2,000 in attendance. It opened my eyes to a broader world. A few Communists were among the delegates, but noisy beyond their numbers. They regularly introduced amendments and made motions, and always were overwhelmingly defeated. But the convention gave me my first contact with a real, live Communist. The gathering divided into subcommittees, and I managed to get named to the one dealing with racial discrimination in education. The student representative of the NAACP at the convention nominated me for the chairmanship, and because I had a touch of a flu bug I declined, but I appreciated the honor not just to me but to the small college from which I came. I first met Cliff Wharton here, later president of Michigan State University and Deputy Secretary of State under Warren Christopher.

Being a college of Christian background, its religion courses all had Christian theologians as teachers. Years later when the Anti-Defamation League gave me their national award for fighting discrimination, together with $10,000 in cash, I gave the money to Dana for hiring a Jewish rabbi part-time to instruct students in a course on Jewish traditions. I have since received letters from two students, one a Muslim from Bangladesh, telling me how meaningful this course had been for them, thanking me.

After announcing my retirement from the Senate, I took $100,000 from my remaining modest campaign treasury and gave it to Dana as a loan fund for students who want to study or travel abroad, with the understanding that they would have no legal obligation to repay but a moral obligation to do so. Once a year Dana will remind former students who have borrowed from the fund that they owe money, and even though they have no legal obligation to repay the loan, my guess is that they will, and do more than repay. The one requirement is that students must do it before their senior year, so that they can return to the campus and infuse the college with a greater sense of international concern. When I mentioned my action to Sol Price, a friend in San Diego, he added $50,000 to that amount. Because such a small percentage of U. S. students study abroad, my hope is that this fund will not only help students at Dana, but serve as an example and inspiration for other schools. I would like to get that total up to $2 million at Dana, so that they can promote study and travel abroad much more actively. And I hope eventually every college and university in the nation will have such a fund. While the United States has many international students studying here, only about seven-tenths of one percent of our students study abroad. The only nation that has a lower percentage is North Korea. Part of the reason for provincialism in the United States Congress and too often in the White House is that at the grass roots level in our nation we are too myopic, seeing only to the edge of our national borders, and sometimes not seeing those much closer who live in our inner cities and rural areas of poverty. Higher education has to take part of the blame when our nation fails to act responsibly in international affairs. I hope that small loan fund at Dana can help to change things.

Dana College was good to me, and in a small way I want to repay that fine school.



In my junior year at Dana I received a telegram from my father saying that the small town of Troy, Illinois, population 1,200, near where my parents lived in Highland, had a weekly newspaper that folded. The local business leaders would arrange for a full loan for me to take over the newspaper if I were to assume ownership.

I wanted to be a journalist, secretly hoping that I could be another Walter Lippmann, a columnist in most of the major newspapers of the nation. People who followed public policy issues, including virtually every public official in the nation read him avidly. He had real influence. (A few years ago a young reporter for the *Christian Science Monitor* asked me what my hopes were as a young man, and I told her that I wanted to be the Walter Lippmann of my generation. I should have explained it more clearly. She reported that I wanted to be the Walt Whitman of my generation.)

Taking over a weekly newspaper seemed like a step in the direction of my ambitions. I took the train to St. Louis where my parents met me. The superintendent of schools in Troy, Fred Wakeland, had explained to my father that the publisher of the newspaper, Ben Jarvis, went to his physician and received the news that he had cancer. In

1948 cancer almost automatically meant death. Jarvis went to his small printshop and office, locked the door, and went home, preparing to die. When I tried to interview him a few weeks later for my first edition, he told me simply to save my energy and wait and write an obituary. Part of the reason for that bluntness undoubtedly came with being "down" physically and emotionally, and part of it probably was seeing a nineteen-year-old come along who thought he could publish the paper, and Jarvis understandably had his doubts. But as a nineteen-year-old, I stammered an inappropriate response to his suggestion that I wait to write an obituary.

My father and I met with several Troy business leaders: Earl and Harold Schmidt, Dan Liebler, Oscar Gindler, James Watson, and a few others, all members of the Troy Lions Club. Watson served as president of the Troy Security Bank. Jarvis wanted $3,600 for his printing and minimal office equipment, and "Pop" Watson said the bank would loan me $3,500, a courageous thing for them to do as I look back on it.

Before I agreed to do it, I contacted Washington University in St. Louis to see if I could get my last year of college there going part-time, waiving a rule they had for one year of full-time attendance to get a degree. They agreed. However, once I started the newspaper I did not have time to attend classes. Years later Chancellor William Danforth asked me to speak at a commencement at Washington University and I received an honorary doctorate. I told the group assembled that I had found a much easier way to get a degree, without attending classes.

I signed a note at the Troy bank, with the understanding that I would spend three more months at Dana College finishing the school year, and then come to publish the newspaper.

I had no idea of the fascinating experiences that awaited me.

---

[1] Author to Simon Family, 4 October 1947, Southern Illinois University (SUI) Archives.

# Chapter 3

# Small-Town Newspaper Publisher

Bill Frangen, a gravel-voiced, retired coal miner who stood an erect five-feet-three-inches invited the local superintendent of schools, Fred Wakeland, to the small office of the *Troy Tribune* and told Wakeland, in front of this new and very green newspaper publisher that the superintendent should get the high school band out for the first edition of the *Tribune*. When he hesitated a moment, Frangen said, "Well, we did it VJ [Victory over Japan] Day didn't we?" With that overwhelming logic, the school scheduled the band to be present when the presses rolled and we handed out that first edition.

In those days (1948) we set newspaper headlines by hand, and Linotypes and Intertypes produced the lead impressions that composed the body of stories. My brother Art helped me with the printing, both of us having learned a little about it from the religious publishing projects of my father. And those first weeks Roy Mayer worked for us, at what I am sure must have been a miserably small wage. Not only were the wages meager, as Roy later related, "I knew I had to work forty hours a week, but I didn't realize I would put in all forty hours in a row!" That exaggerates the situation slightly. But to make our Thursday morning deadlines which grocery stores wanted, we frequently worked through the night on Wednesday. We had old equipment and far too little experience in any aspect of publishing, and the product showed it. My college classmate Ray Johnsen agreed to come from Nebraska to help for the summer. I met him at the train depot in St. Louis on a Thursday morning after working through the entire night. I barely had him and his luggage in the car when he observed, "It must be great just putting out a newspaper once a week!" He soon learned the truth the hard way.

But for that first edition of the *Troy Tribune*, to be published after the *Troy Call* had ceased publication more than six months earlier, we struggled mightily. We wanted to have that initial newspaper ready for the band and Troy's hopeful citizens. We finally got everything into the forms (called chases) and loaded the type onto the old press, started the noisy motor running and we prepared for our masterpiece! Unfortunately the gelatin-type rollers that ink the type had not been used for six months and when we started the presses the rollers crumbled into uselessness. I had to go outside and with great embarrassment tell the waiting band and small gathering of citizens that the newspaper would not come out for another week.

We finally put it out the following week and slowly, issue by issue, the product improved. People in a small town want to read in their weekly newspaper the stories about a family visiting their friends in New Orleans, about a birth, about an automobile accident, about the myriad small things that never make the news of a metropolitan newspaper but are the lifeblood of a community of 1,200. Yes, we had an occasional crime story, but rarely. Unless we planned to be out of town for more than one day, we did not lock the doors of our home, literally. While the newspaper campaigned for improvements, and ran "major" stories about weddings and graduations, we mostly printed items like this: "Mr. and Mrs. George Steinhaus of St. Louis visited Mr. and Mrs. Thomas Lewis Friday."[1] I was nineteen years old when I began publishing the newspaper, and my immaturity showed in much of my writing. I also had to learn how to run a business. Meeting even a small payroll, filling out Social Security and unemployment compensation forms, and the details which business people usually acquire at least in a primitive way before they take over a business were all new to me.

I stayed at the home of Ann Kueker, a woman in her late fifties (I considered her elderly) who took in other roomers. I paid her three dollars a week, and often she had to wait for her three dollars. I discovered that getting started in business is not easy.

Occasionally I would pontificate about some national or international issue, hoping that other newspapers would pick up my writings and notice a journalistic gem hidden in a weekly newspaper in Illinois. But rarely did my profound thoughts get reprinted, and no one suggested that I had gem qualities, just another piece of gravel on the road of life.

Slowly I began to look at the needs of the community. And we had them. Our small newspaper plant in the center of town had running water but no toilet. The wooden outdoor toilet gave us a mighty cold welcome in winter, and gave off a horrible odor in the warmer months, a more than daily reminder that the town could stand improvements. When I started editorializing for a city sewer system, one of the city's biggest landlords called the proposal "socialistic," which of course it was, if socialism means that government sees that everyone gets certain basic services. By that standard, of course, our roads and public schools and many other things are also "socialistic."

The campaign to have a city sewer system reached the point of front-page editorials after a little more than a year in Troy. "As you count the dollars it will take for city sewers," I wrote in one front-page commentary, "also count the outdoor lavatories near the grocery stores, restaurants and taverns — where disease-carrying flies and mosquitoes breed and thrive. . . . Before too many months are over the people of Troy should know whether they have a weak-kneed, spineless city council or a courageous city council. They will know whether their aldermen vote for what is right or what is easy."[2]

A year later we still had no sewer system and I ran a by-lined front page commentary titled "Of Mice and Men," castigating the city council for not moving ahead. One reason they gave for their resistance was that they wanted to wait until the price of construction came down. I noted, "The price is now roughly $60,000 higher than 17 months ago when the Tribune favored the council going ahead with the project." I had a sound basis for suggesting the sanitary needs and that a sewer system would be helpful to the community. In my enthusiasm, however, I also said it would "be a big boon to business in Troy," which did not turn out to be an accurate prophesy.[3] But three months later the city voted to have a sewer system, a small triumph in the life of the city and of the newspaper.

Success did not always follow advocacy. Troy had no library and rather than vote a small library tax the city council decided to have a referendum on the question. The special August election on the library proposal, which I strongly supported, lost 152-137. Eventually the Troy Woman's Club, together with local leaders Allen and Millie Shaffer as well as Jeanne and me, got a library going on a voluntary basis until it finally blossomed. Today the community has a fine library, but my early efforts at influencing city officials and citizens did not impress anyone.

Most of my editorial efforts, while commendable, caused few ripples outside our newspaper. When I learned that residents of the county tuberculosis sanitarium did not have a record player, I wrote about it and we collected enough money to buy one television set, two record players and people contributed more than 100 records and fifty-five books. When a train hit a car and killed a man at an unmarked railroad crossing near Troy, I pushed for flashing warning lights and we got them.

Little by little the newspaper advocated improvements, and working with others, we obtained them. A newspaper can be a powerful force for good, even when operated by someone with almost no experience.

Running a small newspaper you also learn about the flaws of humanity. In a three-way race for mayor, Les Hazzard went door to door, visiting every home in Troy, while his opponents did no visible campaigning. The night of the election I went into the city clerk's office (also his appliance store) and watched the vote count. When they finished I walked out and the three candidates listened as I told them the results: R. R. Moore, 260 votes; Ed Wise, 134; and Les Hazzard, 81. Les, who obviously had differing expectations after his door-to-door endeavors, commented in disgust, "All I can tell you is that this is a town full of liars."

The problems of crime were so minimal that the city saw no need to give a car to the person designated as the local marshal, Ernest Spencer. He walked around town wearing a badge but no uniform, most weeks dealing with nothing more serious than finding a student who skipped school. When he retired, the city bought a used car for law enforcement to be really up-to-date. The Supreme Court had not handed down its Miranda decision and other rulings requiring a professional police force. The city simply handed a badge to someone the mayor and council felt qualified and told him (always him) that he could be the city marshal. After Ernie Spencer's retirement the mayor named a marshal who earlier had drinking problems, but the mayor assured me they were a thing of the past. Not too long after being named, the new marshal walked into the newspaper office and told me, "If you print anything about my hitting that telephone pole with the police car, I'll resign." Up to that point I had not known about it! Of course, I got the facts and then published the story. He didn't resign, but a few weeks later he received his dismissal notice.

As circulation and advertising slowly — oh so slowly — increased, I gradually acquired a small but permanent staff. Charles Klotzer helped on the editorial side and advertising. Born in Germany, his family fled, prior to the crudest assaults on the Jews by the Nazis, to China, where they lived during the war. I placed a classified ad in the *St. Louis Post-Dispatch* for an editorial helper, and the most intriguing response came from Charlie Klotzer with his unusual background. Shortly after he came to Troy one of the local businessmen came to me and said, "Troy is proud of having no Negroes and no Jews here. We would appreciate it if you hired someone else." I tactfully told him that I didn't expect to be running his business and I had better run mine. I didn't tell Charlie about it at the time, but a few months later I saw the two of them chatting like old friends. Charlie wrote a regular column of comment. Charles Klotzer later founded the *St. Louis Journalism Review*, as well as a typesetting business, and with his wife Rose has been a force for good in the St. Louis area.

Others who helped at one point or another included Art Benz, Lucille Schmalz, Arlene Bellman, and Eldon Scholl. Eldon added some verve to the place because he was a militant atheist. On the rare occasions when all of us ate lunch together, we had discussions that would have brought credit to a philosophy department of a great university. Later Ray Johnsen came aboard permanently, as did another long-time friend, Elmer Fedder.

As I went about the routine of publishing a small newspaper, I read in the three St. Louis newspapers about wide-open gambling and prostitution in our county, Madison, which had a population of 187,000, and is across the river from St. Louis, north of East St. Louis. Living in the rural part of the county, twenty miles from the population centers along the river, I editorialized in behalf of better law enforcement, but I didn't get too excited because the problems seemed somewhat remote.

However, one day I had a hamburger at a small restaurant in Troy run by Charlie Struckhoff. On the counter — there were no booths in the tiny place — were several punchboards, something older readers may recall. They were approximately one-half inch thick with a metal device which could be used to punch in at a large number of spots on the board. From the rear would come a piece of paper, having been punched through, which would say that the person won $5 or $3 or more likely nothing. You paid ten cents or a quarter for a chance. I didn't even know they were illegal in Illinois when I chatted with Struckhoff. This occurred during a cultural period in the nation that was vastly different. The only legal casinos in the nation were in

Nevada, and most states outlawed virtually all forms of gambling. I asked Charlie how much he paid for them and how much money he makes. "Ordinarily you would pay $3, take in $90, pay out $30 in prizes and the rest is profit. But if you don't buy them from a man named Carl Davis someone from the sheriff's office comes and tells you that punchboards are illegal. And I have to pay him $30 instead of $3. That cuts my profits in half."

He told me this with the understanding I would not use his name in a story. I checked and in our small town of 1,200 we had thirteen places with punchboards. Most people said they "didn't remember" what they paid for the punchboards or to whom, but a few confirmed Charlie Struckhoff's story. All of this in a state where any form of gambling other than horse racing wagering was illegal.

The sheriff's office refused to comment.

I published an article about this on June 23, 1949, almost a year after coming to Troy. The St. Louis newspaper stories about the Hyde Park Club and the 200 Club, two big illegal gambling casinos in the county, suddenly took on more meaning for me.

The sheriff and state's attorney (called district attorney in most states) brought those operating bookies and gambling casinos and those involved with prostitution, as well as Carl Davis of the punchboard business, into court every three months, fined everyone $50 plus court costs and permitted them to continue to operate. They did not enforce the law, and virtually everyone "understood" that for these things to happen there had to be big payoffs. Sheriffs at that time in Illinois were limited to one four-year term and received $4,000 a year compensation. After a four-year term one former sheriff built a huge home with published reports that it cost $350,000 to build — a great deal of money today, much more in those days. C. W. Burton, the predecessor to State's Attorney Austin Lewis, earned $8,000 a year in that post but the Internal Revenue Service charged him with underpaying his income tax for three years by $78,960. Obviously he had some other source of revenue, and no one found it difficult to guess the source. Seven months before I arrived in Troy someone bombed Burton's house. The explosion, which injured no one, could be felt eight blocks away but Burton claimed he slept through it and neither he nor the police pursued the perpetrators. A year after he stepped aside as State's Attorney he and his wife suddenly disappeared, with great speculation as to why. When the federal government later acted to collect the unpaid income tax of $78,960, former Sheriff Dallas Harrell, acting as agent for Burton, paid the money, the first indication that most people had that the Burtons were still alive. Rumors had them in Mexico or Canada. Whether they suddenly fled because of fear of retaliation from some offended criminal elements, or fear of the federal government, or some other cause is still debated.

After I published my article about the punchboards, people started calling me from around the county with other stories. I started writing open letters to the sheriff and state's attorney, getting tougher and tougher in my language. They ignored me, but other newspapers in the area gave publicity to my attempts to force change.

Not long after I ran the punchboard story, Sheriff Dallas Harrell and State's Attorney Austin Lewis announced with great fanfare that they had closed two houses of prostitution about seven miles from Troy, and had taken away their liquor licenses. Both located on Highway 40, a main road, it soon became obvious to the most casual traveler that the "closed" enterprises still were flourishing.

I did some personal scouting and ran the following story:

> The houses of prostitution along Highway 40 known as the Plamor Inn and the Club 40 which were "closed" by the sheriff in cooperation with the state's attorney's office are now operating in full swing again — except that no liquor is being sold over the counter as it formerly was.
>
> I know. I was there.
>
> Sunday night I stopped at the Plamor Inn and asked for a coke. I was the only person in the place and after serving me the coke he asked, "Do you want a girl?"
>
> "Not tonight," I answered. I took a few more sips from my coke and then asked, "How much do they run?"
>
> "Depends on what you want. It starts at five dollars."
>
> "Will you be open later in the week?" I asked.
>
> "Yes," he said, taking a puff from his cigarette with a hand which looked as if it were suffering from arthritis. "Anything you want when you come back."
>
> "Thanks," I said as I walked out of the door. . . .
>
> My next stop was the Club 40 where I again ordered a coke and where activity was more in evidence.
>
> A good-looking young lady served it to me, then came

around in back of the counter, picked some lint from my suit coat, stroked my back, and said, "Say, if you're interested in entertainment I suggest we go out to one of the bedrooms and talk things over. They won't let us make propositions at the bar."

"OK," I said, and we walked into a small room in which was a very small dresser and a single-size bed, the spread neatly covered over it, with a few cigarette burns on the spread.

"How much is it?" I asked.

"Five dollars for once and ten dollars for twice. For ten dollars I can give you a nice long party, honey."

"That's a little much for me," I said.

"Listen, honey," she cooed back, "for five dollars I'll give you a good long stay and arrange for some drinks for both of us on that too."

"Will you be here later in the week?" I asked. By this time she seemed set on my staying there and I was wanting to get out of there just in case anyone might identify me.

"No, honey, this is my last night. Won't you give me just a little satisfaction tonight. We'll have a nice long party in the bed and then if you don't have quite enough money we can settle up afterwards."

"I think I'd better come back later in the week," I countered, and headed for the doorway.

At this doorway of one of the many small bedrooms sat a large, heavy-set woman in a yellow-print dress.

I placed my coke bottle on the counter and saw this girl start a conversation with a wild-eyed fellow nearby. I headed for the doorway and some much-needed fresh air.

I walked out of the place with five dollars still in my pocket — and undiseased. Which is probably more than many a fellow can say.

However I also walked out of the place with a still lower opinion of the activities of our county sheriff, Dallas Harrell and the state's attorney, Austin Lewis.

> With five dollars per person and many times ten, and with the mass production which seemed to be going on there, the operators might even afford to pay county officials a little. [4]

Not yet twenty-one when I wrote that story, it will not be recorded as great literature, but it made the point clearly. In order to protect myself in the event of a lawsuit, I had a friend in Troy, Paul Lewis, make the same two stops. Five weeks later the sheriff "raided" the two places, but victories came slowly through county officials who had no eagerness to enforce the law.

In what would become a significant comment, Gov. Adlai Stevenson wrote to a minister who complained about the situation: "As for [law enforcement in] Madison County, it is an obstinate problem and we have not yet found a satisfactory answer."[5] Three months later, in summing up his first year as governor, Adlai Stevenson said that commercialized gambling was his "biggest headache." The way to end it, he said, is to elect "conscientious, vigorous officials and insist they enforce the law. . . . It can only exist where local officials tolerate it, either because they are corrupt and profit from it, or because they think the people don't care or because it's politically expedient."[6] He said the activities harmed the good name of Illinois. In those days anyone who wanted to participate in gambling, legal or illegal, had to get a federal stamp, and the center for gambling in Illinois clearly was Madison County. The *St. Louis Globe-Democrat* editorialized in response to Stevenson's message: "He should be prepared to back it up with vigorous action. Illinois can be made too hot for the gamblers, and we believe that if Gov. Stevenson acts he will have the support of the people of that state."[7]

The comments of both the governor and other newspapers had added significance, because a race for sheriff had just begun, and all the candidates declared their belief in "common sense law enforcement," which meant not enforcing gambling and prostitution laws, except selectively. Because of Madison County gambling ties to underworld elements, no one with a differing viewpoint either dared to surface or felt that there would be a chance of being elected with all the gambling money on the other side. We had no campaign disclosure laws in Illinois then, but everyone knew the great source of campaign money.

I had lunch with Governor Stevenson, urging action on his part, but Illinois had the tradition that the state police would be used only for traffic problems, except for unusual emergencies. They bore the title, Illinois State Highway Police.

In the meantime I tried to put increasing pressure on the State's Attorney. I addressed an open letter to him with these questions: "When you took the oath of office of state's attorney you took an oath to uphold the law. Do you still feel that is your duty? Do you recognize that there is wide-open gambling in Madison County which is illegal, or do you attribute this to 'myths' which the newspapers create? Do you believe that gambling laws should be strictly enforced? Do you believe that you are doing everything possible to enforce these laws? If you say you believe the laws should be enforced, and if you also admit that there is wide-open gambling in the county, then how long must Madison County's citizens wait before there is a genuine house-cleaning and not a mere face-saving token raid?"[8] I wrote to Illinois Attorney General Ivan A. Elliott, a rigidly upright man, urging that he look at exercising his options if local law enforcement breaks down. He replied, "I am much disappointed with Mr. Lewis and I believe the suggestion of your letter to be a good one."[9]

Other things helped build pressure for action. The same criminal syndicate people who illegally operated the two big gambling casinos in the county tried to move in on the jukebox business in the area. Also, the *St. Louis Post-Dispatch* published a story that the slayings of Charles Binaggio and Charles Gargotta in Kansas City were arranged at a meeting of underworld figures at the Hyde Park Club in Madison County.

I received a letter from James Mulroy, executive secretary to the Governor, in which he wrote, "I am of the considered opinion that in a comparatively short time the better known gambling places in your county will be closed either due to action taken by your own authorities or by some other type of action which might have to be taken."[10] Jim Mulroy previously worked as a journalist, and he knew his letter went to an editor and if he did not want it published he should have indicated that. So the *Tribune* came out on Thursday with a headline "Big County Gambling Places to Be Closed."

Delivered by mail, my small weekly newspaper got to Edwardsville, the county seat, on Friday morning and that noon the sheriff, state's attorney and a few of their friends had lunch at Musso's restaurant and one of them held up a copy of my newspaper and asked, "Did you see what Simon had to say this week?" They all laughed uproariously.

That afternoon at 3:20 the first state police raid in Illinois history took place when fifty-one officers from the northern part of the state swooped down on the Hyde Park Club and the 200 Club. The raid, featured in *Life* magazine, changed state history. Never again could any county official so brazenly ignore the law. The sheriff, a Republican, and the state's attorney, a Democrat, were enraged. I stayed in the outer office of the state's attorney's office until the early morning hours as the attorneys for the gamblers worked out bail arrangements. The lawyer for some of them, Scheaffer O'Neill, like the others involved, was livid. "Adlai Stevenson is another Adolf Hitler," he told me. Ironically, two years later he seconded the nomination of Stevenson for the Democratic nomination for President within the Illinois Democratic caucus, saying the nation needs Stevenson's leadership. The general feeling was that O'Neill, State Rep. Paul Powell, and a few others who worked together closely wanted to get rid of Stevenson as governor, hoping to go back to "the good old days" of lax law enforcement. Adlai ran for president, rather than reelection as governor, but their hopes of completely reversing the role of the state police and going back to "common sense law enforcement" proved futile.

The State's Attorney, working under the thumb of the Illinois Attorney General, filed charges against fifty-four men arrested by the state police. At the time of the raids the two places had between 800 and 1,200 gambling customers, none of whom they arrested. At the Hyde Park Club the State Police picked up $67,000 off the tables and at the 200 Club $21,000—not small amounts for 1950. The State Police did not know that a bookie operated a few doors from the Hyde Park Club. One of the leaders of the raid observed, "When we were going through the Hyde Park Club we looked out of the window and saw people running out of the other place like mice."[11]

In the midst of all of this, Joe Healey, a county official who occupied an obscure elected office that no longer exists, probate clerk, said he had to talk to me urgently and off the record. He did not want to meet me either in his office or mine. When we met he said that he heard the sheriff and state's attorney talking, half joking and half serious, about having someone throw a bomb in my newspaper office. I will never know whether he came as a friend or as a messenger. I told him that I had old equipment and good insurance and they should go ahead. That was the nearest to a threat I ever received. I had one advertiser who dropped out, and the man from whom I rented my place talked to me, genuinely concerned that we might get a bomb, asking me to stop publishing "these controversial things." I told him

I would move my equipment if I had to, but I would explain to the readers why I had to move. He never mentioned it again.

While the state police raid reduced the most obvious violations of the law, whether for fear or avarice the county officials continued their former practices, permitting gambling and prostitution but at a lower level of activity. Not only did the illegal activities diminish, unfortunately so did national and regional attention to our county. It irked many of us to see "business as usual" and we felt that the sheriff and state's attorney should enforce the law, out of embarrassment and pride if nothing else.

Eight months after the raid, with illegal activities continuing but at a reduced level, a new sheriff took office — they were then limited by Illinois constitution to one four-year term — and I decided to fire a legal shot that would be a warning to the new sheriff as well as to the state's attorney. I filed a formal complaint against the former sheriff, Dallas Harrell, for "palpable omission of duty," the legal phrase, which required that the matter be brought before the Grand Jury. And I filed a complaint with the Illinois Bar Association asking that Austin Lewis, the state's attorney, be disbarred.

One of those two actions turned out to be effective.

At the age of twenty-two, I did not understand fully how intertwined the entire judicial/law enforcement system was. I knew that a prosecuting attorney anywhere has huge sway over a grand jury. But I thought the fact that the state's attorney had a threat over him from the Illinois Bar Association might help. However, I asked for a special prosecutor. The attorney I asked to represent me in the circuit court to request a special prosecutor did not show up. He told me later he decided at the last minute that he faced too much danger if he made his appearance for me. Whether that caused his nonappearance or someone paid him not to be there I can only guess. But when Judge Edward F. Bareis asked me, "Who is your attorney?" I could only say, "I am representing myself." Even if I had prepared to make the presentation I do not know how effective I would have been, but under the circumstances I am sure I did not do well. But I explained to the judge how the sheriff and state's attorney had worked together to ignore the law, and I did not see how the state's attorney could vigorously prosecute the former sheriff. That could hardly have been news to the judge. But he ruled against having a special prosecutor.

Eight members of the grand jury resided in the home township of Sheriff Dallas Harrell, and at least one of the members of the grand jury had business ties to the gambling operations. The maximum penalty that could be assessed for "palpable omission of duty" was a fine of $10,000.

Austin Lewis called sixteen witnesses to testify before the grand jury, including me. The grand jury determined that the former sheriff should not be indicted, although there had been "great laxity" in the enforcement of the law. The grand jury also "commended" State's Attorney Austin Lewis for his prosecution.[12] However, they did say that if there were further violations of the gambling laws during the one month remaining in their term they would reconvene, and that put a temporary damper on things.

My action against the sheriff did cause the spotlight to shine on Madison County again, and that helped. But the good that came from this particular action was minimal.

However, the simple step of asking the Illinois Bar Association to initiate steps to disbar Austin Lewis, the state's attorney, turned out to be powerfully effective. My letter to the Bar Association included these words:

> You may consider this letter a request for the proper committees of the Illinois State Bar Association to institute disciplinary proceedings against Austin Lewis. . . .
>
> [He] served as assistant state's attorney for a number of years prior to his election in 1948. After his election he continued what he called "common sense law enforcement" but which I have termed dollars and cents law enforcement. Under this system Madison County was opened to big-time gambling, and the gambling kings became the big contributors to political campaigns of both parties, thereby wielding an influence far and above the weight they would carry as citizens ordinarily.
>
> Periodically the gamblers were brought to court and given a nominal fine, but they continued to operate with the full knowledge of the state's attorney. The procedure followed by Lewis brought the legal profession into ill repute and made a farce of legal procedure by his failure to mention that the defendants were guilty of more than one offense. There is no question but that his actions brought the courts of Madison County into disrepute.

As a result of his failure to take action he was approached by the governor of this state and the attorney general with a request to eliminate this flagrant abuse of the law in Madison County. The close cooperation of those who violate the law with the law enforcement officials was too binding a thing to allow Lewis to act. Finally, the governor ordered state police into our county to do what Austin Lewis, with the cooperation of the sheriff, should have done. . . .

I therefore am requesting that you refer this complaint to the Committee on Inquiry, the Committee of Grievances and the Board of Governors of the Illinois State Bar Association for appropriate action.[13]

The *St. Louis Post-Dispatch* editorially urged the Bar Association to act. Others did the same. My impression is that at first the state's attorney considered it a minor nuisance, but when it became clear that the Bar Association took the matter seriously, suddenly — that is the right word — Madison County became the cleanest county in the state, and it has never since reverted fully to its former status. The Illinois State Bar Association rendered a powerful public service by taking this seriously. While they did not recommend disbarment of Austin Lewis, their stern approach sent a powerful signal to all prosecuting attorneys.

During this time Senator Estes Kefauver of Tennessee held hearings on the problem of organized crime in the nation. Equally significant, television, still in its infancy, for the first time galvanized the nation on a public policy issue by broadcasting the hearings, making a national celebrity of Kefauver and creating concern about underworld criminal ties to public officials. Kefauver asked me to testify. My statement included these words: "The big-time gamblers and others who would violate the law have formed an unholy alliance in our county with those charged with the responsibility for enforcing the law. I have little respect for the gentry of the gambling profession and the hoodlums they bring with them. But I have even less respect for men in our county who have prostituted public office and betrayed the public for a few dirty dollars."[14] Kefauver called what happened in

Madison County "most shocking," and that it could only have occurred because of "protection and payoffs."[15] In a much too generous appraisal, *Newsweek* called me "a star witness."[16] What the Kefauver testimony did, however, was to make me a mini-celebrity for a short period, people recognizing me from the televised hearings as I walked down the street of any community in our area. And a few people — only a few — suggested I should run for public office, something I had considered off and on but took a little more seriously now.

Occasionally the same unsavory elements continued to raise their heads.

In 1953 — two years after the Kefauver hearings — a place called Club Prevue operated with neon lights, ostensibly as a night club but clearly much more. Always worried about being sued if I falsely charged a gambling operation, Charles Klotzer, no longer with me but a volunteer for this assignment, went there first, providing detailed descriptions, and added: "Gambling in Madison County has passed the stage of being an undercover operation. It is wide open. Anyone, without any inside connections, can participate. There was absolutely no indication that any of the guards feared that the state or county would interfere."[17] Then Ray Johnsen and his wife Nancy went one evening, and I followed later that same evening. Guards at the place recognized me and stopped me from entering, but Ray and Nancy made it in and saw the same things Charlie had. Nancy had her watch either stolen or lost during the visit. Ray and I notified the new state's attorney, Fred Schuman, that we stood ready to sign a complaint and testify if he wished to prosecute. The place closed the next day. No prosecution occurred. Two days *after* it closed, Illinois Attorney General Latham Castle sent the sheriff and state's attorney a letter ordering them to stop gambling in the county.

Leader of the Capone element for our area, according to the St. Louis newspapers, was "Buster" Wortman. The *Chicago Sun-Times* described Wortman as "a multimillionaire in trucking, building construction, juke boxes and loan companies. . . . All of this nice money came to him after he joined up with the Chicago gangsters upon leaving Alcatraz prison in the mid-1930s."[18] In 1958, Wortman's Rite Way Cigarette Company muscled its way into a monopoly of the cigarette vending machines at the Fairmount race track, operated privately but licensed by the state and supported with state-funded prizes. I objected. The Illinois Racing Commission said they would do nothing about it because the company's executive was not "Buster" Wortman but his brother Ted. I responded:

- Ted Wortman . . . has been arrested 13 times and has served two terms in prison.

- He and "Buster" operated the Paddock Bar together in East St. Louis.

- In 1947, when Ted was arrested in connection with a big jewelry theft by federal officials, a search of his bar "found an army carbine, 1000 rounds of ammunition and a .32 caliber revolver. At his home they found a .38 caliber revolver and a quantity of dynamite concussion caps." (*St. Louis Post-Dispatch* quotation)

- When the Kefauver Crime Investigating Committee was looking for him he conveniently disappeared. . . .

- Rite Way and the Plaza Amusement Company have the same address in St. Louis. Plaza also has a controlling interest in Rite Way, making it clear that Rite Way is a front for the Plaza Amusement Company in which a number of the more famous names of the St. Louis crime world have an interest. The Governor of Missouri has been trying to kick Plaza out of the state — while Illinois appears to be welcoming them with open arms.

- Kefauver Committee records indicate that Ted Wortman has used four aliases, and in going through newspaper files I found a fifth . . .

- He and "Buster" and Harold Grizzell were arrested for robbery in 1934. Grizzell later was killed in a gang slaying by machine gun bullets.

- A St. Louis accountant told the Kefauver Committee that he had been hired by Ted and "Buster" for four firms: Plaza Amusement, E and W Loan, Reliable News Agency, and Pioneer News Agency. All four have been in difficulties with the police . . .

- When Rite-Way tried to move into Belleville and Collinsville . . . Belleville Mayor Jerome Munie stated that he would close any tavern using the Rite Way machines. "We don't intend to tolerate that kind of people in Belleville." Collinsville Mayor Al Delbartes reaffirmed that he wants to keep Rite Way out . . .

We intend to stick by our guns concerning the threatened infiltration by hoodlums in the coin-vending machine business here."[19]

After this editorial blast, the Illinois Racing Commission backed off, but apparently trying to hurt me politically — I was then in the legislature — refused to sell *any* cigarettes at the tracks for a few days and told patrons that I had forced them to stop selling cigarettes. I received a few phone calls of complaint, but when I told people the background, they sided with me.

All of this makes it sound as if my newspaper devoted itself almost solely to the corruption/gambling/prostitution problem in our county. Far from it. The shortest editorial I ever ran said simply: "Our State Senator Milton 'Mink' Mueller, in November the friend of all people regardless of race, creed or color, voted against a Fair Employment Practices bill this week."[20] I wrote frequent book reviews, something rare for a weekly newspaper, which I am sure almost no one read. I had commentary on nuclear problems, had a friend in Japan, Lloyd Neve, write an article about Japan's defense expenditures, but mostly I had matters of purely local interest. The lead stories included such items as the local high school adding an agriculture course, and that the Baptists would have a vacation Bible school. My political prejudices showed when I had a banner headline and a front-page editorial noting that Sen. Paul Douglas would speak in Troy the following Monday. Dial phones would replace the system we had, where you picked up the phone and told the operator, Lucille Auwarter, whom you wanted. A major story! Whether that really meant progress was a matter of great local dispute. Our newspaper's phone number was "4" before the new system came. Knowing numbers helped, but if you simply told Lucille whom you wanted to reach, she almost always knew the number and just plugged you in. A simpler life was disappearing. The neighboring Troy Post Office shared a wall with our newspaper, and frequently late at night I could hear the postmaster, Wheeler Davis, hand stamping the letters that people brought in that day to mail. But suddenly they got a small machine that handled more of those envelopes in a minute than Wheeler could hand stamp in an hour, and that welcome sound disappeared.

I maintained my interest in a variety of social causes. The chaplain of the Menard State Penitentiary contacted me, telling me of David Saunders who killed a store owner in a struggle over a gun after having too much to drink at the age of seventeen. He not only had an exemplary record at the prison, he edited the prison newspaper and won national awards for his journalistic efforts. I had worked with him a little. He recommended an improvement in our parole system that called for releasing prisoners on good behavior ninety days earlier and then giving them much more supervision while on parole. I introduced the measure, which became law, reduced the recidivism rate, and saved taxpayers money. But to get a parole he needed work. I checked with the prison warden who spoke highly of Dave. I offered him a job, thinking we could handle things quietly in the community. But the *St. Louis Globe-Democrat* had a heading on a story, "Murderer to Work for Troy Newspaper." It shocked people in our small town. The woman at whose home we had arranged for him to stay said she "didn't want a man like that staying at her place." I intended to explain this to her before Dave came. But once he came and people got acquainted with him, we had no problem. He became editor of the weekly paper we bought in Carterville, and then worked at public relations and enrollment management for Southern Illinois University, doing an excellent job until his retirement.

A small thing added to my knowledge. After my newspaper business operated reasonably well I wanted to affiliate with the International Typographical Union, both for philosophical reasons — believing that unions can raise the standards of pay and safety, both important to our nation — and because it could be of help to get a Linotype operator or printer if I needed one on short notice. But the Edwardsville local would not take us. I couldn't believe it — or understand it — until I learned that the county government had a rule that certain legal documents and printing had to go to a union shop. The ownership of the *Edwardsville Intelligencer* (since changed at least twice) didn't want competition and got their union people to keep us out. Eventually we solved the problem by affiliating with another nearby union, the Mascoutah local, and then did take some business from the *Intelligencer*, which pleased me for more than the few dollars involved. For the same philosophical reasons, I affiliate with a teachers' union when teaching at a university, even when, as in my present position, the legal counsel says that I am part of the administration and the union cannot represent me.

Facing military duty was something male Americans assumed. No one fled to Canada. Some claimed health problems or married early to avoid the draft, but in this post-World War II era we accepted both the right and the wisdom of the federal government to protect our borders and to help stabilize the world. I joined a military government Army reserve unit in St. Louis, twenty miles from Troy, under the leadership of Col. Arthur Jacobs. One of those in our unit, Warren Billhartz from New Baden, Illinois, later became a solid member of the Illinois General Assembly where we served together. Our unit prepared itself to take over the temporary operation of government in the northern part of Korea. But events changed dramatically in Korea with the entrance of China into that fray, and it soon became obvious that no military government unit would be needed. But I wanted to get my military service behind me. I talked it over with my friends Elmer and Wally Fedder, and the three of us decided to enlist, also hoping that by going in at the same time we might be stationed together. We stayed together three days! They eventually went to Japan and I went to Germany. In the meantime I had persuaded my classmate from Dana College, Ray Johnsen, to leave teaching in Blair, Nebraska, and come down and run the newspaper while I served in the Army.

As I went through the various enlistment forms and the physical examination, I saw a man check off that I had a chest x-ray which I did not have. He also asked if I knew any foreign languages, and I told him that I had a little Spanish and German. He checked "fluent" in front of Spanish and German, about as accurate as his x-ray marking. I took my Army basic training at Fort Riley, Kansas and heard that the FBI (actually military intelligence as it turned out) was checking on me, and I couldn't imagine why. "Perhaps I shouldn't have covered that speech that Henry Wallace made," I said to myself. But one day the platoon sergeant sent me to the orderly room, and there they asked, "Would you like to become a Special Agent for the Counter Intelligence Corps?" I had not the slightest idea what that meant, but our basic training unit was heavy infantry, and anything sounded better than hauling those heavy mortars around. So after basic training I went to Fort Holabird, Maryland, for CIC training and ultimately to Germany, thanks to the inefficiency of the man who designated me as fluent in German.

While at Fort Riley, on a weekend pass I went to Topeka, knowing that Alf Landon who ran for President on the Republican ticket in 1936 against Franklin D. Roosevelt lived there. I looked up his address in a phone book, took a bus there, and walked up to a woman sweeping the front porch of a large, attractive home and told her that I simply would like to shake hands with Landon. She said, "Just a minute. I'll wake him up." I asked her not to, but she insisted, and then he and the family visited with me. They were marvelous hosts. But they also had an attractive daughter, Nancy. So when I got back to Fort Riley I wrote and asked her for a date the next weekend. She responded that they were leaving for their annual summer vacation in Colorado, but could we do it some other time. In the meantime the Army transferred me to Fort Holabird, and Nancy almost disappeared from my memory until I read one day that she had become a candidate for the United States Senate. A few years later I served in the Senate with Nancy Landon Kassebaum of Kansas, one of the finest members of that body. (More recently when Jeanne and I attended Senator Ed Muskie's funeral, Nancy walked into the service with former Senator Howard Baker. I nudged Jeanne and said, "Now there is a great couple." Nancy had been divorced many years and Howard's wife had died. Nancy and Howard have since married. Howard, a class act, would have made a fine president had he been able to get the GOP nomination when he sought it.)

One weekend I went to Emporia, Kansas, to get a little flavor of the community where William Allen White, the great Kansas journalist and friend of Theodore Roosevelt, lived. I visited with the woman who had been his maid. I stopped at the tiny grocery store near his home where he frequently shopped. He always fought the railroads, and I figured it would be interesting to visit also with a railroad executive. White had been dead seven years, and I thought that time would have mellowed whatever personal antagonisms might have existed. But the Santa Fe railroad man I talked to blasted William Allen White as the worst thing that ever happened to Emporia and Kansas. History does not share that assessment.

Army basic training in 1951, when we had a draft, brought people of every type of background together and we shared the same physically demanding routine. We learned that whether we were white or black, Polish or Irish, Protestant, Catholic, or Jewish, some couldn't resist a dice game that blew our meager earnings, some couldn't resist the allure of a too-well painted female, some couldn't handle liquor, but there was no ethnic pattern to these things. We formed friendships across all the traditional boundaries. I have long favored one year of compulsory service for everyone at the age of eighteen or after graduation from high school. If the person chooses the military, fine. If you want to work for a park district, or a homeless shelter, or in another capacity, fine. In the process of screening people for this year of service, if basic skills have not been acquired because of learning disabilities or a poor education situation, this could be part of the year of service. It would lift the nation. And it would provide many people with a broader opportunity to know others as my Army basic training did, to make this more "one nation, under God, indivisible."

A few of the friends I made in Army basic training I kept in touch with for a number of years, but most I have lost contact with. I heard that Thomas Young of Lacygne, Kansas, one of the finest men in our platoon, an African American, died in the Korean conflict, and I assume others may have too. But what happened to Bill Daugherty and Johnny Vasas of Gary, Indiana? What happened to Dick Sherrill of Evanston, Illinois? To Louis Piper of Merriam, Kansas? To Bob Romich, Gene Laks, Joe Schaper, and Floyd Vinita of St. Louis? To Ed Petrak of South Bend? To Ed Schaub of Grosse Pointe, Illinois? To Francis Kuhn of Victoria, Kansas? To "Tex" Rudder of Corpus Christi? To Hugo Schulte of New Baden, Illinois? To Bob Sloan of Granite City, Illinois? To Dick Stewart of Kansas City? To Ken Swain of Grand Rapids? To Ed Steppes, Lowell Ressler, Bob Jones, Jim Thompson — a great ping pong player — and Gene Tripp of Detroit? To David Vickers of Paola, Kansas? A glance through the old "yearbook" for those who graduated from the first platoon of Company I of the 10th Infantry Division brings back good memories.

From Fort Riley I went to Fort Holabird, Maryland, just outside Baltimore, a small army base which prepared people of all the branches of the armed forces for counter intelligence work. Those stationed in the United States did security clearances for people being considered to handle classified material, as well as other military intelligence work, and those based overseas did clearance work for civilians who might work for the U. S. armed forces, or, as in my case, collected information on movements of Soviet and East German troops.

The training we received came in an atmosphere of hostility to free speech, generated in large part by Senator Joseph McCarthy of Wisconsin who made reckless charges about Communists massively infiltrating the United States government. A few had, and obviously where we had Soviet espionage that had to concern us. But the gross exaggerations by McCarthy, often attacking people with no basis whatsoever and ruining their careers, brought about a hysteria that harmed the nation.

Because of the McCarthy-created tensions, and because security people frequently look at every possible danger without a sense of balance, the training we received often portrayed a totally distorted picture of the realities in our nation and the rest of the world. I remember, for example, the instructor who gave us documentary evidence that the actor Frederic March contributed to Yugoslavian Children's Relief, and therefore must be a Communist. Instructors provided us literature from the far right fringe. I occasionally disputed the extreme conclusions in the classes, but as a private dealing with officers teaching the classes I proceeded with caution. At the end of several months of training, they asked each of the students to evaluate our instruction. Much of the technical information about gathering intelligence was superb, but I gave a very negative evaluation of its extreme political tilt. I feared my statement might get me removed from work as a CIC agent. I also wrote a letter to an editor of the *St. Louis Post-Dispatch*, a newspaper known for its civil liberties championship, telling him the distortions that were taking place at Fort Holabird. I thought the *Post-Dispatch* might do a story on it. Instead, the editor wrote back to me that it is not safe to write that kind of letter for someone in the armed forces.

A small thing may have saved me for service in the CIC. I read in the *Baltimore Sun* that the Americans for Democratic Action would be holding a dinner in Baltimore and that the speaker would be Owen Lattimore, one of McCarthy's favorite targets. I sensed that McCarthy had no basis for his attack, and I wanted to hear Lattimore's side, not a prudent thing to do as a CIC trainee. They seated me at a table with two White House staff people, Richard Neustadt and James Loeb. When they learned that I knew Governor Adlai Stevenson, they pressed me with questions with an uncommon intensity. Before the evening program finished, they said they would like to talk to me more about Stevenson, and would I please refrain from mentioning their interest in Adlai to others. A day or two later someone ran into the barracks where I had a cot along with many others and excitedly told me, "There is a call at the orderly room for you from Operator 34 at the White House. They would like you to call right away." That call may have saved my hide. The word about it spread quickly. Trainees who are privates — I may have been a private first class by then — are not accustomed to receiving phone calls from the White House. When I reached the White House operator she put Dick Neustadt (later on the faculty at Harvard) on the phone and we arranged to meet the following weekend at the White House. He again asked me not to mention their specific interest. When my classmates at Holabird asked why I had received the call, I told them I could not reveal that, and of course that added to the mystery, and perhaps my security.

What Dick Neustadt and Jim Loeb did not spell out for me, but I accurately assumed, was that Harry Truman would not run again and that at least some of the White House staff favored Adlai as the candidate. Just before I entered the Army, the Governor had written to me:

> I hear today from Carl McGowan that you are shortly to be inducted into the Army. I find myself of two minds: I am delighted on the one hand that you are going to be serving in the armed forces, and disappointed on the other hand that your emphatic and clear voice is going to be stilled here-abouts for a while. I hope it will not be long before you can resume your very important and helpful contribution to the revival of law enforcement in Illinois.[21]

That kind of thoughtful gesture to a twenty-two-year-old impressed me a great deal, and I spoke in glowing but candid terms to the White House staff about Stevenson. Some weeks later when Truman made his announcement that he would not run again, national speculation immediately centered on Stevenson.

After finishing CIC training, they assigned me to Germany, probably because of the man who filled out that form when I entered the Army.

In March 1952 I went overseas by troop ship — and within twenty-four hours got sick and stayed that way until we landed at Bremerhaven, Germany. With little to do for ten days, gambling preoccupied the time of many in the crowded ship, officers occasionally stopping a game but generally understanding that the men needed some type of self-entertainment. Stacked four cots on top of one another in "the hold" for sleeping, the midwinter seas rough, and with so many of us sick already, terrible odors in the sleeping area were enough to force everyone onto a crowded deck except for the worst weather. Too sick to read, I played bridge for the only time in my life, traveling both ways on the Atlantic. (Since my retirement from the Senate, two universities have asked me to teach a semester on one of their cruise ships. I quickly declined!)

I spent a few days in Stuttgart, headquarters in Germany for the CIC. In 1952 the physical scars of war in the buildings in Germany dominated the landscape, except for rural areas. I kept a diary (only for a few days, I regret to say) and in Stuttgart I wrote, "Across from the railroad station I saw a boy whom I would judge to be about 11 with one side of his face and part of his forehead horribly scarred.

What is probably even more tragic is that his mind is probably also scarred and that of his parents too." I have seen devastation from many mini-wars since that time, but that first acquaintance with the grim results of war are vivid to me to this day.

Still in uniform, I went from Stuttgart to Bayreuth in Bavaria, our sub-regional headquarters. I stayed for a few weeks in part of composer Richard Wagner's home, Villa Wahnfried. The Wagner family lived in the main home and the Army had taken over the guest villa next to it. The Wagners were strong supporters of Hitler. Wagner's daughter-in-law still lived there and I saw her regularly but never met her; she resented our presence. But the young great-grandchildren of Wagner were exceedingly friendly and enjoyed our heavily accented attempts to speak German. I could see the grave of the composer from the window of my room. Across the street was the home in which composer Franz Liszt spent part of his life after becoming Wagner's father-in-law. As a lover of music but no fan of Wagner's philosophy, I appreciated this brief but indirect brush with musical genius. The guest house where we stayed had been used by Hitler when he visited the Wagners. I bathed in the same bathtub in which Hitler presumably bathed.

One of the men I met in the Army there, Lorne Macarthur of Waltham, Massachusetts, I kept in touch with through the years. He became a high school teacher, and when I sought the Democratic nomination for President in 1988, he supported me, among other ways, with a big neighborhood rally he and his wife organized for me.

Then I received my permanent assignment, the City of Coburg on the Soviet Zone border, where I had Army orders to live in a home and wear civilian clothes and avoid regular contact with Americans in uniform. I had an office in the courthouse, lived next to the Duke of Coburg, a relative of Prince Albert, an earlier Duke of Coburg who married Queen Victoria. The Duke was seriously ill. I never did see him though I saw and met members of his family. Coburg, a picturesque city of 40,000, traces its roots to 531 A. D. Dominated by a huge castle/fortress on a hill overlooking the city, I lived on the side of the hill and when I walked to the top I looked down into Soviet territory. Martin Luther lived in that castle in 1520, and preached in the local church, St. Morizkirche, named for an African Christian missionary who came to Germany to convert the barbarians there. In part because of the dukedom being there, Coburg has a tradition of rich culture, and when I lived there, despite all the desperate privations of the people during that period, Coburg had a full-time, professional orchestra, opera company, and theater company. And because it received relatively little damage in World War II and rested just out-side of Soviet territory, refugees streamed into Coburg until the Soviets sealed the border. Roughly one out of three citizens there was a refugee, a very unusual situation for Germany, where most people trace their roots in their home towns back for centuries.

We had one small sour note. The United States maintained a place called Amerika Haus in Coburg and other cities where Germans could borrow books and read U. S. newspapers and magazines. But when Sen. Joseph McCarthy started questioning the patriotism of certain authors and called many books Communist-tainted, Amerika Haus got rid of those books, doing the very thing Hitler had done early in his regime. The parallel did not escape the notice of the German populace.

I had a German car with German license plates, as the Army wanted me to blend in with the rest of the population as much as pos-sible. My extremely limited German posed one huge handicap, though by the time I left I could speak a passable "street German." The Army gave me civilian clothes to wear. At that point people in Germany still suffered economically. For example, I could buy a fine steak dinner for four Deutschmarks, then the equivalent of one dol-lar. But the clothing they assigned to me included all white shirts. No one in that area of Germany could afford the luxury of wearing white shirts! My basic job was to interview people who had escaped across the Iron Curtain, Winston Churchill's apt phrase, to learn what they knew about troop movements and about leaders on the other side who might be sympathetic enough to slip us information, and bits of trivia that helped to inform us about Soviet activities. In addition, I regu-larly met a few people from the Soviet side who risked their lives to come across to give us information, for which we paid them well. The border not only had East German and/or Soviet military personnel with machine guns, and spotlights at night, but about a ten-yard plowed strip in which land mines had been placed. Roads that origi-nally crossed the border had deadly barriers to any attempted vehicu-lar escape. But despite all of this, some of our regular informers knew how to make it across in relative safety. A few were probably double agents. Other people sometimes made it across the border too, but many who attempted to escape died in the process. The harshness and cruelty of that border I will never forget. A fourteen-year-old boy I interviewed ate a piece of chocolate someone had slipped over the border, and he said if they had things like that in the West he wanted to go there, and risked his life to do it, successfully.

Every Thursday evening several of us in Coburg gathered in a small tavern (gasthaus) called the Half Moon where we had our special table (stammtisch) and drank wine (for me) or beer and talked about the world's problems. Regulars were Mr. and Mrs. Joachim Behrens, the local newspaper editor and his wife; Mr. and Mrs. Paul Horn, a court official and his wife; and Karl Schweizer, an elderly but mentally acute retiree from the German military of many years earlier. Occasionally others joined us. I enjoyed their company and we had great exchanges of viewpoints, all of us learning in the process. They talked of the inevitability of Germany and France fighting again, and I said I felt that did not have to happen. The editor said, "You are a typically idealistic and unrealistic young American." Today hardly anyone would say such a struggle is inevitable.

People in Coburg were marvelous to me, and I hesitate to mention specific people because I should be acknowledging so many, but the young assistant pastor and his wife of the church I attended, Johannes and Ruth Hanselmann, took me into their small apartment on Christmas Eve, a gesture I will never forget. Later he became the bishop of the Lutheran church for Bavaria and international presiding officer of the Lutheran World Federation.

I had never been outside the United States until my Army service, and the assignment to Germany gave me a chance to see much of Europe, including visiting London when the Yugoslavian leader and dictator Tito paid a state visit. I sat in the gallery of the House of Commons and saw Tito as well as Prime Minister Anthony Eden, and an elderly Winston Churchill and Clement Attlee.

The Army assignment to Germany also gave me the chance to visit France and Spain and to broaden my horizons.

Officers of the CIC tried to get me to stay on for eighteen more months and become a commissioned officer. Instead I eagerly headed home.

I had always viewed running for office eventually as a possibility, but my two years in the Army gave me time to reflect on Madison County and the reality that I could more likely effect real change through public office than through my journalistic efforts. I also recognized that I would never become a Walter Lippmann. In addition, I wanted to show that someone with my beliefs could not only physically survive in Madison County, but actually have a chance to win.

Ray Johnsen had a good handle on running the newspaper business and I trusted him completely. I am not an attorney so I could not run for state's attorney, and I had no interest in being a sheriff. State Representative seemed to fit my interests.

Six months after my discharge from the Army I announced that I would become a candidate for State Representative. The following evening the Democratic executive committee of Madison County met and unanimously voted to oppose me.

It was not a great way to start a campaign.

[1] *Troy Tribune*, 21 October 1954.

[2] *Troy Tribune*, "The City and Sewerage," 29 December 1949.

[3] *Troy Tribune*, "Of Mice and Men," 28 December 1950.

[4] "'Closed' Prostitution Houses Again Operating," *Troy Tribune*, 20 October 1949.

[5] "Governor Calls County 'An Obstinate Problem,'" *Troy Tribune*, 20 October 1949.

[6] "Stevenson Calls Gambling Biggest Headache in State," *Troy Tribune*, 5 January 1950.

[7] "Gambling in Illinois," editorial, *St. Louis Globe-Democrat*, reprinted in *Troy Tribune*, 5 January 1950.

[8] *Troy Tribune*, 16 June 1949.

[9] Elliott to author, *Troy Tribune*, 11 August 1949.

[10] *Troy Tribune*, 11 May 1950.

[11] "Hyde Park, 200 Club Raided by State Cops," *Troy Tribune* 18 May 1950.

[12] "Grand Jury Reports Harrell 'Not Guilty,'" *Troy Tribune*, 19 April 1951.

[13] Author to Charles Stephens, *Troy Tribune*, 25 January 1951.

[14] "Organized Crime in Interstate Commerce," Senate Report, April 1951, 782.

[15] "Kefauver Calls Madison County 'Most Shocking,'" *Troy Tribune*, 3 May 1951.

[16] "Simon Pure," *Newsweek*, 12 February 1951.

[17] Charles Klotzer, "Club Prevue Still Operating Full Blast," *Troy Tribune*, 20 August 1953.

[18] Ray Brennan, "Downstate Hoodlum's Riches Told," *Chicago Sun-Times*, 4 July 1958.

[19] "Gangster Element Tries to Move In," *Troy Tribune*, 7 August 1958.

[20]*Troy Tribune*, 26 April 1951.

[21]Edward P. Doyle, ed., *As We Knew Adlai* (New York: Harper and Row, 1966), 129.

# Chapter 4

# *State Legislator*

Illinois had an unusual system for electing members to its House of Representatives in 1954, the year I first became a candidate. Voters could mark the ballot for one person, who then would get three votes, for two who each would get one-and-one-half votes, or for three who each would get one vote. In the fall, ordinarily there would be two candidates from each party and three of the four would be elected, assuring minority representation even in a district that leaned heavily Democratic or Republican.

Part of my calculation in seeking the nomination for State Representative was that if people voted only for me I would get three votes. Of the three incumbents, two were Democrats in this heavily Democratic area. The Democratic organization backed the two incumbents, Lloyd "Curly" Harris from Granite City and Leland Kennedy from Alton, both cities of approximately 40,000 people. I came from Troy with 1,200 people. At no time did I attack either Harris or Kennedy, because I liked both of them personally and because the real issue was not their candidacies but whether the corrupt system in the county would continue.

Traditionally the organization hired cars in each precinct, and for a precinct committeeman to get money he (still no women then) had to agree to support the candidates the organization wanted. The big money for all this came from the gamblers. Few people thought I had a chance. But I had a small folder printed and started going through business districts and going door-to-door in residential areas. One of the few committeemen to support me, Walter Nonn in Granite City, told me if I covered his precinct door to door he would support me. And he did. My brother Art, then a student at Concordia Seminary in

St. Louis, went room to room in the dormitory soliciting people for Saturday door-to-door activity for me, getting several dozen seminary students to volunteer at least one day for me. Other people volunteered. A middle-aged St. Louis man whom I had never met but who had read about me, Walter Hoops, came across the river Saturday after Saturday to go door to door. No candidate for any office in the area worked as hard at it as I did, and I thought I had a chance until the day of the primary, when I saw the organization cars smothering the county. Some precincts (rarely 300 votes in a primary) had as many as twenty cars hired. My family and I and two or three friends gathered in the Troy City Hall to take in the returns that night, but I told them I thought I had lost. When the votes started to come in, it became clear that all those paid cars took my voters to the polls. The *Alton Evening Telegraph*, under a large front-page banner headline, "Paul Simon Is Nominated In Upset," noted: "Paul Simon, crusading young editor of the *Troy Tribune*, scored a sensational upset when he won one of the Democratic party's two nominations for state representative. The newcomer who wasn't supposed to have a chance topped two veteran vote-getters to lead the field of three."[1] The small city of Troy and the rural area of that township turned out en masse, giving me 1,083 votes, more than 1,000 votes ahead of the other two candidates combined. That vote, where people knew me, gave me special satisfaction. The official total returns gave me 30,141 votes, Harris 20,684, and Kennedy 18,584. I won in the fall easily.

One of the judicial candidates in the fall recalled: "After a Democratic rally in Godfrey, a few of the candidates retired to a restaurant and lounge in Alton for some quiet rest and relaxation and maybe have a beer or two. . . . But you couldn't stand seeing all the potential voters in the room unattended and proceeded to shake every hand in the room. Realizing we were discovered, the rest of us had to pool our resources and buy a drink for the house. We ended the occasion broke, but you got all the votes."[2]

At the age of twenty-five I became a state representative-elect. My total expenditure for the campaign was $3,852.18 which I accounted for in detail, though Illinois had no disclosure laws then. I had no contribution of more than $100. My next campaign, for reelection, cost $2,130.80, of which $512.50 came in contributions, $185 of that from my parents and $1,618.30 came from my pocket. Because of the widespread corruption in the county, I announced that each year in public office I would disclose my personal income in detail, which I have always done, down to a refund of $1.58 from Land's End.

For my first year in public office I received $5,000 for being a state legislator, most of the rest of my total income of just over $7,000 coming from the newspaper business. Other small items included $15 for speaking to the Madison County School Institute. I noted: "My experience confirms the common knowledge that other fields are more profitable financially than the political arena. However, I have no regrets."[3] Eleven years later my income reached $23,038.72, $7,586.78 of that coming from the State Senate, the rest from my newspapers, book royalties, and $5 from the Grantfork PTA for speaking to them.

The first significant piece of legislation I passed came partly from my own experience with government bodies that held secret meetings. But a note from a veteran reporter on the Springfield scene, Don Chamberlain, stimulated it. "*The Illinois State Journal* some time ago carried an editorial entitled 'The Right to Know' suggesting Illinois enact a law similar to one in California requiring actions and deliberations of governing bodies of that state be conducted in public. . . . I am not lobbying, just looking for a story. I have a clipping of the editorial if you would like to have it."[4] He sent that to me two weeks after I had taken the oath of office. I drafted the bill, modeling it after the California statute, providing exceptions for a governmental body meeting in private to discuss personnel matters and for when property was to be purchased or sold, both legitimate exceptions. I gained support from a surprising source. The big abusers of the public's right to listen to deliberations of a government body were school boards. The Illinois School Board Association believed this to be harmful for public relations for schools, and Bob Cole, their chief lobbyist, contacted me and said they would strongly support the proposal. But many government bodies opposed it, saying it would hinder their ability to do business efficiently. Typical was the statement from the Regional Association of South Cook-Will County Municipalities: "This bill would hamper and hamstring the effective administration of municipal government."[5] One reporter told me I was "heading uphill on roller skates." I stressed over and over that the public had a right to know what decision a public body reached and how they reached it. Harold Cross, a New York attorney and the nation's leading authority in the field, praised my proposal and newspapers, gradually, editorially supported it. The most vocal opposition came from "the West Side Bloc," a small group of legislators identified in the newspapers as having ties to the Chicago criminal syndicate. Their opposition — in this case — helped my bill. It passed and became law, my first big victory. Harold Cross, the national champion of open meetings, wrote, "Large gains were scored in the measure which passed."[6]

During my fourteen state legislative years I passed forty-seven significant pieces of legislation for which I served as the chief sponsor, and aided in many others. They varied from my proposal to establish the Illinois Arts Council, modeled after what New York had done, to measures that received virtually no public attention. An example of the latter occurred when a man in my legislative district wanted to take his high school equivalency test (GED), but the local school superintendent refused to offer it. I called the superintendent. He didn't want to give the tests because he said it would encourage people to drop out of high school. At that point school superintendents were the only people authorized to give the tests. In checking around I found that this example was anything but isolated, and I introduced legislation to give the county superintendent of schools in each county the authority to administer the tests. A small change, but almost overnight the numbers of people taking and passing the tests escalated dramatically, providing greater opportunity for tens of thousands.

Perhaps more significant than bills some of us passed were measures we stopped or got amended. I worked closely in the House during these early days with Representatives Alan Dixon, Abner Mikva, Anthony Scariano, and Jeanne Hurley, as well as others. The fact that we looked at legislation carefully probably prevented some of the worst abuses. But we did not have a record of uniform success. Far from it.

Illinois had no minimum wage law and I introduced a measure proposing a 75-cent minimum. I called as a witness before the committee a woman with two children, trying to feed, clothe and house herself and her two children on 57 cents an hour. She told a heart-rending story. I couldn't believe anyone would vote against the bill after hearing that, but they did. My bill went down in a straight party vote, Democrats supporting it, Republicans opposing it.

In my first term two measures became inextricably linked: an increase in the state sales tax from two percent to three percent, and a reduction of one-third in the tax on the two downstate race tracks, one in my district. Race track legislation almost always had a distinctive odor to it. Prior to my entering the legislature, a measure passed to aid Chicago Downs, a track in that area. Rep. Paul Powell handled the measure and then bought 16,900 shares of stock at ten cents a share, and the first year it paid $1 per share in dividends. Not a bad investment! Three years later — my first year in the legislature — it paid $5.75 per share or $57.50 for each dollar invested. All of this is part of the public record. But before many weeks in the legislature I heard from others who had bought 100 shares of Chicago Downs, with the understanding with Powell that all on the inside of this deal would be able to buy an equal number of shares. When the record became public and Powell had 16,900 compared to a handful for others, there were some unhappy legislators. The old saw about "honor among thieves" is much more myth than reality. Powell claimed "the stock was not purchased until after the law was passed and the passage of the law had no connection with the purchase of the stock."[7] No one believed that.

So when the race track tax reduction came up the same day as the increase in the tax on a loaf of bread and a pound of butter from two cents to three cents, I attacked it. And from the emotional reaction of a few of my colleagues it became clear that many of them had money riding on the outcome, and my action represented a potential threat to their income. At first I thought I was alone in the fight, and then Rep. Richard Stengel joined me and called it the worst steal he had seen in his years in the legislature. Powell responded, "You're just angry because you're not in on it." To no one's surprise, it passed overwhelmingly and then Stengel and I used a rarely utilized tool in the Illinois legislature — used by Abraham Lincoln in 1837 on a measure dealing with slavery in the District of Columbia — we filed a formal protest, urging the Governor to veto the race track bill. Any two members can do that. This simple action caused a storm to erupt around Stengel and me. My assumption — and I do not know this for a certainty — is that Governor William Stratton, who had obviously made the deal with the tracks in order to get his sales tax increase, feared the whole thing would explode and told Powell and his henchmen that they would have to take the heat off him. State legislators saw sizable income disappearing. Powell's close ally, Rep. Carl Preihs, introduced a resolution of censure against Stengel and me, calling us "men who lack integrity" and that we had "disgraced" the legislature. That apparently took the heat off the Governor, who signed the two bills quickly the day after passage, the only non-emergency bills acted upon so quickly during that session, and they quietly dropped the censure resolution.

The blatant corruption in the legislature startled me. Coming from Madison County I did not expect a legislative body free of weaknesses. But members talked openly about certain measures being "money bills," others being "fetchers," introduced for the sole purpose of having some industry come and pay the legislator for not moving a bill forward. When a community in my district, East Alton, issued bonds at interest rates that far exceeded the interest rate that a heavily industrialized community should pay, I checked into the law and found we had no requirement for competitive bidding on bonds. So I introduced such a proposal. That resulted in the only direct bribe offer I have ever received in all my years in politics. Shortly after I introduced it one of my fellow House members came and asked, "What are you doing with my bill?" "What bill?" I asked him. "That bond bill," he responded. "I always introduce it and I do rather well with it. Why don't you kill it. If you do, it could be a good thing for both of us. We'll split the proceeds." I declined his offer and quickly scheduled the bill for a committee hearing and vote, fearing that someone might think I was playing the same game. I had prestigious groups like the Taxpayers Federation of Illinois and the Farm Bureau testify for it. Virtually no one voiced opposition, and then the committee voted it down 20-0. Several of the members thanked me.

Lobbyists were told that for $7,500 or more (the figure varied) a legislator would get the lobbyist votes.

We had quality members in both political parties who had far too much self-respect to stoop to this type of thing, but we also had many members who obviously came to Springfield with boodle in mind. Several of us talked about it from time to time, concerned but also wondering what we could do that would be effective. I talked to two Chicago newspaper editors about it, one of whom I learned later owned race track stock. It would not surprise me to learn that he acquired that stock at bargain rates. But the two editors showed little interest in devoting considerable time and money to a thorough investigative reporting job. We did not have something that could be easily proven. About this time Al Balk, who wrote feature articles for national magazines, approached me about working with him on an article about corruption in the legislature for *Harper's*. I respected Al and felt that the problem should be exposed, even if it meant the end of my political career. The article appeared in September 1964, under the title "The Illinois Legislature: A Study in Corruption." It caused a storm. In it I quoted Rep. Noble Lee, a Republican who also served as Dean of the John Marshall Law School in Chicago (the father of Congresswoman Nancy Johnson of Connecticut) as saying that he thought one-third of the members took payoffs. I would have put the figure higher, but I used his more conservative estimate. Mike Royko had a tongue-in-cheek column in the *Chicago Daily News* expressing is shock that two-thirds of the legislators were not getting anything, calling it a threat to the legislative process.[8] Many of these bribes were cloaked as "campaign contributions" or public relations services or legal fees, providing a veneer of legality. Until July 1998, legislators in Illinois could take campaign contributions and legally spend them on a fur coat for a spouse, for college tuition for their children, for sports cars, or to buy a house — all of these real examples.

The spring prior to the *Harper's* article the Illinois legislature did something unexpected: It passed a bill to create the Illinois Crime Commission. It passed only because the day before it came up for a vote Chicago Alderman Ben Lewis was slain gangland style and members hesitated to vote against it. But when it came to appointing members of the commission, with two or three exceptions, those appointed should have been subjects of an investigation. I recall vividly having dinner with a few people who gathered in a Chinese restaurant in the St. Nicholas Hotel. Three or four of us were legislators and the others lobbyists or visitors to Springfield. When the question of bribery came up, Sen. Bob McCarthy commented, "I suppose there will always be some people who will be willing to pay money to buy votes." And then a legislator later appointed to the Illinois Crime Commission responded, "Let's hope so!" The appointments to the Crime Commission were so bad that they led Rep. Abner Mikva to comment, "We should have made it clearer and called it the Anti-Crime Commission."

Ordinarily a chief sponsor of a commission bill is named to the commission, but Rep. Anthony Scariano, with his militant attitude against underworld ties to state and local government, did not receive an appointment despite being chief sponsor. When asked if the West Side Bloc, a group of legislators identified with ties to the old Capone interests, had stopped him, Tony replied, "It wasn't the YMCA!" Strongly opposed to the creation of a Crime Commission, the West Side Bloc members — everyone knew who they were — voted together on all issues. When Jeanne Hurley (soon to become Jeanne Hurley Simon) sponsored a measure which I cosponsored to curtail wiretapping in Illinois, we found unexpected allies from the West Side Bloc. In 1953, Rep. Clem Graver differed from other bloc members on a matter concerning what eventually became McCormick Place, helping his friend George Tagge, the *Chicago Tribune* political editor. Not long after that unusual break from solidity in the bloc, Graver drove into his home and his wife saw "several men from another car leap on Clem, stick guns against him and hustle him into their car."[9] No one ever heard from him again. No one ever found a trace of him.

The bloc members took their politics seriously. And through simple bribery they influenced many more votes than their solid bloc. Rep. William Murphy, the sponsor of a bill to legalize bingo in Illinois, said on the floor in 1961: "The Chicago papers have said the hoodlums are interested in this bill. You know that can't be true or it would have received more votes."[10] Having the West Side Bloc strongly opposed to the creation of a Crime Commission — together with others with illegal activities — stopped its passage for several years.

When my *Harper's* article appeared, Rep. Scariano, long on both courage and integrity and later a Justice of the Illinois Court of Appeals, immediately said I was right and that the Illinois Crime Commission should investigate the charges. The media took up his suggestion and soon the Crime Commission slowly, reluctantly backed into an investigation. I went before them; Tony Scariano did; and a series of other witnesses also testified, some because I had mentioned them. The legislator who had suggested that we split the proceeds of killing my competitive bidding on bonds bill testified, and a friend told me he was terrified about what might happen. I told the Commission of a group that came to me hoping to pass some legislation. Two years before they went to a suburban state senator and gave him $25,000 in cash to get their bill through committee. He did nothing for them, but pocketed the money. "We've decided to do it the honest way," they told me. I politely declined their request, even though the proposal appeared to have merit, because I knew that if I introduced that bill the suburban senator who previously got the money would think I was now the beneficiary. I provided the Commission with my limited knowledge of information, and they went through the motions of a thorough investigation but finally voted, to no one's surprise, that the charges were groundless — with two dissents, two members appointed by the governor, Prentiss Marshall and Harlington Wood Jr., both men of impeccable character who later became federal judges. The majority found that "charges of wholesale corruption made against the Illinois General Assembly are unjust and unfounded." In their dissent, Marshall and Wood stated that under the Commission rules they could not release information of cases where they found substantial evidence. Scariano and I issued a joint statement: "The net result of the majority report is to discourage Illinois citizens from coming forward with information to the Crime Commission."[11]

In the *Harper's* article I suggested that the rumors around the legislature had one influential member making $100,000 a session on bribes, a none-too-veiled reference to Paul Powell. The Commission asked him to testify, and Powell, then Secretary of State, afterwards called me to his office and asked where I got that figure. I told him that was a widely circulated rumor. "You can't prove that," he told me. I assured him I could not. "You shouldn't say it if you can't prove it," he responded angrily. At no time in our fifteen-minute conversation did he deny the truth of the report but he obviously felt I had violated the unspoken rule of silence that legislators should follow to protect each other. That this estimate erred on the conservative side is suggested by a *Chicago Daily News* story that reported that he received $70,000 from a lobbyist for the race tracks while still a legislator. When asked about it he called it a business arrangement that made it possible for him to serve in the legislature without taking bribes.

My relationship with Powell was a strange up-and-down one, though more down than up. I did not successfully stop most of his maneuvers, such as his race track bills, but I provided an irritant and public exposure of the games being played. I sensed that he both hated and admired me. At one point he got a bill passed requiring all trucks in Illinois to have certain hard, plastic contour mud guards. Truckers hated them because they broke off after accumulating dirt and caused a traffic hazard. I always opposed the truckers when they asked for more weight and longer trucks; they reportedly paid well to get that legislation passed. But on this matter I volunteered to introduce a bill to get rid of the contour mud guards. Rumors had it that Powell had an interest in the business. When Powell got up to oppose the amendment, he said that reports that he or his friends had an interest in it were absolutely false. I then read the names of the officers of a specially created corporation to which the patent had been assigned. They were Scheaffer O'Neill, John Stelle, and George Edward Day — Powell's close associates in race tracks and other endeavors. When Powell and I would have these clashes, the ordinarily noisy House would become deathly quiet.

But we never reached a point of not talking to each other. One day he had a bill whose aim looked highly suspicious to me and I let my colleagues know I would oppose it. He came over to me and asked why I was resisting this. I smiled and said, "Paul, you know why I'm opposing you on this." He responded vigorously with his colorful country language, "Paul, you're wrong! If I stole a pig on this bill I would tell you." Of course he would not tell me. Even though he later tried to defeat me for the State Senate, when I went there our relationship improved — until the *Harper's* article — in part because I was out of his hair in the House. During a hospital stay, I sent him a note wishing him good health and he replied that he would be happy to help me on my Senate legislation in the House "providing I am in accord with same."[12]

My status with my colleagues after the appearance of the *Harper's* article is illustrated by a gesture at the biennial Senate dinner, an event I regularly avoided because it took in large amounts of money from lobbyists and then divided that money among the legislative leaders. At the dinner, they called on Sen. Hudson Sours of Peoria, who had a good mind and could recite dates and facts of history *ad nauseam*, though the meaning of all these things totally bypassed him. He stood up at the dinner and, to great cheers and laughter, announced that I had won the "Benedict Arnold Award" and that previous recipients were Judas Iscariot and Aaron Burr.

Some legislators said they admired me for writing it, and even those who obviously did not recognize that they needed my vote on key measures and tolerated me. I think they all sensed I had no personal animus in the matter, but simply believed the situation had to change. One legislator who encouraged me told me he wished I had started much earlier, that he had become already part of the system. He said he made enough in bribes to buy a new car every two years. He felt poorly rewarded for the risks he took. He did not have a role of prominence in the legislature, and obviously others did much better.

Something that lightened my load occurred when someone illegally taped a conversation between two lobbyists staying in the Leland Hotel, telling how they were spending $30,000 to kill a bill. The person who recorded the conversation (and George Mahin of the Better Government Association had a room next to theirs) then got the tapes to Jack Mabley, a clean-as-a-whistle reporter and columnist for the *Chicago American*. Jack's story is that he received a key to a lock in the Greyhound Bus Station in the mail with a note telling him he would find something of great interest. It was! While my article did not mention names, the transcript of the tapes in the *American* had names and all the details that we knew to be authentic. When that newspaper arrived in the capitol it sold out immediately and all business stopped. I have never seen anything like it. Legislators, reporters, everyone who could secure the newspaper read it, sometimes chuckling at something they read, sometimes whispering in amazement to a friend. That article made my *Harper's* story look anemic. It also had little insights into humanity. The legislator (whom we knew as crooked) who paid off members for the lobbyists referred to $200 he had given one millionaire member for a vote. "Why does a millionaire want $200 for a vote?" the one lobbyist asked. The other replied,

"How do you think he got to be a millionaire?" (Because of my service in the U. S. Senate I got to know several millionaire members well, some of them my best friends. I have observed that when they see a penny on the ground they pick it up! But none, to my knowledge, during my time there was guilty of the boorish and criminal behavior of some of these state legislators, though that would not be true of an earlier period in the nation's history.)

In those days we had no offices. We received our mail at our desks and a secretarial pool served several legislators. Patricia Nattermann helped me more than anyone, but since I received more mail than most legislators I always had mail to take back to Troy where a loyal, dedicated woman, Eleanor Ellis, helped me. A native of Mississippi, she gradually grew to tolerate my views that differed substantially from those she grew up with as a white in segregated Mississippi. Eventually, she not only tolerated my views but gradually grew comfortable with them and embraced many of them. And she was gracious to everyone, smoothing over some of the bumps in the road I created.

During my first term in the Illinois House, the Supreme Court gave its "one man one vote" decision which caused state legislative bodies all over the nation to redistrict themselves. Under the old system Illinois had thirty-nine times as many people in one House district as in another. A much-needed change, it would never have occurred without Supreme Court action. But the forces of reaction and status quo liked the old ways and pushed for a national constitutional convention to force a reversal. While I favor a constitutional amendment to require a balanced budget except for emergencies, and I supported the amendment giving eighteen-year-olds the right to vote, and the Equal Rights Amendment, having a constitutional convention could cause havoc to the basic liberties in our nation. It is permissible under the constitution, but it should never occur, and I helped lead the fight to stop this. One of the few groups that consistently supported an enlightened position on this was the League of Women Voters. But in the process of fighting this proposal I wrote an article for *Saturday Review*, an excellent publication edited by one of the finest people I have known, Norman Cousins. In that article I praised the League of Women Voters, but noting the opposition, quoted one of my State Senate colleagues as referring to them as the League of Women Vultures. I did not quote him favorably, but simply quoting him caused a mini storm to descend on me from some of the more sensitive members of the League of Women Voters around the nation. This battle we won, both because of the soundness of our position, and because once reapportionment had taken place legislators were not eager to go through the process again.

I turned out to be a major beneficiary of the Supreme Court ruling and redistricting. One of the people elected in the process, Jeanne Hurley from Wilmette, made an excellent impression on me. It was not "love at first sight," but as we worked together on issues more and more, I learned of our philosophical kinship. We were, for example, the only two white legislators to list ourselves as affiliated with the National Association for the Advancement of Colored People in the memberships shown in the *Illinois Blue Book*. When friends tried to match me with one person or another, I would occasionally say I was looking for "a Lutheran Jeanne Hurley." I heard reports that she said she wanted "a Catholic Paul Simon." Finally — two years after serving together — I asked her for a date. We saw "The Music Man" together. On the next date I proposed and she accepted.

We shared being Democrats, but politically independent Democrats. Both of us won initially when the traditional powers predicted that we would not. In the cumulative, three-vote system that I have explained, Jeanne's heavily Republican district north of Chicago nominated two Republicans and two Democrats, but everyone knew that only one Democrat would be elected, and an able nominee from more heavily populated and more heavily Democratic Evanston, Russell Packard, was expected to win, but the leaders said the process of running would give Jeanne political experience for whatever might develop in the future. Jeanne worked hard, helped particularly by her brothers Bill and Bob, and on election night startled the political old-timers by winning.

Jeanne's father and brothers went to Notre Dame. Her father, Ira Hurley, an attorney, died before Jeanne and I met; I have always regretted not having the chance to know him. Jeanne's Irish Catholic mother, Margaret Reilly Hurley, grew up in a firm religious family, and she had doubts about Jeanne marrying a Lutheran, just as my strong Lutheran parents had doubts about my wedding a Roman Catholic. Jeanne went to Barat College of the Sacred Heart and then attended Northwestern University Law School. She worked as an Assistant State's Attorney in Cook County and later as an attorney for the Brunswick Corporation. Our engagement and wedding took place before Vatican Council II, when Pope John XXIII changed the church and ushered in a period of improved relationships between religious bodies.

We married April 21, 1960, and took our "first honeymoon" to — where else — Washington, D.C. We drove through West Virginia to get there, sampling a bit of the atmosphere of the John Kennedy vs. Hubert Humphrey primary. In the capitol, Congressman Melvin Price arranged for us to have seats for a joint session that General Charles De Gaulle addressed. What he said I do not remember, but what is vivid in my mind is that though he was seriously nearsighted he was vain enough — we all have our vanities — that he did not want to make that obvious. He had memorized his speech. We had a copy of the French text and he delivered it word for word as in the printed document, even though he could not read it.

On our honeymoon we periodically checked by phone with relatives in Illinois and on our return trip we received word in West Virginia that the Governor had called a special session of the legislature, already meeting. We drove back to Illinois quickly because the House had a one-vote Democratic majority, and we represented two votes. But the question arose whether Jeanne could vote. Under the old Illinois law a wife's residence automatically became the same as her husband's after marriage. Could Jeanne, as a resident of the southern part of the state, represent the Wilmette area? The Attorney General ruled quickly and informally that the Illinois constitution established residential criteria for a candidate for the General Assembly, but not for an incumbent, so Jeanne voted in that special session.

Our "second honeymoon" three months later took us to the Los Angeles Democratic convention that nominated John F. Kennedy, and we became actively involved in that campaign (See Chapter 14).

Marrying Jeanne was the wisest thing I have ever done. We have been partners in the fullest sense. We share the same hopes for our society and world and for our children and grandchildren; we travel together and campaign together, and when we campaign or speak or volunteer separately we touch base each evening by telephone. Whatever I have been able to accomplish has Jeanne's stamp on it as much as mine, though she has provided her own distinctive leadership in many areas. Currently she chairs the U. S. National Commission on Libraries and Information Services, an appointment by President Clinton, not secured at my request but because of the urgings of the library community. It is not a full-time position, but a voluntary effort, one of many she provides.

Our two children, Sheila and Martin, and our four grandchildren, to whom this book is dedicated, have given us immense pleasure. Sheila, born eleven months after we married, is now an assistant state's attorney in Jackson County, Illinois, and teaches at Southern Illinois University Law School part-time. Her husband, Perry Knop, is an attorney and teaches at John A. Logan College. The two met at a rally for Adlai Stevenson III. Their children are Reilly and Brennan. Martin (named for my father) Hurley (named for Jeanne's family) Simon came along three years after Sheila and is a professional photographer, with two cover pictures in *Newsweek* and one in *Time* in addition to a wide variety of others, including a two-page spread in a book on classic pictures put out by *Life*. Martin's wife, Julie Jacobsen Simon, taught in the public schools in the District of Columbia. A talented teacher and writer, she is now a full-time mother taking care of Martin and our other two grandchildren, "CJ" and Nick.

From the early years on, whenever we could do things as a family we did it, whether the menu called for campaigning or vacationing or other unexpected turns in the life of a public official. We tried to make their childhood as normal as possible. Sheila belonged to 4-H, where she learned to sew. Before I came to Congress, legislation passed banning sexual discrimination in education. We had engineering and architectural schools that would not admit women, nursing schools that would not admit men, high school agricultural programs only for boys. The most immediate visible result of the anti-discrimination actions by Congress was in athletics, where girls for the first time got their own teams. In junior high school, Sheila participated in track. In high school she won the Maryland state girl's high jump. A few years later as a student at Wittenberg University in Ohio, she won the national high jump for Division III schools. Martin excelled in punt, pass, and kick contests and made the Carbondale area all-star Little League baseball team, the most exciting baseball I have ever seen. And sometimes poor conduct by parents made it even more exciting.

When Sheila and Martin were in the dating years we sometimes held our breath — and our tongues — as we met their friends. Fortunately, both ultimately chose well. Jeanne and I are pleased to have Perry and Julie in the family. We are proud of the four of them and of our four grandchildren.

A surprising number of issues that are similar mark my trail from state government to the federal government. "The more things change, the more they are the same" is an old saw with much truth. Some issues emerge later or disappear, and of course at the federal level I had much more involvement in defense and foreign policy matters.

Sometimes legislative colleagues can play a major role in determining positions. For example, at the federal level I instinctively opposed the value added tax, always taking a stand against it on the rare occasions when someone questioned me about the possibility. Senator "Fritz" Hollings of South Carolina made a few speeches on the value added tax that were so compelling in their logic, that I became a convert to a properly crafted proposal for such a tax.

One matter that I did not seriously consider before coming to the legislature is capital punishment. I do not remember my father, who had strong opinions on many things, ever discussing it with me. Like most citizens, I accepted it without any serious thought. Rep. Robert McCarthy, later a member of the state senate, opposed capital punishment, showing great courage in doing so, and forcing me to rethink my position. The fact that so many innocent people have been executed and that it is a punishment we reserve — with extremely rare exceptions — for those who cannot afford the best lawyers compelled me to accept the McCarthy position. That and the fact that there is no evidence that it is a deterrent: of Canada, Mexico, the United States, and the countries of western Europe, we are the only one that retains capital punishment — and we have by far the highest rate of murder of any of these nations. Only six countries in the world still legally execute people under the age of eighteen, the United States, Iran, and Iraq being three of the six. And disproportionately those who are minorities are more likely to be executed for the same crimes as whites, just as men are more likely to be executed for a murder conviction than women. The American Bar Association now opposes the death penalty. The late Supreme Court Justice Felix Frankfurter wrote: "I am strongly opposed to capital punishment for reasons that are not related to concern for the murderer or the risk of convicting the innocent. . . . When life is at hazard in a trial, it sensationalizes the whole thing unwittingly; the effect on juries, the Bar, the public, the judiciary, I regard as very bad."[13] In 1963, the director of the Chicago Crime Commission — no relation to the anemic Illinois Crime Commission — issued a statement that still makes sense: "Capital punishment probably hampers, rather than aids, law enforcement and the administration of criminal justice. The long delays that invariably occur in capital cases also are a hindrance to the proper administration of criminal justice. Following the imposition of the death sentence, one appeal follows another until frequently many years elapse before the case is finally disposed of. Under such circumstances justice is neither swift nor certain and public interest suffers. The entire issue of capital punishment is so charged with emotion that its abolition would probably aid the orderly processes of justice."[14] I recently asked a class of twenty-one students how many favored the death penalty. A large majority did. Then I asked how many felt it served as a deterrent to crime, and no one raised a hand. If, as I sense, the reason for capital punishment is revenge, an understandable reaction, then the government should not serve as a tool for assisting in revenge. One of the things I have learned in life is that violence breeds violence. Just as citizens should exercise self-restraint, so should government. Those who represent a threat to society should be jailed, but don't incarcerate our consciences with the death penalty.

While I served in the legislature, I continued my newspaper ownership, gradually acquiring other newspapers with some assistance in the investments from my legislative colleague, Alan Dixon, as well as Ray Johnsen and Elmer Fedder. We acquired thirteen small weekly newspapers, and four printing plants. But one day I had to make a major decision on a piece of printing machinery, whether to repair or replace it, and the call to me in Springfield where I was ill equipped to make the determination moved me to decide on something I had contemplated earlier: to divest myself of my newspaper holdings.

My newspapers, all small weeklies, were too small to present any real conflict of interest between my political ambitions and the position of newspaper ownership. While my initial announcement of my candidacy for state representative made the front page of the *Troy Tribune*, and perhaps did not in other newspapers, I generally played it down rather than stressed it, both to be fair and, frankly, because I felt that if I used my newspapers to promote myself it would be self-defeating. Ray Johnsen and Elmer Fedder took over the bulk of the newspaper operation. By 1966, when I divested myself completely, I knew that soon I would make a plunge into statewide office and I wanted neither the bother of having to make business decisions, nor the problem of someone charging that I used the newspapers for political purposes.

I also had a gradually growing interest in international affairs and the weekly newspapers did not provide me with a good avenue for that interest. After my first six-month session of the Illinois General Assembly I took a trip to Central and South America, hoping to at least pay my way by selling free-lance articles. It didn't work. I sold a few stories, and had a great experience, but my meager finances would not permit many expeditions of that type. Two years later I talked to a travel agency that suggested I get other state legislators together for a trip; that they would pay their full fare and I would get a free fare. That appealed to me! I sent an announcement to every state legislator in the nation and pulled together a group to visit parts of Western and Eastern Europe and to meet with leaders in those countries. I also managed to sell a few stories, actually making a little money on the enterprise in addition to enlarging my cultural horizons. Two years later I did the same on an Asian trip, but corralling a dozen state legislators has its drawbacks and I decided that on future trips I would risk a little more financially but enjoy my independence.

In 1962 Senator Everett Dirksen's term expired, and I made clear to the powers that be — really one power, Mayor Richard Daley — that I would love to make that race. I stirred some interest around the state without formally announcing my candidacy, received a surprising amount of encouragement, including help from Senator Paul Douglas. A poll of newspaper editors in the state conducted by the Paddock Publications of suburban Cook County showed me ahead of the other four possibilities mentioned, with 44 percent favoring my being the Democratic nominee, with Paul Powell running second at 27 percent. The poll, skewed by the fact that I also had background as a newspaper editor, encouraged me nevertheless. At one point the name of Adlai Stevenson, then serving as Ambassador to the United Nations, surfaced. I tried unsuccessfully to reach him by phone to urge him to run and say I would support him. I then sent him a telegram. Adlai wrote to me:

> I have been playing tag with you on the telephone and I am deeply distressed that we have not connected yet. I have wanted to thank you for your very kind and thoughtful telegram and I take this means of doing so now.
>
> I was flattered by your graceful and generous encouragement about the candidacy for the Senate. However, I hope — and believe — you will approve of the decision I made. Now you can continue your "personal efforts" without any anxiety about your old and devoted friend.[15]

Stevenson's withdrawal shifted a limited amount of attention in my direction, but Mayor Daley chose not pick a thirty-three-year-old state senator. Instead he selected Congressman Sidney Yates of Chicago, a genuinely fine legislator who would have made a national name for himself in the Senate. When it became clear that Sid would be chosen, I immediately endorsed him. While I am immodest enough to believe I would have made a stronger candidate than the congressman, I cannot honestly say that I would have made a better senator. Sid had experience on Capitol Hill, and while our views on issues are remarkably similar, he would have started with greater strength, knowing the Washington legislative scene.

I then announced my candidacy for the State Senate. Those whose toes I had stepped on and who resented my independence thought this would be the time to remove me from the political scene. The son of Scheaffer O'Neill, Judge Patrick O'Neill, left the bench to become a candidate, a sacrifice he lived to regret, and — my guess is — would have regretted even if he had won. Judge O'Neill's father collaborated closely with Paul Powell and others in the downstate gambling/race track crowd. I am reasonably sure that Powell's not-so-delicate hand played a principal role in this, Powell hoping to get rid of me from the legislative scene. While I had won my state representative races decisively, in those races people who cast only one vote for a legislative candidate (three of four candidates to be elected) gave three votes to that single candidate. I had sizable numbers of those three-vote ballots. Since I have always run much stronger in a general election than in a Democratic primary, Powell and his friends assumed that in a head-to-head Democratic primary where my supporters' votes would count only for one each, they could defeat me. The Democratic organization in dominant Madison County went on record against me, again. Two of the members told me candidly that they could receive considerable financial assistance in the primary from O'Neill but knew they could not get it from me.

O'Neill's ads stressed that he was a family man, showing a picture of his six children, but provided little of substance other than loose charges. Jeanne resented his "family man" ads. Our one small child, Sheila, could not compare numerically with his large family — Martin arrived two years later — and I simply ignored the ads (to Jeanne's chagrin) and concentrated on matters of substance where I felt I could outdo him.

O'Neill made a number of charges, and a week before the primary I ran a large ad in all the district's newspapers titled "The Charges and the Facts."[16] The charges, designed to defeat me in a Democratic primary, included:

- "Simon is an independent, not a Democrat. He frequently does not support the programs of Governor Kerner and other Democratic leaders."

- "Simon has done nothing for the Democratic organization in eight years in office."

- "Simon is opposed to basketball in our schools."

And other similar charges. Most of them did not resonate much with the public, the basketball charge being a slight exception. I had suggested that the main thrust of education ought to be the traditional learning areas, and that sometimes high school and college athletics take a higher priority role than they should.

The race stirred great interest throughout the state and I won 26,788 to 13,876. Four years later I won again, this time with the endorsement of the party in the primary, and no primary contest.

Southern Illinois is southern, the good and the bad. Schools in much of that portion of our state remained segregated long after the Supreme Court's Brown decision. Movie theaters either did not permit African Americans to enter or required them to sit upstairs while whites sat downstairs. When I came into the legislature cosponsoring and sponsoring civil rights legislation, it was hardly the expected conduct of a legislator from the southern third of the state. It got me some attention, negative and positive. One of my opponents ran a full-page advertisement attacking me for supporting "forced civil rights," whatever that is, but he thought it was not good. I also participated in a group that promoted civil rights through the churches, the Lutheran Human Relations Association, and there I met Rev. Robert Graetz of Montgomery, Alabama, one of only two white ministers to associate with Martin Luther King Jr. in that city. The other members of the white clergy, in the words of the biblical story of the Good Samaritan, "walked by on the other side." As a result, Bob Graetz had his house bombed twice. He asked whether I would accept an invitation from Dr. King to speak at the second anniversary of the Montgomery Bus Boycott. I told him I would be proud to do so. That invitation came and Dr. King and I arranged to meet in St. Louis and fly to Atlanta together. He had just spoken in Chicago. I was a month and a half older than he, and the two of us "hit it off" right from the start. At the Atlanta airport this distinguished leader and member of the clergy and I got off the plane and headed for the men's room. Suddenly I saw the signs: white, colored. I hesitated. He laughed, patted me on the back and said, "This is not where we make our fight." But I still remember the sudden crudeness of it, and I felt dirty after walking out of that men's washroom. The law in Georgia said that this man with a doctorate from Boston University was not good enough to go into the same restroom as those with my color of skin. I spent two days with Dr. King, Ralph Abernathy, and others, primarily going from meeting to meeting to explain to black citizens how they could fill out the long forms Alabama required if they wanted to vote. Whites did not have to fill out the forms. I visited with the King family in their modest white frame home. I also met volunteers in Montgomery, one of them Harris Wofford, with whom I would serve in the United States Senate years later. At this point Martin Luther King had reasonable name recognition around the nation, but nowhere near the acclaim and hatred he would engender in a few years. I came away most impressed by his vision and practicality. The day after his assassination the judges of Madison County asked me to speak at a brief memorial service for Dr. King at the courthouse. I closed my remarks with these words: "The nation bleeds today, not just from this one tragic death, but from violence and hatred that sometimes seem to engulf us. . . . No one person can take the place of Dr. King, but all of us can — and must."[17]

Working on problems of discrimination is a consistent pattern as I review my legislative record, and I credit my parents for that. When the teacher placement officer of the University of Illinois told me he had a hard time placing some of his most talented teachers at a time of a real shortage, it startled me and I asked why. "They're black," he told me simply. He cited one female student with a straight A average except for one B who could not be placed and was preparing to accept a clerical job. I introduced legislation that required all school districts to sign a statement that they had no discrimination in the employment of teachers in order to get state school aid. It passed. Suddenly administrators who had paid no attention to the matter invited me to their meetings and the state picture changed for the better.

This illustrates, however, that someone who is not a minority or not disabled or does not face some of these barriers does not automatically think of the obvious. It is why we need more minorities, more women, more disabled, more people discriminated against, in policy-making positions, to help sensitize the rest of us to these needs.

Before my measure passed I did what I could to call attention to the situation. I wrote an article for *The Christian Century* and noted:

"The Illinois Teacher Placement Association is . . . trying to get a list of Illinois schools which would be willing to hire Negro or Jewish teachers. 'The names are coming in slowly,' one official said."[18] I noted that a survey of businesses in Illinois showed that one-fourth would not hire Jews and a much higher percentage would not hire African Americans. In my column I wrote: "It is worth noting that many of the people who complain loudest about so many Negroes being on our relief rolls are the same people who oppose measures that would give them an opportunity to work."[19]

Providing opportunity for the disabled occupied a priority in both my federal and state legislative years. Visiting the state institutions for the retarded and seeing their appalling conditions provided some of the incentive for this. Part of it is that when Jeanne and I married, both in our thirties, the commonly accepted truth — less commonly accepted now — is that if you are older you are much more likely to have a disabled child. We mentally prepared ourselves for that possibility, and were immensely pleased when that did not happen.

I played a role — not the leading role — in passing legislation in Illinois requiring that all disabled young people should be helped by the public schools. Illinois was far ahead of most states in passing this, though two years before we finally enacted the legislation we failed to pass it in the state senate by one vote. That one vote caused a two-year delay and I have often wondered how many children suffered for the rest of their lives because of that one vote. One vote! When I went to the U. S. House in 1975, I helped pass Public Law 94-142 that basically did the same thing for the nation. Until that time public schools could say to young people, if you are deaf or blind or in a wheelchair, sorry we can't help you. A majority of the retarded did not receive help. I remained active in this field throughout my legislative years, and one of the contributions I made was to get Judy Wagner of my staff, who started as a secretary in my U. S. House office, interested in this cause. She eventually became my subcommittee staff director and one of the most knowledgeable people in the nation on disability policy, and has received several much-merited national awards — and the awards I have received in this field should really belong in large part to her.

My limited financial status did not prevent my opposing a proposal for a Korean bonus in 1957, one for which I would have been eligible because I served in Germany during that period. I pointed out the dire straits of mental hospitals, and the need for more money for schools. I would like the $240 and the measure is popular, I told my colleagues, but it should not be the highest priority. Rep. George Dunne, who also served in the Army during this period, joined me and two others in casting lonely votes against it.

My dual status as a publisher and legislator generally meshed without the serious problems most people envision. However, it got me into trouble on one occasion. Looking around for places to save money, I noted that the lengthy legal descriptions of constitutional amendments people vote on were printed three times in the newspapers of the state, paid for by Illinois government. Since few people read them, and those who read the lengthy legal descriptions generally could not understand them, I thought it made sense to save money by printing them only once. One publisher told me, "You're just trying to take advantage of inside information." Russ Hoffman, the respected editor of the *Highland News-Leader*, wrote: "As soon as Paul introduced the bill to limit that sort of unnecessary expenditure, two press associations in the state immediately jumped on him."[20] Newspapers who had great editorials about saving money didn't favor it in their back yard. I have observed that same thing over and over. A group of farmers came to see me, suggesting that a good way to save money would be to cut back on welfare payments for poor people, and then a few minutes later asked for larger farm subsidies, obviously not labeling them as welfare for farmers. Bankers who preach about the free enterprise system fought hard to get high guaranteed interest rates for banks written into the law in the student loan program. Every group is guilty of this.

But sometimes, in looking over the record, it is hard to distinguish between my role as publisher and legislator. I sent two letters to the manager of the state fair and commented editorially about the fair having "a freak show." I told him of my shock "to see physically deformed children on display so that someone with no sensibilities could make some money . . . For people to profit off the deformities of children and hold them up to public stares and ridicule seems to me an extreme violation of good taste."[21] My guess is that it didn't happen again, though I can find no acknowledgment of my letters in the files.

Among other activities that occupied me as a legislator:

- Sponsoring, together with Rep. John Merlo, a bill to provide kidney dialysis treatment for those who need it. A neighbor in Troy with serious kidney problems told me that he could not afford to pay for kidney dialysis to extend his life without mortgaging his house, and then he probably would die anyway, so he had decided to die. And he did. He did not want his children to lose their home. We prevented more of these tragedies with our bill.

- Opposed Sunday closing laws as unfair to Seventh Day Adventists and Orthodox Jews.

- Wrote about matters that I would continue to favor in later years, such as outlawing professional boxing (70 percent of professional boxers end up with brain damage); aid to education ("Illinois spends more in subsidies per race horse than we do per child in our schools"); the abuses of the patronage system in Illinois, a state in which patronage and the corruption and abuses that went with it dominated Illinois politics ("Illinois has 15,000 patronage jobs out of 60,000 state employees. . . . Iowa has 35, Wisconsin 26, California 60."); guaranteeing all employees who work for someone with six or more employees health insurance coverage; the need for campaign finance reform; pension reform and stability; and the danger of concentrating too much economic power in the hands of a few banks.

Civil liberties issues arose then and always will. When I first arrived in the legislature, State Senator Paul Broyles sponsored measures to require every government employee in Illinois to sign an oath that they were not Communists. It finally passed and, of course, caught no Communists, just piled up paper work. A few Quakers, who would not take oaths, lost jobs as teachers or government employees. Leading the charge against the measures was my House seatmate and future colleague in the United States Senate, Alan J. Dixon. I joined him in this fight. The issue stirred strong emotions on both sides. The atmosphere and hysteria of that period caused otherwise rational people to do things that clearly were contrary to the spirit of our Constitution and those who founded our nation.

The American Legion backed a proposal to set up a commission to evaluate textbooks to make sure no Communist textbooks got into the classroom. I led the opposition, defeating it, pointing out that we don't solve this with government censorship. When the question of outlawing the Communist party arose, I observed, "Our system is strong enough to resist Communism without adopting Communist methods."[22]

Education efforts of every kind stirred my interest, and working with Senators David Davis and John Gilbert we established a state community college system, called junior colleges initially. We made progress slowly. First I had a bill to increase the number of people who could constitute a junior college district from 30,000 to 50,000 and the governor vetoed it. Eventually we followed the example of California in establishing a statewide system. When I appeared before the Budgetary Commission, headed by Sen. Everett Peters of the district that included the University of Illinois, he bluntly said he opposed the idea. "Look what you'll do to the University of Illinois football team if you do this," he said in all seriousness.

As editorials around the state noted my work favorably more and more — though sometimes unfavorably — Jeanne and I talked about the idea of higher public office. We took an active part in the state scene, as well as helping statewide candidates locally. In a three-way race for the gubernatorial nomination in 1960 among Otto Kerner, endorsed by the state Democratic organization, Sheriff Joe Lohman of Cook County, and former Democratic national chairman Stephen Mitchell, we helped Mitchell. Even though he ran third statewide, he carried Madison County 8,198 to 6,560 for Otto Kerner, the eventual nominee. We had a reception at our home for State Rep. Sam Shapiro, running for Lieutenant Governor that year. When Adlai Stevenson III ran for State Treasurer in 1966, we had 500 people at our home at an outdoor reception for him.

That same year we worked hard for the reelection of Senator Paul Douglas without success. I recall particularly when Bobby Kennedy came and campaigned for Douglas, when Republicans were hitting on the age issue — subtly, but doing it. The appearance of the youthful Bobby Kennedy and the aging giant unfortunately reinforced the issue. One day at the Douglas headquarters in Chicago a woman from Rockford called and seriously suggested that we get a young woman to file a paternity suit against Douglas. "It will eliminate the age issue overnight," she assured me.

At the suggestion of one of Mayor Daley's aides, I hosted a breakfast for him with forty-five Protestant ministers when he sought reelection in 1967, a group with which he felt less than complete comfort.

And because of my interest in foreign affairs, and because I knew Vietnam policy concerned many people, I flew to Vietnam to do a few

free-lance stories. I also wanted to settle my own opinion on that conflict. When it started I supported our efforts, but I gradually grew
more and more uneasy.

After filling out endless forms at the U. S. Embassy in Saigon
(now Ho Chi Minh City) I became a full-fledged correspondent eligible to be transported around the country by hitching rides with
helicopters. My base was the Majestic Hotel in Saigon, an inaptly
named hotel. One of my first and lasting impressions of that trip came
from walking down the street by the hotel at night, with artillery
shells booming in the background and along the street jukeboxes blar-
ing their music at a high decibel level from massage parlors, small
restaurants, and brothels. The sounds of death and entertainment and
phoney gaiety all competed in a disquieting way.

I saw old friends Peter Lisagor and Ray Coffey, reporters for the
*Chicago Daily News,* and went with other correspondents to the reception honoring the incoming President of South Vietnam, Nguyen Van
Thieu. We heard shelling, and General William Westmoreland, in his
Army formal dress attire, assured us that he knew the sounds and
these were outgoing shells. We learned quickly he had miscalculated.
As a reporter from Minneapolis and I left the palace, about 300 feet
from us a mortar shell hit a car, which exploded. We ducked behind a
tree temporarily and then hurried away.

Vice President Hubert Humphrey visited South Vietnam for the
inauguration, and I joined the correspondents following him to Da
Nang, Hue, and Chu Lai.

I went home more knowledgeable about Vietnam, but more
uneasy.


During all these legislative years I also championed the causes of
the poor, the people who too often are voiceless. Our modest efforts
in this field have brought modest results. There is an underclass and
until we invest in jobs and training and better education for them, the
nation will be neither as productive nor as humanitarian as it should
be. In one article I quoted Bill Boyne of the *East St. Louis Journal:* "We
will not beat the problem until we stop thinking in terms of how much
it costs."[23] Solely focusing on costs will cost us more. There will have
to be an investment. There is no cheap way out of this. I learned that
early in my legislative career, and experience has reinforced it over
and over. Most of those with simplistic solutions have spent little time
walking in the worst streets of our nation.

[1] *Alton Evening Telegraph*, 14 April, 1954.

[2] Judge Joseph Barr to author, 26 June 1996, SIU Archives.

[3] *Troy Tribune*, 16 February 1956.

[4] Don Chamberlain to author, 22 January 1955, ISHL.

[5] B. W. Osterling to author, 22 May 1959, ISHL.

[6] Harold Cross to author, 15 May 1958, ISHL.

[7] "Powell Interviewed on Race Track Stock, Mudguard Bill, Other Issues," *Southern Illinoisan*, 2 November 1958.

[8] 4 September 1964.

[9] Details in *George Tagge Memoir*, an oral history project of Sangamon State University (now the University of Illinois at Springfield), 1986, 16-17.

[10] John Dreiske, "Rep. Murphy's Change to Disown Blocsters," *Chicago Sun-Times*, 11 March 1963.

[11] "Two Legislators Criticize Crime Board Report," *St. Louis Post-Dispatch*, 9 June 1965.

[12] Paul Powell to author, 27 February 1963, ISHL.

[13] Memorandum in the ISHL, undated.

[14] Virgil Peterson, *A Report on Chicago Crime for 1962*, Chicago Crime Commission, 28 June 1963.

[15] Quoted in Edward Doyle, ed., *Adlai As We Knew Him* (New York: Harper and Row, 1966), 135.

[16] *Troy Tribune*, 5 April 1962.

[17] 5 April 1968, SIU Archives.

[18] "Let's Integrate Our Teachers," *Christian Century*, 20 February 1957.

[19] "Sidelights from Springfield," *Troy Tribune*, 16 February 1961.

[20] Editorial, *Highland News-Leader*, 8 July 1965.

[21] *Troy Tribune*, 11 December 1958.

[22] "Sidelights from Springfield," *Troy Tribune*, 28 May 1959.

[23] Quoted in "Sidelights from Springfield," *Troy Tribune*, 9 May 1963.

# Chapter 5

# *Lt. Governor*

As I neared my sixth year as a state senator, I felt the time had arrived either to move ahead politically or to go into some other arena of service. Senator Everett Dirksen's term would expire in 1968. I had eyed that seat in 1962, but now it looked more possible to secure the nomination. I assumed that I would have to get through a contested primary to be nominated, but the power of Mayor Daley and the old-line political leaders was on the wane. Adlai III said he would not be a candidate for the Senate, and commenting about my possible candidacy told the *Moline Dispatch*, "I am one of his most enthusiastic supporters."[1] He told the *Chicago Daily News* that I would make "a very strong candidate."[2] The Lerner newspapers did a poll of editors in the state and 60.1 percent favored my being the Democratic candidate, the rest scattered among five others.[3] *Chicago American* columnist Jack Mabley wrote: "If I thought I could influence Daley, I'd ask him to pick State Senator Paul Simon of Troy to run against Dirksen."[4] And former Senator Paul Douglas sent me notes of encouragement and a check for $200 to help pay political expenses.

I moved around the state, not too subtly indicating my intent. Then one day Joe Knight, a wealthy gentleman farmer from Dow ("the Duke of Dow") phoned me. Knight, a bachelor, had his whole life wrapped up in politics. An extra-long cigar almost always in his mouth, his large frame looked even larger with the expensive double-breasted suits he wore, always unbuttoned. He served at one point as treasurer of the state party, but he had more influence than that title indicates. Daley, State Democratic Chairman James Ronan (one of the finer people I have met in political life), and the small circle of people who really ran the Democratic party in Illinois liked him and trusted him. In his slow-talking deep voice Joe said to me, "I've been authorized to ask if you were slated as lieutenant governor, would you take it?" When he said "authorized," I knew that came from Daley. I told him I would get back to him quickly. Jeanne and I talked it over, and felt that the office would give me a chance to campaign statewide, and if elected be a stepping stone to either governor or senator. And I wouldn't have a primary fight. I told Joe I would do it.

In those days the Democratic State Central Committee met and heard candidates for various posts, and then the members of that leadership group in theory caucused and decided whom to endorse. If a genuine contest — which it rarely did — the decision would be weighted by the Democratic vote cast in a previous election. At that time Cook County cast two-thirds of the Democratic votes in the state, and that meant whoever controlled Cook County made the choice. Daley not only controlled Cook County, but much of downstate because they respected and/or feared him.

After all the potential candidates made their three-minute presentations, and answered a few questions, the group would recess. Daley would go into his office, take out a small slip of paper and write the names of the candidates who would be endorsed, and hand the slip of paper to a key aide, who would then spread the word. The motion to endorse candidates would not be made by Daley, but everyone knew whose not-so-fine hand had wielded the power.

Daley placed me on the ticket as a way of reaching out, something any effective political leader should do, and he was good at that. While he never told me this, my instinct is that he also admired my stands against corruption. When he handed the leaders the slip of paper with my name on it as lieutenant governor, Rep. Clyde Choate expressed the concern of some others, "But Mayor, he might become governor!" Daley, ordinarily a man of few words, said simply, "It's Simon."

Illinois Attorney General Bill Clark, later a justice of our state supreme court, became the Senate nominee; and for governor, Samuel Shapiro, the lieutenant governor who had moved into the governor's chair when Otto Kerner resigned in order to become a judge on the U. S. Circuit Court of Appeals. They slated others for the remainder of the state ticket.

Sam really wanted to become a judge, a small consideration in my accepting the lieutenant governorship. If Shapiro as governor became either a federal judge or a member of the Illinois Supreme Court, I would become governor. More significant, however, the two of us had worked together in the House. I liked and trusted him. After Kerner's

In 1930, the way I looked before I entered politics.

My grandparents, Traugott Simon and Eleanor Elbert, at their wedding on July 14, 1899, in Illinois.

With Eleanor Roosevelt and Adlai Stevenson at a banquet in Chicago in 1958. At the time I was a state representative and 29 years old.

Jeanne, myself, Jeanne's mother Margaret Hurley, and my parents, Ruth and Martin Simon, in January 1969, on the day of my inauguration as lieutenant governor.

This was the unpleasant scene in Cairo, Illinois, during the racial strife there while I was lieutenant governor.

Campaigning with John F. Kennedy in 1960.

Greeting Senator Robert F. Kennedy at a reception, with former Illinois Senator Paul Douglas joining us.

Campaigning in my home town of Troy in 1962 with President Harry Truman (with hat), Congressman Sidney Yates (seated in the rear), and Governor Otto Kerner.

A tribute to Hubert Humphrey I organized while I served in the House. Hubert and Muriel are in the front row. He died a few weeks later.

The city of Coburg in Germany where I spent more than a year with the Counter Intelligence Corps while in the Army. The castle is on a hill and the other side of the hill is Soviet territory.

On a visit to South Vietnam in 1967.

With Vietnamese children in 1967. Note the sandbags in the rear for
protection from shells; and the small boy with the toy gun.

Jimmy Durante with Martin and Sheila when they were younger. The highpoint of my "show business career" came with an appearance on *Saturday Night Live* with the singer Paul Simon.

As a congressional delegate to the United Nations in 1978, I made it a point to visit with those I could not meet in Washington. Here I chat with members of the Chinese delegation.

resignation, when Sam became governor, he would occasionally call me for suggestions I might have. The one I remember most vividly concerned a country club in Springfield that had these traditions: not admitting blacks and Jews to membership, and giving an honorary membership to the governor. After Sam became governor, they sent a letter advising him of his honorary membership. Sam called and asked what he should do. "If you weren't good enough for them before you became governor," I told him, "you're not good enough for them now. I would turn them down." He did.

Bob Dwyer, a businessman of some means, became my Republican opponent. He outspent me, probably by a considerable amount, but we had no disclosure requirement in Illinois then, so I can only guess the amount. A person of ability, he had never run for public office before.

I received a number of strong endorsements from newspapers around the state though the *Chicago Tribune* in endorsing Dwyer referred to me as "talkative State Senator Paul Simon, an advocate of many ultra-liberal causes."[5] Mike Royko, in a *Chicago Daily News* column, opposed Dwyer: "Unless a man holds a lower office first, there is no way to know if he can be distrusted."[6]

Three of us on the Democratic state ticket worked hard at campaigning: Paul Powell, running for reelection as Secretary of State; Michael Howlett, running for reelection as State Auditor; and myself. During the 1968 Democratic convention we had a meeting to coordinate our campaign efforts. Mike, Paul and I had a long list of speaking commitments, the others hardly any. Powell and I developed a begrudging respect for each other in the campaign, despite our wide philosophical differences; each of us campaigned hard. After the convention we flew to southern Illinois together and I remember Powell saying, "The three of us are working hard and the others hate campaigning and are doing only the minimal amount you have to do. There probably won't be any difference in the total votes that we get."

He turned out to be wrong. Howlett, Powell, and I won; the rest of the ticket lost. On election night many places receiving the unofficial results did not bother taking a separate tally on governor and lieutenant governor, assuming that whatever happens to the governor would also apply to his potential successor. When early in the evening Sam Shapiro trailed, I assumed that would be my fate too. We received the returns in the small American Legion Hall in Troy. When the early Shapiro vote came in, our small gathering of family and friends was very subdued. I could tell the negative returns were particularly hard on my father. But soon we received scattered votes showing me running stronger than Sam and by the early morning hours I knew I would become the first Illinois lieutenant governor elected with the governor of another party.

Early in the campaign, on a call-in radio program in Joliet, a man asked why the Democrats had two Jews heading the ticket, assuming the name Simon — often a Jewish name — and Shapiro were both Jewish. Jack Fishbein, publisher of the Jewish publication *Chicago Sentinel* had an article after the election asking whether anti-Semitism caused Sam's defeat. He concluded that it was a factor, but not a major factor. My impression is the same.

Wednesday night Jeanne and I flew up to Chicago and the next morning held a press conference. While running for lieutenant governor I frequently held press conferences — often attended by no reporters. For someone seeking the office of lieutenant governor it is a huge success to have a press conference with one TV camera and one print reporter. Thursday morning after I won the election I walked into the room of the press conference jammed with cameras, mikes, and print reporters. I started by asking, "Where were you when I needed you?"

The Republican elected as governor, Richard Ogilvie, did not have what might usually be called "a political personality," and that modest style, accentuated by a war wound to the face that made it difficult for him to give a full smile, caused some to underestimate him. Commenting on me after the election, he told the Associated Press: "I think he is a high-class legislator. I think he is a high-class gentleman. I feel confident we can work together."[7] While he and I had our occasional differences, he had courage and integrity, both qualities not found in abundance historically in Illinois politics. Illinois schools needed additional revenue, and Ogilvie had the backbone to ask for an Illinois income tax, and I supported him in that endeavor.

One small gesture for which I shall always be grateful to Dick Ogilvie: He invited my father to give the invocation at the inauguration ceremonies. Senator William Harris, in charge of the inaugural events, played a role in this too. Ogilvie and Harris could have pleased any number of high-ranking clergy, but instead asked the pastor of a small rural Lutheran congregation to invoke God's blessings. I particularly appreciated it because my father campaigned hard for me, taking midweek days off to travel to small communities to distribute my literature. I still encounter people who met my father during that period. My brother Art and his wife Kaiya came from New York City and campaigned for me. Art also wrote a campaign booklet we distributed, an unusually substantial document for a candidate for lieutenant governor. My mother took the telephone route, making calls around the state. Jeanne made appearances in the far corners of Illinois. During the school vacation months, Jeanne and our two children and I piled into a station wagon; the four of us, plus two marvelous student volunteers, Greg Nathanson and Johnny Seder, and a high school student neighbor, Jane Gephardt, who served Sheila (then seven) and Martin (then four) as sitter from time to time. It made a crowded station wagon. We went from county fair to county fair, from village festival to village festival. Campaigning became a real family event. At one stop where they lettered T-shirts, Sheila and Martin requested the message: Vote For My Daddy. Those T-shirts got well worn. And they thought campaigning was fun!

My father's participation became more meaningful for me because in August, eight months after my January inauguration, I received a phone call from his physician, Dr. Jerry Beguelin, who told me he had just examined my father and believed he had leukemia. Within hours the physician confirmed that verdict. As minister of a small rural parish near Okawville, Illinois (population 992), my father considered this pastorate a semi-retirement, but he remained active. While mowing the lawn one day, he felt unusually tired, and eventually visited the doctor's office. Dr. Beguelin immediately sent him to the Washington County Hospital in nearby Nashville, Illinois, the boyhood hometown of Supreme Court Justice Harry Blackmun. My father had never spent a day of his life in a hospital. The diagnosis was acute leukemia, and in 1969 treatment for the dread disease remained primitive. Four weeks from the day he went into the hospital he died. It was the most personally difficult thing I have ever gone through. He had no living will, so the physician and hospital felt obliged to provide the transfusions and the oxygen and other measures taken that postponed his life a matter of days at most, possibly only hours, though I know my father would have preferred not having those steps taken when he had no chance to live. But much more than that, I regret I did not tell him how much he meant to me, though I think he sensed that. He was the finest man I have ever known.

Because my sense of loss was so great, I still remember small details; I recall the handwritten note from Cardinal Cody, the Roman Catholic leader from Chicago, the letter from Judge Abraham Lincoln Marovitz, the flowers from Patrick O'Malley, the Chicago business leader, and the telegram from Paul Douglas; and the presence of so many friends, political friends of both parties including Adlai Stevenson III, Michael Howlett, State Senator John Gilbert, and State Representative James Holloway. During the service at the packed rural church he served, those attending — about one-fourth of them Lutheran ministers with leather lungs — sang the stirring hymn, "For All the Saints Who From Their Labors Rest." It rang in my mind — and still does — when we buried him on September 26, 1969, in the country cemetery next to the church, looking out on a field of corn, a scene his rural roots always found comfortable.

As Lieutenant Governor I made the usual visits and speeches. The first official visit was to Sheila's Brownie troop in Troy. Because of our differing parties, Dick Ogilvie gave me no formal assignments. Without opposition on his part I took on the role of voluntary "ombudsman," someone who worked with people and the problems they had with government, and sometimes with the private sector. I served as the principal case worker in the state. I enjoy helping people, and I also knew that providing assistance could be meaningful politically. Describing my office, Richard Icen wrote in the *Champaign-Urbana Courier*: "Simon's presence . . . gives the place an air of aggressive urgency, a feeling that in one way or another time must be found to solve all the problems now being brought to his attention by the people of Illinois."[8] However, my growing visibility in the role of ombudsman caused the Republican leadership in the Senate to introduce a measure setting up an independent office of ombudsman, to be appointed by the governor. The proposal so clearly had a partisan aim against me that the media of the state shot it down quickly.

Under the constitution then in effect, since changed, the lieutenant governor had the full powers of the governor whenever the chief executive left the state. For that day or days I received the governor's pay, $125 more a day on top of my $25,000 a year salary. Jeanne and I looked forward to the governor's absences! During these periods I did not sign bills, make appointments, nor do other things I might have in such a situation. I only handled emergencies, once during a small racial eruption, but more routinely only doing things like signing extradition papers that needed fast action. Ogilvie learned he could trust me following the death of Senator Everett Dirksen when the governor had to be out of the state for two days. Mayor Daley called and said I might think about appointing a senator; it was an oblique request, tactful but clear. I told him that I felt it would not be wise. Ogilvie knew about the request and from that point on trusted me in so far as abusing his out-of-state visits. However, while we were on good terms, it did not translate into a close relationship because increasingly reporters and political leaders talked of an Ogilvie-Simon clash for governor in 1972. And I made no secret that such a contest seemed a clear possibility. Adding a little to that tension were observations like those of one newspaper editor at a meeting of the Illinois Press Association that both Ogilvie and I attended: "Paul Simon was continually being called [upon] . . . to answer questions of reporters. It is plain, he gets more attention than the governor."[9] The reality is that a governor always gets more attention than the lieutenant governor, but my unusual situation brought me more spotlight than most in my position receive, and that did not please my possible future opponent, even though we respected each other.

Our small staff in the Lieutenant Governor's office included Gene Callahan, Dick Durbin, Yvonne Rice, Ray Johnsen, Craig Lovitt, Mary Lou Speaks, and Lorraine Gillespie in Springfield, and Bill Colson, who headed the Chicago office. Gene Callahan, a former political writer for the *Illinois State Register*, knew how to get coverage, in part because he worked hard at it. Dick Durbin, a young attorney I had first met when he volunteered as a student to help Senator Paul Douglas, succeeded me in the United States Senate after serving fourteen years in the House. Ray Johnsen, who worked with me in the newspaper business, headed our bookkeeping efforts to make sure nothing amiss happened. Yvonne Rice, Mary Lou Speaks, and Lorraine Gillespie acted as secretaries but far more than that, handling endless details of problems that people had. Bill Colson headed the Chicago office, working effectively with Alma Sbarboro, Jim Conley, Rick Jasculca, and Dolores Sidlik, who was a tornado on the typewriter, the fastest person with whom I have ever worked.

For young people who get discouraged at the slow progress in race relations in our nation — and I share their desire for needed progress — when I selected Yvonne Rice, who had been the secretary to State Senator Fred Smith, to be my personal secretary it made news around the state and big news in the *Chicago Defender*, the daily newspaper with a predominantly African American readership. Calling it a first for an Illinois state official, the headline read: "Lt.-Gov.-Elect Simon Picks Black Secretary."[10] Yvonne did a great job for me, but I am pleased that that type of small action no longer makes the headlines; we are inching ahead.

One thing I did irked a few of the other Democratic and

Republican state officials. As Lieutenant Governor I inherited a huge black Cadillac limousine. I felt pretentious in it. I am not a limousine type. I bade farewell to the Cadillac and acquired a Ford as my official car. It felt better to me, though some of my fellow officials resented it. For the same reason, when I fly to speak somewhere and I am told that they will have a limousine for me, I tell them that I don't want it. I generally also ride tourist class in planes, except for overseas flights or lengthy domestic flights when I accept the frequently offered gesture by the airlines to upgrade me to first class or business class. I also don't like black tie dinners. I do have a black tie suit and sometimes feel I have to attend. If it is a "black tie optional" dinner, you will not find me wearing a black tie. All of these things do not make me any better than those who ride the limousines or like the glittery dress, but each of us has to do what fits his or her personality.

The Illinois State Police assigned one officer to be with me at all times. Fred Perry volunteered for that assignment, serving as driver of the state car, and security person when I needed it. If I worked a twenty-hour day, he did. Worse than that, he had to listen to all my speeches. I am not a good joke-teller as a speaker. I had three that worked and were well used. One always got a good audience response, and Fred — anticipating the reaction — would start laughing before the crowd did.

Like most states, Illinois has no Lieutenant Governor's official residence, and then had no housing allowance. A small third-floor apartment became the Simon family's home when I stayed in Springfield.

Because the only duty assigned to me by the Illinois constitution or statutes was to preside over the State Senate, being Lieutenant Governor gave me the chance to branch out, to learn more about problems, and to call attention to areas of need. For example, I appointed a task force to look at the effects of pollution on the human system, a group headed by a distinguished physician on the medical school faculty of the University of Illinois, Dr. Bertram Carnow. At that point we had reached only the infancy of today's environmental concerns and knowledge.

A truck driver in Peoria, Charles Harshbarger, wrote that I couldn't possibly understand the condition of the roads of Illinois without riding the cab of a truck. Every night he rode a big truck to Alva, Iowa, leaving Peoria about seven in the evening and returning about 4:00 A.M. He wanted me to ride with him to compare Illinois and Iowa roads. I agreed to do it, and Gene Callahan saw the possibility of good media coverage. I accepted Harshbrger's invitation to have dinner with his family before we started, but he did not expect four television cameras to be in his dining room catching each bite as we ate. And as we bounced — yes, bounced — along the road, NBC Today had a crew ahead of us in a truck with the back open, filming the first fifty miles or so of our trip. Charlie had never ridden his truck under such circumstances! Among other observations, he pointed out that Iowa had "No Passing" triangular signs on the left side of the road wherever needed, an added reminder of danger. The idea impressed me favorably, and I requested the Illinois Highway Department to do the same. They did it on an experimental basis first, and found the safety experts and the public liked it, and now those signs are everywhere on state roads in Illinois. Perhaps the state eventually would have had them anyway, but they arrived more speedily because of Charlie Harshbarger's invitation to ride with him. I am sure Charlie Harshbarger's action saved lives.

Several months after I became Lieutenant Governor, violence erupted in racially troubled Cairo, Illinois, a river city of 8,000 at the southern tip of the state, a city approximately sixty percent white, forty percent black. Martin Brown, editor of the *Cairo Evening Citizen*, called and said he could get no action from the Governor's office or the Attorney General and he felt that the town — already torn by violence — would explode if someone didn't act. When I informed the State Police that I intended to go to Cairo for two days, they advised against the trip for security reasons. When I proceeded anyway, they provided protection I had never experienced before, similar to the assistance provided by the Secret Service years later when I sought the presidential nomination.

After visiting in Cairo with the principal players on both sides, I called a meeting of the clergy, black and white. Amazingly, in this small town it was the first time that they had such a meeting. Some of the talk caused tensions, including vigorous disagreement between the two Roman Catholic priests who attended. But at least they talked, and all agreed that further violence should be avoided, though they differed on the causes for tensions in the community.

I went to Pyramid Court, the all-black public housing project whose people charged that members of the White Hats, a sort of White Citizens Council vigilante organization, would stand on the levee that abutted the housing project, firing at the residents and when residents called the police, the police did nothing. A group of Catholic nuns sent me a telegram asking that I investigate the White Hats. I talked to the chief of police, Carl Clutts, and when I relayed the complaint from the people at Pyramid Court, he responded, "We can't go in there sometimes. It's too dangerous." Later he changed his message in testifying before an Illinois House Committee, saying they make "more emergency runs to Pyramid Court than any place in the city. But I feel that other people . . . deserve some protection too." Since he had an all-white police force in which the black community had no confidence, there might have been a little validity to his initial claim of danger to the police. My first recommendation to the community was to fire the chief of police. I proposed that the semi-vigilante, semi-law enforcement group known as the White Hats be disbanded, and that if a vacancy occurred in the all-white city council that a black be appointed. My staff and I talked to literally hundreds of people in this small city before issuing our report, which still looks solid after three decades. It was blunt but fair, pointing to needs in both the white and black communities if Cairo wanted to avoid further bloodshed. The *Cairo Evening Citizen* editorially said that the report "in its totality is likely to please very few citizens," and noted that my action "is more likely to result in political suicide rather than political gain." But the editorial concluded: "We at the *Cairo Evening Citizen* applaud Paul Simon for his willingness to help Cairo solve its problems and thank him for his courageous and forthright approach."[11] Reaction from white extremists around the state to anything constructive I did in Cairo was discouraging. A typical letter: "There is no doubt in my mind that the niggers in Cairo are responsible for the trouble there. These overprivileged blacks should be punished and I am sick and tired of you politicians favoring the lazy arrogant niggers and you are one of these politicians."[12] But I felt that we had acted carefully and spoken plainly; we had done the right thing. And there were balancing letters. A Catholic priest wrote: "I just finished reading the report compiled by you and your staff. When I finished reading it . . . I had tears in my eyes. You have, in my estimation, seen the problems. . . . [We] will work to achieve these goals."[13] Vocal whites in the city reacted negatively initially to most of my recommendations. Slowly people came to see the necessity for change. Henry Bolen, president of the Cairo Chamber of Commerce, told the *St. Louis Post-Dispatch* that its board of directors "read Simon's report and concluded that he sincerely, honestly tried to make a report that he thought would be helpful. It was a down-the-middle report. The Lieutenant Governor said our chief has been ineffective, and the evidence shows he has been ineffective. But the chief is appointed by the mayor and council. As long as they are satisfied, nothing can be done."[14] The articulate and thoughtful head of the National Association for the Advancement of Colored People in

Cairo, Preston Ewing Jr., told an Illinois House Committee looking at the city: "All that is required now for a man to become a policeman is to give him a gun and the keys to a police car. An immediate end to illegal practices and the establishment of law enforcement that the black people can have confidence in is a top priority. . . . Law enforcement is being maintained here in such a manner as to relegate [black people] to an inferior position in the community."[15] Ewing and others also testified that "Negroes cannot win court cases in Cairo and they don't have funds for appeals. White lawyers generally don't take Negro cases to court." Witnesses also testified that officials developed a system "so that there are no Negroes on juries."[16] Eventually not only did the police chief resign, but the mayor did too. Though two of every five citizens were of African heritage, the city had only one black city employee, who worked for the water department. I recommended that the Police and Fire Departments be integrated.

Aggravating the situation, the prosecuting attorney for the county, Peyton Berbling, was widely believed to head the White Hats. I did not ask him that specifically, but he made clear that he did not welcome my involvement "and other outside agitation." He told a number of people, "Simon is staying at the Morse Motel with his nigger secretary." My secretary did stay there, along with two other members of my staff, but his attempts to portray something illicit backfired even with people who tended to be sympathetic to his cause. Some who had racist leanings supported my proposals because they knew the danger the community faced. My recommendations received praise from the U. S. Civil Rights Commission and gradually met with favor from responsible elements of both races in Cairo.

A few days after we issued the report the *Cairo Evening Citizen* noted the "tension [still] gripping all our community leaders" that could lead to more bloodshed. It editorially added:

> One part of Lt. Gov. Paul Simon's report on Cairo has not received much attention by local leaders, evidenced by statements and counter-statements that continue almost daily.
>
> "All community leaders, clergymen, school officials and others should weigh their words carefully," the report states. "Sticks and stones may break my bones but words can never harm me we all learned as children. . . . and it is not true."
>
> Simon emphasizes that words injudiciously used by all sides of the Cairo issue can cause further bloodshed.

Shortly after my initial visit and suggestions, the *Cairo Evening Citizen* reported: "In accord with his recommendations regarding Cairo, Lt. Gov. Paul Simon sent Dick Durbin, a member of his staff, to the community to consult with leaders on the feasability of organizing a police-community relations council."[17]

Cairo police arrested forty-two protestors, most of them black, though two were white Roman Catholic priests. At their trial the defense called me as a witness. When I walked into the courtroom the forty-two defendants knew it would not be appropriate to applaud, but felt they should pay some type of tribute, and they all quietly stood, a silent tribute that has meant more to me over the years than almost all the honors and awards I have received.

Tensions and violence did not disappear after my first visit there. Five months later a heavy exchange of gunfire occurred, compounded by newspaper reports that machine guns had been sold in Cairo, an apparently unfounded report but one that fueled fear on both sides. Arson started a new fad of violence. Then for a short period the minority in Cairo expressed fear about any meeting with the white leadership "unless Simon is present," but slowly calmer heads prevailed. Mayor Lee Stenzel issued a proclamation of sweeping proportions:

1.  Effective immediately all gatherings of people of two or more individuals is prohibited.

2.  It is further ordered that no person shall take part in or become a part of a parade or engage in any picketing within the corporate limits of the City of Cairo.

3.  No person shall loiter in and upon any public street within the corporate limits of the City of Cairo.[18]

Trying to restore calm to the community, Governor Richard Ogilvie sent in a company of National Guard troops; and large numbers of Illinois State Police visited Cairo regularly. Later Ogilvie announced that the State Police would furnish professional training for the Cairo police, a move that also helped to ease tensions. Occasional outbursts of gunfire occurred but they gradually became increasingly infrequent.

For months afterwards when my phone rang in the middle of the night, Jeanne and I accurately assumed that someone from Cairo needed help. Frequently it would be Sister Joan Marie and the nuns from the Catholic hospital there. What logic anyone ever found in firing at a hospital serving all citizens in need has always baffled me. But I would then call the State Police who responded quickly.

Gradually reasonable voices prevailed, and today it is a far different community, a better community. It remains, however, a city with great economic potential that is largely untapped.

The death of Senator Everett Dirksen meant a 1970 contest for his unexpired term. Presumably the Democrat would face the Ogilvie appointee to that position, Senator Ralph Smith, former Speaker of the Illinois House. The speculation immediately centered on State Treasurer Adlai Stevenson III, son of the former governor, and myself. I would have been pleased to run but leaving the position of lieutenant governor would have meant the Democrats sacrificing any chance to secure the governorship, in the event of death or resignation by the governor — and more and more political leaders talked about my running for governor in 1972. In addition, the Adlai Stevenson name has political magic, much more magic than the name of Paul Simon had at that time and probably still has. The Democratic leaders chose Adlai and he went on to win and do a solid job as Senator, taking on inglorious but significant tasks like reorganization of the Senate.

After my election as Lieutenant Governor, the Senate majority leader, Republican W. Russell Arrington, decided to take over the office traditionally held by the Lieutenant Governor. Against the advice of many friends, I did not fight him on it. Arrington took the large office — probably twice as large as the oval office of the President of the United States — and I took space perhaps one-quarter the size. It was not something that had great importance to me. But it became a *cause célèbre* with the media. I told the Associated Press, "In 1784 John Jay was named Secretary of Foreign Affairs and they gave him just two small rooms, but they became the most important rooms in the United States at that time. I find some consolation from history in that."[19] Eventually Arrington's embarrassment mounted; and when a change in Senate leadership occurred two years later I took over the larger office.

One of the great assets of Chicago is its great ethnic variety, something to which neophytes in politics don't pay much attention, except for the large-number groups. I appointed ethnic advisory groups in the Lithuanian community, the Ukrainian, the Cuban, and many other groups that were relatively small compared to the Irish or the African Americans or the Poles or Mexicans. It helped me politically but I also enjoyed it, giving me the chance to understand other cultural backgrounds, and learn about their particular concerns. Adjusting to various ethnic foods usually brought pleasure — but sometimes hiding my reaction became an unpleasant necessity.

State Auditor Michael Howlett visited our home and asked Martin, then six, what he wanted to become when he grew up. "Lieutenant Governor," Martin quickly replied, at which Howlett and the rest of us laughed. "Well, who else is there?" Martin asked. It was a good lesson in how sexism and proprietary feelings creep into our culture. Without our ever saying it, he assumed the Lieutenant Governor had to be male, because he excluded his older sister from the position, and he assumed it belonged in some way to the Simon family.

The stirrings of independent Illinois Democrats continued, engendered in part by the need to open the process of our party, and in part by those who saw others in power and wanted it themselves. I tried to encourage the more independent forces without splitting the state Democratic party. A group calling themselves the Independent Democratic Coalition formed and asked me to speak to them about a month after I became lieutenant governor. I quoted from Will and Ariel Durant's book, *The Meaning of History*:

> Nothing is clearer in history than the adoption by successful rebels of the methods they were accustomed to condemn in the forces they deposed. . . .
>
> It is good that new ideas should be heard, for the sake of the few that can be used; but it is also good that new ideas should be compelled to go through the mill of objection, opposition, and contumely; this is the trial heat which innovations must survive before

being allowed to enter the human race. It is good that the old should resist the young, and that the young should press the old. . . .Out of the strife . . . comes a creative tensile strength.[20]

I urged them to "recognize that any effective political party is a coalition. . . . [and to] be issue-oriented rather than personality oriented," a none too-subtle suggestion that they should be for something more than an anti-Daley stance. Then I commented on a problem that unfortunately has not diminished:

> Plutarch noted in Athens in 594, B.C. "the disparity of fortune between the rich and poor . . . so that the city seemed to be in a dangerous condition."
>
> Solon emerged in Athens; he relieved the oppressed of many of their burdens, restructured much of the government and saved Athens from ruin. Today our nation needs not one Solon but many, and hopefully you and I can be among them.
>
> What we must pursue are not only the heady cheers which surround the victorious, but also the deadly indifference which haunts those who believe no one cares; we must not only follow the hero who raises the banner, whose dramatic fight stirs us, we must also enter the bowels of the city and help lift those who have forgotten there is a sun and sky.[21]

My new state-wide office gave me an opportunity to do more than the visible things like trying to keep the party together or answer questions about my small office.

One of the proposals that passed the legislature overwhelmingly with both Democratic and Republican support called for a $2 billion bond issue to build roads in the state. A few years earlier the nation had gone through this struggle when President Dwight Eisenhower suggested the Interstate Highway system, a great step forward and a huge blessing to our economy. Eisenhower proposed that we issue bonds to build the system, but Senator Albert Gore Sr., the father of our current Vice President, said we should raise taxes and do it on a pay-as-you-go basis. Fortunately Gore prevailed, and the estimate is that the nation has saved more than $750 billion — yes *billion* — in interest because of that leadership. I knew that if we voted $2 billion in bonds in Illinois it would take more than ten years to build the roads. I also knew that once the state started down the path of building roads through bond issues, it would never stop. Bond issue would follow bond issue, and the losers would be the taxpayers and our economy and our roads. Under the old Illinois constitution one of my functions was to preside over the Senate, and as the official President of the Senate, I signed bills that went to the Governor's desk. For good cause, I decided that I would not sign this bill. That provoked a mini-storm. The Illinois Supreme Court ruled in 1906 that a bill could not become law without the lieutenant governor's signature. My refusal to sign the measure caused fury among highway contractors — who are large contributors to candidates — as well as state legislators and the Governor. I said I would sign it only if Attorney General William Scott ruled that my signature was routine, and in no way indicated my approval of the legislation. I wrote to the Attorney General: "If a measure passed without complying with the statutes, am I mandated by the state constitution to sign the bill?" Media attention suddenly intense, within twenty-four hours the Attorney General released a statement to the press: "I have informed the lieutenant governor that it is mandatory for him to sign the road bill in his position as presiding officer of the Senate. A presiding officer cannot thwart the will of the legislature by refusing to execute his ministerial function." But the measure which quietly had been working its way through the legislative halls suddenly received front-page headlines. More and more people understood that it didn't make sense. In order to issue the bonds, the state had filed a *pro forma* suit challenging its legality but not challenging it vigorously, with the anticipated result being approval. I called William Kuhfuss, president of the Illinois Farm Bureau, the only organization that had opposed the bond issue. I told him that I believed it to be unconstitutional but unless someone filed a careful and thorough challenge it would be approved — that the challenge then pending in the courts aimed at selling the bonds, not stopping them. He said he would take it up with his lawyer and his board. They did challenge the proposed bond issue, and the Illinois Supreme Court unanimously ruled that it had violated the technical requirements of the Illinois law and constitution, and tossed it out. Illinois requires a fiscal note to pass with any legislation, giving a reasonable estimate of the effect of a proposal on state revenue and expenditures. Counting the interest, the $2 billion road bond issue in this form would have ballooned to a total cost of approximately $5 billion, something the supporters were not eager to detail. I pointed out that to pay for the measure there eventually would have to be a 10¢ increase in the gasoline tax, seven and one-half cents of which would go for interest. The measure had an unusual provision that delayed for ten years the start in paying the principle on the bonds, meaning that the political leaders of our decade could build the roads and then hand the bill to the leaders and taxpayers of the next decade, a procedure soon to be acquired with eagerness by federal legislators and administrators. That approach "may be good news for the bond holders but will not be to most Illinois taxpayers," I told the press. "If we start this, we will never again have pay-as-you-go roads in Illinois." Supporters assumed that if a measure had a $2 billion price tag it needed no further fiscal note, but the Illinois Supreme Court stunned them with their sound and resounding opinion.

Anyone who deals with personnel for any length of time will encounter some unusual circumstances. The phone rang one day while our family ate a Sunday dinner and the voice on the other end of the phone said, "This is Colonel Tom Parker, Elvis Presley's manager. I just wanted to let you know that we'll take care of that boy you wrote to us about. We'll introduce him to Elvis at the edge of the stage."

"Are you sure you want Lt. Gov. Paul Simon, or do you want the singer?" I asked, because the two of us have become confused a few times.

"No, the Lieutenant Governor. I got your letter about the boy who is dying of cancer and his last wish is to meet Elvis."

"What is the boy's name?" I asked.

"Paul Lis," he responded. Then it all clicked. Paul, in high school then, worked in my Chicago office part-time under Bill Colson. Paul showed a great deal of ambition and creativity early in his career — and an occasional willingness to compromise with the truth. He had taken a letterhead from my office and fabricated a great story. Paul is active in politics in Illinois to this day.

In 1970 Illinois had its first state constitutional convention since 1869. I spoke to the delegates in what the *Chicago Daily News* too generously called "a scholarly address" in which I "proposed sweeping changes in state government that would greatly strengthen the power of the governor."[22] The delegates did not accept several changes I recommended, such as appointment of the Illinois Supreme Court, subject to the approval of the Senate, a reform still needed; non-partisan election of circuit judges; making clear there is legislative authority to require full income disclosure by public officials; and requiring a two-thirds majority of the House and Senate for the state to issue bonds, an easy and unnecessary habit most states (and the federal government) have acquired. They did accept the suggestions that others and I recommended to appoint the State Superintendent of Education rather than elect that official and to reduce the size of the General Assembly; and a suggestion that I pushed that I doubt would have happened without my effort — giving the governor authority both to have a line item veto that can be overridden by a three-fifths majority of the legislature, and to reduce appropriations, the latter just as significant as the former. I strongly favor giving the President similar authority. The power to reduce appropriations gives a chief executive the ability to control essential expenditures that a legislative body may in its enthusiasm fund beyond need. If, for example, the legislature or congress votes $100 million for construction of bicycle paths in parks — a worthy goal — but the chief executive believes that $50 million is a more sensible expenditure, there should be an ability to at least force a legislative body to vote on the smaller number, probably saving a substantial amount of money in the process. Illinois and five other states now have this procedure, and the same is needed at the federal level. I also recommended to the delegates that the office of Governor and Lieutenant Governor be tied together in a general election; Dick Ogilvie suggested the same. Ironically the two of us got along better than our immediate two successors as governors and lieutenant governors, even though they shared party affiliation.

The election year 1970 not only brought opportunities to travel up and down the state supporting Democratic candidates, but to do things as varied as serving as a Politician in Residence at Hunter College in New York City for one week and dealing with student leaders on campuses during the turmoil that the Vietnam War brought with it. Jackson County State's Attorney Richard Richman asked me to appoint a commission to deal with a tense situation on the Southern Illinois University campus at Carbondale. I appointed a 22-person committee headed by Judge Paul Verticchio, a highly respected jurist, and their recommendations helped to calm frayed nerves on the part of both students and the administration. A particularly key suggestion called for students to be temporarily included in the police patrols.

Sometimes in politics you get bad breaks you don't deserve, and sometimes you get good breaks you don't deserve. The November 1970 election gave the 58-member Illinois State Senate twenty-nine

Democrats and twenty-nine Republicans, and as presiding officer under the then existing constitution the assumption was that I would break the tie to organize the Senate and on key legislation. Suddenly by the most unusual of circumstances I found myself daily on the newspaper front pages and on television and radio. At first everyone assumed I had the power to break a tie, and the post-election headlines centered not on those just elected but on this non-candidate. "Senate Standoff Puts Simon in Driver's Seat" read the headline of one Chicago newspaper.[23] Then some questioned whether I legally would be usurping a legislative privilege as a member of the executive branch. That kept the news alive for about six weeks. Attorney General William Scott handed down an opinion at the end of December, with headlines in the *Illinois State Register* almost as big as a declaration of war: "Scott Rules Simon Can Break Senate Tie."[24]

The furor almost turned to chaos. The constitution designated the day and time of the swearing in of the new senators and of the election of the president pro tem, who then named the committee chairs. Not too many minutes before the legally designated noon hour we realized that one of our Democratic members, Senator Robert McCarthy, was missing. One of the ablest members of the body, Bob at that point in his life had a drinking problem. No one knew where to find him. Gene Callahan of my staff phoned the motels in Springfield and soon discovered him. A Supreme Court Justice waited impatiently in my office to swear in the new senators and I had the Senate Republican leader, W. Russell Arrington, who had a short fuse anyway, telling me, "Let's get things going." I did not dare tell him the cause for the delay. Perhaps twenty minutes after the legally designated time for starting the session Bob arrived and we quickly proceeded with the organization of the senate. Had we gone ahead temporarily without Senator McCarthy we would have had political turmoil as one side would have prevailed temporarily and then the other side would have claimed power.

Mayor Daley actually picked the senate president pro tem because of his patronage control of Chicago, which had a majority of the Democratic senators, though if he had selected someone I found obnoxious I would have resisted. He picked Senator Cecil Partee, a capable legislator with whom I had served in the House. I had a good relationship with him. Born in Arkansas, as an African American he attended segregated schools there and when he came to the point of going to law school, rather than suffer the indignity of having a black in their law school at the University of Arkansas, that state paid his way to Northwestern University Law School in Illinois, something for which Cecil was always grateful, though not for their motivation.

As president pro tem he followed me in the succession line for the governorship, if anything happened to the governor and me. Because of the constitutional provisions that succession followed even for temporary vacancies, one day when I knew Governor Ogilvie would be out of the state I made it a point to go over to St. Louis so that Illinois had an African American governor for the first time, even if only for one day. And I'm pleased Cecil Partee had that honor.

Senators and presiding officers had the privilege of naming their children honorary pages after the end of the school year. Sheila and Martin enjoyed that role, and the chance to get acquainted with the cavernous state capitol. What particularly impressed them: Senator Bernard Neistein asked for a glass of water and then gave each of them a five-dollar bill, something their father had never done for them.

A few days before the November 1970 election John Rendleman, the president of Southern Illinois University in Edwardsville, called and said it was urgent that he get together with me. He said the matter was so sensitive he could not even take the risk of discussing it over the telephone. I explained that I had campaign commitments through the night before the election, but I could come over to his office — about ten miles from my home — the morning of the election. I gathered it had something to do with the recent death of Illinois Secretary of State Paul Powell.

John started the conversation that morning: "Remember years ago when we had a late night bull session in my apartment in Carbondale, and you told me that Paul Powell was a crook, and I told you that he was not?" I said I did, but I added, "After many years of fighting each other, Powell and I recently got along reasonably well. He assured me that he was playing it straight now as Secretary of State, and I tend to believe him." John responded with a laugh, "You were right years ago and you're wrong now."

Powell died October 24, 1970, and named John Rendleman to handle his estate. He had served as counsel to the university before being designated as the President of Southern Illinois University at Edwardsville. Paul had seen John in action and saw his ability, but more than that, trusted him, which was not true of some of those much closer to Powell politically. Powell had been having health problems and went to the Mayo Clinic in Minnesota for a checkup and died there one afternoon. No one in an official position in Illinois knew anything about it. That evening the State Police called and asked whether I knew where the governor might be. I did not. They said they wanted to reach him because Powell had died. In the meantime a few close associates of the former secretary of state had gone to Powell's office in the capitol, opened his safe and removed his personal items. That part of the story has not been fully told yet, and probably never will be.

Powell's friends — he had no surviving relatives — contacted John Rendleman who the next day went to Paul's apartment in the St. Nicholas Hotel to inventory the items and among other things found shoe boxes full of money in a closet. John went downstairs immediately, pulled his car into a no parking zone in front of the hotel and then as nonchalantly as possible loaded the shoe boxes full of money into the trunk of his car. On his last trip down, the car had disappeared! The police, totally unaware of its content, had towed the car from a no parking zone. After he retrieved his car he arranged with a Springfield banker, A. D. VanMeter, to take the money to the bank, a sum of approximately $800,000.

After John told me the story he said, "You, VanMeter, and Attorney General Bill Scott are the only people who know about this and it is essential that we keep it quiet. We need to look for any other places Powell might have cash hidden. Because you and he fought so much and you knew more about him than most people, do you have any idea where he might have more money hidden?"

I assured John the only other spot I could think of would be Powell's home in Vienna. He said they had checked every crevice of the place.

My assumption is that Powell got the money everywhere he could, everything from payoffs on jobs to payoffs on vending machines, plus from people handing him cash in election contributions that frequently did not make it to the campaign treasurer. He symbolized an era of Illinois politics, an era that was colorful but fortunately is largely behind us.

His estate was estimated at $3 million.

---

[1] "Stevenson Says He's Not Candidate for Office in 1968," *Moline Dispatch*, 3 January 1968.

[2] Henry Hanson, "Adlai Spurns Race in '68," *Chicago Daily News*, date uncertain, SIU Archives.

[3] *Glenview Life*, 21 January 1968.

[4] 12 February 1968.

[5] Editorial, *Chicago Tribune*, 1 November 1968.

[6] 31 October 1968.

[7] "Ogilvie Praises Simon," *Alton Evening Telegraph*, 7 November 1968.

[8] 19 January 1969.

[9] Phil White, *Tuscola Journal*, 22 May 1969.

[10] *Chicago Defender*, 8 January 1969.

[11] Editorial, 23 April 1969.

[12] John Hansen to author, 19 November 1970, ISHL.

[13] Rev. Gerald Montroy to author, 22 April 1969.

[14] Robert Collins, "Cairo Forces Maneuvering To Oust Chief of Police," *St. Louis Post-Dispatch*, 11 May 1969.

[15] Ibid.

[16] John Taylor, "Charges Asked in Cairo Case," *Metro-East Journal*, 29 April 1969.

[17] "Simon Sends Staff Member to Cairo to Consult With Community Leaders," *Cairo Evening Citizen*, 26 June 1969.

[18] 11 September 1969, ISHL archives.

[19] *St. Louis Post-Dispatch*, 2 May 1969.

[20] Will and Ariel Durant, *The Lessons of History* (New York: Simon and Schuster, 1968), 34.

[21] Paul Simon, "Simon Discusses Demo Coalition," *Metro-East Journal*, 11 February 1969.

[22] Henry Hanson and Frank Maier, "Simon: Increase Governor's Role" *Chicago Daily News*, 15 January 1970.

[23] *Chicago Today*, 5 November 1970.

[24] *Illinois State Register*, 28 December 1970.

# Chapter 6

# *Candidate for Governor*

Life is not a uniform series of successes, and politics reflects and magnifies life.

The logical office for a lieutenant governor to seek is governor. I had decided to run, whether or not I received Mayor Daley's blessing. I would not bow out at the last minute if someone closer to him and more to his liking would be chosen by the party hierarchy.

I did not have a bad relationship with Daley, but not a close one either. Few people were close to him. Others worked with him much more than I did, particularly people on his staff and in the city council. He and I discussed matters frankly when we did meet, and he learned he could tell me things without reading them in the newspapers the next day. Little things indicated that he did not harbor hostile feelings toward me. When a reporter for a downstate newspaper asked Daley who the strong downstate Democratic leaders were, Daley replied: "Paul Simon has made quite a record for himself. Some others who have done all right are Al Dixon and Paul Powell."[1] But I also sensed that I was not his first choice and that I would have to prepare for a fight in the primary, and in the process make it more likely to get his endorsement.

I did my work as ombudsman while Lieutenant Governor, and covered the state speaking at every civic club or Democratic group that would listen to me. But inevitably some of my actions stepped on the toes of leading Democrats as well as Republicans. I talked frankly to the press about the problems sometimes making public officials unhappy. When people complained about conditions of public housing I visited with them. When migrant laborers had temporary housing in Illinois counties that endangered their lives, I spoke out, offending landowners as well as officials who tolerated these abuses.

Democratic slate-makers scheduled their meeting for December 1971. I privately started telling key leaders some months before that I would ask for the blessing of the Democratic leaders, but I would run regardless. I knew the word would get to Daley. In May, Rowland Evans and Robert Novak had a national column titled "Lt. Gov. May Buck Daley Machine" with a sub-head "Belief Grows He'll Run for Governor Regardless of Chicago Democratic Backing."[2] They wrote: "The privately stated intention of Lt. Gov. Paul Simon to run for the Democratic nomination for governor next year even if it means bucking Mayor Richard J. Daley in an open primary puts the power realities [in Chicago] in a new, highly complicated perspective."

In the meantime, what I viewed as a small cloud on the horizon came with the announcement of Dan Walker, who said he would run no matter what the organization did. Dan, a prominent attorney, had chaired Adlai Stevenson III's successful campaign for U. S. Senator and written a report on the 1968 Democratic convention that received much attention. A man of unquestioned ability, he also had a reputation for duplicitousness that did not help his stature among political insiders. During Adlai's campaign Walker asked for my list of contributors, and with both spoken and written assurance that no one else would get it, I gave it to him, wanting to help Adlai. After Walker announced we quickly learned Dan had violated his word and used my list for his own campaign. At this point I viewed him as a threat primarily if I faced a Daley-endorsed candidate, fearing that Walker would divide the forces opposed to the officially blessed candidate.

In June I had a fund-raising dinner in Chicago, raising money for an unstated office. Daley was there. The strongest labor leader in the state, Joe Germano, district director of the United Steelworkers, introduced me with these words: "Whatever office Paul Simon seeks, the Steelworkers will be in his corner. I give you Paul Simon, the man I hope is the next governor of Illinois."[3] His introduction meant he did not support Mike Howlett or Tom Foran, the other two most prominently mentioned possibilities, and it also meant he would not wait for Daley's nod, as labor leaders in Illinois traditionally did.

By the time of slate-making we had a sizable body of endorsements, including eighty-seven of the 101 downstate Democratic county chairmen and the Illinois AFL-CIO, the first time that organization had endorsed before the party officials met. A group calling themselves Citizens for Simon began circulating petitions for me, co-chaired by Newton Minow, former head of the Federal Communications Commission; C. Virgil Martin, chairman of Carson Pirie Scott, a major Chicago business; Robert Johnston, regional director of the United Auto Workers; and Donald Prince, the 1966 Democratic candidate for State Superintendent of Public Instruction. And semi-helpful were stories appearing all over the state, with headings like "Paul Simon May Have the Machine Painted into a Corner."[4] Personally meaningful to me was a ringing endorsement from former Senator Paul Douglas.

A *St. Louis Globe-Democrat/Chicago Sun-Times* poll under the heading, "Simon Solidly Ahead of Ogilvie," also helped. It showed me beating Ogilvie in the heavily Republican suburbs of Chicago and carrying populous Madison County by an astronomical 64-22.[5]

At the end of November I sent Daley the results of an Oliver Quayle poll we had commissioned based on 455 interviews in a letter marked "personal and confidential." It showed me defeating Ogilvie, and all the other possible candidates behind him. The pollsters significantly noted — and I included this with my letter to Daley — that I could not "take the nomination for granted even assuming Simon receives his party's designation. Dan Walker could become a major threat in a Primary contest because . . . the Chicago attorney shows signs of becoming the kind of anti-Establishment candidate which voters around the nation have increasingly been turning to in recent years."[6]

The first solid clue I had that Daley would be in my corner came when the state Democratic chairman, Jim Ronan, asked me to give him three names of people I would like to have as Lieutenant Governor candidates. Ronan promised me nothing, but I knew he would not be asking this if things were not moving in my direction. I gave him the names of Neil Hartigan, a respected young Democratic leader in Chicago who had worked on Daley's staff; State Senator Phil Rock, a person of ability; and State Senator Cecil Partee, then serving as President of the State Senate. I told Hartigan of my conversation but neither of the other two. I sensed accurately from Ronan's reaction that it would be Hartigan.

After listening to the possible candidates in Springfield and Chicago sessions, the Democratic leaders adjourned until Sunday. That morning Daley called me at home and said that a few of the leaders had misgivings about my running for Governor and thought I should be a candidate for the Senate. I told him to tell them I would run for governor and nothing else. "That's what I told them you would say," the mayor told me, laughing as he said it. Jeanne and I went to a St. Louis Cardinal football game with the Green Bay Packers in St. Louis that afternoon and left word with officials at the stadium where I could be reached because I expected an important phone call. It arrived just before Green Bay made a touchdown. Jeanne and I took off in a chartered plane for Chicago, thanked Daley and the other Democratic leaders, and prepared for what we thought would be an eleven-month hard but successful campaign.

Bill Colson headed our political effort. He had been in charge of my Lieutenant Governor's office in Chicago. Yvonne Rice of my Springfield office led the downstate campaign. Ed Joyce, a lawyer and CPA, served as treasurer of this campaign and subsequent statewide election efforts.

The Democratic leaders not only endorsed the state ticket — Congressman Roman Pucinski for Senator, Tom Lyons for Attorney General, Michael Howlett for Secretary of State, and Dean Barringer for State Comptroller — but also the county Democratic ticket, including Ed Hanrahan for reelection as State's Attorney. Hanrahan had been indicted in connection with a badly botched police raid on the Black Panthers in which two people were killed. (He and thirteen other law enforcement officials were acquitted after a thirteen and one-half week trial.) Hardly had the ticket been selected when reporters asked all of us whether we supported Hanrahan, would we support him if a jury found him guilty, and other questions. In the black community most believed him to be a racist, a judgment probably unfair but hard to disprove, particularly after the raid indictment. Roman Pucinski called and said, "You have got to talk to Daley. All I'm getting are questions about Hanrahan. We have to get him off the ticket." I called Daley, who also was receiving the same questions from reporters. We met with Daley and soon Judge Raymond Berg replaced Hanrahan as the endorsed Democratic candidate for Cook County state's attorney. But Hanrahan, always feisty, stayed in the race.

Walker, in the meantime, attacked me as a puppet of Daley, and started to walk the length of the state, a legitimately good campaign gimmick that caught public imagination. He attacked me for not making public my knowledge of the Paul Powell shoe-box money as soon as I knew about it, an action that would have been irresponsible on my part because officials were still investigating other possible places he had money hidden. When both of us appeared before the Illinois Education Association, I promised to meet the current obligations to the teacher pension system — which the state was not doing — and to take the actuarial deficiency, what in theory should be there for future retirements, and over a period of forty years get it paid, $2\frac{1}{2}$ percent each year. In my four years I would reduce the accumulated deficiency by 10 percent, and each year after that the amount needed would be reduced. It would not be easy but I knew I could do it. Walker got up and told the group that he would not only meet the annual responsibility but eliminate the accumulated future indebtedness in one year! His speech brought cheers but had no possibility of fulfillment. (When he became governor he did not meet even the current year obligation.) But he looked good, had a dramatic flair, portrayed himself as the champion of the people against the evil political organization. And thousands in Illinois legitimately yearned to defeat the only old-time political machine left in the nation, and Walker gave them the opportunity. The 1968 Democratic convention also left a residue of ill will four years later among many Illinois Democrats who saw this as a chance to protest.

But so many leaders endorsed my candidacy that it lulled us into an unreasonable self-confidence. Even the probable Democratic nominee for President, Senator George McGovern, when speaking in the state, all but endorsed me, an unusual action in a primary: "I have known Paul Simon more than twenty years. . . . I know of no one in public life whose integrity and character and devotion to the public good that I would put confidence in any more than I would Paul Simon."[7]

I hoped, once I had the endorsement, not to have a primary so divisive that I would lose in the fall. My most serious problems generally have been in the primaries, within my own party. In general elections I have always had sizable Republican and independent support. But I did not want to take a chance of diminishing my Democratic base. I wanted to win the primary but remain strong for the fall. After receiving the nod of party leaders, the United Press International story about me said, "Seldom has a challenger started a campaign for governor with such a lead in popularity over the incumbent governor. The respected *Chicago Sun-Times* and the *Prairie Farmer* polls both show Simon would out-poll Gov. Richard B. Ogilvie even among traditionally Republican farmers."[8] I wanted to keep that lead but hold the Democrats, so I met Walker's strong attacks with soft answers, "I'm sure he's sincere but he's wrong." And then I explained to reporters why. At no time did I go on the offensive against him. If I had won the primary, that would have been sound strategy. That was my error, no one else's.

A second factor that compounded our problem was the Hanrahan-Berg race which brought out a great many anti-Daley and anti-black voters in Chicago. Hanrahan won in the primary and lost in the general election. The Hanrahan voters in the primary tended to be angry at Daley, angry at me, and at anyone who had anything to do with dropping Hanrahan as an endorsed candidate.

Complicating things, federal courts in Illinois and New York handed down opposite opinions about state laws limiting cross-overs in party primaries. Twelve days before our primary a three-judge federal panel in Illinois struck down a ruling restricting people of one party from crossing into another party in a primary. Walker hailed the ruling, and it did concern us, particularly because the Republicans had no serious primary contests.

That became significant when combined with a sound stand I took but did not handle well. Illinois relies heavily on the real estate tax for support of our schools. The difficulty with that is there are huge inequities both in its application and in the level of support that schools receive. Someone out of work temporarily must pay the same real estate tax as someone who is earning income. School districts can be rich in students but poor in assessed valuation for real estate taxes, frequently the impoverished areas not getting what they need. Through the years I had consistently advocated less reliance on the real estate tax, shifting the burden to the income tax so that there would be greater equity in expenditure per pupil. In mid-February I reiterated that stand in a press conference, but unfortunately I had no precise figures on how it would be carried out. Walker jumped on it, claiming my proposal would "triple the state income tax," so preposterous a claim that I didn't pay that much attention to it, and the newspaper editorials in the state sided with me. I did issue a press release, saying "It's clear that I haven't asked for a bigger tax bite, but only a fairer one. I think the people of Illinois have more common sense than some other candidates give them credit for. Glib speeches about easy cuts in taxes without increases elsewhere are pure political hokum."[9]

Walker went on television with commercials urging citizens to "stop Paul Simon from tripling your state income tax," and urged Democrats, Republicans, and independents to go into the primary and vote for him, a significant appeal in view of the court decision.

But our signals continued to run favorably. The fact that Senator Adlai Stevenson strongly endorsed me after Walker had managed his campaign we felt meant something to on-the-fence liberals. Our staff called the county Democratic chairmen in the state and only one indicated that he thought Walker would carry his county. The newspaper editorials lulled us into too much confidence, every newspaper but one that endorsed supported my candidacy. Most significantly, all five Chicago daily newspapers had strong endorsements. Their editorials were summed up by the Tribune's comment: "We find him [Simon] by far the better man."[10] And our poll of those who voted in previous

Democratic primaries showed me winning, but that did not include those who would vote in a Democratic primary for the first time. I followed a cautious path, one that did not convey urgency to my supporters around the state. I worked hard, but our campaign did not send signals that we felt we had a serious challenge.

Walker also sensed accurately the potential of television commercials — which we did not — and hired an able New York producer, David Garth, to assist. Walker loaned his own campaign $250,000 of the approximately $1 million spent in the primary, about twice our expenditure, and used part of that for some effective last-minute TV commercials.

The night of the primary our family, joined by Alan and Jody Dixon — Alan then served as state treasurer — flew from southern Illinois to Chicago. The first sense that we might lose came from Alan, who said that he heard bad reports from two precincts in Belleville that should have been for me. Gene Callahan, a key member of my staff, met the plane in Chicago and said it did not look good.

Walker carried fifty-two of the 101 downstate counties, but more significantly carried the suburban areas around Chicago by a wide margin. The vote total for the state: 735,193 to 694,900. I lost by 40,293 votes. A huge crossover vote in the suburbs made the difference, though when you lose by that close a margin almost all theories about what is the key can be accredited as accurate. In part because of the Hanrahan factor, I carried Cook County by only 20,957 votes.

The post-election analysis by one suburban newspaper typified most of them. "Walker Won, Thanks to GOP Crossovers" headed the editorial. Along with a statistical analysis of what happened they commented: "The massive GOP crossover was apparently stimulated by a court decision of little consequence that was announced only two weeks before the primary, which made it at least more socially acceptable to cross over. . . . DuPage and western Cook County Republicans provided Dan Walker with more than the 40,000 votes he needed to defeat Lt. Gov. Paul Simon, apparently doing it to secure what they thought would be an easier target for Gov. Ogilvie in November. The Illinois polls had for months been giving Simon an important advantage over Ogilvie."[11] The theory that people in large numbers crossed over to nominate a weaker Democratic candidate is not one that I have ever believed. A few did it for that reason, but I don't believe that most citizens will do that, either Democrats or Republicans. My sense is that they either wanted to cast an anti-Daley vote, or they believed Dan Walker's commercials about my tripling their state income tax, and cast an anti-tax vote. And Walker's claim that he would increase aid to schools by eliminating waste and corruption had simplistic appeal to the unsophisticated.

When it looked like I would win both the primary and general election I had two offers of substantial contributions, $250,000 and $100,000 — each with a condition. One group wanted to name the chief highway engineer and the other wanted to designate the dates at the race tracks. I declined both offers and turned the information over to the FBI. My assumption is that the FBI made a cursory investigation and that the parties who made the offers denied doing it. On another occasion a man I knew approached me in the lobby of the Bismarck Hotel and handed me an envelope which he said contained $10,000. All he wanted, he told me, was assurance he would be named to a key and sensitive spot in my administration, which he designated. I handed the money back to him and went to the campaign office and told Gene Callahan that I wanted him to make sure that man received absolutely no position if I should be elected.


What lessons did I learn from my defeat?

First, win elections one at a time. If you have a primary fight, worry about the general election later. Second, if you're attacked, don't turn the other cheek. Respond quickly and vigorously.

I learned these two lessons the hard way.


Walker defeated Ogilvie in the general election by a narrow margin. He had a controversial governorship. Marital and legal difficulties followed. The Annapolis graduate and one-time governor ended up serving eighteen months in federal prison, a sad ending to the career of a capable man.

Shortly after the primary Roman Pucinski, then our candidate against Senator Charles Percy, called and said that I should file an appeal of the primary result on the basis that the New York court decision on cross-over primary votes and the Illinois court decision differed and the New York court had ruled correctly. I did not encourage Roman on this. Within an hour Mayor Daley called and urged the same, commenting that he had talked to a member of the Illinois Supreme Court and had reason to believe they would rule favorably for me. Because I had friends on the Court, but primarily because of

Daley's influence, I had no serious question that the Court would rule in my favor, but I felt it would look like "sour grapes." It would get tangled in endless litigation and would not create either the image or atmosphere I would want to enter the general election or the governorship. I declined the mayor's suggestion.

Perhaps two weeks later Roman Pucinski called with a different suggestion, that he withdraw from the Senate race and that I take his place, and that he then run for reelection to his congressional seat. His theory was that since the primary defeat had strangely made me a semi-hero in the state that I could run well. He also sensed accurately that with Walker and Hanrahan as candidates it would be an awkward few months campaigning with them and the probable results less than positive for Roman. At that point I did not know what I wanted to do, but jumping into another campaign did not have appeal.

After the primary I issued a statement congratulating Dan Walker and indicated my support. I added, "He must now show that he has the ability to unite the party; that will be no easy task. And then he can have the chance to heal the wounds of poverty and bitterness which afflict our state."

I thanked various people, including Mayor Daley "who never asked for any commitments and acted like a gentleman throughout despite the abuse heaped upon him." And then I added: "I am sorry that I have let my supporters down. I regret the inadequacies of my campaign, inadequacies which others may see more clearly than I do. But I do not regret telling people the truth. I hope I never become so eager for any prize that I corrupt the truth, as vile a corruption as any other."

Losing an election, a hard-fought election, is never easy. Someone has said it is almost like a death in the family, and that contains an element of truth.

The praise that came from a great variety of sources softened that blow. The words that meant most to me came from Paul Douglas, interviewed by the *Chicago Sun-Times* for his eightieth birthday a few days after my defeat. Asked about the primary, he said, "Paul Simon is everything that a politician should be. I have followed him and tried to help him over 20 years. When Emily came in and said it looked as though he was going to lose, it cast a pall over my entire day. I think that the voters made a great mistake. They thought that the most independent man was not independent, a cruel judgment. . . . I am deeply disappointed, disappointed for the state and personally disappointed, because I love and trust that boy."[12]

That is a finer tribute than I deserved, but it added balm to the wound of defeat.

[1] Robert Hartley, "Interview with Richard Daley," *Metro-East Journal*, 16 November 1969.

[2] *Post-Crescent*, (Wisconsin), 26 May 1971.

[3] John Dreiske, *Chicago Sun-Times*, 23 June 1971.

[4] *Metro-East Journal*, 7 November 1971.

[5] *St. Louis Globe-Democrat*, 11 November 1971.

[6] Author to Richard Daley, 29 November 1971, ISHL.

[7] Students for Simon Press Release, from remarks of Senator George McGovern to Farmer's Union convention, ISHL.

[8] Thomas Pledge, "Pucinski Over Dixon in Senate Endorsement," *Collinsville Herald*, 7 December 1971.

[9] Taylor Penseneau and Bob Ellis, *Dan Walker* (Evansville, Indiana: Smith-Collins, 1993), 146.

[10] Editorial, *Chicago Tribune*, 13 March 1972.

[11] *Itasca Record*, 24 May 1972.

[12] Tom Littlewood, "Paul Douglas, 80 on Sunday, Talks of Genius and Politics," *Chicago Sun-Times*, 26 March 1972.

# Chapter 7

# *Religion*

My Christian heritage and beliefs are part of me, but through the years I have become more sensitive to the great harm that religious beliefs can cause as well as the great good they can create.

To read through the history of civilization in the books written by Will and Ariel Durant is to recognize that in the name of Christianity those of the Jewish faith suffered death and torture through centuries, not simply during Hitler's time; that Protestants killed Catholics, and Catholics killed Protestants, all in the name of religion; that Muslims killed Christians, and Christians killed Muslims; and Hindus can be added to the role of the oppressed and oppressors. The list goes on and on.

In 1997 I spent a little time in the former Yugoslavia. I witnessed the intense hatred that caused the deaths of tens of thousands of people, hatred still vividly alive, hatred ultimately exploited by cynical leaders on the basis of religious affiliation. Roman Catholics hating Orthodox Catholics hating Muslims, and all killing each other, or at least doing it until U. S. and other international troops arrived to stabilize the situation. It is disheartening to visit a small city and see that the first buildings destroyed were the Roman Catholic and Orthodox churches and the mosques. And in some places not a building of any type without shell damage.

When President Clinton visited Northern Ireland and spoke at a factory outside of Belfast, newspapers reported that the factory had separate entrances for Catholics and Protestants. The killings in Northern Ireland diminish, thanks to successful negotiations and the referendum that followed it. However, the slaying of people in other regions because of being Sunni Muslims instead of Shiite Muslims, and the other way around, continues as does other religious oppression.

Religion is a powerful force for evil — and a powerful force for good. Religion kills, and religion heals.

As I grew up, we had devotions in our home twice a day, after breakfast and after our evening meal. Usually my father read a short lesson, followed by prayer. Sometimes my mother read it, and as my brother and I grew older, sometimes we read the lesson. We always attended church and Sunday School, and when we neared the age of twelve took confirmation lessons and went through the rite of confirmation, in which we professed accepting the doctrines of Christianity as enunciated by the Lutheran Church-Missouri Synod. Religion played a central role in our family life. (The title, Lutheran Church-Missouri Synod, goes back to the Missouri roots of the founding of this branch of Lutheranism, representing about one-third of Lutherans in the United States. I often wonder how someone in Hong Kong or Nigeria explains why he or she is a Missouri Synod Lutheran.)

When I was fifteen, leaders of a Lutheran youth organization called the Walther League elected me the Oregon district president, an opportunity to acquire leadership skills as well as grow in understanding of religious beliefs and how a church organization functions. Not too long after we moved to Illinois I had the opportunity to serve as the Southern Illinois district president of the same organization, and then later on its national board. From about the age of twelve to eighteen, Art and I spent a week each summer at a Lutheran youth camp, learning a little, being inspired more, and thoroughly enjoying ourselves.

My father would be placed on the "liberal" side of this conservative branch of Lutheranism. His attitudes undoubtedly played a role in the development of my thinking. I recall one of the teachers at Concordia, the pre-seminary school I attended, estimating that 95 percent of the people in heaven would be Lutherans, a remarkable claim that even as a young teenager I found offensive. Anti-Catholicism played a significant role in the thinking and theology of Missouri Synod Lutherans then, as well as much of the non-Catholic religious world. Anti-Catholicism was a sort of respectable Ku Klux Klanism, without the sheets and violence. Some years ago the Missouri Synod refused to have what we call "communion fellowship," with the American Lutheran Church because they did not teach as doctrine that the Pope is the anti-Christ, a vague Biblical reference that people have ascribed to various unpopular persons and groups over the centuries. Some years later I picked up a magazine and saw a picture of Lutheran leaders with the Pope, including the head of the Missouri Synod. The current Missouri Synod president sent a letter to the Pope addressed "Dear Brother in Christ." Attitudes had changed, thanks in large part to Pope John XXIII, who "opened the windows of the Vatican," and John F. Kennedy, who showed our nation the ridiculousness of anti-Catholicism's claims. One of the Catholic doctrines Lutherans regularly denounced was that of papal infallibility. At the same time part of the general prayers offered during a Missouri Synod service thanked God that we had been blessed with pure doctrine, words obviously meant more for the congregation than for God, who was probably not much impressed by our assertion. We denounced the papal claim, but made virtually the same claim ourselves. If it is true, as some suggest, that we now have "a post-denominational religious culture" that is not all bad.

Anti-Catholicism has diminished, as has anti-Semitism, but in 1960 when a marvelous Roman Catholic young woman, Jeanne Hurley, and I decided to marry, it shook up some members of our families and we ran into religious stereotypes and prejudices. Before we married, we read everything we could about Catholic-Protestant marriages, and the information was so uniformly negative that we decided if we married, and if despite the predictions our marriage lasted a month or two, we would write something constructive for Protestants and Catholics who want to wed. One book suggested that if despite all the advice a couple married, they should never invite guests to their home because this would inevitably lead to religious controversies. We later wrote a book together, *Protestant-Catholic Marriages Can Succeed*, which I'm pleased to say is outdated, thanks to Vatican Council II and the growing tolerance and understanding between religious groups that is now more a part of our U. S. cultural scene.

When we married in my wife's Catholic Church, my Lutheran clergyman father could not participate in the wedding ceremony. Twenty-seven years later when my daughter Sheila, a Catholic, married Perry Knop, a Lutheran, my brother Art, a Lutheran clergyman, took part in the marriage ceremony in a Catholic church. Things have changed for the better. Some Sundays Jeanne and I attend both Lutheran and Roman Catholic services. We support each other's churches. And we differ with both Catholic and Missouri Synod Lutheran positions opposing the ordination of women, a throwback to an ancient culture that will not survive long in either of our churches.

When I went to Dana College in Nebraska, I took a religion course from a Lutheran theologian, Paul Nyholm, and he startled me by saying that while the message of the Bible in general has validity, we could not claim that God had inspired each individual word. I argued with him because I had read in my church publications that God inspired each word, a position my father also held at that time. Three years later my brother went to Concordia Seminary, and told me that he thought the literalist interpretation of the Bible for historic minutia wrong. That startled me also, and as I reexamined my thinking came to the conclusion that Paul Nyholm and my brother were correct. The position of Paul Nyholm and my brother is that the Bible is inspired and an accurate guide on Christ's life and mission and on issues of faith and morals, but does not require that a person accept creation in six days or that Methuselah lived to be 969 years old.

Thoughtfully reexamining positions that often are based on emotion more than anything should be part of the search for truth. And careful analysis should include looking at the context and culture and times in which those who wrote ancient documents lived.

I am still offended when, during the Lenten season, Scriptures are read describing how "the Jews" did various things that led to Christ's death. I am pleased I have no Jewish guests with me on those occasions. A more accurate reading would be "the organized religious leaders" headed the efforts which resulted in Christ's death, and such a reading might result in reexamination of attitudes instead of anti-Semitism.

While I accept the Christian beliefs, I reject the absolutism and rigidity which is too often part of Christian followers as well as those of other faiths. I believe that logic can lead to a belief in a Supreme Being, whatever the name. But then people have to make what Danish theologian/philosopher Søren Kierkegaard called "the leap of faith." For most of us who have been reared in one particular religious background, that leap came almost with birth. To understand through reason what the ultimate realities are is impossible, though we make leaps of faith frequently in our lives without understanding. I do not understand why a light brightens when I turn on a switch; I do not understand how it is possible to sit in Illinois and be on a television show in New York with someone from South Africa; I do not understand how a computer lets me speak to my son Martin in Maryland or an academician in Russia. Without understanding I accept these realities. There is truth to St. Augustine's words: "Understanding is the reward of faith. Therefore, let us seek not to understand [so] that we may believe, but believe that we may understand." With flawed understanding, I try to reach reality in religion. But I know my understanding is flawed, and that helps to avoid excessively dogmatic assertions. The danger with the self-search for reality is that it becomes easy to adapt beliefs to our weaknesses. When someone told President Ulysses S. Grant that Senator Charles Sumner did not believe in the Bible, Grant responded, "That is because he did not write it himself." There is the Sumner weakness in all who thoughtfully search. With the command of Jesus to his followers to wash each other's feet, we say that was a different culture so we don't do it. When we read the directive that wives should submit themselves to their husbands, we — largely male decision-makers — decide we should follow that directive. Cultural differences don't seem to apply in the latter case; ignored is St. Paul's admonition to "be subject to one another."

In the arena of religion — as well as politics — it is sometimes too easy to say with certitude, "I'm right and you're wrong," and then slip into saying, "I'm good and you're bad." The latter leads to intolerance and bloodshed. Swedish Lutheran Bishop Krister Stendahl warns against what he calls "churchification," when faith "hardens hearts instead of enlivening."[1]

Religion is the only field where many leaders assume all truth has been revealed. In chemistry and mathematics and all other areas, truths are built upon truths. In mathematics, for example, whoever came up with the formula that two and two are four did not say, "I have found the truth. Let's stop here." The search for truth continued, building on the base of knowledge already acquired.

But mysteries about life remain and always will remain. I do not understand the presence of evil. I do not accept the easy generalization, "It is God's will," when there is death or disaster. I do not believe God willed the Holocaust; I do not believe God wants a six-year-old girl to die of a brain tumor; I cannot believe that an Almighty Power decided to have a tornado and rip apart the bodies of twenty-three people; I cannot accept that my lifespan as an American is seventy-six years, and that of a person in Zambia is forty-two years, and that that is the wish of God. In the Old Testament book of Judges, Jephthah is reported as promising the Lord that if he could lead Israel to victory over the Ammonites, then Jephthah would offer as a burnt offering the first person he saw when he returned home. The first person he saw was his daughter, his only child, and he offered her as a burnt offering. I do not accept that God wished that upon the daughter of Jephthah.

In 1739 King Philip V of Spain refused to renew an agreement to give English ships the right to take African slaves to Spanish America. For that action, England declared war on Spain to great public rejoicing "and throughout England church bells rang."[2]

Again and again in history, the cruelest actions are demanded by a religion, or approved in the name of religion. Listen to this account by Ashurnasirpal, the Assyrian leader:

> All the chiefs who revolted, I flayed, with their skins I covered the pillar, some in the midst I walled up, others on stakes I impaled, still others I arranged around the pillar on stakes. . . . As for the chieftains and royal officers who had rebelled, I cut off their members. . . . I burned three thousand captives with fire, I left not a single one among them alive to serve as a hostage. . . . These warriors who had sinned against Ashur [the sun god] and had plotted evil against me. . . from their hostile mouths I have torn their tongues, and I have compassed their destruction. As for the other who remained alive, I offered them as a funerary sacrifice. . . . Their lacerated members have I given to the dogs, the swine, the wolves. . . . By accomplishing these deeds I have rejoiced the heart of the great gods.[3]

If in the name of religion, so much evil is consummated, why accept Christianity or any other religion?

There is another side to this. A knife can be used to stab someone, or it can be used as a tool to prepare food.

I read St. Paul: "And now these three remain: faith, hope and love. But the greatest of these is love." That strikes me as an essential truth that the world needs, and each of us should strive to live by, however inadequately we do it. The words of Jesus about helping the hungry, the naked, those in prison, and others desperate seem to me to ring true and are so contrary to the actions taken over the centuries by so many in the name of Jesus. When I read Amos demanding justice for the poor, that resonates with me.

But when people in the name of any religion claim to have the sole possession of truth, they have crossed the line from faith to arrogance. That is an easy temptation for any group. My own Missouri Synod Lutheran denomination — which has done many good things — does not want even to sully itself by praying with other Lutherans, justifying it by a strange interpretation of one scriptural passage. These inconsistencies are part of every group, and part of each of us as individuals. We gain from listening to others, not that we accept all assertions of truth as equally valid. I do not have to become a Christian Scientist to recognize the validity of their insight that many who claim physical ailments in fact have nothing organically wrong with them. I do not have to accept Mormonism to recognize that the Latter-Day Saints have done great work in taking care of the physical needs of their people. I do not have to join the Nakshbandi order of the Muslim world, but I can appreciate their appeal for tolerance and understanding.

However inadequately I follow the dictates of my faith, I am better for having it. It is no accident that those who attend religious services and express a religious belief are less likely to become drug addicts; are more likely to volunteer for charitable activities.

When people ask me to be precise in how my religious faith has had an impact on my votes or the stands I take, that is difficult to assess. When I served in the Illinois State Senate, Jerry Williams, then a call-in host for station WBBM in Chicago, asked me that question and I responded by saying that I know that my religious background affects me, but precisely how I could not say. I mentioned that a few seats from me in the state senate sat Sen. Robert Cherry, later a distinguished judge. I said that he is Jewish and I am Lutheran but our records are virtually identical. The next day I saw Bob and told him I had mentioned him on the Chicago station. "Yes, thanks," he said with a chuckle. "You told everyone I am Jewish." A few weeks later I spoke to the men's brotherhood of the synagogue to which Bob belonged, but an out-of-state engagement prevented him from being there. "I took care of you, Bob," I told him the next day. "I told them you are not Jewish." Having a sense of humor helps in politics — or religion.

Until my father's death from leukemia, I believed that wakes drained the family and, in my experience, too often placed the visitor in an awkward situation, not knowing exactly what to say. But I changed my mind after my father's death, the most difficult experience I have ever had. At his death he served as pastor of a small rural parish near Okawville, in southern Illinois. I shall always be grateful to Governor Richard Ogilvie and his wife Dorothy for being there, as well as other officials, but the people who really impressed me were the farmers, the laborers, the housewives, the people with rough hands and unpolished English. As they came through the line many told stories about how my father had helped them. He had a real gift as a preacher, talking in understandable language. But after his death

I realized that the great sermons he preached did not come from the pulpit but in what he did. He volunteered every Thursday morning to help at a school for the retarded. If someone needed food or comfort, he helped. I mention this because I know of no one who is now a Lutheran who was not born a Lutheran, who read the Augsburg Confession and said, "I want to become a Lutheran." I know of no one who is a Roman Catholic today who originally did not have that affiliation, who read the papal encyclicals and said, "I want to become a Roman Catholic." I know of no one who is Jewish today who had a different heritage, who read the Torah and said, "I want to become a Jew." Generally we see something in the lives of others that persuades us to change course.

Those who practice rigidity and absolutism in the name of religion, whether simply by word or with arms, will not persuade. Part of humanity's history is that if a Protestant or Catholic or Muslim or some other belief conquered an area, people "converted" in overwhelming numbers to save their lives. But the world is different today. The Protestants who kill Catholics in Northern Ireland, or the Catholics who kill Protestants, do no favor to their professed faith. Muslim extremists in Algeria who decimate villages cause their faith to be held in ridicule by people around the world. However, those who kill have been stimulated by others who preach fanaticism. Religious leaders who advocate with excessive zealotry share the guilt with the murderers who wield the knives and pull the triggers.

At the age of sixteen, I knew I had found all ultimate truths in the field of religion. At the age of sixty-nine as I write this, I am less set in concrete in my beliefs. I accept certain truths but I respect those who have made a different leap of faith, and my search for truth and insights into the meaning of life continues. The day I stop searching for truth should be my last.

---

[1] Address to Lutheran Bishops of the United States, 1998.

[2] Will and Ariel Durant, *The Age of Voltaire* (New York: Simon and Schuster, 1965), 102.

[3] Quoted in Will Durant, *Our Oriental Heritage* (New York: Simon and Schuster, 1954), 275-276.

# Chapter 8

# *The Pause*
# *That Refreshed*

Part of the rehabilitation process from the blow of losing the race for the nomination for Governor was receiving different job offers and contemplating what we might do. My uncertainties complicated this process.

The first academic offer came from Southern Illinois University, where I would teach many years later. I explained to them that while I had written a number of books and had more honorary doctorates than I deserved, I had not finished college. They said that would be no problem. They had another faculty member named Buckminster Fuller who did not have a bachelor's degree.

One of the offers came from Dr. Robert Spencer, president of a soon-to-be university in Springfield. That appealed to me because I liked Bob Spencer, and we talked about creating a public affairs reporting program which I had long felt the state needed, and because of my part in creating the university.

The Illinois Board for Higher Education, in a period of rapidly growing enrollment at all schools, recommended the creation of four new state universities. The independent colleges felt threatened by that. A remarkable business leader, Ben Heinemann, headed the Board for Higher Education. Governor Kerner called a meeting of representatives of the independent schools and state universities, together with representatives of the Board, and three or four legislators during my years as state senator. The first meeting, while not acrimonious, got nowhere. The governor called a second meeting and it became clear quickly that it also would not result in anything. I suggested to the Governor that he appoint a subcommittee of four or five people to see if a compromise could be fashioned. Always a dangerous move! The Governor agreed and within thirty minutes after the close of the meeting called and asked if I would chair the subcommittee.

We worked out a proposal to have two universities offering only junior, senior, and graduate courses, and to greatly increase the grants and loans to students going to public or private colleges in the state. That had something to please everyone. We suggested that one new school be placed in suburban Cook County, and that eventually became Governors' State University, and, the other one, on my insistence, in Springfield, the state capital. I had just finished reading a biography of Robert LaFollete, the Wisconsin Progressive, who in a short time as Governor not only led Wisconsin, but provided the nation with everything from unemployment compensation to political primaries. He was able to do it because of the location of the University of Wisconsin and its rich human resources at Madison, the state's capital. I felt that a university dedicated in a special way to public service located in Springfield could be of help to Illinois. Our recommendations received virtually unanimous approval from various groups and from the legislature. The university in Springfield, Sangamon State University, named for the river flowing through that area, eventually became the Springfield campus of the University of Illinois.

So I felt some ties to that embryonic Springfield university, even though it had no campus yet. I accepted that offer, plus an opportunity to lecture for one semester at Harvard, as a Fellow of the John F. Kennedy Institute of Politics. I enjoyed the change in Springfield but the break at Harvard really gave our family free time we have not enjoyed so fully before or since. No one asked me to appear at Rotary or Kiwanis clubs, no candidates asked me to speak at their rallies; membership on various boards and commissions existed in some far-off place called Illinois, and they did not expect me to attend. We had evenings to ourselves, and weekends. About once a week I accepted speaking engagements at places like Brandeis and the University of Rhode Island, and occasionally spoke to classes that faculty members at Harvard wanted me to address. But otherwise my sole obligation was to lecture once a week to "my" students, and to enrich myself in every way I could at Harvard. And what a great place to enrich yourself!

I had a small office in the old home that then housed the Kennedy Institute. Our family rented the home of Prof. and Mrs. Karl

Deutsch, a political philosopher lecturing in France for the semester. Ordinarily I walked to the office down Brattle Street, past Henry Wadsworth Longfellow's home and the old Episcopal church in which George Washington is supposed to have worshipped, past the oldest buildings on the Harvard campus, a marvelous walk.

We had a fascinating weekend driving to the boyhood home of Senator Paul Douglas in Maine, visiting with a former teacher of his in her nineties, seeing the village of Onawa with its twelve houses where he spent his early years, and the one-room school he attended where his stepmother taught. I always respected Paul Douglas but I gained even more appreciation for him seeing the base from which he rose.

The Public Affairs Reporting program at Sangamon State University enlisted — and helped — some fine potential journalists. Bob Secter, Mitch Locin, Pam Huey, Bill Lambrecht, and others who are graduates of the program have done a solid job of reporting for major outlets in the nation. Succeeding me in directing that program have been Bill Miller and Charlie Wheeler, both of whom have been excellent.

One thing I did learn: Faculty meetings are a plague. It takes two hours to make a two-minute decision, and faculty members are much more likely to get bitter and personal over an exchange of views than professional politicians. After leaving the Senate and accepting a teaching post at Southern Illinois University in Carbondale, one of my stipulations in taking the position was that I would serve on no faculty committees.

In the summer of 1973 I received a phone call from Gene Callahan, a long-time friend and former staff member, and his boss, Alan Dixon, who then served as State Treasurer. They said that Congressman Kenneth Gray had just announced that he would not run for reelection and they urged me to become a candidate. Gray's district, the southern tip of Illinois, started about eight miles south of Troy, where we maintained our home. I told Gene and Alan that earlier I had urged a former state legislator for whom I had a high regard, Jim Holloway, to make the run if Kenny Gray should ever retire. I felt committed to Holloway. Callahan and Dixon called him and in a few minutes Jim Holloway phoned and said he didn't want to run, that I should. Then Ray Chancey, the Democratic County chairman of the largest of the twenty-two counties in the congressional district called and urged me to become a candidate, as did State Senator Kenneth Buzbee. Jeanne and I decided to explore the possibility immediately, drove to Carbondale and talked in greater detail with Chancey and others. Then we decided to do it, but we knew that living just outside the district would not be practical. Once we made the decision, we felt that living in a university community had many advantages, and Carbondale, home of Southern Illinois University, is in the center of the district. We rented a home temporarily while we looked for one to buy. And we started working on all the practical details of petitions, announcements, how we would raise money, and where we could have a campaign headquarters.

We stuffed envelopes with announcements and petitions in the home of Randy and Mae Nelson one Sunday evening. Randy, a Marine veteran blinded in the war, taught political science, and Mae served on the Jackson County Board. Four faculty members provided significant help and advice; John Jackson, now provost of the university; Roy Miller, who teaches political science; Keith Sanders, who taught political science and then became president of the University of Wisconsin at Stevens Point and is now executive director of the Illinois Board for Higher Education; and Gene Trani, a diplomatic historian who drove me around in his little VW bug and is now president of Virginia Commonwealth University. Those four provided invaluable service.

We had superb volunteers. People came from all over the state to go door to door. One of those who came from Springfield and knocked on doors is now the junior senator from Illinois, Dick Durbin. (If there is a theme that runs through this chapter, it is that faculty members who want to move ahead and people who have political ambitions should volunteer to help Paul Simon!)

The *St. Louis Globe-Democrat's* Tom Amberg spent two days covering the campaign and wrote:

> Snow was beginning to fall and it was near the end of a long day of campaigning, but there was another shopping center to cover.
>
> As the candidate walked into a small shop he greeted three women at a counter with the same enthusiasm and warmth he had generated all day.

"Hi, I'm Paul Simon and I'm running for Congress," he said, shaking hands with the first two women. "What's your name?"

After he greeted the two ladies he turned to the third who was writing on the counter and had not turned around when he came in.

"She's a deaf mute and doesn't hear you," one of the first women said after the woman at the counter failed to respond to the Simon greeting.

At that, Simon tapped the woman on the shoulder, and when she turned around, greeted her in the sign language of the deaf. The woman beamed, obviously touched and pleased that a politician had taken the time to learn to communicate with her.

After leaving the shop, Simon waded through a busy supermarket, greeting people with a firm handshake and exchanging quips. If he met someone in the produce aisle and saw them 10 minutes later in the canned vegetable aisle he unerringly remembered their name. "Nice to see you again, Mrs. O'Keith". . . .

The pace of Simon's campaign is hectic and intense, yet his greetings are personal and warm. . . . He has been into each of the 22 counties in the district. His plans call for street campaigning in virtually all the cities and villages of the district, and his organization is being made watertight.

Each precinct of the approximately 500 in the district is being watched and canvassed by Simon people. If the precinct committeeman needs help, he can get it from a Simon volunteer. If a precinct is wavering in support, special attention is given.

So while there is a personal candidate and a warm smile out front, there is a tightly organized campaign organization behind.[1]

I had primary opposition from Joe Browning, member of a prominent Franklin County family and a radio sports announcer. He and his followers made an issue of the fact that I had moved into the district, a legitimate concern. I countered with the argument that the question is not where you are from, but how well you can serve the district. I also countered their appeal to provincialism with my own appeal to provincialism. All of our folders and advertisements stressed the theme: "He Can Do More for Southern Illinois." But Joe Browning and I conducted a campaign that by today's standards is almost angelic. In a front-page story titled "Vigorous Race for Congress Nomination," one newspaper article noted, "Neither [Browning nor Simon] has yet been known to make a derogatory remark about the other."[2] We differed on a few issues, but that is what a campaign should be focused on. And we did it civilly. I won the primary by a 2-1 margin. Joe helped me in the general election and we have maintained contact through the years. He now edits the *Daily Californian* in El Cajon, California.

The general election presented a tougher challenge because there would be substantial amounts of Republican money coming into the district to help my opponent, Val Oshel, a likable and capable public figure who ran a small business but also sang and recorded Gospel songs. Geographically the congressional district is south of Louisville and south of Richmond. You are served grits for breakfast at many area restaurants, and the dominant religious affiliation is Southern Baptist. So running against a Gospel singer posed problems.

Terry Michael, who came aboard as press secretary and general troubleshooter, conceived the idea that since tourism had great appeal as a source of economic development in our region, that our family should rent a camper and spend two weeks visiting the attractive tourist sights in the district, having coffee hours in nearby communities as we went around. With a little reluctance we agreed to do it. His theory that it would generate favorable publicity worked well. We loved the lakes we saw, and historic homes we visited, but Jeanne and I discovered that we are not camper types. Taking a shower in something I could barely get into did not have great appeal; a lack of privacy in squeezed space, where we bumped into each other constantly, was fine for about two days. At the end of two weeks we welcomed the luxury of a home with more than a few square feet per person.

To raise money we did the usual things, but a few unusual.

On the theory that as people gave money the more committed they would feel to our cause, we pushed a drive for $3 contributions, headed by "Cork" and Eloise Armstrong of Carmi. That generated large numbers of contributors.

A Shawneetown farmer and manufacturer, Einar Dyhrkopp, volunteered to head a committee to have a fund-raising dinner. We secured Senator Edward "Ted" Kennedy as the speaker, and charged

$100 a ticket, an unheard of sum in Southern Illinois in those days. We packed the hall with more than 800 people, the biggest fundraising dinner in the history of southern Illinois. Einar also helped in other ways, as did Gordon Allen, Jerry Sinclair, John and Muriel Hayward, Steve and "Kappy" Scates, and many others I should be mentioning. Einar has assisted in other campaigns and is now a member of the Board of Governors of the United States Postal Service, where I hear he is doing an excellent job.

My mother again cranked out one-page mimeograph machine appeals to every small community. Part of the message read: "Why should anyone from Addieville (or whatever the name of the community) vote for Paul Simon for Congress?" I would mention local people I knew and whatever ties — however remote — I could make to that community. Then I added a more general appeal. Addieville got 137 mimeographed sheets, Mt. Vernon 7,990, Simpson 41, and the right amount to fit the number of households in 182 communities. I am sure many of those letters never reached the homes — true of all campaign literature — but enough did that it had an impact.

Managing the congressional campaign were Bob Hays and Ray Buss. Among our student volunteers was Penny Severns, later a state senator and candidate for lieutenant governor. A few students and faculty members said they would help set policy on health care or China, but had no interest in stuffing envelopes or walking a precinct. We thanked them politely, but did not use their services.

For election night at headquarters, an abandoned service station, our children Martin and Sheila designed a series of wall charts for each county, showing the numbers of precincts reporting, those yet to report, and the totals for Val Oshel and myself. It would do credit to a national campaign.

Because of limited finances, we had no professional polling. Few House races did. We had the sense that we would win, but it is easy to deceive yourself in politics. We knew we had outworked the opposition with all the volunteer activity, but there is nevertheless some apprehension as the night of election approaches. And it turned out well. I won 108,417 to 73,634.

---

[1] Thomas Amberg, "Running Hard, Running Scared," *St. Louis Globe-Democrat*, 31 December 1973.

[2] *Benton Evening News*, 28 January 1974.

# Chapter 9

# *The U. S. House*

After the election Jeanne and I drove to Washington and looked for housing. We earlier decided that Sheila and Martin should finish their school year in Carbondale. Jeanne would be there until the end of the school year and then the family would move to Washington. Having a separate existence from the family had no appeal to me. And I knew that weekends in the district I would spend most of my time traveling to meet with people and speak to meetings if I intended to survive politically. Weekends would not be an opportunity to be with the family much.[1]

For philosophical reasons, we did not want to join the congressional families who sent their children to private schools. However, the public schools in the District of Columbia were not good, so with some reluctance we decided to move to the suburbs. We bought a home in Potomac, Maryland, and lived there until our children graduated from Winston Churchill High School, then sold that house and for two years rented a home on 9th Street Southeast, near the Marine Barracks, in a neighborhood integrated both racially and economically. The family across the street from us received welfare payments. We loved the area, but when the owner sold the house we moved into an apartment complex in the southwest part of the city, Harbour Square, where Hubert Humphrey lived when he served as vice president, and where two Supreme Court justices and several members of Congress live. The complex is integrated racially, but not economically. African Americans and whites who live there serve in capacities like ours, or were teachers or physicians or diplomats. But we had good neighbors and a great landlord, Dr. John Holden, and felt comfortable and free of security risks, unfortunately not true everywhere in the District of Columbia.

My initial House committee assignments: Labor and Education, which I requested, and Post Office and Civil Service, which I did not request. I served only one term on the latter committee, long enough to learn more about the subjects than I originally cared to know, but it proved valuable to me. I fought for survival of many third and fourth-class — small — post offices. When the Postmaster General said he could save money closing those post offices, I said he could save even more money by closing all post offices. In many small communities the only visible sign of federal government existence is the post office, as well as the source for information for United Parcel Service and others who want to deliver packages or find homes. Eventually I went into federal court to get an injunction to force the Postmaster General to live up to their regulations before closing smaller post offices. Judge John Lewis Smith issued a restraining order on February 27, 1976. I did not oppose closing any and all offices, but I believed strongly — and still believe — that small communities need encouragement, that the flight from rural areas to the cities is often not healthy either for the rural areas or the cities. When Postmaster General Ben Bailar, who came from being chief executive of a can company, took over the Postal Service, I had breakfast with him and mentioned that a postal supervisor in Herrin, Illinois, Bill Miriani, made suggestions for improving postal service that made sense to me, and I would appreciate Bailar taking ten minutes to talk to him and at least listen to his ideas. He said he would. But he didn't. And the more I pushed the more I got a nothing response, an experience I had not had with any cabinet officers or other government leaders. When I pushed his staff, they said that he did not have time to meet with 700,000 postal employees. I understand, I told them, I'm not asking him to meet with 700,000 employees, just one.

Eventually Bailar came before the committee and I asked him about it. He said he got his information through a chain of command. I responded that I used to be in business and I felt that I should know as much as possible about it in order to make sound decisions. Different executives have different styles, he told the committee.

I then asked if he had ever talked to a mail carrier, not the head of the union, but just an individual mail carrier about his or her job. "No," he said. I then went through the same on a rural carrier and other Postal Service jobs, and always received the negative answer.

"I don't mean any disrespect to you," I said, "but you would be a better and stronger Postmaster General if you took off two weeks and spent two days walking a route with a mail carrier, and one day on a rural route." I outlined a two-week program for him. He did not react with enthusiasm to my idea, and did nothing. He did not last long as Postmaster General. Maybe he was good at running a can company, but I have my doubts.

The Labor and Education committee gave me the continuing opportunity to provide leadership in education, everything from college loans and grants to creating greater opportunities for the disabled. The labor part of this assignment stirred my interests in the labor-management field. One bill I introduced in the House, and later in the Senate, made no headway but is still sound. Under the federal statutes a company that has "a pattern and practice" of violating our civil rights laws is not eligible for federal contracts, a good restriction. We have companies that flagrantly violate the National Labor Relations Act, and yet the federal government gives them billions of dollars in contracts. I proposed that we follow the example of the civil rights laws with a proviso that the Secretary of Labor or the President could waive this if the national interest required it. If, for example, a defense manufacturer violated the laws but made a key component of something vital to our defense, the Secretary of Labor or the President could waive it. The closest my bill came to passage occurred when I introduced it in a Senate Committee as an amendment. To my great surprise it received two Republican votes as well as the Democratic votes and passed. But the next day, when the impact of it undoubtedly had been carefully explained to the two Republicans, the motion to reconsider it passed, and my amendment died. Senators who make great speeches about "law and order" when it comes to blue collar crime sometimes are less enthusiastic about enforcing the law when big contributors are involved.

In the House I continued a practice I started in the state legislature of visiting offices unannounced to find out what is happening. In the legislature I discovered that when I stopped at a mental hospital without prior announcement I found a very different situation than when I arranged for a visit well in advance. When I stopped at a federal office I would say to a startled employee, "Hi. I'm Paul Simon, a member of Congress. I'm just stopping to see how things are going here. Are there ways to improve this program?" Usually I received an initial response, "You want to talk to my boss. His office is over there." "No, I don't want to talk to your boss," I would reply. "I'd like to talk to you and a few of your co-workers." After a little reluctance, they would tell me the changes they would like to see. Sometimes they were off-the-wall suggestions impossible to fulfill, but frequently they were practical ideas, often things that could be implemented without changes in the law. Usually within five minutes of my arrival, the supervisor would come and listen, but I found that once people started talking they were surprisingly uninhibited by the presence of their boss.

The CBS program *60 Minutes* heard about my forays, and asked to follow me on a few visits. I told them I had no objection but I did not know whether people would talk freely with a television camera staring at them. The CBS people said that I would be pleasantly surprised, and I was. The camera made little difference. Occasionally as I closed an interview someone would ask, "Is he filming this?" But people had no objection. The program they ran was pure gold for a politician.

I was part of "the Class of 1974," a large group of Democrats swept into the House in the wake of Watergate. By the time we took our oaths of office, Gerald Ford served as President. The class initiated reforms that reduced the power of the automatic seniority system and instituted other changes that made the House more responsive to the wishes of the members, and less under the control of the leadership. In retrospect we served the House and the nation poorly with some of our reforms. While each of the changes individually is defensible, the net result reduced the ability of the House leaders and committee chairs to exercise restraint on a body that sometimes needs it. In some ways — campaign finance reform, for example — the House is not as responsive as it should be to a clear public need and wish, but in too many ways the House too easily becomes a mob, swayed by the latest quirk in public opinion.

Carl Albert served as Speaker during my first term. An Oklahoman from a town with the unlikely name of Bugtussle, he did not dominate the House, but was respected and provided a stabilizing force when we needed it. He appeared at a fund-raiser for me in southern Illinois when I first sought the House seat, and went out of his way to be good to me on many occasions. He also had a skilled sense of when Congress should act, and when we should not, when we should leave things to the President. He also had some surprising views coming from a conservative portion of Oklahoma, being clearly more liberal than his constituency, but they took pride in this small (five feet, four inches) man who had gained national stature, and they also recognized his sincerity. Driving with him one day the subject of abortion arose, and he said, "I'd sooner lose my seat in Congress than vote for that constitutional amendment to outlaw abortion."

Thomas P. "Tip" O'Neill succeeded Albert. He did not know as much about the details of legislation as his predecessor or his successor as Speaker, Jim Wright, but he had a great instinct for what would be good for the nation, and what would not be. He tried to reduce our involvement in the Vietnam War. He looked like a lineman for the Chicago Bears with white hair, and his physical presence dominated a room when he entered. He loved to tell stories, particularly stories with a point. And he had a genuine, deep-seated commitment to help those less fortunate. I really liked him as a person and a leader.

Jim Wright of Texas succeeded Tip, potentially the strongest Speaker among those I worked with in my twenty-two years in Washington. A gifted orator, he showed a willingness to press members into action that he believed to be in the national interest even if the stands were temporarily unpopular. No Speaker can do too much of this and remain in that position. But his strength annoyed Republicans, and one of them, Newt Gingrich, spotted a vulnerability in Wright's armor — the way he handled the sales of a book he wrote, with lobbyists purchasing some of the books in small quantities. While his action appears minor compared to many abuses made public over the years, nevertheless he handled it in a way that violated House rules, and Jim resigned from the Speakership and the House. It was bitter medicine for Jim Wright, who had fought through the years to become Speaker, and had the potential to become the strongest Speaker since Sam Rayburn, also from Texas, with whom Wright had served.

Ironically, when Gingrich became Speaker, he also faced questions over a $4 million advance on a book he wrote, a sum vastly greater than the amounts involved in the Wright maneuverings, but Gingrich's actions did not involve any clear-cut violation of the House rules. Gingrich has been a forceful Speaker, but somewhat unpredictable. He is bright and glib — too glib for his own good. When I came to the House, the Senate had a historian but the House did not. I thought it important that the actions of the House and records there be preserved carefully for future researchers. I sponsored a bill to create the position of House historian, and Newt cosponsored my measure. It passed, and Tip O'Neill asked Rep. Lindy Boggs of Louisiana, Newt, and me to serve as a committee to select the House historian. The staff screened the lists for a few applicants who sounded particularly good. We interviewed them and the three of us recommended the person who received the appointment, and so far as I know he did a good job. I was a bit startled, then, to note that after Newt became Speaker, in one of his first actions he fired the House historian and attempted to replace him with a Georgia historian who immediately engendered controversy over comments she had made about the Nazi era. He then backed off that action. As the old children's nursery rhyme goes, when Newt "is good he is very, very good and when he is bad, he is horrid." He recently (as I write this) took a trip to the troubled Middle East and undercut U. S. policy there by indicating to Prime Minister Netanyahu and his Likud supporters that they will have strong support in Congress if they do not follow the Clinton efforts to bring about reconciliation, even referring to Secretary of State Madeleine Albright as a Palestinian agent. His action did not help Israel, the Middle East peace process, the Clinton administration, or even himself. It was both inappropriate and harmful, a not very subtle attempt to endear himself to a small segment of donors in the United States who do not represent the bulk of Jewish opinion here. On the other hand, Gingrich at his best is creative, not bound by the usual molds and patterns of thinking that too often circumscribe political leaders. In minutes, he understands an issue like the need to find less expensive ways to desalinate water, including its global context.

Preceding Gingrich as Speaker was Tom Foley, who lost his House race in Washington. Now ambassador to Japan, Tom Foley was much more the diplomat than any of the Speakers with whom I worked, but somewhat less the leader.

Currently the Democratic leader of the House is Dick Gephardt, like Foley a good consensus person. He has presidential ambitions, and has the ability to serve in that capacity. My hesitancy in being enthusiastic about that prospect is that a strong President has to have strong convictions. Gephardt has the same weakness of President Bill Clinton and Vice President Al Gore of following the latest polls too much. The nation needs someone with Harry Truman backbone, and you don't get backbone from a poll or a focus group.

Part of the nature of the legislative process is that strong leadership is the exception. To a large extent you have to be a consensus person, particularly under the present rules. In perhaps my third term in the House, when the bottom rung on the leadership ladder, chairmanship of the caucus, became open Rep. Fred Richmond of New York came to me with a petition he was circulating on which he had twenty-nine names, urging me to seek the post, as a way of moving up. I thanked Fred, but explained that I like my independence, and if I wanted to be the only Democrat to vote a certain way on an issue, I wanted to be free to do that. I had no objection to achieving a subcommittee or committee chairmanship, because seniority locks that in unless your conduct is viewed as too egregious. But I did not want to move into the House leadership role in any capacity and have to constantly be worrying about pleasing my troops. "My voting record was a lot better before I became majority leader," Senator George Mitchell once commented to me.

I involved myself in a number of national issues; "Freshman on Hill Sets a Torrid Pace" headed a story in *Farmland News*.[2] In my second year in the House columnist Jack Anderson named his picks for the twenty-four best members of that body, and included this freshman. While I took some unpopular stands, I felt that the favorable publicity coming my way politically compensated for that. Four years after being sworn in, the Associated Press carried a story: "Rep. Paul Simon . . . has developed considerable influence for a congressman who was first elected in 1974."[3]

I organized a small bi-partisan group that met for breakfast every four to six weeks to talk about world food and population problems. Those who attended included people like Dan Glickman, later Secretary of Agriculture; Tim Wirth, later Assistant Secretary of State and point man for Ted Turner's huge contribution to fostering the United Nations; Pat Schroeder, a leader on women's issues and defense spending restraint; and Bob Edgar, later president of the Claremont Seminary in California. We had speakers, some of whom heard about our group and asked to come. Jacques Cousteau, the famous ocean explorer, was one of these. Others we asked to give their perspective, such as Bob McNamara, president of the World Bank. I cannot point to any specific attainment as a result of these meetings, but we created greater sensitivity to the developing nations and their difficulties.

I continued writing my column, sending it to the newspapers in my district and those that came close to my district as well as to any others in the state or outside Illinois that requested it. I wrote it myself, frequently saying conventional things, sometimes taking controversial stands like defending the Panama Canal Treaty, not popular in my district, and saying that what is wrong with congressional trips is that there should be more of them, not fewer, except they should more frequently take members to developing nations instead of Paris and London. The latter column was provoked by a House colleague who showed me his political brochure which boasted that in twenty-two years in the House he had not left the country. Probably politically popular, but wrong. If a few members of Congress had visited Vietnam before our involvement in the war we might have understood the situation better and prevented the loss of 58,000 American troops, at least hundreds of thousands of Vietnamese killed, and scars in our society yet today. But many agreed with the *St. Louis Globe-Democrat* editorial: "The case for more extensive foreign travel by congressmen is weak."[4] The *Washingtonian*, a magazine for the capital area, had a picture of the two members of Congress who wrote their own materials, Rep. Barber Conable, later president of the World Bank, and myself, saying our writings constituted "political science at its best."[5]

Patricia O'Brien, a reporter for the Knight-Ridder newspapers who formerly worked for the *Chicago Sun-Times*, approached me to do an in-depth story on what happens day-to-day in the office of a House member. My staff divided on whether the offer should be accepted. She spent six weeks in our office, with access to everything with the understanding that meetings she would sit in on would have to be off-the-record if they involved personal problems that people have. She worked assiduously, getting to know all of us well, and the story that resulted — used by some newspapers as a big feature and by others as a three-part series — provided the best single story glimpse into the real life of a member and staff that I have ever seen. It should have received a journalism prize.

Both because of the economic needs of my district, the poorest on a per capita basis in the state, and because of the realities of politics, I did not ignore my district in either time or legislation. I spent most weekends in the district, going into different communities, holding open office hours. People approached one at a time to tell me of problems with Social Security or with some government agency, or sometimes with an insurance company or a furniture store. Many former coal miners came to get help with their black lung disease problems, an issue that I spent considerable time trying to deal with through legislation. I was an ombudsman again, but didn't call myself that. I helped many people and many I could not help, but even where my efforts did not succeed people usually expressed gratitude that I had tried. Sometimes I simply listened to families and their problems and tried to give good counsel. Occasionally simply getting a problem off their chest helped, as they discussed alternative solutions with me. We had a few who claimed the FBI or the CIA was following them, or had implanted radios in their teeth. One man had a terrible rash situation, and dropped his pants to show it to me, startling me and the others there at the time.

Sometimes even accidents helped politically. Attending my son's Little League baseball game, I slipped in the stands on some soda someone had spilled. The largest newspaper in the district ran a story under the heading "Simon Breaks Bone at Baseball Game."[6] I received sympathy, and everyone learned that my son played Little League baseball like their sons did (daughters entered this later). However, I would have preferred another way of getting the coverage and sympathy.

The Shawnee National Forest, the only national forest in our state, occupies a good portion of the southern part of the district but it creates problems as well as being a great asset. I asked President Gerald Ford to agree to a study of the possibility of a National Recreation Area in the Shawnee National Forest, with the probability that he would support the result of the study. He agreed to it. I told people in the district I would move favorably on the result if all the counties most affected would support the recommendations. But when the study results became public, quarrels developed between the counties as to which would get what benefits and I quietly buried the idea. Counties and political leaders and nations too often are like small children who fight over toys. They have a hard time learning that if they share their "toys," everyone will be better off.

Pope County has 3,800 people and 370 square miles, but 40 percent of the county is occupied by the Shawnee National Forest, meaning that its tax base is minimal. Per capita income is one of the lowest in Illinois, and the county could not pay its bills, not because of any extravagance, but simply by doing the things mandated by the state and federal governments. I drafted a proposal to provide 75¢ an acre in lieu of taxes for public lands for counties throughout the nation faced with this situation. I asked Rep. Frank Evans of Colorado, chairman of the subcommittee of jurisdiction, to introduce the measure which helped his district also. It became law. Not much money, but it meant the difference between solvency and insolvency for Pope County and almost the same for Hardin County. Actions like that met real needs, and helped to soften the political edge on stands I took like opposing legislation for prayer in the public schools.

Oil companies received leases for exploration in the national forests at 50¢ an acre. As a freshman I put in an amendment to require competitive bidding, and as I spoke in the well of the House, I saw Wilbur Mills of Arkansas walking down the aisle telling members, "Let's help Paul on this." Thanks to the high regard members had for him, my amendment passed despite oil company opposition. Wilbur Mills, chair of the Ways and Means Committee, had come through a

serious alcohol problem when his un-Mills like conduct showed
something seriously wrong. Among other things he squired a burlesque queen, Fanne Fox, around town and even appeared on the
stage with her on one occasion. He sought help and got himself
straightened out.

Serious drinking was much less a problem in Washington than in
the state legislature, perhaps in part because in Washington we usually had our families with us while in Springfield legislators did not
have that companionship and restraint. I do remember that one member from Alabama early each day had an obvious problem. Between
votes some of us had gathered in the Democratic cloakroom behind
the House chamber, Wilbur Mills among those there. The Alabama
member, already well lubricated, turned to Mills and said, "Wilbur,
why did you call yourself an alcoholic? Why you're no more an alcoholic than I am." His statement produced a roar of laughter, but is also
indicative of the mind-set of most alcoholics in denying what is obvious to others.

One of my strong supporters in southern Illinois was George
Bader, a generous contributor and genuinely liberal Democrat despite
being one of the largest landowners in the area and a sizable investor
in the stock market. But George had a serious alcohol difficulty, which
he acknowledged. He occasionally called about two in the morning,
obviously drunk. But because of George's good-hearted nature, I
could not get angry with him. He was enough of a friend that I talked
to him candidly about the need to face his problem. One day he called
and asked whether Wilbur Mills had really stopped drinking. I
assured him he had. I told him that Wilbur had joined Alcoholics
Anonymous and George should do the same. "But you have to be religious to do that," he said. "I'm not religious." I responded, "I've never
thought of Wilbur Mills as being particularly religious." We talked on
and he said he would try to quit. I then got Wilbur to write a note on
an official letterhead, saying simply, "George, I know you can do it.
Wilbur Mills." About a week later my southern Illinois friend called
and said, "Did Wilbur Mills really sign that?" I assured him that I
stood by him while he wrote it. "I've carried that in my billfold since
I got it and I haven't touched a drop since then." I asked Wilbur to
call him. The nationally known congressman then gave George Bader
his home phone number and told George that if at any time, day or
night, he ever felt the urge to take a drink to call him first. Bader
became a rejuvenated man, and until the day he died I don't believe
he touched a drop of alcohol again. When people would half-jokingly
refer to Wilbur Mills, I told them of another side of this man who for

many years played a dominant role in Congress and once he got past his personal problem showed a willingness to help others.

A small footnote to all of this. About the time Wilbur Mills was squiring Fanne Fox, the burlesque queen, we acquired from the Humane Society the finest dog our family ever had and the children named her Fanne Fox. When we moved to Washington and took the dog with us, I hoped that Wilbur would not discover this minor indiscretion, which I don't believe he did.


I gradually put together a quality staff. Margaret Bergen, Ray Johnsen, Judy Wagner, Vicki Otten, Joe Dunn, Betty Pyrros, David Solomon, Karen Steele, plus Terry Michael, an excellent press secretary, succeeded by David Carle, who had been working for Congressman Gunn McKay of Utah. Dave stayed with me the remainder of my legislative career. Hard-working and capable, he is also simply a genuinely fine human being. But I should pass that compliment to the rest of the staff, many of whom I have not named. In Illinois Ray Buss, Paul Gayer, Virginia Ottersen, Joe Bob Pierce, and others contributed both to my legislative ideas and keeping me in office through their good constituent service.

The Vietnam War still dominated discussions during the early part of my House service and I joined those who wanted to wind it down and make an early but honorable exit. After our exit from Vietnam, at the start of my third term a small bipartisan group, Members of Congress for Peace Through Law, elected me as chair, with Senator Adlai Stevenson III and Rep. John Heinz of Pennsylvania vice chairs. The organization worked for sensible arms control steps, as well as pushing diplomatic efforts to settle disputes.

The Communist system dominated the Soviet Union, China, and other nations, and the residue of the McCarthy era remained, with many seeing Communist penetration where it did not exist. However, the charges could not be dismissed lightly. Rep. John Ashbrook of Ohio felt that the programs under the jurisdiction of Sam Brown looked suspicious. Sam headed both the Peace Corps and Vista, a domestic program to help the poor through volunteers, under the general title of Action. Sam (now serving the nation in Vienna, Austria, as a representative to the Organization for Security and Cooperation in Europe sometimes called the Helsinki Group) and some others in Action were involved earlier in the anti-Vietnam War protests and though the Ashbrook charges occurred in 1979, Sam and a few others still had the sixties hairstyle and dress, and even some of the language. These all sent Communist signals to John Ashbrook, who had opposed Richard Nixon for President because of Nixon's liberal views. But John, unlike Senator Joseph McCarthy, had no alcohol problem, was a genial person to work with, and could be convinced to change his mind on something, if slowly. I viewed his motivation as good, even though he had an exaggerated view of the internal threat of Communism. I chaired the subcommittee of jurisdiction. He talked to me about his concerns and I agreed to hold a hearing, to bring any witnesses he wanted to testify. My theory, which fortunately turned out to be accurate, was that open hearings would puncture his balloon and show no substance to his fears. The first day of the hearings we met for fourteen hours, with Sam Brown and many other witnesses. I particularly recall Heather Booth, who headed Midwest Academy and later steered Citizen Action, coming with Joseph Rauh as her attorney. Joe, a long-time liberal advocate known and respected by all of us, need not have been there. Heather defanged Ashbrook's charges so adroitly that she left him breathless. As a result of the hearings we found a few people who had made mistakes in their zealous advocacy of programs for the poor, but no Communists and no subversion. John did not become a Sam Brown fan nor an advocate of the Peace Corps or Vista, but he did learn that they were not trying to overthrow our government.

The subcommittee I first headed, the Subcommittee on Select Education, had as its major responsibility dealing with the problems of the disabled. Judy Wagner, who had become knowledgeable, in that area headed the staff, but as with all subcommittees things that didn't seem to fit naturally into any other area would be added to the assignment, which is why I handled the Action oversight. Two years later I had the opportunity to chair the Higher Education Subcommittee. I asked William "Bud" Blakey who worked for the then Department of Health Education and Welfare in the field of higher education to head the staff. Both "Bud" Blakey and Judy Wagner did an excellent job, but both were more pioneers than they should have been, Judy being one of the few female subcommittee staff directors in the House and "Bud" being the first African American subcommittee staff director in the House outside of the Subcommittee on Africa. I had no idea that was the case when I chose either, selecting them for their abilities. Both went over to the Senate with me when I shifted chambers.

Through two subcommittees I helped to shape responses to needs, and during the early Reagan years those two subcommittees — plus my House Budget Committee assignment — permitted me to help resist the president's proposals for cuts in higher education. But launching significant new offensives became impossible, except in small ways.

While I advocated more spending in education, health care, and some other social programs, I also worked to save money in areas as huge as the defense budget, or on small items. The Corps of Engineers always sent telegrams to members of Congress and other key players on projects approved, at a cost of $4 per telegram. I requested that they notify everyone by first class mail, which they agreed to do. When a Gallatin County, Illinois, farmer who graduated from Harvard told me the agriculture census form confused him, that he couldn't figure out how to fill it out, I was able to get the census people (working with the Department of Agriculture) to reduce the form for farmers from sixteen pages to four pages, and make it more understandable. (I agree with people who write and complain about too much red tape, but I am helpless to do anything if their complaint is general. When people write and are specific about their criticism, like the agricultural census form, then policy-makers can deal with it, and sometimes get something done.) But we were less successful on other things, such as getting rid of the Postal Rate Commission, which most citizens don't even know exists. Its sole official function is to approve or disapprove rate requests of the Postal Service. Its unofficial role is also to provide positions for political favorites. My amendment would have done away with it, limiting the Postal Service increases to the inflation rate. We lost. The Army spent — and probably still spends — $1 million a year to ship beer to U. S. personnel in Germany. I said that is "like sending high sulfur coal to southern Illinois,"[7] with much logic but few votes. "This is a costly subsidy of the U. S. beer industry. Congress never voted a direct subsidy of that industry."[8]

Sometimes our personal experiences help to shape our decisions and legislation. In high school our son Martin dated a friendly, petite, and striking girl, Rachel Mann. Rachel had cystic fibrosis, the largest genetic killer of children in our nation. Rachel came to our home frequently and sometimes we saw the difficult time she had breathing. One day her parents, Larry and Susan Mann, called and said the National Institutes of Health (NIH) planned to cut back on research on this dread disease. Because frequently these type of rumors prove to be false, I told them I would check it out, but I had doubts about its veracity. I called the head of NIH and he said it was true but he wanted to talk to me about it. We had breakfast and he reported that he faced a budget crunch and since Dr. St. John, who headed the research on cystic fibrosis, planned to leave he felt he could cut back there. His statement appalled me. In the meantime, two other parents I knew, journalists Marty and Sue Tolchin whose son Charles had cystic fibrosis, also took an interest and encouraged me. I then introduced an amendment on the House floor to *increase* funding for cystic fibrosis research and it passed. This story has both a tragic and happy footnote. Rachel Mann died from the illness in her early twenties. Charles, thanks to research, received a double lung transplant, is now twenty-nine, in reasonably good health and working. At the dedication of the Mark Hatfield[9] Clinical Research Center at the National Institutes of Health, Charles spoke: "When I was diagnosed at the age of five, life expectancy was eight. Now I'm twenty-nine and life expectancy [for someone with cystic fibrosis] is thirty-one." He now drives a car and swims.

Years later I had another brush with someone's death that influenced me. We had a person assigned to my office for one year from the Department of Commerce under a program in which the executive branch trains future leaders in the legislative process. The person assigned, whom I will call John, did a good job and worked well with the staff. I did not see him for about two years after he left our office and encountered him at a reception and after the usual exchange of greetings, I asked tritely, "How are you doing?" "Not well," he replied, "I have AIDS." It stunned me. A few months later his companion called and said that John had died, and one of the last things he asked was for me to attend his funeral service, which I did. Later I wanted to write a column about John and AIDS and called his parents to get their approval to use his name. Understandably, but to my regret, they declined, so I wrote a column about him and the disease, but it did not have the small details that would have made it come alive. I supported AIDS research prior to his death, and had met with people with AIDS, but John's death spurred me to do more.

Critics say that politics should not play a role in which area of research gets how much money. But even the technically trained people ultimately make their decisions in part because of personal experiences. One area I have promoted, mental health research, does not receive anywhere near the funding it should when compared to the devastation it causes. People who have cancer, diabetes, arthritis, and many other problems — or their relatives have the affliction — stand up and say, "Put more money into research here." But there is still a stigma with mental health. People don't stand up and tell about their afflictions, nor do their relatives. Two people among those who have stood up are Katharine Graham, former publisher of the *Washington Post*, and Ruth Edelman, wife of Chicago public relations leader Dan

Edelman. I am grateful to both of them. While the stigma is diminishing, it still results in less funding than should be allocated. Both "experts" and political leaders have failed. I frankly don't care whether it is political pressure or the wisdom of technicians that changes this; I want change. While the distribution of health care to our people remains a major national disgrace, with 41 million Americans not covered by health insurance, we lead in research and that has been a great lift to our health and our economy. However, Senator Tom Harkin of Iowa reminds us again and again: We have spent more money on military research in the last seven years than on health research in this century. We are doing a good job in medical discovery, but we could be doing much more. Polls show that the public would not only tolerate, but would welcome, a small tax increase for this purpose.

In the House — and later in the Senate — I introduced a measure that some day must come: guaranteeing a job opportunity to all Americans. It would be a substitute for much of today's welfare program. The idea is based on the Works Progress Administration (WPA) of the Franklin D. Roosevelt administration. Under my proposal, anyone out of work five weeks or more who cannot find a job in the private sector could get a job at the minimum wage, four days a week. The fifth day he or she would have to try to find a job in the private sector. Even at the minimum wage, if a five-day-a-week job is found, that person's income would increase by 25 percent by working five days a week instead of four. Local districts carved out by each state's governor would have a board of thirteen people, at least one from labor and one a business person, and either the labor or business person could veto any of the projects so that there would not be a problem of substitution by these temporary workers for regular workers, or taking away from businesses. These thirteen people would decide the projects. People working would be screened. If they had limited reading and writing abilities, or none, they would be entered into a program. If they had no marketable skill, they would attend a community college or technical school. We would lift people's abilities while we offered them temporary help. And two persons in a household could get these jobs, encouraging people to live together rather than as our present welfare programs do in most states, discouraging people from marrying. The annual cost, estimated at $12 billion several years ago, would be somewhat higher today but there would also be substantial offset from savings on welfare, and ultimately huge savings both in dollars and humanity. Under one small part of the WPA more than 1.5 million Americans learned to read and write — and their increased taxes alone over the years probably paid for the WPA program. We also enriched ourselves in so many other ways: art works commissioned, plays written, mountain hiking trails created, lodges built in state and national parks — the list goes on and on.

And perhaps the most important benefit, people who lack self-respect, who do not get it from a check sent to them, will suddenly see themselves contributing in a meaningful way to society. I have yet to talk to an audience that is not quickly sold on the idea, whether conservative or liberal. In the Senate, David Boren — now president of the University of Oklahoma — took my idea and introduced a bill to try it as a pilot project in two states. Even that didn't pass. We need to do something creative, positive, and helpful for the nation's underclass. A few days ago — as I write this — I asked a prominent United States Attorney what percentage of the crimes he has to deal with are caused by poverty. "Eighty percent" came his quick reply. That is not a scientific study, but I am convinced that a program like this that starts to move people out of poverty would be the greatest anti-crime program we could have, far better than endlessly building more prisons.

Education continued to take more of my time than any single subject. It is the key to lifting people out of poverty and aiding our nation economically. A 1996 survey by Coopers and Lybrand of 428 high-growth companies found that 60 percent considered the lack of skilled and literate employees their greatest barrier to growth. To help lift people from domestic poverty and encourage skill development, I successfully pushed everything from improvements in the Tribally Controlled Community College Act to setting up a program to encourage endowments in colleges that serve primarily low income students. The latter program I developed with Dr. Frederick Patterson, better known as "Dr. Pat," former president of Tuskegee Institute and the founder of the United Negro College Fund. It has been a real help to many schools, particularly some of the historically black colleges. I salvaged meager funds for international education, a battle I won several times, but always narrowly. I pushed for help for libraries, for international faculty and student exchanges, for making it easier for students to consolidate their loans, for monitoring more carefully the school for congressional pages, and for a series of efforts to put greater stress on foreign language instruction.

I have always been aware of my own international language deficiencies, and sometimes appalled by Americans who pride themselves in not speaking another language. When the western and Soviet Bloc nations signed the Helsinki Accord in 1975, it moved the world one small step away from nuclear annihilation. The agreement calls for cooperation, but its requirement that all of the signatory nations have to agree before any action can be taken makes it a difficult instrument with which to work. But it represents progress. Congress set up a joint House-Senate commission to monitor the Helsinki Accord and the Speaker named me as one of the House members. In reading the document I came across language which said the "the signatory nations agree to promote the study of other languages and the understanding of other cultures." I suggested to the co-chairs of our commission, Senator Claiborne Pell of Rhode Island and Congressman Dante Fascell of Florida, that we should ask the president to appoint a special committee to look at our foreign language deficiencies and see what we could do. They both said, "It's a great idea. *You* talk to the President." I did. President Carter responded favorably, mentioning that he had once suggested something similar to the Southern Baptists, and added, "You know the Mormons are way ahead of us on this." He asked me to work with Commissioner of Education (no Secretary of Education yet) Ernest Boyer in putting the group together — and asked me to be on the commission, an inevitable part of making any such suggestion. The President designated as chair of the group James Perkins, former president of Cornell University, who did a first-rate job. It turned out to be one of the hardest working and most dedicated committees with which I have ever served. We made a series of recommendations, some of which have been adopted, some have not. We still remain the only nation in the world in which you can go through grade school, high school, college, and get a Ph.D. and never have a year of another language. I believe — I am not certain on this — we are the only nation in which you can go through grade school and not study another language. One of my favorite quotes is from H. L. Mencken, the Baltimore journalist. During the anti-foreign language hysteria of World War I, with tongue-in-cheek he said he agreed with the anti-foreign language crowd. He wrote, "If English was good enough for Jesus Christ, it's good enough for me." Our deficiencies cost us in cultural enrichment, in trade opportunities, and in security risks. When Iran seized fifty-five U. S. hostages in the late 1970s, only six spoke Farsi, the language of the people of Iran, according to the testimony of one of the former hostages before my subcommittee. We spoke to the elite in English, and missed what was happening on the streets of the nation. One of several amendments I did get adopted — over State Department objection — was to designate two demonstration embassies where everyone, including the Marine guards, had to speak the language of the nation where they served. They picked Senegal and Uruguay. The State Department's inspector general later reported to the Senate Foreign Relations Committee that this raised morale at the embassies and improved the effectiveness of their work significantly. But it costs a little more money and requires a little more effort. Congress has cut State Department funding because the State Department's an easy political target. These cuts reduce U. S. influence abroad. But the cuts gave the State Department an excuse for not expanding on this successful language experiment. That, plus the simple reality that the State Department is no different from the Senate or schools or religious organizations or businesses or labor unions — we all get in ruts and it is easier to defend the status quo and live with it than to change.

Success in politics and life involves doing the little extra things that ultimately make a huge difference. I read an Associated Press story about a six-year-old boy, Etan Patz, who went to school in New York City one day and disappeared. The story quoted his parents as expressing dissatisfaction with the cooperation they received from the federal government. I called and asked what they meant. Among other things, the father said, the FBI computer keeps track of missing automobiles but not missing children. I felt sure he must be wrong, but I checked and discovered him to be correct. I introduced a bill mandating the FBI to include a list of missing children in their computer. Then, someone told me that if an unidentified body is in a given state the details are not forwarded to the national FBI computer so that other states will know about it — and I added a provision to change that too. The FBI, also liking the status quo, resisted my bill. It appeared I had less than a 50/50 chance of getting it adopted when John and Reve Walsh of Florida appeared on the scene. Their son Adam had been kidnaped and slain. John didn't just grieve; his tragedy made him a zealot, and soon he buttonholed House members asking them to approve my bill, and persuaded Senator Paula Hawkins of Florida to sponsor similar legislation in the Senate. After it became law, we introduced legislation to establish the Center for Missing Children, again with John as an unpaid lobbyist. That center became a reality and is doing great work. John Walsh has written about his experiences in the book, *Tears of Rage*, and now hosts the television program, "America's Most Wanted," helpful in capturing violence-prone criminals. Most of this would not have happened if Etan Patz's father had not talked candidly to a reporter. Small things make a difference.

Bob Farmer of Steeleville came to one of my open office hours and told me his sad but engrossing story. As a young man in the Navy, he served in the Pacific when our nation tested the first post-World War II atomic bombs. Officials did not fully understand the indirect radiation threat. Navy officers told Bob and his buddies to duck behind a truck on the beach of a nearby island when the explosion occurred. Wearing swimming trunks, they hid behind trucks as a radio broadcast the countdown. Suddenly the sky lit up brilliantly and as Bob looked at his buddies he saw their skeletons, a sort of x-ray that lasted for a few seconds. After the blast they played in the ocean and the next day scrubbed down the boats placed near the center of the blast, but far enough away not to be too obviously damaged. Some years later Bob developed cancer, and so did a disproportionate number of his buddies. Bob and his wife — neither of whom had any history of special genetic problems — had nine children, and only one at birth appeared to have a genetic deformation. But soon it became apparent that all had problems. Bob tried to get help from the Veterans Administration, but it would not acknowledge that any of these difficulties were service-connected, the key words essential for getting help. The VA, in its attempt to save money, ignored reality. While what Bob Farmer suffered did not fall into the same category as a gunshot wound easily identified as service-connected, it nevertheless was clearly a service-connected disability. I introduced legislation that made Bob and his counterparts in that situation eligible for VA help. Some of them had walked into Nagasaki a few days after the atomic bomb exploded in Japan and experienced the same difficulties. Rep. Lane Evans, a leader in the Veterans Committee in the House, offered the same legislation there and eventually we achieved at least partial coverage for people with difficulties from this radiation exposure.

I worked on many amendments, small changes to improve things. *Time* magazine once referred to me as having more amendments adopted than any other member of the House. That may be true, but I am not sure. Amendments do provide a tool for change. Often I would have an amendment drafted and the sponsors, wanting to avoid any fights, would agree to accept it, or accept it with some modifications. And sometimes my better amendments would get dropped in the House-Senate conference committees. My service in the House was by no means only a series of successes.

The big deficiency then — and now — is the lack of courage that so many members have. The overall ability of those elected to the House and Senate is much higher than the public perception. However, the public accurately perceives that we lack courage, that we are excessively partisan. They see us playing political games, and too often that perception is accurate. That harmful tendency grew during my twenty-two years in the House and Senate. While I am a Democrat, and proud of that affiliation, most problems do not involve political philosophy. They are nuts-and-bolts problems for which people of good will should sit around a table and find solutions.

The gutless nature of too many members hit me when, after I spoke on the floor supporting foreign aid, Rep. Richard Kelly of Florida said he really admired the stand I took, and he wished he could be with me on the vote. "Why can't you?" I asked. "The people in my district are against it," he assured me. How do you know, I queried? "The letters I receive," he told me. How many in the last month I asked him. "Perhaps six," he responded. Six letters frightened him into voting against what he believed to be in the best interest of the nation!

Dick Kelly later went to prison for accepting bribes. In a sense those six letters also were bribes. In both cases — the money and the letters — he knew what was right but the short-term gain overrode his judgment. When radio-evangelist Jerry Falwell's Moral Majority gave me a zero rating and Dick Kelly a 100 percent rating, and Dick was subsequently indicted and convicted, I used his rating to defend myself. When asked about my Moral Majority rating, I told reporters, "I knew I was morally imperfect. I just didn't realize the extent of my imperfection."[10] One of the "immoral" votes I cast, according to the Moral Majority, was one for foreign aid to help poor and hungry people.

The only House race that I barely survived came in 1980, with the confluence of several factors that worked against me.

Senator Edward "Ted" Kennedy's race for the nomination against President Carter, in which I endorsed Kennedy (details in Chapter 14), hurt me both with the public and political leaders. "Early Political Grave for Simon?" headed an editorial in *The Marion Daily Republican*.[11] The president worked my area hard, made many phone calls, and lined up state legislators and county chairs on his side. Ted, a superb legislator but a person who lacked a good public image, lost my district by a wide margin in the March primary. We had a residue of the primary race in the general election. In the primary I had a Catholic priest opposing me, someone so militant on the abortion issue that at one point the Bishop called me and apologized. Father Edwin Arentsen had resigned from a pastorate and from the Belleville diocese. But he attacked me on everything from the Equal Rights Amendment to "the give-away of the Panama Canal." (Archbishop Marcos McGrath, the Roman Catholic prelate in charge of Panama, strongly supported the Panama Canal Treaty and said not to approve it would play into the hands of the Communists.) And of course Father Arentsen attacked my position on abortion. I have never had so many Catholic priests openly supporting me as in that primary. While I defeated Father Arentsen decisively, 38,005 to 14,183, all those minor wounds from his attacks had not healed completely by the general election. Compounding that problem, my general election opponent had the name John Anderson, the same name as a popular and highly respected Republican member of the House also from Illinois who had sought the GOP presidential nomination that year. We found many voters confused. But the major obstacle came from Ronald Reagan. He carried the district overwhelmingly — and I just barely squeaked in, with a majority of 112,134 to 110,176.

My narrow win in 1980 encouraged some of those who wanted me out of the House. When the Reagan tax cut came before us, the National Conservative Political Action Committee approached fifteen House members, including myself, and said that if we voted against the Reagan plan they would buy radio ads attacking us, and if we voted for it they would buy ads praising us. The combined popularity of Ronald Reagan plus the appeal of the phrase "tax cut" would have made his bill attractive anyway. But on top of everything, the President said the passage of it would balance the budget by fiscal year 1984. I saw it — correctly — as creating much larger deficits. I voted against it and the radio onslaught started. Part of the ad stated, "Did you know that since he's been in Washington Paul Simon has been associating with people like Tip O'Neill?" It made Tip sound like an underworld character rather than the Speaker of the House. But their ads backfired, with many local people sending letters to the editor supporting my stand and my independence.

The Illinois House delegation worked together well and had strength. Bob Michel, the House Republican leader, cooperated with members in both parties when he felt it would not reduce or impair his effectiveness as GOP leader. We liked him. He is genuine. Dan Rostenkowski unfortunately ended his career with legal problems, but his contributions as chairman of Ways and Means helped the nation immensely. He had a quality not in abundance, backbone. Henry

Hyde is a class act, with strongly held convictions that we respected. Eloquent and compassionate, he could have played a much larger role on the national stage had a few breaks gone his way, or had he pursued such goals. Sidney Yates was our dean, and a strong supporter of the arts, national parks, and other good causes. And effective. Lane Evans, a soft-spoken House member showed much more courage than I anticipated. John Porter has emerged in a position of influence in the House Appropriations Committee and could be a strong candidate for state-wide office for the Republicans, but his moderate positions on abortion and other social issues have reduced the likelihood of his being a GOP nominee. Ed Madigan, popular within the delegation, became Secretary of Agriculture. Ed Derwinski, also well-liked, became Secretary of Veteran Affairs. I could go down the list. We had no lemons in the Illinois delegation. Dick Durbin, clearly a superior House member, went on to serve in the Senate, taking my seat. Hard-working Glenn Poshard became the Democratic candidate for Governor in 1998. Dennis Hastert is a low-key House member who wears well and is effective. He is not a headline-grabber but a member whose influence will grow. A relatively new member, Ray LaHood, took Bob Michel's seat after serving on his staff. Ray shows real leadership potential. I am impressed by him. The only member of the House delegation who is not that popular with a few of his Illinois House colleagues is Jerry Weller, and my guess is that he will gradually develop a better relationship with other members.


On two occasions in my House service Democratic state Chairman John Touhy and others tried to get me to run for governor, but having shifted to the national scene the governorship had less appeal to me. In late 1977 several leaders, including Vice President Walter Mondale, Speaker "Tip" O'Neill, the state Democratic chairman, and others publicly appealed to me to run for the Senate against Charles Percy. I told the Decatur newspaper, "If ten years ago someone had told me that such an array of leaders would urge me into a Senate race and I would decline, I would not have believed it."[12] When Adlai Stevenson III left the Senate in 1980 there was talk again about my seeking the Senate. But Alan Dixon, then Illinois Secretary of State, indicated to me he wanted to run, and both because of pragmatic reasons, knowing the office of Secretary of State is a great crowd-pleaser, and because of my friendship with him over the years, I endorsed Dixon and said I would not run.

But in 1984 Senator Charles Percy's term expired and he faced reelection. That year marked my tenth in the House. I liked the House, and while I knew I would enjoy the Senate more, I had no plans to run, not eager to take on a statewide race and all the fundraising that goes with that. But more and more people urged me to run, even two of my House Republican colleagues from Illinois who said they thought I could win. A representative group of labor and business leaders came and urged me to make the race.

Tipping the scale as I weighed what to do, leaders in the Jewish community urged me to run. The Percy record on Israel was not strong, and his domestic votes became increasingly conservative. In running for reelection he said he was "for the Reagan program 100 percent." I could not make the same claim for any Democratic program. But the combination of his international and domestic record shift concerned Jewish leaders. My friend, former Congressman Paul Findley, has written about this as though the Jewish community bought votes from me and others. My record of strong support for a homeland for the Jewish people and my strong opposition to anti-Semitism predated my entrance into politics by many years. I also oppose discrimination against Arabs and Muslims, and I have never felt my strong support of Israel was an anti-Arab stance. But the Jewish community has been generous in campaigns, and their support of me would make a difference.

Two long-time friends, Bob Schrayer and Stan Weinberger, urged me to run, both respected in the community, but at that point they were not "the heavies." Bob held a breakfast for me with perhaps fifteen leaders, and sitting next to me was Bill Levine, clearly one of the strong members of the community, who leaned over to me during the breakfast and said if I ran he would help in a major way. That meant something. And then a nationally respected Jewish leader from Chicago, Bob Asher, called. While I did not know him well, I knew him well enough and knew his reputation so that if he said he would do something, he would really do it. Most people who pledge money, for example, mean it when they say they will do something, but you will not be far off if you discount political financial pledges by 50 percent. Asher had a different reputation. He said he would go all-out for me if I became a candidate. I took the call in the kitchen of our 9th Street home in D.C. When I put down the receiver, I thought I would become a candidate. Jeanne and I talked it over and quickly made the decision. I knew that with Bob and his friends, plus my strong labor support, and with other indications of aid I had received from a surprisingly diverse base, I could make it a serious contest. I knew that

Chuck Percy, whom I respected, would outspend me but he would have a serious fight on his hands. Others in the Jewish community who helped significantly included Lester Crown, Larry Hochberg, Judd Malkin, Harvey Wineberg, and Mike Cherry. I write about this in some detail because during the contest Percy charged that I entered the race because of pledges of contributions from the Jewish community, a partially valid claim but with innuendos that were not good and not valid. He said, "I'm not going to kowtow to [the pro-Israel lobby]."[13] The implication of this and other statements was that because we differed on Mideast policy, I had sold my soul to pro-Israel elements. I opposed selling weapons to Arab nations who would not work out peace agreements with Israel, for example, while Percy favored such sales. However, I always favored direct talks between Israel and the Palestine Liberation Organization, and took other stands that differed from official Israeli policy, but he spoke accurately in stressing that I strongly supported Israel.

The large majority of my funds came from outside the Jewish community, and I had far more small contributions than most candidates receive, a healthy sign. The indications of support from African-American and Latino leaders did not surprise me, but I welcomed them. Many had supported Percy in his previous races. People who helped lead the way for me financially included Ed Joyce, John Schmidt, Dick Phelan, Al Friedman, Al Johnson, and Greg Harris.

It became clear that I would have serious primary opposition: State Senator Phil Rock, Democratic leader in the Senate and chair of the state party; Alex Seith, business leader who ran against Percy in 1978; and State Comptroller Roland Burris, the first African American to hold statewide public office. The state party had endorsed Rock, and that meant many political leaders automatically went to his corner. The poll also showed Percy beating me 47-27, though Copley Press columnist Robert Estill wrote: "Simon is the one the Percy camp would least like to face in a general election."[14] In the meantime the two who headed the state Democratic ticket in 1982, Adlai Stevenson III, candidate for governor, and Grace Mary Stern, candidate for lieutenant governor, endorsed my candidacy. And from Washington Rep. Claude Pepper of Florida, a legitimate hero to senior citizens and Senators Howard Metzenbaum of Ohio, Chris Dodd of Connecticut, and Frank Lautenberg of New Jersey came and campaigned for me.

The only action that stunned me came in a switch from Congressman Bill Lipinski, who early in the campaign endorsed me at a public press conference. Then a few days before the primary I heard his ward sample ballots were marked for Rock, not for me. When I called him he said he was under great pressure from the Cook County Democratic leaders to switch and so he did so. Prior to that he had indicated that he really would like to get back to Chicago and head my office there if I was elected. While I made no promises to him or anyone, if he had stuck with me I probably would have offered him the post. After my experience in the primary, I obviously did not do that. In all my years in politics, I have never had another experience quite like that.

While some of the polls showed a tight primary, I headed all the published polls and I won the primary with 31.4 percent. Burris had 20 percent, Seith 18.5 percent, and Rock 17 percent.

My full-time campaign manager in the primary, James Wall, a member of the Methodist clergy and editor of *The Christian Century*, had indicated that he did not want to manage the fall campaign. After an interim manager, I then secured David Axelrod, a *Chicago Tribune* reporter, and David Wilhelm, a Democratic political aficionado and later Democratic National Committee chair, to head my campaign. They did an effective job. Robert Squires did my television work, Paul Maslin my polling. Rosemary Cribben headed my fund-raising. It was an excellent team. I asked Illinois House Speaker Michael Madigan to chair the campaign. Mike is a person of few words, who understands practical politics and is completely reliable. After my election to the Senate, the two pictures most prominently displayed in my office were of Abraham Lincoln and Paul Douglas, and Mike Madigan held the third most prominent spot.

The polls all showed Percy leading, by a wide margin at first. The lead narrowed, but the polls continued to show Percy ahead through election day.

Percy and I differed on a number of issues, but unlike most campaigns we focused many of our differences on international and defense issues. I did oppose the Reagan tax cut, which he voted for. I called it both imprudent, when facing a huge deficit, and skewed to primarily help those in the upper income brackets. He supported the MX missile, a Defense Department fantasy to which I led the opposition in the House. It called for a complex, massively expensive mobile railroad system in the west carrying missiles, requiring approximately as much land as the state of Connecticut. After I denounced it as idiotic, key people in the Defense Department got word to me that most of them agreed with me. When I pointed out the military vulnerability of the missiles traveling above ground, the Pentagon shifted to an underground system for the missiles, but it took several hours to get the huge missiles from their underground moorings to the point where they could be fired. However, attack missiles can go anywhere on the face of the earth in twenty-five minutes. "The new system is a great system if the Soviets agree to send us a postcard telling us they're going to attack," I said to laughter in the House. Through amendments I postponed its construction but I never could kill it. Finally the Latter-Day Saints (Mormons), headquartered in Utah, formally took a stand against it, one of the rare instances in this century of their leadership taking a formal stand on a political issue. After that happened, President Reagan dropped the idea. But before Reagan dropped it, Percy supported it. I favored a nuclear freeze, stopping all testing and production of nuclear weapons. The United States had a clear lead so that an agreement by nations to a halt would not jeopardize our security situation and might make the world safer. Percy opposed the freeze. Percy also criticized me as too liberal, and not sufficiently supportive of President Reagan, running for reelection at the time — and extremely popular.

In Percy's primary against Congressman Tom Corcoran, which the Senator won handily, a Californian, Michael Goland, spent money independently attacking Percy. His ads backfired in the primary and I knew they would do the same in the fall. After the primary I wrote to Goland, whom I had never met, urging that he refrain from further involvement. "I believe your advertising deflects from the major issues of the campaign and can only serve to hurt my candidacy."[15] But toward the end of the campaign he had billboards showing a lizard, saying "Dump the Chameleon. Beat Percy." I believe the billboards hurt me, though no one will ever know with certainty. People asked why I would put up such a billboard. I assured them I did not. Goland later injected himself into a campaign in California in a way that clearly violated the law and he served time in prison.

Percy attacked me regularly in debates on my opposition to a school prayer constitutional amendment. The Supreme Court had ruled that students cannot be forced to pray, and that the state cannot prescribe prayer, both sound decisions. Public opinion did not recognize the niceties of Supreme Court decisions and many believed in a conspiracy of "secular humanists" to take God out of the schools. I had never heard the phrase "secular humanists" until I listened to a House speech that they were taking over the country. I said that teaching religion should be the primary responsibility of homes and religious institutions, not public schools. And I cited a story told me by Rep. Dan Glickman of Kansas, my House colleague and later Secretary of Agriculture. When he was a fourth grader, each morning his classroom had prayer, and each morning little Danny Glickman, a Jew in an overwhelmingly Christian community, would be excused as they started the day with prayer. "Each day," I would respond to Percy, "little Danny Glickman was being told he is different, and so were all the other fourth graders. That shouldn't happen in America." One of our last debates was at a Reform Jewish temple north of Chicago. This time *I* brought up the school prayer issue because I knew for once my audience had sympathy with my position. When a reporter on the panel of questioners asked Percy how he would respond to a Danny Glickman, Percy said, "The Danny Glickmans have to learn to live in the real world." The audience groaned. While most debates are near-draws, I knew I won this one.

The Reagan economic agenda became a focal point of the campaign toward the end. I pushed Percy to reveal his income tax returns to disclose how much the Reagan tax cut had benefitted him. Political columnist Steve Neal wrote in the *Chicago Tribune*: "The normally unflappable Percy looked as if Simon had hit him in the face with a pie when the downstate congressman issued his challenge [to make public his income tax returns] during their recent debate."[16] I said that we should raise $50 billion a year revenue by closing tax loopholes, and Percy had a TV ad that said I wanted to raise taxes $200 billion a year, "more than double the $85 billion [a year] tax raise" that Walter Mondale, the presidential candidate, had talked about and then backed away from. In the final debate on WBBM radio in Chicago, I noted that General Electric had paid no income taxes the previous year because of the Reagan tax bill Percy supported. I pointed out that the "radio station engineer monitoring this program," whom we could both see, paid more income taxes than General Electric.[17]

Our vigorous debates mostly centered on the issues but sometimes wandered from them. I quoted Senator Barry Goldwater: "It's not that Percy is too liberal. It's that he's too inconsistent. He wanders all over hell's half acre." Percy responded by saying he consistently supported the Reagan program, and added that the president had called me an "ultraliberal." The *Chicago Tribune* account then noted:

> "I think you fool yourself if you think by tossing out labels you're going to get anywhere," said Simon. "People are not looking for liberals . . ."
>
> "Reagan called you that," Percy interrupted.
>
> Simon: "You handed him a document to sign, and I'm sure he never even saw the thing."

Percy: "That's what we in Chicago call clout."

Simon: "If it's clout, it hasn't brought any jobs to Illinois."[18]

A small thing happened a few days before the election. President Reagan made an appearance in Springfield. Sitting next to Percy and unaware that a radio mike was close at hand, Reagan leaned over to Percy and said, "See that brave bastard out there with the Simon sign." Some people thought Reagan had called me a bastard. Members of the United Auto Workers had fun with that at the expense of the Republicans. They made signs: ILLEGITIMATES FOR SIMON. Union members showed up at two or three major Republican rallies and the signs caused comment, none of it hurting me.

Newspaper editorials generally were predictable. The liberal *St. Louis Post-Dispatch* found me the right person and the conservative *St. Louis Globe-Democrat* headed their editorial: "Simon's Place Not in the U. S. Senate."[19] The *Chicago Tribune* endorsed Percy, finding me "wedded to a philosophy of government intrusion and social spending."[20] *The Collinsville Herald* found me "thoughtful, informed, compassionate, liberal, decent, all the things that are cliches to describe the ideal politician."[21] But the much less predictable *Peoria Journal-Star* endorsed me, an editorial with weight in that section of the state.

I personally monitored every television commercial we put on, and vetoed two that I felt were too negative. But our ads hit hard. Percy had gone from being a liberal senator to being "100 percent for the Reagan program." One advertisement said: "If you feel strongly about arms control summits, then Charles Percy has a position for you. He's been for them. And against them. Paul Simon. A Senator we can count on."[22] Percy had one that temporarily was powerful, but backfired. The commercial showed our hostages being taken in Iran, the American flag being burned, a picture of the Ayatollah Khomeini, and the voice message said: "Paul Simon has called the Ayatollah 'a just and holy man.' Do you want him as your Senator?" We couldn't figure out where this came from, but the Percy people said they had a letter quoting me as saying that. We finally tracked it down. Shortly after Iran seized the hostages the State Department asked several of us to write to the Ayatollah urging that he release them. In the middle of the letter I wrote, "As a just and holy man I hope you will release the hostages." It was simply an attempt to appeal to his better nature. When we got the letter and background we released it to all the media, and Mike Royko had a column in which he said, "Charles

Percy's commercials would make the shadiest used car salesman blush."[23]

The day before the election I started campaigning at "L" stops in Chicago with Mayor Harold Washington who said I was "going to run like wild fire." Percy countered, "His only hope lies in Chicago and a big delivered vote by City Hall. . . . Downstate, collar counties and the suburbs are really going to respond to that."[24]

After voting in Makanda in southern Illinois, our family flew to Chicago. After checking into the hotel we rented a car and drove to Barrington in the Chicago suburbs to visit Jeanne's mother. On the way we heard a radio report that exit polls showed Percy winning. That did not startle us knowing that all the public polls showed me losing, but it discouraged us. We went back to the hotel where we gathered returns, scattered at first. But before we had many vote tallies, ABC called Percy the winner. However, Hugh Hill, the analyst for the ABC television station in Chicago, said that might be incorrect, that ABC assumed that the downstate vote would go heavily for Percy and that could be wrong. NBC and CBS did not call it, and we found that encouraging. We had a narrow lead starting with the first votes that came in. That never changed. I finally won with an 89,000 majority out of 4.7 million votes cast. Reagan carried the state by more than 600,000 votes. I became the first United States Senator elected from deep southern Illinois in 147 years.

I have defeated candidates who never congratulated me. I understand their feeling but it shows a lack of understanding of how our system should work. Chuck Percy not only called and congratulated me the next morning, he asked to talk to Jeanne and to Sheila and Martin and congratulated them, because he knew it had been a Simon family joint effort. It was a generous act on his part. Since that election Percy and I encounter each other perhaps every six months, and we have a cordial relationship.

A few days after the election, Congressman Dan Glickman called and asked if I would speak at an Israeli Bond dinner honoring him in Wichita on April 21st of the next year. I told him I would love to do it but April 21st Jeanne and I would be celebrating our 25th wedding anniversary and I had to turn him down. "Bring her along," he said with his usual enthusiasm. I told him I would call Jeanne. She said, "After using Dan Glickman's name on the religious issue throughout the campaign, we can't turn him down." So we went to Wichita. I started my speech by saying, "Twenty-five years ago Jeanne and I got married, and we dreamed that some day we might celebrate our twenty-fifth wedding anniversary by going to Wichita!"

They roared. It was an appropriate way to celebrate for a political couple.

---

[1] We continued to have a home in Illinois, as well as in the Washington area. In 1981 we built a home in the country, south of Carbondale, where we still live.

[2] Undated scrapbook clipping, SIU Archives.

[3] Mike Robinson, "Downstate Congressmen Are Hodgepodge," *Decatur Herald and Review*, 15 January 1979.

[4] Editorial, 8 May 1980.

[5] *Washingtonian*, September 1982.

[6] *Southern Illinoisan*, 19 May 1975.

[7] "$1 Million a Year Spent to Send Beer to Troops," *St. Louis Globe-Democrat*, 20 September 1997.

[8] Edward O'Brien, "Coals to Newcastle: Beer-Lift to Germany," *Birmingham News*, 20 September 1977.

[9] Named for Senator Mark Hatfield who pushed for more medical research.

[10] Robert Reid, "Simon Doesn't Deserve Moral Majority's Barbs," *Southern Illinoisan*, 22 March 1981.

[11] 28 January 1980.

[12] "Simon's Decision Simple," editorial, *Decatur Herald*, 4 November 1977.

[13] "Percy: I Won't Bow to Pro-Israel Lobby," *Southern Illinoisan*, 31 October 1984.

[14] Robert Estill, "Simon Candidacy Would Be Bad News for Percy," *Aurora Beacon-News*, 2 July 1983.

[15] Author to Michael Goland, April 1984.

[16] "Percy's Tax Returns: Skirmish in a War," *Chicago Tribune*, 8 September 1984.

[17] Lynn Sweet and Mark Brown, "Debate Finale Hushes Discord," *Chicago Sun-Times*, 2 November 1984.

[18] Phillip Lentz and Marianne Taylor, "Percy, Simon Spar in Debate," *Chicago Tribune*, 8 August 1984.

[19] *St. Louis Globe-Democrat*, 2 November 1984.

[20] Editorial, *Chicago Tribune*, 21 October 1984.

[21] Karl Monroe, "Herald Helped Paul Simon Get Started," *The Collinsville Herald*, 20 February 1984.

[22] Quoted in Andrew Malcolm, "Illinois Senate Rivals Focus on Reagan in Debate," *New York Times*, 8 September 1984.

[23] *Chicago Tribune*.

[24] "Simon, Percy Make Last Push," *Southern Illinoisan*, 6 November 1984.

Chapter 10

# *The U. S. Senate-*
# *Part One*

I thought I would like the Senate, but it turned out even better than I had hoped. I knew the members before my arrival but I did not know the procedures, many much different from the House, procedures that give individual members more power than in the much larger House. In the Senate anyone can put "a hold" on a piece of legislation or on a nominee who needs Senate approval, and though that does not totally stop action, except at the end of the session, it is a barrier to action. And the "hold" and the desired action may have no immediate relationship other than the Senate sponsor. If, for example, I want a colleague to have a hearing on a bill of mine, and he or she refuses to do it, I can look for a proposal of that senator's on the calendar (which I may favor) and put a "hold" on it. That senator then comes to me and asks why I'm doing that, and I explain that I'll be happy to take the "hold" off if I can have a hearing on my bill. It usually works. There is no such procedure in the House.

Because as a senator you have more power, including the ability to approve or disapprove presidential nominations and treaties, people outside Congress respond more quickly to a senator than to a House member. As a senator you can call the president of the United States or the president of General Motors. Few people turn down a call from a senator, and that in itself gives you more influence. Being a senator also proved helpful for occasional "think tank dinners" I held on subjects of interest to me with six to eight experts from around the nation, people eager to bend the ear of a senator. So we had "think tank dinners" of real quality.

Because the Senate is smaller, getting action is easier. For example, during ten of my twelve Senate years the Subcommittee on Immigration had only three members: Senator Alan Simpson of Wyoming, Senator Ted Kennedy of Massachusetts, and myself. While some times we had differing opinions, the three of us worked together well. Alan and Ted were my seniors both in Senate service and knowledge in this area. We met informally from time to time to talk over the problems. It made possible legislative action in the Senate that the much larger House subcommittee could not have taken.

One of those who urged me to become a Senate candidate, Senator Lloyd Bentsen of Texas, assured me that if I ran for the Senate and won that I would serve on the Labor and Human Resources Committee, which deals with education issues among other topics. Lloyd headed the Democratic Senatorial Campaign Committee and was eager for me to run.

The Democratic leader in the Senate when I arrived was Senator Robert Byrd, an old-fashioned Roman senator except for the missing toga. He led in more than title. Byrd called and asked if I would take Judiciary as my second committee. I told him that I am not a lawyer, but if that did not present a barrier I would be pleased to serve there. He said he had confidence that would not prohibit me but that he would check. I served there, and dealt with matters as diverse as abortion and constitutional amendments and confirmation of Supreme Court Justices.

Those two committees filled my quota. But senators can get a waiver of the rules and serve on more than two committees. The Senate is like a church or Rotary club or any other organization: If they see you are willing to work, they assign it to you, and in any organization about one-third of the members do the bulk of the work.

Senator Lawton Chiles of Florida — governor there after his Senate service — asked me to become a member of the Budget Committee. I had served on the Budget Committee in the House and I agreed to do it if he asked for the waiver, which the Senate granted. Senator Claiborne Pell of Rhode Island approached me about serving on the Foreign Relations Committee, another strong interest of mine, and once again I agreed to do it if he requested it and the Senate approved, which it did.

The last six years of my Senate career I served on one other committee, which came about in an unusual way. I had always resented the use of American Indian mascots for athletic teams. To have, for example, the Washington Redskins along with the Chicago Bears and the St. Louis Rams is a denigration of Native Ameicans. We would not tolerate a team called the Washington Blacks or the Washington Jews, and even that is not an apt analogy because Redskins is not a term of respect. A closer comparison would be to have a team called the Washington Niggers or the Washington Kikes. Native Americans resent this abuse of their heritage, except for a few defendants of the status quo who are trotted out, as segregationists used to display a few African Americans who would assure us that their people liked segregation.

In the midst of my campaign for reelection in 1990, I caused panic among my staff by signing a petition for the Native American community to do away with Chief Illiniwek as the mascot for the University of Illinois. I knew it would cause difficulties, but I did not know how much. It suddenly became a *cause célèbre*. The Saturday after I signed the petition, I attended the University of Illinois-Michigan football game where at halftime they had scheduled me to receive a 4-H recognition and award. University officials said they thought the event now should be conducted privately, and I agreed with that assessment, knowing that introducing politicians at athletic events is always a risky business for the office-holder, even without this controversy. At halftime, in the nationally televised game, my opponent, Congresswoman Lynn Martin, had a plane circle the field trailing a message: KEEP THE CHIEF, DUMP SIMON. The crowd cheered. All of this on national television. Jeanne and I watched the game from a glassed-in box high above the field, away from the crowd. The university appeared to be doing its best to keep me from the more boisterous fans, a few of whom always "bend the elbow" excessively at tailgate parties before a game. At a meeting in Springfield one of the state's Democratic leaders said I had blown any chance I had of winning, that I should withdraw from the ticket and have the State Central Committee name a replacement. My Senate colleague from Illinois, who campaigned for me, nevertheless said he was "prepared to lead a fight to keep the mascot."[1] Devoted alumni explained to me that Chief Illiniwek is almost a sacred symbol, done with great respect to Native Americans. They said that the dance done at halftime in games is a religious dance copied carefully from Indian ritual. As to whether it shows great respect to Native Americans, I told them they should let Native Americans make that determination. And on the religious significance of it, I suggested that for one game they try having a Catholic priest or a Jewish rabbi dance around at halftime with religious garb and carrying a chalice or a

Torah, and see what the reaction would be. The uproar gradually died down, though I heard about it — largely negatively — everywhere I went in the state. Since that time the Student Senate and the faculty at the University of Illinois have voted to do away with this racist symbol, but the board of trustees, good but insensitive people, have voted to keep it. One of these days the University of Illinois will join Dartmouth and Stanford and Syracuse and Miami of Ohio and other schools in doing away with this affront to Native Americans. And I applaud the University of Iowa officials who will not permit the Chief Illiniwek mascot at their athletic contests with the University of Illinois.

After this episode, editorials appeared generally opposing my stand, with either the theme "Why should Simon worry about this when there are so many important issues facing the nation?" or "With only 22,000 Native Americans in Illinois, which has 12 million people, why is he spending time worrying about the 22,000 more than the rest of us?" The only time I had spent on this initially: ten seconds to sign my name to a petition. Springfield political columnist Anthony Man wrote: "The Illiniwek imbroglio allowed [Lynn] Martin and every other Republican to portray Simon as strangely out of touch with what the real people of Illinois are thinking. The fact that the chief's antics offend some Native Americans matters little in the Illinois political world."[2]

Not everyone who supported Chief Illiniwek was racially insensitive, but the outpouring of prejudice against Native Americans startled me. I had visited reservations, as well as worked with inner city Native Americans, and I understood some of the difficulties they face — for which most Americans are far too callous. After my reelection I asked to be named to the Select Committee on Indian Affairs under the effective leadership of Senator Dan Innouye of Hawaii and Senator John McCain of Arizona. That made my committee assignments heavier than desirable, but I wanted to help at least a little on a problem that remains an American tragedy.

Most issues in which I became involved in the Senate followed the House pattern, the major exceptions being the immigration field and constitutional amendments, plus a few items that did not fit any pattern. Unexpectedly I came across a grant of $186,710 from the Office of Juvenile Justice and Delinquency Prevention to Jerry Falwell's Liberty University to prepare materials on the Constitution for high school students. What that has to do with delinquency prevention escaped me, and with more than 100 companies in the United States in the business of preparing material for schools, I saw no need for the federal government to get involved, whether the grant was to Harvard or Liberty University. The next edition of Falwell's *Liberty Report* had me on the front page — a drawing with me scowling — with the words: "Sen. Paul Simon: A Religious Bigot?" The article inside had the heading: "Sen. Simon Locks Arms With Religious Bigots." The story did not criticize Senator Arlen Specter, the Republican chair of the subcommittee, who to his credit also objected to this kind of political pork. The grant clearly was a small gift tossed Falwell's way by the Reagan administration with the hope that no one would notice. The radio evangelist accused me of "a complete lack of tolerance." The *Chicago Tribune* commented editorially that the charge by Dr. Falwell "cheapens his own credibility."[3]

An area where we are inching ahead, but much more needs to be done, is basic literacy. We have, by the most conservative estimate, 23 million adult Americans who cannot read a newspaper nor fill out an employment form. Four million adult Americans cannot recognize their name in block print. Every major business in the United States is concerned about the skill level of the work force we have, and many of the jobs lost to other countries are lost because of the inability of corporations to find the employment force here with a minimum quality background.

I entered the field of literacy accidentally. When I had open office hours during my House service, if people wanted me to look at their background information on Social Security or anything else involving federal records, regulations required them to sign a consent form. Frequently someone would say, "Is it OK if my wife signs?" or "Is it OK if my husband signs?" I realized they could not even write their name. Frequently someone would carefully and slowly draw his or her name, and I knew they could not write anything else. Then when people came in desperate for a job, seeking my help, I started by asking the question, "Can you read and write?" When there was an awkward moment of silence before the answer, I knew what the reply would be.

I then held subcommittee hearings on the question of illiteracy, the first such hearings in the history of Congress. The late Secretary of Education Ted Bell wrote that he held the top education post in the nation and did not know anything about illiteracy until I asked him to testify. After his testimony, we talked and I suggested that we should have a series of breakfast meetings with a few who are concerned about this, to see what we could do. We had about fifteen who attended, one of them being Barbara Bush, whose husband then served as Vice President. She already had an interest in literacy.

As a result of the hearing and breakfast meetings, the Senate adopted my amendments to create a Literacy Corps as part of the Vista program, to encourage libraries to offer literacy training, to foster literacy programs in federal prisons (82 percent of those in our nation's prisons and jails are high school dropouts, many illiterate), and to encourage literacy as part of the assistance to the homeless, who have a high illiteracy rate.

At a town meeting I held in the small town of Teutopolis, 45-year-old Gloria Wattles stood up and said she wanted to read the first letter she had ever written. In the letter she thanked me for establishing the Vista Literacy Corps, but the letter told her life story, the tragedy of being unable to read and what it meant. She related being asked to read in a church service as a twelve-year-old, rushing out of the church crying and not going back until many years later when she could read. She told about her three-year-old son asking to sit on her lap and have a story read to him, and how he burst into tears when she couldn't do it. Before she finished reading the letter she was crying and had the whole town meeting in tears.

When I moved to the Senate, I again held hearings — Gloria Wattles testified — and then I introduced a bill that is now known as the National Literacy Act, which established the National Institute for Literacy and inches the nation ahead on this front. Rep. Tom Sawyer of Ohio was the House sponsor. When I first introduced the measure, the White House announced its opposition. At a meeting I attended with President Bush on another subject I told him he might get lobbied at home on this. I called Barbara Bush and explained the situation, and the administration position suddenly reversed itself 180 degrees, supporting the measure. At the White House signing, the President started to hand me the pen he used to sign the bill, customarily given to the chief sponsor. I said, "This time the pen should go to your wife." Everyone present laughed and applauded because they knew the background. Barbara accepted it. I asked Gloria Wattles to be present for the signing, and introduced her to President and Mrs. Bush.

We have made progress on literacy but we are basically just nibbling at the edges of this huge drawback to greater productivity. We really need a massive assault on this problem. We should involve religious groups, voluntary organizations, government at all levels, as well as libraries, and community colleges. A major difficulty is that the problem is hidden. People who do not have these basic skills try to hide it from their friends and neighbors and often from their own families. A woman I met a few days ago as I write this, Kay Burner, told me a story that is typical. Her husband enrolled in a real estate broker's course, and asked Kay to help him study for the test. She said she had trouble with words. "Any words you have trouble with I'll spell out and tell you," he responded. "That would be all the words," she told him as she broke down and cried. She enrolled in a Laubach literacy program and now is about to begin nurse's training in West Virginia. Her world has changed dramatically. She told me this at a dinner at which I spoke. After the dinner a big, rough-hewn man perhaps fifty-five years old came up and suddenly gave me a hug. "I read at the fourth grade level. It was like I was in prison. You helped to make my life complete." He had tears in his eyes. There are thousands of such stories — but thousands upon thousands who need help but hide their problem. When little Johnny or Jane asks an illiterate parent to read, he or she is usually "too busy" to do it. And so instead of enriching that child's life, the problem may be handed from one generation to the next. Because of the stigma of illiteracy, enlisting people who need help must be handled carefully. They will not walk into a high school or grade school and say, "I need help." But they can be tempted to go into a library, or a community college, or a church, or an office. When I introduced the bill I announced that my aim was to eliminate illiteracy in the nation by the year 2000. We are a long way from achieving that goal. We have taken no more than a step in that direction. If we were to spend one percent as much on promoting literacy as we did on salvaging the savings and loan business, we would enrich the nation immensely — and salvage a great many lives.

A small but wise decision I made in the House and followed in the Senate relates to receptions. Members are barraged with invitations to reception/cocktail hours each evening. When I first got to the House I tried to attend if some local constituency wanted me to be there. I found it took me ten or fifteen minutes to get to the reception; you have to stay at least twenty minutes; and then another ten or fifteen minutes to get back to your office. Rarely is anything serious discussed. The local grain dealer or chiropractor or shoe manufacturer wants to show you off to a few of his or her friends. I saw this as a huge waste of time when I already had a shortage of that commodity. I started a policy of telling the lumber dealers or whatever the group might be that I would be happy to meet with them in my office for ten minutes rather than go to the reception. And about half the time they didn't even want to do that.

In the Senate I started a Thursday morning "breakfast" (coffee and rolls) for anyone who wanted to stop by at 8:30, a suggestion of Floyd Fithian of my staff. We secured a committee room and made a town meeting out of it, and if I had not had time to meet with some group they could ask their question or make a brief statement at these events. I am pleased that Senators Carol Moseley-Braun and Dick Durbin are continuing these events. I found them helpful.

In the Senate it is easier to be involved in many issues, because the Senate has a virtually unlimited amendment rule and because, unlike the House, the Senate is less a committee-oriented body. In the House if a member rises and proposes something in an area that is not part of his or her committee jurisdiction, often there is grumbling and opposition by members of the committee, assuring the House member who offers the amendment that "We're looking at that" or "We will look at that." The result for me, with a wide range of interests, is that in the Senate I could stick my toe into a number of bodies of water. Among the issues I tackled:

- **DNA**. I read about this British experiment in working with genetic testing that could have an immense impact on crime detection, both in convicting the guilty and proving innocence. I called the director of the FBI, Judge William Sessions, and he came to my office with some of his key staff aides to talk about DNA. They were looking at it. As a result of our meeting I held a hearing on DNA and then obtained the first appropriations for the FBI to use this valuable new tool. It continues to grow in importance, though like fingerprints when they first became a law enforcement tool, we are still struggling with refining some of the standards.

- **Amusement parks and rides.** People who attend a festival and ride a Ferris wheel generally assume that someone is looking at the safety standard of that or other rides. That is not necessarily the case. The major operations, like Disney World, operate carefully for fear of being sued if for no other reason. But many operations are marginal, carry no insurance or in some cases little insurance. Every year we read about a few children being killed on various rides. I wanted to give the Consumer Product Safety Commission jurisdiction over this — a jurisdiction they once had — but I lost this effort. It continues to be a need.

- **High-speed rail corridors.** Rep. George Sangmeister of Illinois led the fight in the House to have the federal government establish five places where we could have high-speed railroads. Spain, Sweden, Japan, Germany, and other nations have them (along with better rail passenger service generally). I handled the bill in the Senate. Our measure passed, the five corridors have been designated, and we are ever so slowly moving toward making this a reality.

- **Business mergers.** Our race into more and more business mergers is generally not healthy, though in some instances it is. Our tax laws encourage these mergers. For example, when U. S. Steel (now USX Corporation) borrowed $5.6 billion to buy Marathon Oil, it did not increase steel productivity, it did not cause any more oil wells to be drilled, it added nothing to the nation's productivity. But the interest they paid on that purchase is tax deductible — ultimately subsidized by you and me. It eats up money on the financial markets, increasing interest. I proposed that only 80 percent of the interest from money borrowed for a merger or acquisition would be deductible. That would not prevent mergers, but would encourage acquisition by issuing stock, making the businesses healthier. If they don't make money they don't issue dividends, but if they borrow money they ultimately have to declare bankruptcy if they can't pay interest and principal, and many have gone bankrupt because of their debt payments. I proposed that the savings from the merger loan deductions be used to make one-half of dividends paid on all stock not taxable. It would be a wash financially for the federal government if that procedure were to be followed, the treasury neither losing money nor gaining. The idea interested a few business leaders, including one of the nation's finest, Warren Buffett, but I could not get anyone on the Senate Finance Committee to champion this cause. The idea remains sound. The federal debt is not the only indebtedness that should concern us. This measure would slow the increase in corporate debt.

- **Surety bonds.** I proposed banning discrimination on surety bonds, still a problem for minorities and women in business to obtain. The bond people opposed my bill, but its introduction caused them to improve their practices, so I gained half a victory.

- **Environment and conservation.** I received consistently high marks from their organizations for my votes and for several measures I proposed and passed, particularly to protect national forests.

- **Hate crimes.** I sponsored the legislation which requires the FBI to keep track of crimes against people or property because of the groups to which they belong. To no one's surprise, the statistics gathered since my proposal became law show that most hate crimes are committed against African Americans. But the most frequently attacked group, in percentage terms, are gays. Those who preach hatred toward any group rather than understanding share in the blame for these despicable crimes. All crimes are heinous, but picking on someone because he or she is African American or Asian American or gay or Jewish or belongs to some other group, and brutalizing someone for the sheer pleasure of doing it because of that person's background, is somehow more reprehensible than stealing money. But with the gathering of statistics we at least have better knowledge of the amount of this poison that is in our national system.

- **Motorcycle helmet law.** I consistently offended the motorcycle crowd. They have one issue: to stop the required use of helmets for motorcycle riders. Sometimes at town meetings about fifteen of them in their leather jackets or other distinctive garb would arrive in a group. One would attack me for my support of the helmet law, I would respond, and then they would walk out, not interested in any other issue. The evidence is overwhelming that helmets save lives, and prevent serious accidents, just as seatbelts in cars do. So I voted to protect their lives — and they disliked me for it. I did make one mistake that unnecessarily irritated them. When one young man became fervent in attacking me at a meeting, and said if he wanted to kill himself by not wearing a helmet he should have that right, with irritation I responded: "If you can guarantee me that you would die, maybe I would go along, but if you end up being paralyzed for the rest of your life it will cost the taxpayers millions of dollars." The next edition of their motorcycle journal had a big headline: "Senator Simon to Motorcyclists: Drop Dead." I should have handled it more diplomatically.

- **Air controllers.** The Federal Aviation Administration released statistics showing that O'Hare airport in Chicago, the world's busiest, while generally safe, had more what non-technicians would call near misses than any other major airport. That caused concerns. My staff and I worked on the issue and came up with a series of recommendations, many of them from FAA people. I invited the FAA officials to my office and they assured us there would be follow-through, but they gave me no dates for action. I said that without dates attached for accomplishing these things, we simply had a wish list, asking them to return with specific dates by which they would accomplish these actions. They did and for a period we had monthly meetings at which they would report progress or lack of it. Two major improvements that resulted from this were a new air control tower at O'Hare, and an increase in pay — technically a bonus — for controllers working at Chicago, Los Angeles and New York, the heavy traffic locations. If an air traffic controller can receive the same pay working in Pensacola, Florida as in Chicago, why take the stressful job? So experienced and senior air controllers opted for the lighter duty stations, until we passed the pay differential. That pay difference has continued though we have had to fight administrations each year on it. Senator Frank Lautenberg of New Jersey played a key role in helping to get this accomplished. The old air control tower in O'Hare simply did not meet today's needs. Even as a non-technician I could see the deficiencies as I toured the facility. O'Hare today is safer.

- **Drugs.** Talking with families who are devastated is part of my education on drugs, a disheartening part of it. Talking with parents about their children on drugs is heart-wrenching. A bright young man who makes an excellent impression, but is about to go off to federal prison, appealed to me for help, thinking that somehow a senator could save him, but I told him that is the job for courts, not legislators. A woman talked to me about her ten-year-old son offered drugs by a thirteen-year-old and when I talked to a police officer his first reaction was to laugh, not typical of police officers but discouraging nevertheless. I also spent part of one day with two Chicago police officers in making their drug rounds. I remember passing a woman sitting on a bench and one of the officers said, "She used to be a respected member of the community. Now she's a prostitute." After talking with chiefs of police, prosecutors, and prison wardens I worked primarily to put greater emphasis on prevention and treatment. I did get an amendment adopted to require federal prisoners to undergo drug testing prior to release, to discourage drug use in prisons, as well as random testing while former prisoners are on parole. However, we are still much too wedded to incarceration as the answer to crime problems — including drugs — rather than preventing the demand for drugs. Put one drug kingpin into prison and unfortunately many others are eager to take his place. Reduce demand and then you solve the problem. But unfortunately the answers to the demand side are not quick and dramatic and don't make good political speeches.

- **Prison sentencing.** People who commit crimes of violence should be locked up, the penalties quick and severe. But spending huge amounts of money on lengthy prison sentences for those not committing crimes of violence does not make sense, except politically. Long ago Plato told us to select good judges and then let the judges determine the sentences. Guidelines are there for judges, but they should have the right to explain why the guidelines may not be followed in an individual case. Recently a federal judge called me and said he is considering resigning because he is forced under the law to sentence a young man to ten years in prison who perhaps should receive a six-month sentence. "If he were white and living in the suburbs, he would have been sent to a clinic instead of being prosecuted," the judge said. When people are guilty of nonviolent crimes, alternative sentencing should be pursued. For example, a bank embezzler is probably not a physical threat to society. Maybe for the first thirty days of his or her sentence there should be prison time, to get the message across of the seriousness of the offense. Perhaps the rest of the time should be served working at a homeless shelter or some other worthy cause, where the prisoner would be helped more, the local cause helped, and the taxpayers assisted.

- **Presidential succession.** This area I studied and then introduced legislation which did not pass, not because of strong
  objection but simply because we had what appeared to be more
  pressing issues before us. We still need a clarification in the law
  as to what happens if a President-elect dies between election
  day and the time he or she is sworn into office. This does not
  require a constitutional amendment. If Horace Greeley had
  won in the election of 1872, it would have happened. He died
  a few days after losing the election. We should spell out procedures clearly when and if this does happen.

My staff deserves much of the credit for whatever I accomplished.
After election to the Senate, I called Floyd Fithian, a former member
of the House and former faculty member at Purdue, and asked him to
become my chief of staff. We entered the House together in 1974. He
served as chief of staff for all of my first term and part of my second
term before moving on to a position with the Farm Credit
Administration. Jeremy Karpatkin, who joined my Senate staff after
heading the New York operation of my unsuccessful presidential candidacy in 1988, succeeded Floyd as my chief of staff. Jeremy
impressed me by his ability and his attitude. He married Susan Fry
from Colorado and moved there. Vicki Otten, who headed my legislative efforts, then took over as chief of staff and performed ably in
that capacity until I left the Senate. I sensed from day one of her service that we were on the same philosophical wavelength. I am grateful to all three — and to the many other staff people I should mention.
Vicki Coupling served as my executive secretary until moving on to a
position at the NAACP headquarters, and then Jackie Williams, who
had been with me in the House before starting a small business,
returned in that position. I do not need to tell any executive who is
reading this how important that job is. In Washington, two other people deserve special mention. Ray Johnsen, my college friend who
worked with me from newspaper days through the Senate, retired
with his wife Nancy to North Carolina. David Carle, my press secretary, now serves in that capacity for Senator Patrick Leahy of
Vermont.

In Chicago Bettylu Saltzman, daughter of former Secretary of
Commerce Phil Klutznick, headed my efforts and pulled together
the initial staff. She headed things for several years followed by
Anne Roosevelt, granddaughter of Franklin and Eleanor Roosevelt,
and Nancy Chen, who became a leader in the Chinese-American

community. Each performed in a different style, but helped me and the people of Illinois ably.

Jerry Sinclair, a longtime friend and businessman, played an overall key role in Illinois. In charge of my Springfield staff were Joe Bob Pierce and Joe Dunn. Both had been with me in the House. Virginia Ottersen and Donna Eastman headed my small Carbondale office.

I should mention each member of the staff. A book publisher or editor reading the above paragraphs already sees them as dull to the general public. That may be, but the staff played such a crucial role that I want to give them credit.

Riding on the Senate subway with Senator Dan Evans, a Republican from Washington, he mentioned casually, "Outside of mine, I believe you have the best staff on Capitol Hill." I did have a superb crew and I will always be grateful to them.

Health delivery occupied much of my time, particularly after Bill Clinton became President. I worked on one of the two committees of jurisdiction for his health proposal and we went over it carefully, emerging with a better bill than he proposed. Unfortunately the distortions provided by opponents through commercials on national television, plus the fact that those who opposed the measure are big contributors, doomed the bill. The next year I had a measure drafted to provide health coverage for pregnant women and children under the age of twelve, but legislators had no eagerness to spend time on something that didn't appear to have much chance, particularly with the Clinton administration abandoning the field. Several times I tried an initiative on long-term care, a growing need, but again did not make headway, even though the need is so apparent.

In addition to legislation on the labor-management front, I tried to be helpful in a variety of specific Illinois situations where someone had to bring the two sides together. My most successful effort came with the looming strike of the Chicago and Northwestern Railroad, which carries tens of thousands of north suburban residents into the City of Chicago. A strike would have caused harm to those employed and to their businesses. Both sides agreed that I should mediate. The president of the railroad, Bob Schmiege, had his office in Chicago and the president of the United Transportation Union, Fred Hardin, lived in Ohio. I was on the phone to the two of them night and day and we came close to working things out as the strike deadline approached. They both agreed that because we almost had things settled that

Congress should pass a law keeping the railroad operating, but the president of the union did not want to publicly have to say he favored the legislation, because unions generally oppose that type of law. I explained it quietly to those I thought might be concerned, and the bill uneventfully passed the Senate and headed to the House. One of the House members, Rep. Charlie Hayes of Chicago occupied the seat once held by Harold Washington, Ralph Metcalfe and Bill Dawson, all respected names in Illinois. He had been an officer of the Packinghouse Workers Union, and when he saw that we were preventing a strike by law, his instincts as an old labor leader told him something is wrong. As soon as I heard that he tried to stop the measure on the House floor I contacted him; we had been friends for many years before he came to Congress. He had a hard time believing that a labor leader could approve the bill. I finally called the head of the UTU and said that I knew he didn't want to surface publicly as favoring this but could he call Charlie Hayes and tell him the situation. He did, the bill passed, and within days we had the settlement.

Firestone, manufacturer of tires, became Bridgestone/Firestone, a corporation totally owned by Japanese business leaders. When the workers went on strike, Bridgestone/Firestone simply started to replace their longtime employees, rather than negotiate. One of their plants is in Decatur, Illinois, a community then plagued with labor-management problems. The head of the U. S. operation refused to take a phone call from Secretary of Labor Robert Reich, who told me he had never had that experience. I tried to phone the industrial leader also without success. In the midst of this the Japanese prime minister visited Washington. I had the Senate proceedings on the television set in my office, and Bob Dole announced that there would be a twenty-minute recess so that senators who might want to meet and chat with the Japanese Prime Minister could do so. I raced over to the floor, bowed appropriately as I met him, and then told him the problem. A day or two earlier I had spoken on the floor of the Senate about it. The prime minister obviously had been briefed by someone alert at the Japanese embassy. He listened patiently while I explained the situation, and then he said, "They should negotiate." About an hour later I called the head of the Bridgestone/Firestone U. S. operation again, and lo and behold, the atmosphere had changed dramatically. "Obviously we would like to work something out," he said. Eventually the older workers had the chance to get their jobs back. The final result did not please everyone, but it was better than all of them losing their jobs.

However, I failed as well as succeeded. I called Don Fites, the chief executive of Caterpillar, headquartered in Peoria, and Owen Bieber, international president of the United Auto Workers, and asked if I could meet with both of them on the years-long strike that hurt everyone, with the understanding that we would not tell the media. We would just explore possibilities. Because a meeting in my office could attract reporters, we first met in the office of John Calhoun Wells, the head of the U. S. Mediation Service. We met for about two hours, and I felt made progress. A follow-up meeting in Louisville brought the key staff members of both sides together with Wells, but not much progress could be seen. I asked Don and Owen to meet with me again in a motel near the St. Louis airport, once again taking steps to keep our limited negotiations quiet. At the top level on both sides it could have worked out. But below the Fites-Bieber level there had been so much prolonged acrimony that I wasted their time and mine. While things are calmer on the Caterpillar scene today, the long strike hurt labor and management and the communities. But at least I tried.

I did not get involved in any mediation outside of Illinois, although a few times people asked me to do so. And I worked on many other Illinois issues with Alan Dixon and later Carol Moseley-Braun, my Senate colleagues from our state.

Thanks primarily to the leadership of Rep. George Sangmeister, and follow-through by Rep. Jerry Weller after replacing Sangmeister, a large block of land in the Joliet area, formerly part of the Joliet Arsenal, is preserved for wildlife, hikes and the beauty of nature in the heavily populated Greater Chicago area. It is known as the Midewin National Tallgrass Prairie, the term Midewin coming from the Native Americans. I shepherded that through the Senate, a surprisingly difficult task for a relatively small piece of legislation.

Rescuing Illinois entities who would lose money because of technical infractions of the law or regulations happened regularly. Chicago school board member Bill Singer, an old friend, called and said the Chicago schools had not been in full compliance with the law requiring them to serve disabled students, and they would lose $106 million. I checked. They had not lived up to the requirements of the law but they agreed that they would comply fully if they could get the money. I worked it out. Depriving Chicago's cash-strapped schools of $106 million would not have helped anyone. We had other problems within the state. The state librarian failed to sign a required document; Illinois libraries would lose $11 million, and the federal agency had no choice but to withhold it. I succeeded in having the law changed and they received their $11 million. Floods and tornados always required a special response and I was pleased to help. I worked with Rep. John Porter to get aid to the schools of North Chicago, an impoverished district with a huge enrollment of the children of families in the military at the Great Lakes Naval Training Base and at the Army base at Fort Sheridan. When Caterpillar needed an $86.2 million Export-Import Bank loan guarantee to make a sale of equipment to Russia, I called the White House staff and they quickly pushed it though. On that one, since Caterpillar workers technically were still on strike, I received criticism from one labor union, the UAW, even though the contract meant employment for 1,200 people around the clock at their East Peoria plant.

Rep. Harris Fawell, a frequent critic of "pork" legislation, sometimes successfully cut favorite projects of his House colleagues. When he advocated an important medical experiment known as the Advance Photon Source project at the Argonne Laboratories, his House colleagues reciprocated. It is to Fawell's credit that he conscientiously went after items of limited merit, but when his proposal came up, its merit had nothing to do with its temporary death. His colleagues wanted revenge. Twice he called me to rescue this in the Senate and I was able to do it.

With my help legislation passed for the Chicago Deep Tunnel drainage project, a program that not only helped Chicago with occasional flooding problems but pioneered in large underground tunnel construction, using the knowledge acquired from building the tunnel between Great Britain and France and a major project in China.

Sometimes when you have a good bill you become a target from both the left and the right. Two ethnic groups have had unique experiences in our history, Native Americans and African Americans. Smithsonian has a Native American museum and we reached an understanding to have an African American museum, to be housed in one of the older, historic buildings Smithsonian has on the mall. I had the agreement of all the African-American House members on this, except one, Rep. Gus Savage of our state. Gus had real ability, but a mercurial disposition. Often it was difficult to tell where he would find himself on any issue. He believed the old historic building in which Smithsonian planned to house the museum to be inadequate; he wanted an expensive new building. All my quiet negotiations went up in smoke. People who wanted an excuse to be against it now had an African American leading the charge in opposition. Two years later I tried again, with Rep. John Lewis, an extremely able African American from Atlanta whom I got to know slightly during the civil rights struggle, as my House sponsor. Gus Savage, in the meantime, had been defeated. But now Senator Jesse Helms of North Carolina attacked the idea and I lost it in the Senate, even losing two votes I expected to get on the Democratic side. Some day I hope it will happen, reminding all of us of an important part of our heritage.

The unhealthy and huge growth of legalized gambling in the nation concerned me, both because it always brings corruption with it, and because many become addicted. It is the only addiction promoted by the state and federal governments. My background made me interested and concerned. Then in my mother's Lutheran church in Collinsville, Illinois, a substitute teacher at its parochial school, unknown to her family, visited the gambling boat casino in East St. Louis and became an addict. Money the family thought went for rent and paying bills went to gambling. One day the family came home and found a note that the mother could be found in the parking lot at the shopping mall. She had committed suicide. Suicide is more common for gambling addicts proportionately than for drug and alcohol addicts. I saw this one incident and the huge growth of the industry, and it all smelled bad to me. I introduced a bill to create a commission to study legalized gambling, and Rep. Frank Wolf of Virginia did the same in the House. Over the objections of the gambling industry we finally passed it, with appointments to be made by the legislative leaders and the president. Asked by the White House whether I wanted to be on the commission, I said that I thought I should not be, that those appointed should be relatively neutral — which I am not — to have the outcome be respected by everyone, but should be people who are fiercely independent and honest, so they could not be bought off. The commission is now working under the leadership of Dr. Kay James and I wish her well, but so many of the appointees have ties to the gambling industry that I am not optimistic that anything constructive will come from my efforts.

In the midst of legislating I also made regular trips to Illinois and held town meetings, literally in every county in the state at least twice and in almost all of the wards and townships in Cook County, more than 600 meetings in all. I did it both for political purposes, obviously exposing my views to many who would never come to a Democratic political rally, and for philosophical reasons. I wanted to make sure that people who are unemployed or facing a huge hospital bill had access to their senator, and not simply the big contributors or those who could afford a trip to Washington. The reaction to the meetings is typified by an editorial in strongly Republican Macomb, where the *Daily Journal* observed: "For a senator to come in just to talk and to listen is a rare thing, and rather pleasing."[4] I continued the practice of holding town meetings after I announced I would not run again, in part because it helped me as a senator to hear the concerns of people, and partly because I thought if I continued the practice it might diminish a little the cynicism so many have toward government and public officials.

[1] "Senators at Odds Over Chief," *Bloomington Pantagraph*, SIU Archives.

[2] Anthony Man, "The Senate Track," *Southern Illinoisan*, SIU Archives.

[3] Editorial, *Chicago Tribune*, 11 July 1986.

[4] "Simon's Visit," editorial, 22 April 1985.

Chapter 11

# The U. S. Senate-
# Part Two

Have I made mistakes in my Senate votes? You bet!

I voted for airline deregulation, in large part because of my confidence in the man who pushed it, Alfred Kahn, a former Cornell professor who headed the anti-inflation efforts of President Carter. Two of the assumptions of airline deregulation were that it would lead to a growth in the number of carriers and to better service for smaller communities. The third assumption, that it would reduce fares, has been partially realized, but as we move ultimately to two or three major carriers, and as they get near-monopolies in various cities, ticket prices inevitably will go up. Trans World Airlines, for example, has the only service between St. Louis and Washington National airport. Almost any day I can fly round-trip from Washington to London or Paris or Frankfurt for less money than from Washington to St. Louis. It makes no sense. And communities like Carbondale, Illinois, with its large university, now has no commuter service when we formerly had good service. Some deregulation probably would have been fine, but what I supported went too far.

When Justice William Rehnquist received the nomination for Chief Justice of the Supreme Court, as Warren Burger stepped down, I voted against him because of my philosophical differences with him. If he were just coming on the Court, that would have been a justifiable vote. But voting against him for Chief Justice changed no votes on the Court, and my friends tell me he has been a fine administrator as Chief Justice. I should have voted for him.

On nominations to the district and appellate courts, I properly did not take into consideration the political philosophies of the nominees, on the correct assumption that the Supreme Court sends the constitutional directions. If someone was extreme in philosophy I would have voted against that person, but generally I looked for competence, though occasionally we had nominees before us and I would say to myself, "I hope nothing too complicated comes before this judge." I did start a policy — now adopted by the full Judiciary Committee — of stopping judges who belonged to country clubs or other groups that discriminate, unless they resigned from the organizations. When Clarence Thomas appeared before us for chairmanship of the Equal Employment Opportunities Commission, I cast one of two votes against him, because I sensed from our questioning that he really didn't believe in the mission of the EEOC. When the President nominated him for the appellate court, I voted for him but the *St. Louis Post-Dispatch* quoted me, "If he were up for nomination to the Supreme Court, I probably would vote against him."[1] Which I eventually did.

Considering the political philosophy of a Supreme Court nominee who will have a huge say in the future course of the nation is not only permissible, it is essential, both for the President who nominates the person, and for the senators who vote to confirm or not to confirm the nominee. Few votes we cast have as long-lasting an effect on the nation as approving or disapproving Supreme Court nominees.

Sometimes it is "voting in the dark." Those who voted for Justice Harry Blackmun, the nominee of Richard Nixon, did not expect him to become one of the two most liberal justices on the Supreme Court. I voted for Supreme Court nominees when after questioning I still had only a slim idea of their philosophical moorings. While I would prefer nominees who reflect my political outlook, what I wanted more than anything were justices who would have an open mind, who would not be rigid. If, on top of that, they showed compassion for those who struggle in our society, that made it even better. Most nominees to the Supreme Court I did not know or just barely knew, Justice Stephen Breyer being an exception, having known him since my days of lecturing at Harvard. When Justice David Souter came before us, he presented largely a blank slate. He had written almost nothing, and his answers to our questions were understandably cautious, but not revealing. I remember Ted Kennedy, Howard Metzenbaum, and I having a conversation about whether or not to vote for Souter. None of the three of us felt solid about how we would vote. Howard and I eventually voted for him, Ted voted against him. Justice Souter turned out to be an excellent member of the Court. But our vote was a gamble.

I voted for Justice Anthony Scalia, a likable and capable person, but he is much more rigid with his far right ideology than I expected. I called my longtime friend who sat on the appellate court with him, Justice Abner Mikva, and Ab told me that Scalia "is probably about as good as you're going to get from this administration." If I were voting again, I would vote against him.

The first big battle for a Supreme Court nomination involved Appellate Court Justice Robert Bork. He had powerful witnesses supporting his nomination, including Chief Justice Warren Burger, President Carter's Attorney General Griffin Bell, and the former White House counsel to President Carter, Lloyd Cutler. But former President Carter opposed him, writing that his presence on the Supreme Court would "have a deleterious effect on future decisions involving personal freedom, justice for the deprived, and basic human rights."[2] Historian John Hope Franklin testified, "There is no indication in his writings, his teachings, or his rulings that this nominee has any deeply held commitment to the eradication of the problem of race or even its mitigation. One searches his record in vain to find a civil rights advance that he supported from its inception."[3]

Some have portrayed the Bork hearings as an example of liberal organizations flooding members of the Senate with mail against Bork. The reality is that we had plenty of mail from both the right and the left. While my inclination, because of his record, was to be against him I had not firmly decided. Bork persuaded me not to vote for Bork.

The American Bar Association's Model Rules of Professional Conduct include the admonition: "A lawyer should render public interest legal service." When Senator Patrick Leahy of Vermont asked him if he had done this (generally known as *pro bono* work) he replied he had not. I then asked:

> I was a little surprised to hear your response to Senator Leahy on pro bono work. One of the things that is important for a Justice on the Court . . . to have is some understanding of those less fortunate in our society. Are there other things that you have done with the less fortunate in your sixty years . . . helping or volunteering to work with the retarded or whatever it may be?

> Bork responded, "No, Senator, I can't claim a record of that sort."[4]

He criticized the Griswold decision of the Supreme Court, which on the basis of the right of privacy, using the Ninth Amendment, set aside Connecticut's ban on the use of contraceptives in that state. James Madison added the Ninth Amendment to the Bill of Rights when, after circulating a draft Bill of Rights, Alexander Hamilton wrote that the courts might ultimately rule that the rights spelled out are the only rights people have. So these words became the Ninth Amendment: "The enumeration of certain rights shall not be construed to deny or disparage others retained by the people." That is the basis for the Supreme Court's recognizing a right of privacy, but for Bork that was not high on his list of constitutional amendments, even suggesting that when they inserted the language that it meant that other rights are reserved to the states rather than as the amendment declares that other rights are "retained by the people."

He also held to a strange mathematical equation on rights. My belief is that when slavery is stopped, that helps the rights of all of us, that when segregation in the south ended, in some immeasurable way that helped me. Bork and I had this exchange:

> Simon: At a speech at Berkeley in 1985, you say, "When a court adds to one person's constitutional rights it subtracts from the rights of other." Do you believe that is always true?

> Bork: Yes, Senator. I think it's a matter of plain arithmetic. . . .

> Simon: I have long thought it is kind of fundamental in our society that when you expand the liberty of any of us you expand the liberty of all of us.

> Bork: I think, Senator, that is not correct.[5]

When the President nominated him, the *CBS-New York Times* poll showed 14 percent for him, 13 percent opposed, and 63 percent undecided. After the televised hearings, the polls showed 32 percent for him, 52 percent opposed. Ronald Reagan's chief of staff, former Senator Howard Baker, summed it up: "Bork was brilliant, but he turned off the committee." What some will not acknowledge is the simple reality: Bork defeated Bork. The Senate voted against confirmation 58-42, the largest vote against any Supreme Court nominee in our history.

President George Bush never felt comfortable with the religious right. He tried to please them. In one speech he assured them he was "born again," a good scriptural phrase but one that Episcopalians don't ordinarily use. The religious right sensed the cultural gap between Bush and themselves. To help bridge that gap, Bush told them on many occasions that before he made Supreme Court nominations he would consult with them. On June 27, 1991, Justice Thurgood Marshall, plagued by bad health, resigned from the Court. Four days later Bush announced that Clarence Thomas would be the nominee, that race had nothing to do with the selection, and that Thomas was the best person in the nation for the seat. If you were to ask 100 lawyers to name the top twenty attorneys in the nation who should be considered for the Court, it is doubtful that Thomas would have been on anyone's list. But the President nominated him.

When Thomas visited in my office I told him I would be concerned about civil liberties and civil rights and his willingness to do the unpopular if the situation demanded it. I also said that I "have observed two trends among those who have been markedly successful after an early struggle: Either they remember that past and help those continuing to struggle, or they assume that 'if I can make it, so can they' and turn a cold shoulder to those who still struggle."[6] He assured me he would remember and help.

The civil rights groups unanimously opposed him. In his testimony he backed away from many of his views enunciated in speeches and articles. "I don't have an ideology to take to the Court," he assured us.[7] A student in law school when the Supreme Court handed down Roe v. Wade, the abortion decision, he said he could not remember discussing it then or since. It simply was not a credible answer, as were several other of his answers. After Thomas responded to a question posed by former Senator Howell Heflin of Alabama, Heflin, who sat next to me, turned to me and whispered, "He's lying." The committee voted 7-7 on the question of approving him, and then the motion to send his name to the floor without a recommendation carried 13-1. I cast the negative vote, believing that if we found him inadequate in committee we should not send the nomination to the Senate floor.

Two days before the Committee voted on the nomination, Ted Kennedy told me that Joe Biden had a statement from a woman alleging sexual harassment by Thomas. The next day Biden related that he had the affidavit but the woman wanted it kept confidential so he felt he could not use it. I agreed. But I told Susan Kaplan, who headed my Judiciary Committee staff, and John Trasvina and Jayne Jerkins, also lawyers on my staff, about the allegation in case anything further developed, but that they should keep it strictly confidential. Within hours I had a phone message that Anita Hill, a law professor at the University of Oklahoma, wanted to talk to me about the Thomas nomination. Susan Kaplan told me that she had authored the affidavit. With the idea that I would find out if she was "off the wall" or a substantial person, I talked to her. She asked if I had seen her affidavit. I told her I had not. She said she would like to have it circulated to all 100 senators, but wanted it kept confidential. I responded that would be impossible, she might as well give it to one of the wire services. I added that she had to make a difficult decision, whether to go public or not, and that it would so change her life that I would not make a recommendation one way or another. She had to make that choice. The rest of the story is history. I became the first senator to say we should postpone the vote and listen to Anita Hill, but within twenty-four hours several others joined me. She testified, and told the story that mesmerized the nation, though those of us on the committee did not realize for a period the immensity of the television audience. Thomas denied the charge, calling it a lynching of his reputation.

In retrospect, we could have handled it better. We should have heard an expert on sexual harassment and looked carefully for other witnesses. Another employee of Thomas had a similar experience, with a corroborating witness, and had told others of it. We should have heard her.

The nation had a graphic lesson in sexual harassment. We will never be the same, thanks to the courage of Anita Hill. What we did not know is that millions of American women who had similar experiences instinctively knew that Anita Hill told the truth. Many tried to call us. We kept both my Chicago and Washington offices open to receive as many calls as possible. Illinois Bell, now Ameritech, keeps track of phone calls attempted as well as the numbers that get through. In the Chicago offices of Senator Alan Dixon and myself, 58,780 people tried to get through but could not. That exceeded anything we ever had experienced. More people watched the hearings that Sunday than watched the National Football League games, and Sunday night the ratings in many large cities dwarfed the ratings for the CBS broadcast of the National League play-off game between the Atlanta Braves and the Pittsburgh Pirates.

In retrospect, it is clear to me that Anita Hill told the truth. If she were making up stories, she would have told a better one, that he physically fondled her, for example. She voluntarily took a lie detector test and passed it. Two *Wall Street Journal* reporters later wrote a book in which they found twenty people who would have either supported Hill's story or contradicted Thomas's.[8] When asked about

Hill's testimony in the Senate hearing, Thomas said he did not watch it. Trial lawyers say that in a criminal trial, if the defendant does not listen to the witnesses describing the offense, ordinarily that is an indication of guilt. Federal trial judges polled by the *National Law Journal* overwhelmingly believed Hill.

Does that mean that someone who perjured himself is now on the U. S. Supreme Court? That is probably correct. Do I favor impeachment? No. While the evidence is strong, absolute proof is missing, and without that the Senate would not provide a two-thirds majority for impeachment and the proceedings would deeply divide the nation. Thomas saw his dream of serving on the Supreme Court blowing up in his face, and in desperation he lied. I do not defend it, though I understand it. Now all we can hope (from my perspective) is that his record on the Court might improve and that others on the Court will continue to generally outvote the Thomas and Scalia extreme. The Senate approved him 52-48. Of the thirty Senators still in the Senate who voted against the Civil Rights Bill of 1990, all thirty voted for Clarence Thomas. He won, but in a real sense, so did the women of the nation who saw their male counterparts learn a lesson in sexual harassment.

One of Justice Thomas's early decisions on the Court involved a Louisiana prisoner, Keith Hudson. While shackled, two guards beat him after a supervisor told them not to have "too much fun" with him. They broke his dental plate, loosened other teeth, caused facial swelling and other bruises on his body. The question the Court faced: Did this constitute "cruel and unusual punishment" outlawed by the Eighth Amendment? The Court ruled 7-2 that it did. Thomas wrote the dissent for Justice Scalia and himself. The majority said the dissent ignores "the concepts of dignity, civilized standards, humanity and decency that animate the Eighth Amendment." And an editorial in the *New York Times* carried the heading: "The Youngest Cruelest Justice."

But sometimes people change. Justice Hugo Black, a great civil liberterian, once belonged to the Ku Klux Klan. I hope Justice Thomas will change. But I am not optimistic.

One of the lessons both a president and the Senate should learn from the Clarence Thomas nomination fiasco is that we should not rush into decisions. The President should not have nominated someone four days after a vacancy, and the Senate — pushed by the Administration to get Thomas approved before the next Court session — should have acted with greater deliberation. If both the President and the Senate had taken two more weeks it is probable Clarence Thomas would not be on the Supreme Court today.

I decided that if Clinton won the presidency, rather than making arbitrary recommendations to the White House for the district federal bench — the prerogative of the senior senator of the President's party — I would follow a few other senators and name an advisory committee for each of the federal court districts, and ask Senator Carol Moseley-Braun to share in the naming of the committees and in the choices for federal judge. I selected the chairs, Illinois Appellate Court Justice Anthony Scariano for the northern district; a former chairman of the Illinois Commerce Commission and a non-lawyer, Susan Stone, for the central district; and a former law school dean at Washington University in St. Louis and at Southern Illinois University, Hiram Lesar, for the southern district. We tried to name similar quality people to the committees, and they recommended three possibilities for each vacancy, not only for district judgeships but for U. S. Attorney and for federal marshals.

Those named by the committees in many instances I had never met. We urged people to apply, telling them this was not a place for repaying political favors. For the two initial judgeship vacancies in the northern district, for example, we had 138 applicants. The committees took their responsibilities seriously and the net result is a higher caliber of appointments. For all three U. S. Attorney nominees, we designated people of eminent quality, but not those favored by the majority of the political leaders. Independence in that position is particularly important. I am pleased that Carol has carried on with the committee tradition. No system is perfect, but this is an improvement.

Reflecting the increasingly partisan nature of congressional operations, Republicans in the Senate markedly slowed the numbers of judges brought for approval, a practice that has harmed judicial service in the nation. We had two distinguished nominees caught in that partisan bickering, Judge Sue Myerscough in the central district, and Prof. Wenona Whitfield in the southern district. A law school professor, Whitfield would have been the first woman and the first African American in the southern district. She had strong recommendations from a number of people, including the chief judge of the district, Phil Gilbert, a Republican appointee. I took her to meet the Republican members of the Judiciary Committee, and all indicated they would support her but one, and he did not indicate opposition. The chairman of the committee, Senator Orrin Hatch, said he "would do everything he could to help her," but he didn't. The excuse used by his staff was that fourteen years earlier she had been an alcoholic. I checked with research authorities and was assured that anyone who has been dry for five years is highly unlikely to have a recurring problem. Plus Wenona Whitfield pledged to resign if a problem developed. I finally persuaded Orrin to give her a hearing. She, along with four other nominees, testified and she was clearly the outstanding one of the group. That made no difference. I sense that his staff saw a black woman and that spelled "liberal" to them, even though on some issues, like capital punishment, she is more conservative than I am. Orrin, sometimes dominated by his staff, would not bring her up for a vote. He kept telling me he would like to but that Majority Leader Trent Lott would stop the nomination. I went to Trent Lott and explained the situation. He said, "You probably don't know this, but both of my parents were alcoholics. I'll do everything I can to help you if you can get her out of the committee." I went back to Orrin Hatch and once again he said he wanted to assist in the nomination but Trent Lott was the barrier. I then told him of my conversation with Trent Lott, and he blushed and stammered for a moment. He knew that I understood he was the barrier, not Trent. In many ways Orrin Hatch is a good person and leader, but his caving in to his staff despite his pledge disappointed me.

State Judge Myerscough faced a somewhat similar situation, partisan bickering stopping her rather than her ability. Two women who would have been outstanding jurists on the federal bench were denied that possibility for no solid reason, other than petty politics. The more either party plays these type of games, the more we hurt the courts and the more we diminish public confidence in congressional action.


The United States has citizens who are not represented in Congress. They are residents of Washington, D. C. — the only capital city among democracies whose citizens are not represented in their parliament — Puerto Rico, Guam, and other possessions. We should find a way to assure them a voice in the House and Senate and in presidential races. France did not have a reputation for being a wise colonial power, but France did permit people in Algeria and other colonies to be represented in parliament.

I favor statehood for the District of Columbia and cosponsored legislation to permit that, but in the near future that will not happen.

Puerto Rico's claim to statehood is strong — if the people of Puerto Rico vote to have it. Their present status, commonwealth, is a fancy way of describing old-fashioned colonialism.

U. S. corporations based in Puerto Rico like the present status because of the tax breaks that they receive. But sooner or later commonwealth status will fall, and the island will either move to statehood or independence. Statehood makes more sense for them and for our nation, but that decision should be left to the Puerto Ricans. Their average income is one-half of that of Mississippi's residents, and the island will not attract either industry or tourism the way it should unless it becomes a state. Puerto Ricans have contributed more personnel to our armed forces per 100,000 citizens than almost all of our states — yet Puerto Ricans continue to be treated as second-class citizens. I helped Puerto Rico with various amendments when I saw them not being treated fairly, but my casual assistance cannot compare to what two Senators and several House members could do — plus a President who needs their electoral votes. I have worked with Baltasar Corrada, formerly their non-voting House member now on their Supreme Court; Carlos Romero, former governor who is now their non-voting House member; with Governor Pedro Rossello; and with State Senator Ken McClintock, a capable and aggressive young leader. They all favor statehood and I hope it happens.

All American citizens should have a voice in our government. We need a constitutional amendment that states that all citizens should have the right to vote for members of the House and the Senate and for the president, and that Congress shall assign their votes to a state if the territory in which they live is not a state. Then the votes of the District of Columbia could be assigned to Maryland or Virginia, Guam could be assigned to Hawaii, and Puerto Rico would become a state, become independent, or be assigned to Florida. But statehood for Puerto Rico makes sense.

For those who object because Puerto Ricans speak Spanish, there is no higher a percentage who speak Spanish on that island than spoke Spanish in New Mexico when that state came into the union. I have not heard anyone suggest that New Mexico is not an asset to our country.

As in all my public offices, I worked hard in the Senate on education. In addition to the Literacy Act, already mentioned, and being chief sponsor of the School to Work measure that encourages cooperation between schools and the workplace, I also headed the successful effort for a major revision and improvement of the Job Training Partnership Act, the type of action that receives little attention but is important to hundreds of thousands of people who need help. I sponsored other measures that have had an impact. But not all of the proposals passed or were implemented. I sponsored an amendment to pay added federal assistance to public schools that move from 180 days a school year to 210. My amendment became law but the funding of it never passed. In Singapore, students in high school and grade school attend 280 days a year, in Japan 243, in Germany 240 — the list goes on. In the United States we go between 175 and 180. Can we learn as much in 180 days as students in Germany do in 240? Obviously not. Why do we only attend 180 days? In theory so that our children can harvest the crops. That was another era! If we increased this to 210 days, by the time a student finished the twelfth grade, he or she would have the equivalent of two additional years of school. But the sound idea, now imbedded in the law, needs to be funded.

Another good proposal that did not come close to passing was to increase the oil import fee $5 per barrel and to use the money to make grants to students in higher education. We have gradually shifted student assistance from three-fourths grants and one-fourth loans to the exact opposite. The $5 a barrel fee would almost double the money available for student aid, and would have been welcomed by conservationists to encourage use of gas-saving cars to reduce carbon dioxide emission. My friends in the oil industry did not like the idea! They prevailed.

President Bush called a summit meeting on education with governors, which I applauded, but I suggested that he should also have a summit meeting on education with key members of Congress where he could have a more direct impact. That didn't happen.

Achieving bipartisan effort is important in education or any area. In an article by Jamie Stiehm, *The Hill* reported: "Throughout a two-day bitterly fought budget battle . . . bipartisanship was more the exception than the rule. Yet one amendment co-authored by Senators Olympia Snowe (R-Maine) and Paul Simon (D-Illinois) won Senate approval."[9] I drafted an amendment to add $9.4 billion to education, paying for it by closing a tax loophole. But I knew that in 1995, with the Republicans controlling the Senate, it would not pass if I were the chief sponsor. I went to Olympia Snowe, who has been strong in support of education, and suggested that she sponsor it and that I co-sponsor. If she could get six Republican votes, I felt I could get all the Democratic votes. It finally carried 67-32.

A major change for colleges, students, and the federal government is the Direct Loan program which I championed. But credit should go to two people particularly: Rep. Tom Petri, a Republican House member from Wisconsin who first suggested the concept, and Bob Shireman of my staff, who liked it and had to persuade me slowly that it really had a chance to pass. He is a superb numbers cruncher. The idea is simple: Cut out the famous middle man. The old loan program — still in existence — has the federal government guaranteeing the loans that the students sign, often without even seeing a banker. We set the rate of profit in the law. All those bankers who hate welfare for poor people love welfare for banks! We set the rate at 3.1 percent above treasury notes into the law.

The system not only guaranteed a profit with no risk, it gave banks no incentive to prevent defaults. One year the chief executive officer of the Student Loan Marketing Association — created by the government to purchase loans from banks — had a salary and benefits of more than $2 million, and his vice president received $1.7 million, all from profits on student loans guaranteed by the U. S. Government. We pay the President of the United States $200,000 a year. Not only banks loved the old system. We have something called Guarantee Agencies scattered around the nation, who reimbursed banks if students defaulted on their loans after getting out of college. We in turn reimbursed the agencies and on top of that, if they were able to collect, we gave them 30 percent [now 27] of the amount collected. These Guarantee Agencies did extremely well! The CEO of the largest agency — a "non-profit" called USA Group — made $619,949 in 1993.[10]

We brought Orlo Austin, in charge of student aid at the University of Illinois in Champaign, to Washington to help develop the bill, working closely with Bob Shireman. I introduced the proposal early in 1991. My chief cosponsor, Senator David Durenberger, a Republican of Minnesota, stood up like a Rock of Gibralter. When bankers told him that the free enterprise system should handle this, Dave responded, "This is not free enterprise. This is a free lunch!" Not long after I introduced it, Governor Bill Clinton, then seeking the Democratic nomination for president, stopped in my office to talk about it. Education is an area he pursued vigorously as governor and where he has been excellent as president also. He understood the basics before he spoke with me. A few nights later he made a speech at Georgetown University endorsing the Simon Loan Plan, the first and last time anyone called it that. After he became president, he continued to support it vigorously, despite great pressure from the banks and the guarantee agencies.

The fight in Congress forced changes that save money for students on their fees and interest payments, $100 million for Illinois students alone in five years. It saves money for the colleges because they reduce paperwork. Instead of dealing with 100 banks, some of whom pay promptly and some of whom don't, they are dealing with one banker, Uncle Sam. And instead of paying out huge sums to the banks and guarantee agencies, the taxpayers get a break. Savings the first five years will be about $4.3 billion. Approximately one-third of the colleges and universities in the nation now use the Direct Loan system. Because of competition — which they claim to like — bankers have made their old program more attractive. That's why some schools are not changing. Another reason is that many colleges and universities have bankers on their boards, and as one university president told me, "We like your idea but I like my job better." Congressman Bill Ford of Michigan and Senator Ted Kennedy played key roles in getting this passed. Under the Direct Loan program, students can pay back through a percentage of their income after graduation, if they wish, rather than a flat fee which causes financial difficulty in many cases.

Because I barely won my 1984 race for the Senate, and because I had taken a series of unpopular stands, I looked like a juicy target to the Republican leadership in my race for reelection. They persuaded Rep. Lynn Martin of Rockford, Illinois, who had been mentioned as a vice presidential possibility with George Bush in 1998, to become the GOP Senate candidate, with assurances she would be strongly backed and receive heavy financial support. Republican National Chairman Lee Atwater said unseating me was their top priority.

Columnist George Will wrote that George McGovern, Birch Bayh, and Frank Church lost senatorial elections after presidential tries. He described Lynn as "the ideal kind of Republican candidate for 1990." He also noted that "just two years ago she learned that she has Polish ancestors — a good career move for anyone seeking votes in Chicago."[11] The only problem with the latter part of Will's statement is that Chicago Poles felt that she knew of her Polish origins all along, and had shunned any identification with the community until the Senate race.

When Poland's first freely elected Prime Minister, Tadeusz Mazowiecki, visited the United States, President Bush had a state dinner for him, but failed to invite the chief sponsor of the bill that got aid to Poland, Paul Simon (See Chapter 19). He did invite Lynn Martin. It made the wire services and helped me. "Simon Snubbed by Bush" headed stories all over the state. They reminded Polish Americans in Illinois that she had "recently discovered" her Polish roots. When the Prime Minister came to Chicago, local leaders of the Polish community had me prominently seated with him. And for the big Polish parade in Chicago I became the first non-Pole to serve as Grand Marshal.

Lynn and I both took what is generally called the moderate stance on abortion, so that issue did not divide us. But I opposed capital punishment, and our polls showed 85 percent of the people of Illinois favored it. I said the federal government should have more revenue to balance the budget, together with sensible cuts in spending; polls showed that was not popular. While I had solid backing from the Jewish community, she had the oil companies and their big dollars with her, with the chairman of her campaign committee the chief executive of Amoco, one of the nation's biggest oil companies. All national early political commentary had me on the endangered list or worse.

Compounding these trials for my campaign staff, I headed the opposition to a constitutional amendment on burning the U. S. flag. Each year we have two to four Americans who protest something by burning a flag. The Supreme Court ruled that is part of free speech. The only way to overturn that Court decision is through a constitutional amendment. And if we had such a constitutional amendment, we would still have *at least* two to four Americans somewhere who would burn flags as a protest. The amendment would do no good, but would trivialize the Constitution. The Constitution should deal only with fundamental problems, and this clearly is not a fundamental problem for the nation. However if you simply poll people without giving the background, they favor the constitutional amendment. Veterans organizations to which I belong strongly favor it. I respect the flag. I served overseas in the Army under it, and if you visit our home in rural southern Illinois you will see a U. S. flag flying. But I agree with an editorial in the *Darien* (Ill.) *Doings*:

> The real desecration of the flag . . . is its use by politicians for self-serving purposes. . . . Maybe a better amendment would read like this: "Congress and the states shall have the power to prohibit the political desecration of the flag of the United States by legislators who use it as a campaign tool."[12]

Making my situation a little more awkward politically, both the Democratic and Republican candidates for governor in Illinois endorsed the amendment, as did my Illinois Senate colleague, Alan Dixon. Lynn Martin observed, "apparently, [Simon] believes that protecting our flag is not worthy of such consideration."[13]

We differed on gun legislation. Her opposition to the Brady bill which called for mild limitations on handguns pleased the National Rifle Association zealots, but not most people — if I could get the message across. Helping me, Jim Brady, a long-time friend and former press secretary to President Reagan, publicly endorsed me.

I met with Molly Yard, president of the National Organization of Women, hoping to get their support. After pointing out various areas where my votes on women's issues were much stronger than Lynn's, Molly said, "We can't be for you. You're a man." That was hard to deny. Softening that, however, the Illinois chapter of NOW endorsed me, much to the furor of the national organization. And Anne Roosevelt, my campaign manager, handled herself well as my spokesperson on issues.

We are still a sexist society in many ways, and my attacking Lynn would not look good, and if she took out after me too much we sensed that she would look shrill. We decided to aim our barbs at her campaign media person, Roger Ailes, who had been responsible for the George Bush negative commercials in Bush's successful 1988 presidential campaign. Whenever Lynn went off on the deep end, we attacked Roger Ailes. He then exploded at a press conference in Chicago, calling me "a weenie," "Paul Slimeman," and a few other things, much to our delight. Asked about his diatribe, I said, "I don't remember being called names like that since I was at a county fair and ran into a fellow who had a little too much to drink."[14]

"Chamber Turns Thumbs Down to Simon" read the heading of one story about a Chamber of Commerce rating, but balancing that columnist Vernon Jarrett of the *Chicago Sun-Times* noted a letter from Chris Edley, head of the United Negro College Fund: "Among our many, many friends in Congress, Paul Simon stands out as the one who has done more for black colleges than any other member of Congress."[15] Things seemed to be turning my way. Jack Germond and Jules Witcover noted in a column about our race: "What once was seen as one of the best Republican shots at winning a Democratic Senate seat . . . Martin now heads against Simon facing an uphill battle."[16]

In the middle of the campaign my first grandchild arrived, Reilly Marie Knop, not planned for campaign purposes but a thrill for

Jeanne and me, and it did no harm in the campaign, receiving statewide attention.

Another non-issue that generated attention was Lynn's reference to people in the southern part of the state as "rednecks." She tried to clarify that she meant it as a compliment, but no one found that believable.

In February the Associated Press reported: "Special interest groups gave more money to Rep. Lynn Martin than to Sen. Paul Simon in the last six months of 1989, but the Democratic incumbent is still sitting on a higher hill of campaign cash."[17] I ended up getting more money than she did, in part because many groups donated to me toward the end of the campaign, when the polls showed me winning, or because groups, like the American Dental Association, said they had given to her but if I won they would give to me after the election. I took their money, but the system is terrible (See Chapter 17).

The only significant bump on the road came with the *Chicago Sun-Times* publishing a story emblazoned on its front pages about pressure I allegedly used to help a campaign contributor.

Housing developer Stephen Ballis, whose wife contributed $1,300 to my Senate campaign, served on the Chicago School Board and made a favorable impression on me, though we barely knew each other. He called one day saying that maybe I could help him. Pathway Financial, a savings and loan in Chicago, contacted Ballis and suggested that if he would develop a condominium complex they would finance it for him. Ballis agreed to do it but as the project neared completion the savings and loan — like many others — folded and Ballis did not have the money to complete the project. He temporarily was in arrears on his payments because construction could not continue as he had originally anticipated, and therefore his income did not start as soon as expected. In the meantime, the savings and loan sold its assets and liabilities to First Nationwide Financial Corporation of San Francisco. Someone in San Francisco looked at the books, saw Ballis in arrears and, instead of calling to learn about the situation, filed a lawsuit. Ballis called me and said he wanted to talk to someone at First Nationwide to explain the situation but couldn't get past the receptionist. Ballis thought it could be straightened out fairly simply without a lawsuit. I called the chief executive officer of First Nationwide and told him that I knew only what Ballis told me, but there appeared to be at least the possibility they could work things out without a lawsuit. I told him I would appreciate it if he would talk to Ballis. They did talk and worked it out to the benefit of everyone. No lawsuit. No big fees for lawyers, which may have caused my difficulty. Not a penny of loss for the taxpayers. And I helped a constituent.

The *Chicago Sun-Times* got the story and had big front-page headlines "Simon takes S & L Heat Off Developer."[18] Then Lynn Martin asked for a Senate ethics investigation of my action, and that produced headlines in the *Sun-Times* again the next day, "Senate Quiz of Simon Urged."[19] But most newspapers and media outlets did not run the story or play it up. The Associated Press carried an article, including my response, but a balanced story. The *Peoria Journal-Star*, the only newspaper to editorialize on it outside of the critical *Sun-Times* editorial called it "no big deal" and added, "Lynn Martin is creating a campaign mountain where even the molehill is small."[20] But what took real courage, *Chicago Sun-Times* columnist Carol Ashkinaze wrote that I had done the right thing, and by implication that the newspaper was wrong. Not too long after that she left the *Sun-Times*.

Not surprisingly, Lynn Martin had a television commercial charging, "Paul Simon called a savings and loan president to fix a $5 million bad debt for one of his contributors." She charged that "the Keating Five has become the Keating Six," referring to serious problems between an Arizona developer and five senators. Carol Ashkinaze wrote a column, "Dragon Lady in Gutter," referring to my opponent.[21] The irony, as Carol Ashkinaze pointed out in her column, was that despite all the pressure from the savings and loan industry to deregulate, I thought it unwise and cast one of thirteen votes in the House against deregulation, while Lynn Martin voted for it. Had my vote prevailed, it would have saved the federal government more than a hundred *billion* dollars.

Otherwise things went well for me, unbelievably well. I won by almost one million votes, 65 percent, the largest victory of any seriously contested Republican or Democratic candidate for either senator or governor in the nation. I carried 100 of the 102 counties in the state. Republicans as well as Democrats obviously had been good to me.

After her defeat, President Bush nominated Lynn Martin to be Secretary of Labor. I supported her, making a few of my followers unhappy. I felt she had the ability to serve well, even though we had philosophical differences.

I had a good relationship with my colleagues in the Senate of both political parties. I first worked with my senior senator, Alan Dixon, as a state legislator and he had invested in some of my small newspapers. In the period when far too many state legislators took bribes, he played it straight. We worked together well. He worked well enough with his other colleagues to be named Chief Deputy Whip. His vote for Clarence Thomas for the Supreme Court appeared to be the popular vote at the time, but women in the state reacted negatively, and strongly. He suddenly faced a primary against Al Hofeld, a wealthy attorney, and Carol Moseley-Braun, the Cook County Recorder of Deeds, an African American. I endorsed Dixon. It looked as if Dixon would win until the end of the campaign. Dixon had the advantage — and disadvantage — compared to me of having fewer people enthusiastically for him, but also fewer people enthusiastically against him. A poll in April 1990, for example, found 25 percent rated my record excellent, compared to 6 percent for Dixon, while 12 percent found my record poor and only 8 percent rated him as poor.[22] But in a primary where he needed enthusiastic backers that turned out to be a problem. Hofeld's attacks on Dixon did not help Hofeld, but they hurt Dixon, and Carol had the base of African Americans, plus women — particularly suburban women — plus Democrats unhappy with Dixon's Thomas vote. That combination provided her with the needed votes in the primary and she won the general election comfortably.

My voting record came closer to Carol's than Alan's. She has been an effective member of the Senate, but she complicated her political life and her personal life by falling in love with the wrong person — easy for someone else to say. She has a strong record in the Senate, where her colleagues elected her to the Finance Committee when members more senior also sought the post, but she has political problems in her base of Illinois. As I write this she is in a close contest for reelection against an opponent who spent approximately $7 million in a primary. Polls show her ahead. I hope she makes it. If judged on her performance in the Senate, she will.

Senators who showed great skill include Senator Jesse Helms, with whom I disagreed frequently but whom I respect, and Ted Kennedy, who is the best legislator in the Senate. Jesse's office, next to mine, gave me a chance to see him in action with his North Carolina constituents. Whether they agreed with him or not, he was always gracious. And he followed his convictions. Fortunately a majority of the Senate had differing views on many things, but none of us felt he acted to try to win a popularity contest. Ted Kennedy's genuine commitment to helping those who struggle in our society resulted in many victories, both helping people who need help and stopping harm from being done. Courage is an essential ingredient for effectiveness, and Ted and Jesse both show courage in abundance. Senator Paul Douglas, who served in the Senate with John and Robert and Ted Kennedy told me several times that Ted was the best legislator of the three, though he respected all of them. If I were to name one outstanding legislator during my twenty-two years on Capitol Hill, it would be Ted Kennedy.

Some come into the Senate with no legislative background, and it is difficult for a period. Senator Herb Kohl of Wisconsin fit that mold. An extremely successful businessman, I sensed that in the first six months he wondered to himself why he had ever run for the Senate. But then he gradually became more comfortable, and more effective.

My closest friend during my Senate years, Senator Howard Metzenbaum, had the courage factor in abundance, plus a bulldog tenacity. Howard, like Ted Kennedy, is a man of wealth who kept his focus on those less fortunate. He probably stopped more bad legislation than any member of the Senate during his years there. He and his staff faithfully combed pending legislation, and did a better job of catching little "goodies" placed in proposals for special interest groups than any of the rest of us.

An outstanding Senator I worked with while in the House, but did not serve with in the Senate, Jacob Javits of New York, frequently rankled his Republican colleagues with some of his progressive stands, but everyone respected him, and his diligence.

When George Mitchell of Maine declared his candidacy for the Democratic leadership, I immediately endorsed him. He often showed understandable impatience with some of us, but he worked hard at his leadership role with great skill. It is generally believed that Bill Clinton offered him a seat on the U. S. Supreme Court and Mitchell declined the offer. After Mitchell stepped down from the Senate, he came close to being named Baseball Commissioner. Mitchell, an avid baseball fan, would have been superb, but the prolonged negotiations between the players and management diminished his interest and the likelihood of it happening. He eventually found himself negotiating the peace agreement in Northern Ireland, a great tribute to him as well as the Irish leaders who supported the final document. But those of us in the Senate with whom he had to negotiate and work prepared him well for the rigid, recalcitrant sides in Northern Ireland. He probably found the Irish negotiations easier.

Senator Robert Byrd, Mitchell's predecessor as Democratic leader, knew the rules of the Senate as no one else did — better on some occasions than the parliamentarian. The son of a coal miner, he had a rugged childhood, worked his way through college and law school, and had a greater sense of the mission of the Senate and loyalty to the institution than anyone. He also has an amazing ability to memorize speeches. Deeply dedicated to projects that help West Virginia, I respected that dedication rather than resented it because economically depressed southern Illinois reminds me of West Virginia. As chairman and later ranking minority member of the Appropriations Committee he wielded that power for West Virginia effectively. His sense of the big picture for the nation also marked him as an above average legislator. And he grew. He voted against the Civil Rights Act of 1964, a popular stand in West Virginia at the time, but one he later regretted. The main complaint of members against him as leader was that he lived for the Senate, and some of the other members wanted to get home evenings and weekends to their families more frequently than the Byrd schedule permitted.

The Democratic leader during my last years in the Senate, Tom Daschle of South Dakota, handled his chores well. In a contest for leadership, Senator James Sasser of Tennessee, one of our best members, at one point challenged Daschle. Earlier I urged Jim to seek the presidency and had he done it I would have endorsed him. But when Jim challenged Tom Daschle, I told him frankly that because Tom Daschle cosponsored the Balanced Budget Amendment and strongly supported it, I felt I should be for Tom. "But I voted with you," Jim Sasser told me. "You can count on me." "I appreciate your saying that, Jim," I responded, "but I know that you have mixed feelings on it. Tom Daschle genuinely believes in it and it is really important to the future of the nation" (See Chapter 20). To my utter amazement, Tom switched 180 degrees on the Balanced Budget Amendment, opposing it after becoming leader. My instinct is that as a new leader he feared Robert Byrd, my main antagonist on this issue. In small ways Tom showed excessive attention to Byrd's wishes during the early part of Daschle's leadership. I made the mistake of not getting a commitment from Daschle. Had I done that, it would probably be part of the Constitution today. But Daschle did not violate his word to me, since he gave me no commitment.

The Republican leaders during my years there, Bob Dole and Trent Lott of Mississippi, did a good job and I respect both of them. Dole's Whip, Senator Alan Simpson of Wyoming, did a particularly effective job in that position but when Bob surprised the Senate by resigning to devote full-time to his presidential pursuits, Trent Lott defeated Alan Simpson by the narrowest of margins, one vote.

Though Bob Dole supportted him and though he showed great ability in pulling coalitions together for legislation, the job of a leader, Alan did not satisfy the hard-right members of his party. His defeat disappointed me. Not only the Republican party but the nation would have been well served by Alan's ascendancy. Having said that, I found Trent a good person to work with during my final months in the Senate, and less ideological than I thought he would be.

I have mentioned the quality of courage as important to a legislator. Among the people who showed that in abundance during my years there were Senator Paul Wellstone of Minnesota — who voted against the popular but misguided welfare "reform" bill when facing reelection, Senator Patty Murray of Washington, Senator Barbara Boxer of California, Senator Robert Kerrey of Nebraska, Senator "Fritz" Hollings of South Carolina, Senator "Pat" Moynihan of New York, and Senator Russ Feingold of Wisconsin on the Democratic side and on the Republican side Senator John McCain of Arizona, Senator Mark Hatfield of Oregon, Senator Robert Stafford and Senator James Jeffords of Vermont, Senator Fred Thompson of Tennessee, Senator Olympia Snowe and Senator Bill Cohen of Maine, Senator Charles Mathias of Maryland, and Senator Nancy Kassenbaum of Kansas. And two mentioned earlier, Ted Kennedy and Jesse Helms.

There are also Senators who are not star performers on the national scene, who simply do a quality job. In that category I would put Democratic Senator Carl Levin of Michigan, former Senator David Pryor of Arkansas, and Republican Senators Jon Kyl of Arizona and Robert Bennett of Utah.


Nearing the point where I had to make a decision about running again, Jeanne and I took off the weekend after the 1994 general election and went to one of our favorite cities, New Orleans. On a yellow legal pad we wrote the pros and cons, and I decided not to run again. Before that weekend we had leaned in that direction but that sealed it. We had basically three reasons for the decision. First, I saw some of my colleagues staying on too long. I could see that in others, but could I see it for myself? Second, when Jeanne and I first came to Washington if some group had a big dinner at which the president or some other celebrity would speak, we eagerly went. During the last years the excitement diminished considerably. Those events may not be about policy-making, but my reluctance was an indication of waning enthusiasm. My colleague Senator Bill Bradley had a statement announcing his departure with a somewhat negative tone, showing that he had soured on his Senate service. I did not feel that way. While there are many deficiencies in the Senate, I enjoyed it; my colleagues were good to me. But the diminished enthusiasm for the peripheral matters like the gala dinners sent a signal to me that leaving would be wise. An effective Senator has to devote long hours and a self-discipline that can only exist with enthusiasm for the work. I did not want to become a half-enthusiastic Senator, doing enough to get by but not serving my nation well. Finally, I raised $8.4 million to run for reelection in 1990 and I did not relish the prospect of doing that again. Newspaper polls showed me more popular than I had ever been. The decision did not rest on the possibility of defeat. We felt the time had come for a change, to refresh ourselves.

At the press conference in which I announced my decision I expressed a strong preference for Congressman Dick Durbin to succeed me. I had confidence he could do a superb job, and he has.

Reaction to my announcement around the nation was generous, from editorials in the *Salt Lake City Tribune* to the *Quad City-Times* of Davenport, Iowa, which headed its editorial, "Simon's Decision a Loss for Nation."[23] The *Capital Times* of Madison, Wisconsin observed: "It will be far easier for Simon, a respected Lincoln scholar, to fill his days than for America to find an adequate replacement for this soft-spoken giant in a bow tie."[24] Newspapers in every corner of the state had generous editorials, including those that rarely agreed with me. The *Belleville News-Democrat*, which always considered me way out in leftfield somewhere, grudgingly said, "He has done much good for Illinois and the nation, and he will be missed. And here's to 1996 and the opportunity to elect a leader more politically in step with the people."[25] Meaning more in step with the *News-Democrat's* thinking.

When a person retires from the Senate, you receive more plaques and honors than you merit — by far — but one tribute I particularly prize. I spoke at a commencement at Chicago State University, which has a Gwendolyn Brooks Center, named for the first black (she prefers that to African American) to win a Pulitzer prize. Her poetry sings and disturbs. For this commencement Gwendolyn Brooks wrote a poem about me and my struggles for the oppressed, and read it at the commencement ceremony. It is one of the few mementoes of my years in public service that hangs on my office wall.

One small thing happened in the Senate during my final days that I appreciate, and shifted the Senate temporarily to a more bipartisan atmosphere. Senator Connie Mack, a Republican of Florida and grandson of the baseball great with the same name, in talking to Senator David Pryor, a Democrat of Arkansas, suggested that the members of the Senate should one day all appear wearing bow ties as a tribute to me. The Arkansas senator said he knew a manufacturer who might donate bow ties for the occasion. I knew nothing of all this. When there is a vote in the Senate, the bells (really buzzers) ring, and we have fifteen minutes to get to the floor. For this vote call my staff suddenly emerged with documents I had to sign, delaying me. I finally escaped to the floor for my vote. On the subway ride to the Senate floor I encountered Senator Jesse Helms, wearing a bow tie. "Jesse, you're unusually well dressed today," I told him. He laughed and said it was the first time in his life he had worn a bow tie. I should have guessed something was happening! When I walked onto the floor, the men were wearing blue polka dot bow ties, and the women members wore scarves tied in the form of a bow. Jeanne, and my son Martin and my staff, all of whom knew about it in advance, sat in the gallery. Everyone enjoyed the occasion, no one more than I did. Small things in life make a difference.

---

[1] William Freivogel, "Panel OKs Thomas for Judge," *St. Louis Post-Dispatch*, 23 February 1990.

[2] Jimmy Carter to Senator Joseph Biden, 29 September 1987.

[3] *Nomination of Robert H. Bork to Be Associate Justice*, Hearings, Senate Judiciary Committee (Washington: Government Printing Office, 1989), Part 2, 2121.

[4] Ibid, Part 1, 438.

[5] *Nomination of Robert H. Bork*, Report of the Senate Judiciary Committee (Washington: Government Printing Office, 1987), 11.

[6] Paul Simon, *Advice and Consent* (Washington: National Press Books, 1992), 80-81.

[7] "Clarence Thomas Hearings," Senate Judiciary Committee, 11 September 1991, 8.

[8] Jane Mayer and Jill Abrahamson, *Strange Justice: The Selling of Clarence Thomas* (New York: Houghton Mifflin Co., 1994).

[9] Article, Jamie Stiehm, *The Hill*, date uncertain.

[10] For much more detail read Steve Waldman's book.

[11] George Will, "Simon or Martin," *Peoria Journal-Star*, SIU Archives.

[12] "Amendment is Rejected: Let the U. S. Flag Issue Die," 29 June 1990.

[13] "Simon Won't Support An Amendment on Flag," *St. Louis Post-Dispatch*, 14 June 1990.

[14] Leon Daniel, "'Weenie' Word Cheap Shot," *Kankakee Daily Journal*, 14 October 1990.

[15] Vernon Jarrett, "Simon Is On Correct Side of Key Issues," *Chicago Sun-Times*, 30 August 1990.

[16] "How to Buck the Bow Tie," *Southtown Economist*, 13 August 1990.

[17] "Martin Gains on Simon in Money," *Peoria Journal-Star*, 3 February 1990.

[18] 24 August 1990.

[19] 25 August 1990.

[20] Editorial, 30 August 1990.

[21] *Chicago Sun-Times*, 30 September 1990.

[22] "Simon Hot, Thompson Not," *Danville Commercial-News*, 1 May 1990.

[23] 16 November 1994.

[24] Editorial, *Capital Times*, 16 November 1994.

[25] Editorial, *Belleville News-Democrat*, 16 November 1994.

# Chapter 12

# *Presidential Candidate*

What combination of circumstances causes someone to announce for a presidential nomination? That differs with each candidate, but one factor is a level of self-confidence that is well above average, some would say excessive. Each person's path to this campaign trail differs.

As a House member, when lists of presidential possibles surfaced, on rare occasions my name would be included. It received slight visibility when Paul O'Dwyer, former president of the New York City Council and highly regarded in that state's political scene, mentioned me as a possibility. But ordinarily if people considered twenty possibilities, my name would not be on the list. If you stretched to a larger list, it might be.

Early in 1985, shortly after my election to the Senate, Congressman William Lehman of Florida, in an interview with CNN, responded to a question about who should be the Democratic presidential nominee by suggesting my name. A few isolated things followed, but my name was not on the minds or lips of many Democratic leaders. While every person elected to the Senate or as a Governor has flickers of presidential ideas now and then, such a race did not occupy my thoughts or conversations, at home or anywhere.

On June 30, 1986, fifteen respected members of the House wrote me a letter urging that I consider a run for the presidency. They were from nine states.[1] This caused a small ripple, but not much more than that. Then nationally syndicated columnist Richard Reeves wrote that the best candidate for President is not running: Paul Simon. That stirred more speculation, and calls from people like the California State Democratic chair urging me to become a candidate. Though I

209

had more years in government than those already actively seeking the nomination, I was new in the Senate, and enjoying my service there. About this time I had a conversation with Senator Dale Bumpers of Arkansas, whose ability and courage I respect. He indicated he would probably become a candidate. To end the speculation about my candidacy, in February I held a press conference and announced my support for Dale Bumpers.

Four weeks later, on March 20, after a knee operation, Dale said he would not become a candidate. Our Washington apartment phone rang until 1:30 that morning. Congressman Berkley Bedell, who had just retired as a House member from Iowa, called and said he would devote night and day to supporting me if I would become a candidate. A long-time friend, Bernard Rapoport of Texas, an insurance executive, phoned and said he would raise money. The nationally recognized pollster Lou Harris — who does not do surveys for candidates — called and said he had just done a poll of 1,638 Democrats as to who they would like to see as the nominee. Gary Hart came in first, Mario Cuomo second, Bill Bradley third, and far down at 3 percent each were Senators Sam Nunn and Paul Simon. "But," he added, "two things are of real significance. First, we have never polled where a front-runner has as many negatives as Gary Hart. He will not be your nominee. Second, while your numbers are small, there is a surprising amount of in-depth support. I believe you have a good chance to become the Democratic nominee and the next president."

Advice — pro and con — descended on us. We discussed it with our children, Sheila and Martin, and sought guidance from a few respected friends. Then Jeanne and I had an opportunity for a weekend in Florida to talk it over. Both of us immodestly felt that I could do a better job as president than any of the others in the field, but we also knew of the great drawbacks, the loss of privacy, and also the haunting thought that we might get little support and just embarrass ourselves and our friends. The decisive moment came when Jeanne turned to me and said simply, "Go for it."

Those already in the field at that point, officially or unofficially, who had been campaigning for some time were former Senator Gary Hart, Rev. Jesse Jackson, Senator Albert Gore Jr., Massachusetts Governor Michael Dukakis, Senator Joseph Biden, former Arizona Governor Bruce Babbitt, and Rep. Richard Gephardt. We heard reports that Arkansas Governor Bill Clinton might enter the race but they were met with general disbelief because of rumors that he had "women problems."

Once Jeanne and I had made the decision, we wanted to get the word out quickly. On April 9, 1987, I made the traditional pre-announcement that I would formally announce later. The press responded with less than rapturous enthusiasm. The *Baltimore Sun* editorialized, "His candidacy seems forlorn."[2] *Chicago Tribune* political writer Jon Margolis wrote: "Most people probably will have these two reactions: Laughter and wonder about what Simon is smoking."[3] The first *Des Moines Register* poll showed me seventh in a field of eight. Gary Hart had 67 percent and I had 1 percent!

In my formal announcement I tried to distinguish myself from Gary Hart who called himself a neo-Democrat and others who appeared to be courting the well-to-do Republican constituency who can contribute heavily:

> I seek the presidency not because I want to live in a large white house or because I want to hear the band playing "Hail to the Chief" or I want to hear the applause of the crowds. I seek the presidency because of the force for good that office can become.

> I seek the presidency because I know we can build a better tomorrow for the nation and for our world and I understand how to get there. I seek the presidency because this nation needs to dream once again, act once again, believe once again, care once again. . . .

> The tradition of fighting for decent jobs for all Americans and long-term care for seniors, the tradition of leveling with the American people and having pay-as-you-go government, the concern for quality education for everyone, the tradition of standing up for human rights — these are the traditions I embrace, not just with this speech, but with my whole heart. Those who tell us to abandon these traditions are telling us to abandon our soul and our chance of winning. I'm pleased there is a Republican Party, but one Republican Party is enough.

> You can't win an election by standing for nothing. Harry Truman said it best: "Give the American people a choice between a Republican and a Republican, and they'll choose the Republican every time" . . .

> You and I are on this planet but a short time. Let us seize this time and opportunity to build a better tomorrow so that generations to come will look back upon us and say, "These were people of uncommon compassion and vision and courage."

Shortly after I became a candidate, the Secret Service offered protection, and at first my inclination was to decline the offer, at least until things became more chaotic at the end of the campaign. Then, in one week we received two threats, and I reversed course. I came away from the campaign most favorably impressed by the Secret Service. They are real professionals who handle their job seriously and effectively. One of my vivid memories is being in a parade in South Dakota after a threat and "the Secrets" — as my children called them — suggested I wear a bullet-proof coat, the heaviest coat I have ever worn, by far!

Gradually — very gradually — the perception that I had no chance to win changed. When a story about Gary Hart's private life garnered national headlines he withdrew. A June 4 *ABC News-Washington Post* national poll, after Hart's withdrawal, showed Jesse Jackson first at 25 percent; I ran second with 13 percent, followed by Dukakis at 11 percent. But national polls had limited meaning.

Debates became part of the routine, the first one in Houston with William Buckley and Robert Strauss as hosts, nationally televised. I participated in more than twenty debates, a few with all the candidates, more with only two or three. A two-hour NBC debate had all the candidates — Republicans and Democrats — participating. In some debates I did well, others less well. Scoring well in debates early in the campaign was easier than later, because early expectations were so low for me. When I surprised people by holding my own with the better known candidates, that helped. When I became more of a favorite, people expected me to win resoundingly and in most debates no one really triumphs. In theory, the staff scheduled time for me to relax and concentrate on debate preparation, but the theory too often did not materialize because of other priorities that emerged.

As expectations for me rose, so did media attention, and that helped raise expectations further. When I first traveled to Iowa we felt fortunate if we had a reporter or two covering anything I did or said, but that gradually changed.

The first two state contests, Iowa and New Hampshire, have a huge impact. A Peter Hart poll showed me running stronger against George Bush than the other announced candidates. That and other national factors started to have an influence in Iowa. Former House Speaker Carl Albert of Oklahoma endorsed me. Early in November the *New York Times* ran this story:

> Governor Mario Cuomo, who had for months hinted at a preference for Gov. Michael Dukakis as the Democratic Presidential

nominee, indicated today that he might not endorse Mr. Dukakis and expressed strong interest in Senator Paul Simon of Illinois.

"He looks strong," the Governor said of Mr. Simon.

Mr. Cuomo stopped short of an outright endorsement. "I'm not saying I'm committed," he said. But a few seconds later he added, "I feel great empathy with him."[4]

Heading my efforts in New York, Rep. Stephen Solarz and Jeremy Karpatikin, could take much of the credit for my strength there. And around the nation the mood had changed. The *Los Angeles Weekly* analyzed the candidates' policies and "ability to carry out those policies if elected" and rated me highest.[5] Former President Jimmy Carter said he would make no endorsement, but added: "The South is wide open now for an approach by a candidate who will tell the truth and who will be quite progressive on social issues, on environmental issues, on human rights, on arms control. . . . Sen. Simon certainly has these characteristics."[6] And adding punch to his words, two members of his family were wearing my campaign buttons. Columnists who had been skeptical now talked about my chances of winning being good. A November 15, 1987 poll by the *Des Moines Register* showed me leading for the first time. I had 24 percent, Dukakis 18 percent, Gephardt 14 percent, Jackson 11 percent, Babbitt 8 percent, and Gore 3 percent. And as I moved in front, the critics increased their sounds, in both Republican and Democratic ranks. George Bush commented: "I wouldn't mind if the Democrats nominated Paul Simon. Next to him, I look like Clint Eastwood."[7] But Senator Bob Dole, one of the Republican aspirants, told Larry King: "I think Senator Paul Simon of Illinois is going to surprise a lot of pundits. I've known Paul a long, long time, and he grows on people. He is a fighter. He is very, very smart. And he is tough."[8]

Winning became enough of a possibility that I started making a small list of people I might appoint to the cabinet. If I won, I wanted to get moving quickly. And the sense that things seemed to be moving my way came in a variety of small ways. The Texas Teachers Association endorsed me. Comedian Mark Russell, who sports bow ties and horn-rimmed glasses, started wearing a button that proclaimed: "I'm Not Paul Simon." He sometimes began his comedy routine walking onto the stage and saying, "I would like to tell you right now, ladies and gentlemen, that I am not Paul Simon. The bow tie is real, the shirt is a clip-on." James "Scotty" Reston, the unanointed dean of political writers in Washington, told fellow reporters that it looked as if I was the "sleeper" in the campaign and would emerge. Godfrey Sperling Jr., who hosts weekly breakfasts and lunches for key reporters, noted in the *Christian Science Monitor*: "A gathering of 40 reporters for this lunch [with Simon] — at a moment when the Gorbachev visit was engulfing Washington and draining desks of their available people — indicated that among the media Simon now is being taken very seriously as a presidential candidate."[9] And Chuck Mannatt, highly respected former head of the Democratic National Committee, came aboard as the honorary chair of my campaign committee.

An early December *Des Moines Register* poll showed:

| | |
|---|---|
| Simon | 35% |
| Dukakis | 14% |
| Gephardt | 11% |
| Jackson | 9% |
| Babbitt | 8% |
| Gore | 0% |

And then the roof fell in. On December 15 Gary Hart reentered the race and immediately took first place in the polls. Fred Barnes wrote in the *New Republic*: "The Hart reentry stopped Simon in his tracks. It had the effect of starting the race all over again."[10] Gary Hart and I obviously appealed to the same people, assuming the polls were accurate. The next *Des Moines Register* poll showed Hart at 33 percent, me at 17 percent, Gephardt and Dukakis each at 14 percent, Jackson at 4 percent, Babbitt at 2 percent, and Gore at 1 percent. But Hart's lead did not last long. In the meantime Gephardt wisely used his House leadership to strengthen himself, bringing in forty House members to campaign for him. I had more volunteers than any candidate, and volunteers who paid their own way to Iowa, but they did not get the media attention that forty House members received. But I have yet to talk to one of our volunteers who did not enjoy the experience and speak of it with pride. Shortly before the caucuses the widely read *Des Moines Register* endorsed Bob Dole for the Republican nomination and me for the Democratic spot. They wrote: "Of the Democratic contenders, we believe Simon has the makings of the best president. . . . What the record shows is a man who has decent instincts and sticks by them. Beyond the record, Simon exudes a simple trustworthiness. . . . Once before in troubled times the nation turned to an unpretentious man from downstate Illinois. The times are not quite as troubled now, and perhaps the man is not as great, but he is good, honest and eager to turn the energies of government toward long-neglected needs. Paul Simon would be the best nominee for the Democratic Party."[11] The last *Des Moines Register* poll showed Gephardt at 25 percent. I followed at 19 percent, the others trailing us.

Iowa does not have a primary, but caucuses, in which individuals stand up and declare their choices, precinct by precinct. I did not carry a majority of the caucuses, but one of the satisfying results came in university and college communities. When I first announced, commentators noted that as the oldest candidate (fifty-nine then) and as one who lacked flashiness and charisma, I would not do well among young people. Precisely the opposite occurred. I carried college and university areas heavily. The *New York Times*/CBS exit poll of Iowa caucus voters showed that among those "with some college and more" I received 29 percent, Dukakis 21 percent, and Gephardt 17 percent. But among those with high school education or less Gephardt carried decisively and won. Before the networks went off the air on caucus night CBS and ABC declared Gephardt the winner, NBC stating it was too close to call. Once the networks went off the air, in many counties they stopped tabulating. When the tabulating stopped, Gephardt had 31 percent, I had 27 percent, Dukakis 22 percent, Jackson 9 percent, Babbitt 6 percent, and Hart and Gore did not score, while 5 percent went uncommitted. The next day Tom Brokaw reported on NBC that Gephardt had won "by less than one-half of one percent." The headline in the *Des Moines Register*: "Gephardt Beats Simon in Squeaker."[12]

But he won.

After the general election which George Bush won, Dukakis's campaign manager told *Newsweek* that they feared my winning in Iowa, believing that I was so well organized in the rest of the nation that I would have been the nominee. But the boost I might have received in Iowa did not happen.

Gephardt's victory did not propel him forward as it ordinarily would have because the big news did not center on Gephardt or Bob Dole's winning on the GOP side, but that Pat Robertson unexpectedly upset George Bush for second place. Dole had 37 percent, Robertson 24 percent, Bush 18 percent, Jack Kemp 11 percent, Pete du Pont 7 percent, and Alexander Haig 1 percent.

Everyone expected Dukakis to carry his neighboring state of New Hampshire. The question was who would run second. Before the Iowa caucuses, the polls showed me running second. After Gephardt's Iowa win, he emerged. The New Hampshire totals: Dukakis 37 percent, Gephardt 20 percent, Simon 17 percent, Jackson 8 percent, Gore 7 percent, Babbitt 5 percent, and Hart 4 percent. Bush revived his candidacy by defeating Dole in New Hampshire.

I had left strict instructions that my campaign should be run in such a way that if we had to drop out at any point there would be no debt. While technically a candidate is not liable for the financial obligations created by his or her campaign committee, you clearly have a moral obligation to pay the bills. On the Thursday before the New Hampshire primary I flew to Washington. The general counsel of the campaign, Leslie Kerman, and the assistant executive director, Barbara Pape, met me at the airport and as we drove in they told me that the campaign had $500,000 in debt and some checks had been written with no funds to cover them.

The news stunned me, and lowered my already sagging morale. I immediately ordered that no more checks be written, and called a long-time friend, Jerry Sinclair, a former bank president who knows politics, and asked him to fly to Washington from Illinois to get hold of things. In the meantime ABC heard that we had $1 million in debt. As it turned out, they knew more than I did. When Jerry Sinclair totaled our debt, it reached $1.3 million. I immediately reduced the staff, and spent valuable time raising money — both for future primaries and for debt. By the time I withdrew, the debt had shrunk to $600,000 and we gradually raised the funds to pay that off, not easy for a losing candidate.

I stumbled along from state to state, doing respectably but not well. Illinois became the key and because of my financial situation I ordered that no money be spent in my home state. Dukakis and Gore invested in substantial television buys in Illinois, believing (with legitimacy) that my campaign appeared to be nearing its end. The front-page banner in the *Chicago Sun-Times*: "Jesse Mobilizes to Whip Simon in Illinois Vote."[13] "Simon Sagging on Eve of Vote in Home State" read the headline in the *Boston Globe*.[14] But when the vote came in I had 42 percent, Jackson 32 percent, Dukakis 16 percent, and Gore 5 percent. The top of the front page in the *Boston Globe* the next morning: "Simon Leads Pack in Illinois."[15] That was the big news around the nation. "Bush, Simon Gain Big Leads in Illinois" headed the news for the *Arizona Republic* of Phoenix.[16] It temporarily revived my flagging campaign. Because of the poor condition of our treasury, we knew we could not effectively campaign in both the next two primary states, Michigan and Wisconsin, so we decided to by-pass Michigan and concentrate on the small population state where our dollars could reach further. If we could win in Wisconsin, then we moved into "Simon states," New York and others where I could run strong. But this all hinged on winning Wisconsin. However, by-passing Michigan made that state a race between Jesse Jackson and Michael Dukakis, with Jesse doing well. Coming into Wisconsin it then looked like a two-person race, and my meager showing in Michigan disheartened my followers. We went through the final days in Wisconsin working hard, but knowing it soon would be over, making campaigning difficult. In Wisconsin I ran fourth; I then suspended my campaign.

I closed my statement to the press with these words:

> I entered this race because I have had the good fortune to understand that vast difference in the lives of millions of people action by government can make. . . . I entered this race because I want this generation to give the coming generations a sound economy, not an uncontrollable debt. I entered this race because I see a nation indifferent to the wasted lives of far too many — children in schools where fear dominates rather than learning; older citizens and their families financially devastated by long-term care needs; hardworking farmers devastated by short-sighted government policies; people eager to work who cannot find a job, who lose pride in themselves and their families and their nation; and communities gripped by the terror of crime. I entered this race because I know that the President of the United States can lead our nation and other nations away from the arms race. The blight of the arms race and unemployment and crime and inadequate health care and educational shortcomings are not the result of acts of God, but the result of insensitive leadership, chosen by a people who sometimes are not as caring nor as careful as they might be. I know we can do better. You know we can do better. I want leadership that will provide that.

Wendy Koch of the Small newspapers wrote of the press conference: "When Paul Simon bade his presidential dreams farewell Thursday, he did so in style. At a press conference packed with cheering supporters, he appeared subdued but in good spirits. . . . He said he had no regrets, that running for the presidency was an 'exhilarating experience' allowing him to learn more about the country. 'I shall be a better senator because of this rich experience,' he said philosophically. He made clear he had no desire to run again for president. His wife Jeanne and two children appeared more emotional. They stood at his side, biting their lips to fight back the tears. Determined to remain upbeat, they proudly waved to the crowd. Mrs. Simon received hearty applause when her husband turned to thank her for her work as a 'superb campaigner' . . . The senator also thanked his son Martin, 24, for being his traveling companion, photographer and consultant. He noted his daughter Sheila, a 27-year-old attorney, and her newlywed husband Perry Knop spent their honeymoon on the campaign trail in places like Audubon, Iowa and Berlin, New Hampshire. The crowd laughed. They smiled. . . . Simon was in good form. He took his defeat graciously. After the press conference, several reporters crowded around to shake his hand and wish him well. A *Newsweek* reporter who had covered him for months on the campaign trail shook her head . . . and sighed, "'That was a class act.'"[17]

Losing is no fun, but there is a sense of relief in being able to go to a men's store and buy something without having the Secret Service and reporters and cameras with you. Jeanne and I went to see "The Last Emperor" and bought popcorn — the first movie we had seen in a long time. The ordinary things of life became more precious. And we enjoyed a week in Puerto Rico with our children, with only tennis, fishing, and loafing on our schedule.

I have no regrets for having made the race. I had the opportunity to see this nation, its many strengths as well as its weaknesses, as few people can. We had a good staff, some of them outstanding, and magnificent volunteers. The "Bow Tie Brigade" (a term created by reporter Mitchell Locin of the *Chicago Tribune*), scores of Illinois people who went to Iowa and other states on my behalf, are typical. Volunteers from Wisconsin headed by Rep. Midge Miller came to Iowa to go door to door, one of them young State Senator Russ Feingold, who a few years later would be elected to the United States Senate. One of my volunteers in Georgia, Cynthia McKinney, later became a member of the U. S. House as did a Michigan volunteer, Debbie Stabenow. I had more volunteers in Iowa and New Hampshire than any candidate. Everywhere I go today I encounter people who come up and say, "I got interested in politics through your presidential race." While we did not have the quantity of votes needed, we had quality in volunteers and supporters. People who offered words of encouragement varied from actress Whoopi Goldberg to architect I. M. Pei to political observer Walter Cronkite. We didn't have the best financed race, nor a glamorous candidate. "He has a great face for radio," one Dallas observer noted. The *Cape Cod Times* noted that cartoonists are for my candidacy: "Those earlobes, those horn-rimmed glasses, that bow tie . . . the man practically draws himself."[18] Then the newspaper practically endorsed me. Jack Beatty, senior editor of *Atlantic Monthly*, asked, "Can a man who looks like Oscar Levant survive on Reagan's medium, television?"[19] His answer: Yes. Columnist Jeff Greenfield wrote: "His haircut comes courtesy of Pop's barbershop, not the $40 coiffeurist's. His glasses — not contact lenses, but glasses — suggest a CPA rather than a fighter pilot. . . . One look at that haircut, those glasses and that bow tie and voters are sure to believe him when he says he is running on his ideas."[20] Columnist Mike Royko, in his usual style said he favored me, but noted: "He ain't pretty, compared to most of the clones. In fact, a friend of mine once asked me, 'Is Simon a drinker? Every time I see him on TV he looks a little hung over.' One of nature's silly pranks. I once saw Simon nurse the same tiny glass of sherry for an entire evening. When the host asked him if he wanted the half-empty glass topped off, he said: 'No, I'm driving.' His idea of a wild evening is reading a biography of Lincoln."[21]

We laughed at the friendly barbs, and had fun with the hard work of campaigning. But I also had the opportunity to tell millions of people in what direction I believed the nation should head, to stimulate at least a little substantial thought about the issues.

In retrospect the biggest deficiency of our campaign was not getting in earlier, not having the ability to plan a careful strategy in advance, not having the chance to pick key staff people long before the campaign officially started. When a candidate makes a sudden if not quixotic decision to run for the presidency, many small details that ultimately are important are not as thoughtfully planned as they should be. That includes the vital area of campaign financing. A June 30, 1988, report showed me running fifth in the funds raised among the seven serious candidates.

My family once again performed yeoman service. My mother, then 81, phoned people in Iowa and elsewhere whom she had never met. Jeanne literally covered the length and breadth of the nation, and each night, no matter how weary we were, we talked by phone and compared notes on our experiences. Jeanne's cousin Marie and her husband Tom McDermott helped greatly in Pennsylvania. Sheila and Perry Knop married in the midst of the campaign. Martin, then 24, a photographer by profession, left his paying work, and generally traveled with me shooting pictures, taking care of the many small details required, often working with the secret service late at night. He also made independent appearances for me. I cannot stress enough how superbly my family performed during the campaign.[22] There are moments of glory, hours of fun and long days and nights of campaigning when you wonder how you can keep going. But they did.

One campaign appearance I made that Martin really enjoyed taught me something about our culture. The NBC television show "Saturday Night Live" asked me to do a skit making fun of Gary Hart and Senator Joe Biden, a candidate for several months. While I would have welcomed the attention from the program, I didn't feel comfortable doing it and I declined. A few weeks later they called and asked me to be on the program with Paul Simon, the singer. I know him and like him and agreed to do it. They began "Saturday Night Live" by saying, "Our host for tonight is. . . . Paul Simon." The two of us walked on, had an argument as to who should be the host, and of course he won. It was fun. Jeanne stayed home and watched it on television, terrified that my total lack of familiarity with show business would shine through. But it worked out well. The next morning I appeared on David Brinkley's Sunday morning show. As I walked down the street, no one mentioned my being on the news commentary show, but "Saturday Night Live" evoked recognition and responses from people everywhere.


Generous remarks greet a departing candidate, but the comments in the *Houston Post* of Bob Krueger, my Texas state co-chair and former ambassador and colleague in Congress, I appreciated as much as any: "Like Truman and Lincoln, Paul Simon is outwardly undistinguished. But the real strength of leadership always comes from inner qualities. A president cannot lead a nation without first finding direction within himself. Paul Simon could. He is a man of heart."[23]


I came away with great respect for the other candidates including the eventual winner, Mike Dukakis. Going through this physically and emotionally draining process tests a person, and the winner emerges with a much better sense of this nation and its people.

In my book on the presidential race, *Winners and Losers* (Continuum) I commented on one of the candidates who did not do well, Senator Albert Gore Jr.: "My sense is that Al is still sorting out who he is and what life means to him. . . . He will be a presidential candidate again and probably a better one the next time he runs."[24] Al Gore's greatest strength, where he differs from most people in political life, is a willingness to look at things long-range, particularly in environmental matters and the arms race.

Dukakis is now teaching and inspiring students at Northeastern University in Massachusetts, and one quarter each year at UCLA. He would have made a solid, strong president.

Babbitt became an excellent and controversial Secretary of the Interior, and as I write this an independent counsel is investigating whether he lied in connection with the influence of a campaign contribution to the Clinton campaign on Babbitt's actions. My instinct is that nothing will come of the charge, other than costing Bruce grief and legal expenses. During a campaign like the one we went through, the candidates get to know each other's strengths and weaknesses well, and my sense is that Babbitt is not only a good public servant but an honest person.

Dick Gephardt has emerged to head the House Democrats, and he is almost ideal for that type of position. He has ability and flexibility on political positions, a strength in a legislative leader but not necessarily in a President, a post that he still desires. But another Missourian, Harry Truman, turned out to be a better President than most people imagined he would and Dick could surprise us too.

Gary Hart is now practicing law, contributing articles occasionally that help us understand the former Soviet Union, an area in which he specializes.

The celebrity among the candidates was Jesse Jackson, also the most eloquent. He has a solid, visceral commitment to helping those less fortunate. It is not an intellectual exercise. In a New Orleans debate at Tulane University, Hodding Carter asked a question too seldom posed to candidates: What should we do about the nation's poor? Jackson responded:

> Hodding, of the people on the stage I was the poorest the longest and the most recently. I was born to a teenage mother who was born to a teenage mother. Now, how do you break out of that cycle? A combination of things: Spiritual, personal and governmental. A mother who cared and who did not surrender was a factor. Love is a factor in making people come alive and dream of their predicament. Secondly, the option to get an education. A public school system that worked for us, and when teachers gave homework, mother made me be home to do that work. It was a partnership

between school and home, of teacher and parent. That was a factor in getting out. A public housing system, Fieldcrest Village, gave us for the first time a concrete floor and heat and a refrigerator. That was a factor in getting out. My father came home from the military service and got those extra ten points and became a janitor at the post office and mama was able to go back to school when I was about twelve to become a beautician. It took a combination of private initiative and government support to break that cycle.[25]

I have known Jesse about forty years. When I first knew him, he wore a dashiki and had an Afro hair-style. His speeches startled people. Today he wears a three-piece suit, and from his haircut to his shoes he exudes success. But he does not feel success; his spirit is restless. And he still startles many with his speeches.

In my 1984 race for the Senate against incumbent Senator Charles Percy, Jackson had mixed feelings. He did not like Percy's embrace of Reagan and Reaganism and felt much closer to me on domestic issues, but Percy had befriended him and his organization Operation PUSH. He also felt closer to Percy's stands on the Middle East than to mine. He endorsed neither of us.

After the election Jesse and I had breakfast, and he asked why I had not pushed him for an endorsement. I explained that I understood the dilemma he faced, and since he had been a Democratic candidate for the presidential nomination in 1984, I should not have to ask for his support. I also told him that I felt I was in reasonably good shape in the black community, with my strong civil rights record and Chicago Mayor Harold Washington's vigorous support. I added, "And Jesse, you're not the most popular guy in the Polish wards in Chicago." He laughed.

"But one other thing is more than political," I told him. "You're a Baptist minister, and I'm the son of a Lutheran minister. We were both involved in the civil rights struggle. The portion of the white community that supported us most strongly in those days was the Jewish community. I am concerned that you are sending the wrong message to people in the Jewish community and about the Jewish community.

"When I get on a radio call-in program with a predominantly black listening audience, occasionally I get anti-semitic phone calls from people who assume that the name Simon is Jewish. I do not suggest that there are not some Jews who have prejudices against blacks. But you should use your immense talents to be a force for reconciliation."

Our conversation became vigorous at the point. He told me of the Jewish merchant who ran a small store near where he grew up in South Carolina, who overcharged people. He asked me to read a speech by Congressman William Clay of Missouri commenting on black/Jewish relations, to understand more fully the black perspective, which I did.

Jesse and I did not see each other for several months, and then I met him at a reception. "I've been working on that sermon you preached to me," he said. No one around us knew what he meant, but Jackson and I knew.

I have seen him grow over the years in this area and in others, and I hope he has seen me grow. I have noted his understandable pride as his talented son, Jesse Jackson Jr., has been elected and reelected to the U. S. House of Representatives, taking on a slightly more conventional leadership role than his father, but not differing in objectives.

Critics of our process suggest that two small states, Iowa and New Hampshire, should not be so decisive in determining presidential nominees. The most widely suggested alternative is to have regional primaries.

This would be a great mistake. The advantage of starting with two small states is that a candidate of limited resources, like myself, has a real chance. Under the present system, prospective presidents cannot simply "campaign" by having press conferences at airports, which is what a regional primary would become. In Iowa and New Hampshire, the candidate has to go into homes, talk with people about real problems. Yes, having money gives a candidate, even in Iowa and New Hampshire, a real advantage, but if I had changed only a few things, without more money I would have carried Iowa, run a strong second in New Hampshire, and been the nominee. Regional primaries would be television commercial contests between well financed campaigns. The two states with early contests do not have to be Iowa and New Hampshire. It might be good to switch to New Mexico and North Dakota, or Vermont and West Virginia, but candidates should be forced to do more than wholesale campaigning where big dollars determine winners.

Former Senator Thomas Eagleton of Missouri has suggested that we move away from primaries and have a genuine convention where Senators, Governors, and House members — or the candidates for these posts who lost — should constitute the conventions. We would nominate people with greater experience in the federal government, and in foreign affairs particularly. I favor his idea, but I don't think it will happen. It would inch us toward a benefit of the parliamentary system that many nations have. It would produce better candidates, stronger presidents, and a finer nation.

---

[1] They were Representatives Fortney H. (Pete) Stark, Barbara Boxer, Richard Lehman, Norman Y. Mineta, and Don Edwards of California; William Lehman and Charles E. Bennett of Florida; Marcy Kaptur and John Seiberling of Ohio; Cardiss Collins of Illinois; Sam Gejdenson of Connecticut; Charles Rose of North Carolina; Wes Watkins of Oklahoma; Stephen J. Solarz of New York; and Robert W. Kastenmeier of Wisconsin. Much of the material for this chapter is found with much greater detail in Paul Simon, *Winners and Losers* (New York: Continuum, 1989).

[2] Editorial, *Baltimore Sun*, 26 May 1987.

[3] Jon Margolis, "Can Paul Simon Make the Doubters Change Their Tune?" *Chicago Tribune*, 14 April 1987.

[4] Jeffrey Schmalz, "Cuomo, Uncommitted, Says Simon 'Looks Strong,'" *New York Times*, 6 November 1987.

[5] Andy Boehm, "Making Mr. Right," *Los Angeles Weekly*, 5-11 June 1987.

[6] Quoted in Mitchell Locin, "Carter Says Simon Can Win Voters in the South," *Chicago Tribune*, 5 October 1987.

[7] "Bush, Simon Images Compare by Bush," *Boston Globe*, 8 November 1987, quoting *Washington Times*.

[8] Quoted in Larry King, "Choice Candidates and Funny Men," *USA Today*, 23 May 1987.

[9] Godfrey Sperling Jr., "I remember Paul Simon" *Christian Science Monitor*, 5 January 1988.

[10] Fred Barnes, "The Sprint," *New Republic*, 8 February 1988.

[11] Editorial, *Des Moines Register*, 31 January 1988.

[12] *Des Moines Register*, 9 February 1988.

[13] 25 February 1988.

[14] 14 March 1998.

[15] 16 March 1988.

[16] 16 March 1988.

[17] Wendy Koch, "The Senator's Departure a Class Act," *Kankakee Daily Journal*, 10 April 1988.

[18] Editorial, *Cape Cod Times*, 7 February 1988.

[19] Jack Beatty, "Paul Simon: A Candidate with a Difference," *Peoria Journal-Star*, 27 August 1987.

[20] Jeff Greenfield, "Simon Leads Us Into Anti-Image Era," *Moline Dispatch*, 21 May 1987.

[21] Mike Royko, "Class Like Simon's Always in Style," *Telegraph (Iowa) Herald*, 15 May 1987.

[22] For the campaign story from Jeanne's perspective see *Codename: Scarlett* (Continuum Press, 1989).

[23] "Paul Simon's Best Asset Is His Decency," *Houston Post*, 16 April 1988.

[24] *Winners and Losers*, 50.

[25] Debate sponsored by the Democratic Leadership Council, 2 November 1987.

# Chapter 13

# *Chicago*

Chicago dominates Illinois, more than its three million citizens out of twelve million in the state indicates. It is the financial center of the state, and much of the nation. Its voters cast a majority of votes in a Democratic primary, so its leaders tend to dominate Democratic politics. Its television, radio, and newspaper outlets reach about two-thirds of the population of the state.

Culturally it is also the most dominant factor, and an improving one. Visitors to other countries frequently find that when they say they are from Illinois, there is no recognition by the resident of the other nation. Then when you add an explanatory note that Chicago is our biggest city, people understand. At that point, often in jest, they act like they are firing a sub-machine gun, and smilingly say, "The gangster city." Today the response is more likely to be, "The Chicago Symphony Orchestra." What a difference that orchestra has made! But it is not that alone, it is the Lyric Opera, now one of the world's finest; it is the still emerging theater and entertainment offerings — Second City which produced the Belushi brothers being the most widely known. The Chicago Bulls, with the almost incredible Michael Jordan, draw huge interest, as do the seldom-winning Chicago Cubs, along with the Chicago White Sox, the Chicago Bears, and the Chicago Blackhawks. And there is the architectural magnificence of the city.

The Chicago ethnic diversity brings ties to others in Illinois and around the nation. The sizable Polish population not only produces kielbasa and other food specialties, but the *Zgoda* and other media contributions. The two largest national Polish fraternal societies are based in Chicago. Political leaders know when they reach the Polish leaders in Chicago they are also reaching Poles in Waukegan and Peoria and Cicero. What is true of Poles is true of other ethnic groups, though most of them are not as large as Chicago's Polish population of approximately 275,000. Greeks, Mexicans, Italians, Ukrainians, Chinese, Koreans, Asian Indians, Pakistanis, Lithuanians, Vietnamese, and other groups have sizable populations in Illinois, with their leadership centered in Chicago. Their restaurants are based in Chicago. Here Afghan, Cuban, Armenian, Japanese, and every other ethnic group imaginable have restaurants. Ethnic parades are part of the Chicago scene for Illinois politicians, whether for pleasure or votes. An Illinois politician who hasn't been booed by a semi-inebriated onlooker at a St. Patrick's Day parade is too obscure to deserve mention.

Chicago politicians tend to be more colorful, though I regret to say that those of us who have imposed political reforms on the state have sapped some of that color. The city still harbored a few of the old really vibrant characters when I started in Illinois politics. Charlie Weber had seats in both the City Council and Illinois House of Representatives. He would occasionally slip me a $100 campaign contribution — in cash — and advise me, "Kid, if you want to win the next election, buy yourself a street sweeper and go around cleaning things up." He did not understand that what worked for him in a Chicago ward would be markedly unsuccessful in rural Illinois. One of his contemporaries in Chicago politics, Alderman "Bathhouse John" Coughlan, opposed a city proposal to have six gondolas, similar to those on the canals of Venice, Italy, purchased for the Lincoln Park lagoon in Chicago. "Why buy seven?" he asked with great logic. "Let's just buy two and let Mother Nature take its course."

Alderman Vito Marzullo belonged to the old school of Chicago politics and hated most of the reforms, but always went out of his way to be good to me despite my part in the reforms. Part of that was his instinct simply to be good to all people. Born in Italy, his comfortable English always had a sizable Italian tilt to it. He married an English wife and the combination of her British accent and his heavy Italian accent somehow made visiting with them more interesting. His keys to success were service and loyalty. Whatever Mayor Daley asked him to do, he would do. That occasionally got him into trouble with his fellow Italian-American officials, but not much trouble, because he was clearly their leader. He kept his political base by working hard at it, spending at least one night a week at his 25th Ward Democratic Headquarters helping people who came in one at a time to talk to him about their problems. They knew he helped them and they sensed accurately that he liked them. His few years of formal schooling did not prevent Vito from being a guest lecturer to a class at the University of Illinois or from lecturing a reporter about the political facts of life. I always knew that in any inner circle discussions among Chicago leaders — and I never got close to being in the inner circle Vito would stand up for me.

One of the brightest and most sophisticated political leaders I have ever met was less universally popular than Vito Marzullo but highly respected, Alderman Tom Keane. He did not fit the traditional mold of Chicago aldermen. He had an impressive knowledge of fine wines. He could carry on a conversation about great art works. He was both quick and eloquent on his feet. Tom chaired the powerful Finance Committee of the Chicago City Council, and next to Daley had more power than anyone else. I enjoyed his company, and found him completely straightforward in his assessments of my political situation. He would half-joke, "Daley got into politics for power, and I got into politics for money." His interest was obviously more than money, because he passionately wanted a better city, state and nation. But he also liked to make money, and had some of the most famous and prestigious people in Chicago as his clients. Where the boundaries of politics and making money meshed, he felt he could legitimately and carefully use his connections and knowledge to help clients, and make money in the process. That eventually got him into legal trouble. In an era when pursuing political leaders helped the careers of prosecutors, Keane landed on the hit list. Tom felt he had not violated the law, but a jury ruled otherwise. Stripped of his seat in the Chicago City Council, he spent time at the federal penitentiary in Lexington, Kentucky. Against the advice of one of my staff members, Jeanne and I visited him during my years in the U. S. House. My staff had concerns about unfavorable publicity. I felt that regardless of whatever the legal merits of his case might be, Tom had stood up for me and I should visit him, and let him know that I remained his friend. We arrived at Lexington at lunch time, and officials directed us to the dining room, where we hoped to see him. It was almost like visiting the Walnut Room at the Bismarck Hotel, a center for lunch and political activity for many years. Not only Tom, but people who had been active in Chicago and Illinois politics, kept coming up to greet us. After he left prison I occasionally called him, or he phoned me. Once Jeanne and I had dinner with Tom and his wife Adelaide, talking politics as usual. But the prison stay dampened his spirits. The day of his funeral I was slated to host United Nations Secretary General Boutros Boutros-Ghali in my office, and I felt I should do that, particularly since the Secretary General was under attack from people who should have been supporting him. When I read the newspaper account of Tom's funeral and only two known political figures attended, I regretted my decision. Of the many people whom Tom Keane helped, I would have expected a few more to show some courage and attend. I should have been there. After the funeral I talked to his widow on the phone, and she told me, "Tom really wanted to clear his name. Not doing that before he died hurt him." Tom Keane grew up in another era of politics, when representing clients to various governmental bodies was an acceptable procedure, even though you held public office. Was he technically guilty of violating the law? Probably. Did he do a great deal more good than harm in his years of public service? You bet.

Another extremely able alderman and frequent critic of both Mayor Daley and Tom Keane was Leon Depres, who would have made an outstanding United States senator if his political path had taken a slightly different course. Leon (called Len) had a great combination of ability, wit, compassion, and common sense. He never expressed to me any desire to become mayor or governor or senator, but he would have filled any of these tasks ably had the political fortunes in Illinois taken a slightly different twist.

An alderman who started on the outside as a critic of the establishment, Bill Singer, ran against Richard Daley for mayor, but gradually became an insider, not as an alderman but as a political consultant and lobbyist. A person with real ability, he came close to launching a major political career on a couple of occasions.

I first met George Dunne when we both served as freshmen in the Illinois House of Representatives. I instinctively liked him, and I watched his gradual growth in political influence in Chicago until he became President of the Cook County Board. He filled that position like he spoke, without great flourish or fanfare, but did a solid job. When I worked with him, whatever the issue might be, his expressed concern on any project would not be the politics of the situation but what was good. I liked that. And I saw him through the years go out of his way to help people, which is what politics should be about.

The first Chicago mayor I met was Mayor Martin Kennelly, who political leaders regarded as honest and able and well-intentioned, but not strong.

Richard J. Daley became Mayor in 1955 and no one ever accused him of not being strong. He served in the State Senate, as Director of Revenue for Illinois under Governor Adlai E. Stevenson, and was county clerk in Cook County. Unlike Martin Kennelly, he knew government and politics intimately before he emerged as mayor.

Daley's keys to strong leadership included the patronage system, which he followed with infinite detail, and hard work, including careful use of his time. Before the courts curtailed the political appointment of all but the most significant policy positions, party leaders appointed people to jobs in Illinois from janitor to state policeman (only men then). People got jobs quickly — sometimes through bribes — and lost them quickly. Daley carefully monitored and followed these appointments, particularly with care when recommended by leaders whose loyalty he had reason to suspect. Cook County state legislators generally held jobs also as assistants to the county clerk, or something similar. If they should ever deviate from the Daley line, they had better come up with a powerfully good excuse or they would be out of their patronage job (which often required them to do nothing, or next to nothing), and soon would no longer be legislators. The precinct captains (called committeemen and women outside of Cook County) knew they had to deliver in their precinct for the list of candidates handed them by their ward or township committee leaders or they would be out of a job. The net result of all of this was a huge concentration of power in the hands of the Mayor of Chicago.

Because of this power, most Democratic legislators followed the Daley line without question and without exception. Downstate Democrats did not have the same job incentive to vote faithfully with Chicago, but they knew that if they voted "right" their reward would be key appointments to committees and commissions. The handful of us who did not vote in lock step on all matters were labeled by the press as "independent Democrats" or "anti-Daley Democrats." The irony of this was that in years when we had Democratic presidents, members of Congress who voted with the President 75 percent of the time were labeled as administration supporters, while those of us who may have voted with Daley 90 percent of the time were called anti-Daley Democrats. I did not vote for or against a measure because of the mayor's position, and never took part in the anti-Daley rhetoric of many of the Republicans and of a few Democrats. I believe he gradually sensed that I would not always be with him, but I was not antagonistic.

Getting to really know Daley was not easy. I did not have the same comfortable relationship with him that I had with Vito Marzullo or Tom Keane or Leon Despres or George Dunne. Senator Paul

Douglas said he had a polite but distant relationship with Daley, even though he deferred to Daley on many federal appointments. Douglas, for example, wanted to name Anthony Scariano, an outstanding legislator, to the federal bench but Daley vetoed that and Douglas chose someone more acceptable to the mayor and the Italian leadership. But Douglas never felt fully accepted by Daley. I had much the same relationship.

My analysis of him is that he provided a good bridge between the world of yesterday's politics and today's, though he would decry the deficiencies of today's politics.

If he gained financially in any improper way from his service in politics, I am not aware of it, and in politics you quickly sense who is playing it straight and who is not. Occasionally you are fooled, but not often. I recall particularly when Daley came to Vienna, Illinois, for Paul Powell's funeral. In a custom much more common in an earlier day in our nation, Powell's body rested in his home until we all went to the memorial service. Powell's "family" were those of us in politics. He had no children, and his wife, whom he saw rarely even when they were married, had died several years before. Daley and I happened to be standing by the casket and somehow got into a discussion of corruption. Daley advanced the theory that if the person on top plays it straight, then those below him do the same. Powell played it crooked, he said, so the people under him did the same. Daley had a habit of speaking quietly most of the time, so others in the room could not hear what he said, but the almost-alive Powell was about two feet from our conversation. I thought he might rise up to defend himself!

Daley appointed outstanding people in many positions, like Tom Donovan, David Stahl, Neil Hartigan, and others. But he did not push reform until at least a mini-scandal occurred and the newspapers played it up. He could then defend his reform efforts to the non-reform-minded political leaders by saying he had to do it because of the media. The politicos could understand that. If he had launched such reforms without the base of a scandal, he would have offended them and eroded his political power. When a scandal within the Chicago Police Department occurred, for example, he brought in a nationally recognized, no-nonsense police superintendent, O. W. Wilson, and told him to clean up the situation. Most members of the police department welcomed this action, almost all citizens of Chicago did, and the more reluctant political leaders who could no longer fix traffic tickets and play more serious cops-and-robbers games grumbled but understood the political necessity of what the mayor did. His procedure was not to interrupt their political games without good cause. But when he did act, it was genuine, not a public relations fix.

Before the current age of so many homeless people — a national disgrace — on West Madison street in Chicago, alcoholics gathered and slept on the streets. None too respectfully, we referred to them as "winos." I talked to Daley about having a place where they could have minimal but safe housing. Daley said he shared my concern and had suggested to the federal Housing and Urban Development (HUD) leaders that they construct a building with one-room units and a bathroom for temporary housing. HUD responded that their requirements were a kitchen, living room, bedroom, closets, and a bathroom — appropriate for most people but not for the needs of these derelicts. Daley's interest combined compassion with a desire to improve the appearance of that portion of the city.

Daley's Democratic political moorings were solid and real. When the McGovern followers kept the Mayor and many other Democrats from being seated at the national convention in Miami in 1972, I would have understood if Daley had given Senator McGovern only nominal support in the general election. Instead Daley did everything he could for McGovern. Once during the campaign McGovern, Adlai III, Daley and two of his sons, and I had dinner together prior to a Democratic rally in Chicago. You could sense the two of them genuinely liked each other. After all that had happened, it would have been understandable if the relationship between Daley and McGovern had been cool. It was not. A small tribute to Daley occurred at his funeral when George McGovern flew from Washington to be there.

In the middle of my term as lieutenant governor I campaigned for the Democratic candidates on the state ticket and went to the Cook County Democratic headquarters to be of assistance on election night. Daley, who also chaired the Cook County Democratic Party, had an office in the headquarters and installed me on one phone in the office while he handled the other. At one point prior to midnight we had no returns from heavily Republican DuPage County. I called the Democratic County Chairman, Rep. William Redmond, later Speaker of the Illinois House, and the person who answered the phone at his home said he had already gone to bed. I turned to the Mayor and told him. Daley, who had a short temper and turned beet red when it exploded, could not contain himself. "Went to bed! Before the votes are in!" He launched into a tirade on responsible leadership and then gradually calmed down.

The Latino population in Illinois had no members of the Chicago

City Council and no one in the state legislature when I served in the Illinois General Assembly and as lieutenant governor. As a state legislator representing rural southern Illinois I became interested in the plight of migrant workers, introduced some legislation to help them, and suddenly because of this became the voice for Latinos in state government, even though I lived 250 miles from the bulk of Latinos in Illinois. Perhaps the most significant thing I did for them was to get the state's universities to become more sensitive to their potential. In visiting with Daley, I suggested that with about 400,000 Latinos in the city, he should get one Mexican American and one Puerto Rican in the city council and one of each in the state legislature. Daley hesitated for a moment before responding, "Paul, they're just not ready for it yet." His sincere answer was the same answer given to every ethnic group over time. Power is rarely handed to people; they must prepare for it and demand it. Today both the city council and state legislators are richer for their presence.

The times I really visited with Daley, in contrast to the formal encounters, occurred when we sat next to each other at dinners. He enjoyed recounting things that happened in the past. His favorite story — one I heard several times — involved a state legislator, Gary Noonan, who bet another legislator that he could keep his leg in a tub of hot water longer than his colleague could. Gary had a wooden leg. He put his leg in, grimaced and groaned, and then finally pulled his leg out of the hot water after about three minutes. The other legislator could not take it for ten seconds. The mayor had a high-pitched laugh and struggled with laughter each time he told the story. True or not, it made a story that Daley enjoyed, as did his listeners.

I have already related (Chapter 7) one instance in which Daley apparently contacted the judiciary. Because Daley played such a powerful hand in deciding who would become judges, people somewhat naturally went to him occasionally to influence judicial decisions. Even in my more remote contact with the judiciary, perhaps once a month someone would come and ask for my help with a judge faced with making a decision. I always carefully explained that I should not do that and could not do that. But Daley grew up in a different era. When I visited with him one day, his secretary buzzed him on the intercom. He took a phone call he had placed and I heard him say, "Judge, I don't want to influence your decision, but you have a stockyards case before you involving a man who really needs help." He gave the name of the man, asked the judge how his family was doing, and then ended the conversation. About three weeks later I read a small item in the newspapers about the decision, which went Daley's

way. Had the judge ruled the other way, Daley would never have criticized the judge. But if that jurist wanted to move up in the judicial
hierarchy to the appellate court or the Illinois Supreme Court, my
sense is his chances would not have been good. Journalist and lobbyist George Tagge of the *Chicago Tribune* told about contacting Daley
when the Tribune needed his help with the Illinois Supreme Court,
and apparently received it.[1] But in an earlier era that type of contact
and conduct was not uncommon. After retiring as Governor of
California, Pat Brown told an interviewer that he "worked very, very
closely with the [Chief Justice of the California Supreme Court] on
decisions."[2]

Daley did have a habit of ignoring those he could no longer use.
Sam Shapiro as a state legislator had followed the Daley line faithfully,
much more faithfully than I did. Sam became Lieutenant Governor
and then Governor, but his real ambition was to become a judge, and
he would have been excellent. But after he lost the race for governor,
Daley did not return his phone calls, and his chance to become a
judge died. After I lost the nomination for governor, I twice phoned
Daley, for purposes I do not recall, but he did not return my calls. Two
or three months later Daley called and asked me to nominate him as
head of the Illinois delegation at the Democratic convention. I
declined, in part because I did not want to get into the middle of an
intra-party fight then brewing, but mostly because he had not shown
the courtesy of returning my calls. It was not my finest moment.
Retaliation in life and politics is understandable, but almost always
wrong. Later Daley and I worked together on the presidential campaign, but the relationship, never close, became more distant.

Alderman Michael Bilandic succeeded Daley, after the Mayor's
sudden death. In talking to me about a state official who had gone to
the Mayo Clinic for a physical examination, Daley commented,
"Don't go to a doctor unless you have to. They always find something
wrong with you." I've wondered since that time if Daley might have
postponed death with regular checkups. Bilandic, alderman for
Daley's home ward, was a solid, capable, thoughtful leader, but not
charismatic. His term as mayor ended abruptly after a huge snow-
storm hit the city just before the election, badly snarling city services,
making it possible for Jane Byrne, a former aide to Mayor Daley, to
upset Bilandic. Bilandic later became a Justice of the Illinois Supreme
Court.

Jane Byrne, a graduate of Jeanne's alma mater, Barat College, had
all the charisma that Bilandic did not have, but a mercurial personality,
lacking Bilandic's stability. Political feuding, often not of her creation,

tended to overshadow some of the constructive things she did. I worked with her on the Kennedy candidacies of both 1960 and 1980. One gesture she made many regarded as either foolish or an empty campaign ploy, but I liked: She and her husband, journalist Jay McMullen, moved into a housing project for a short period, at a time when crime and violence had escalated there. Attention focused on the problems in the project as they had never focused before. If there had been more widespread follow-through on their stay by the media, by civic and religious groups, the impact could have been greater. But the gesture showed concern, one of the ingredients not felt in most public housing projects and by the poor generally.

During my House service Jane Byrne sent her aide, Steve Brown, to Washington to urge me to become a candidate for governor. It was one of several attempts by various party and elected officials to get me to be a candidate for that post again. I have great respect for the office having sought it once, but I had moved onto the national stage and my primary interests had shifted. It is one of the ironies of politics that the more you say no, the more people want you to run.

At the end of her first term, Jane Byrne faced primary opposition from the son of the former mayor, State's Attorney Richard M. Daley, and from Congressman Harold Washington. For whatever reason, Rich Daley and Jane Byrne did not get along even though his father gave her significant responsibilities in his administration. Harold Washington and I became acquainted during our activities with the Young Democrats, when I first served in the legislature and shortly before he went there. We both liked to read, both shared a strong desire for government to help those who struggle desperately, and the media categorized both of us as independent Democrats. Harold had a great personality; people who knew him liked him. Early in his career the African American community in Chicago had a dominant figure: Congressman Bill Dawson. I knew him slightly. One of the first blacks to serve in Congress, he had pioneered in many ways, but he achieved strength by going along with the dominant white powers-that-be. The senior Mayor Daley and Dawson worked together closely, so closely that a few leaders in the black community whispered privately their unhappiness, but rarely publicly. After Dawson died, Daley worked with several key aldermen and ward committeemen, but no one person took Dawson's place. Alderman Ralph Metcalfe, later a member of the U. S. House, became the first major black figure to break with Daley and display independence frequently. Ralph not only had ability, he had been an Olympic champion as a runner, and that gave him a special status in both the white and black communities. Successfully breaking the mold and becoming independent might not have been possible at that point for anyone else. Without Metcalfe's leadership, it is doubtful that Harold Washington could have succeeded. Harold followed the same path, eventually also serving in Congress. When the mayor's race faced Chicago, black independents felt that the time had come for them to show strength, perhaps not winning but, by demonstrating power, getting greater consideration on everything from city streets to judgeships. Ralph Metcalfe turned down the appeal to run, and then the attention focused on Harold. He reluctantly agreed to become a candidate. I served in the U. S. House with him then, and he told me several times that he felt obligated to make the race, even though he thought he could not win. That changed dramatically after a televised debate between Jane Byrne, Rich Daley, and Harold Washington. The most articulate one of the three was Harold. He won the nomination — barely — and faced the Republican candidacy of a former state legislator, Bernie Epton, and, in 1987, the independent candidacy of another respected Chicago leader, Tom Hynes. Bernie, inaccurately portrayed by some as a racist, unquestionably had sizable segments of the city in his corner who feared having a black mayor. In racially divided Chicago, more segregated in housing patterns than most American cities, those fears were real. After receiving the nomination, Harold asked me to campaign for him in the white areas, and the reception I received was not warm. I remember the driver assigned to me, who happened to be black, saying afterwards, "I've never heard a white man booed like that." Not only did Harold win, but to the great credit of the Jewish community which had its first serious candidate for mayor in Bernie Epton, the Jewish community — unlike most white areas — gave Harold Washington a majority. The black areas voted overwhelmingly for Harold, whose combination of personality, charisma, and racial identity gave them special pride.

The city council then divided largely along racial lines, with Alderman Ed Vrdolyak leading a majority of 29 whites against the coalition of 21 aldermen who generally supported Harold. I respected both men, but each became captives of his followers; Harold could not appear to be compromising with Ed, and Ed had to maintain his leadership by fighting Harold. I always felt that if I could have brought the two of them together on a fishing trip for a few days, they would have enjoyed each other's company, and perhaps worked together more. The division limited the contribution that Harold made.

The division also made it awkward for candidates. I would not have won my 1984 race for the U. S. Senate without the strong support of both. But when I had a fund-raiser, we had to arrange for the two to make appearances at different times. Even on the night of the election, when it appeared finally that I might win, we arranged for Harold and Ed to stop at my suite at different times. Ed, as chairman of the Democratic Party of Cook County, exerted himself in every way possible for me, and Harold would get up early in the morning and go to stops on the elevated train with me. He enjoyed campaigning, and sent a clear message that his support of me was more than perfunctory.

After his reelection, Harold Washington started to reach out more, and had he been able to serve his full four years, there would have been greater reconciliation both in the city council and in the city generally. Once Jeanne and I appeared with him at a Lithuanian Festival in Chicago. There are not many black Lithuanians! The mayor had been given the phonetics for a greeting in Lithuanian. He butchered it. The crowd laughed; he laughed at himself. But you could almost touch the good will that everyone felt that day, a good will that the city needed and he had started to spread. The last time I saw him I mentioned that someone had shown me a picture of the two of us when we were youths attending the convention of Young Democrats in Oklahoma City. "I looked a lot thinner then, didn't I?" he said with a laugh. I confessed to him that he did. He then told me his difficulty in cutting back on eating. He had become a large man, but when he cut out snacks, he became so desperately hungry in the evening that he ate two meals. I think he ate himself to death. When he died suddenly of a heart attack, the outpouring of grief in the city was overwhelming. The new Chicago library, underway during his administration, was named the Harold Washington Library, a tribute that avid reader Harold Washington would have appreciated. Author Studs Terkel, in a tribute to Harold, said that he was the most widely read mayor in the history of Chicago. I am sure that is true.

The sudden death of Mayor Washington caused a furious fight in the city council over designating his successor. Alderman Gene Sawyer, an African American, finally received the appointment, but found himself in an almost impossible situation, with many blacks criticizing him for accepting votes from the Vrdolyak supporters, and people in every corner maneuvering for the next race for mayor.

State's Attorney Richard M. Daley, the son of the former mayor, emerged as the next mayor. In some ways he is similar to his father — both having a short temper — but in other ways different. He has reached out to the minority and gay communities in Chicago as his father never did. He is less the political creature than his father, but different times require different responses. My relations with him have been more distant than with his father, and they were not close with his father. We simply have a different style of doing things. Not helping the relationship has been the requests for appointments at the federal level. I decided early in my Senate years that if the Democrats ever won the presidency, I would designate U. S. attorneys and federal judges of the finest quality, no matter what the political pressure. I tried to do that, and the results showed. When it came to the appointment of U. S. attorneys, in all three districts the dominant political pressures from Democratic leaders were fair, but I wanted to see that these key prosecutors would be free to do their duty without concern for offending sponsors. In the northern district, virtually every major Democratic leader contacted me urging the naming of Richard Devine, a former chief assistant prosecuting attorney in Cook County. I did not know him well, but I liked him. However, I also felt that having a U. S. Attorney who was too close to all the king-makers in Chicago would not be good. My internal vibes told me not to do it. I consulted with my colleague Senator Carol Moseley-Braun, and we designated Jim Burns, who served well in that capacity, indicting Democrats and Republicans without fear or favor. Rich was unhappy with me on this appointment, and also on some federal judicial appointments also filled on the basis of merit. Dick Devine, his choice for U. S. Attorney, later became State's Attorney of Cook County and appears to be doing an excellent job.

If I were mayor of Chicago — a position with exciting possibilities — my style would differ from Rich's. But in fairness I must add that he has made changes in the Chicago school system that have required courage, and that ultimately will reap huge benefits for the city and region. People who flee the city do it largely because of deteriorating schools. If the schools can be turned around, and that is starting to happen in Chicago, then that flight will be reversed. If Rich Daley did nothing more than to stand up to a variety of special interests — in this instance primarily unions — and start schools moving in a better direction, he would earn high marks for his years as mayor. No mayor in recent memory — probably ever — has done as much for the Chicago public school system as Rich has done.

Compared to former mayors like "Big Bill" Thompson, who pledged to punch King George in the nose, and compared to the city council of "Bathhouse John", "Hinky Dink" McKenna, Paddy Bauler, and Charlie Weber, this is a dull crowd indeed. But the dull crowd is giving Chicago better government.

[1] *George Tagge Memoir*, an oral history project of Sangamon State University (now the University of Illinois at Springfield) 1986, 28.

[2] Marc Reisner, *Cadillac Desert* (New York: Penguin, 1986), 366.

Chapter 14

# National Figures

Franklin Delano Roosevelt's wife Eleanor became the first wife of a President in this century to play a significant non-traditional and public role. Woodrow Wilson's wife played an important, but non-public, role. Political opponents and newspaper cartoonists lampooned Eleanor Roosevelt. She was both one of the most respected figures on the American and the world scene and one of the most hated. In the eyes of her opponents, her sins varied from refusing to play the usual tea-pouring, smiling role of a President's wife who did nothing else, to showing concern for minorities and people like coal miners. I grew up in a home that had huge respect for her.

My chance to get acquainted with her came through a circuitous route.

The Democratic political club movement achieved strength in California, and some felt that the path to greater independent strength for Democrats in Illinois would be a club movement. Independent Democrats — meaning those not under the thumb of Mayor Richard J. Daley of Chicago — gathered in Springfield in 1957, determined to follow the California example. Dissatisfaction with both the corruption and the insensitivity to social problems in the two political parties served as the catalyst. I knew they would be meeting and had sympathy for the cause, but I had previously scheduled a trip, my first, to the Middle East and the Soviet Union. In the Mena House Hotel in Cairo, Egypt, near the Pyramids, I received a call from James Clement, a respected patent attorney and political activist. He asked if I would be willing to serve as president of the newly formed Democratic Federation of Illinois. Then in my second term in the Illinois House of Representatives, and twenty-eight years old, I

somewhat reluctantly agreed, not being sure what it meant, the crack-
ling, primitive overseas phone service in Egypt then not making it
easy to ask even a few basic questions. The club movement grew, but
as clubs succeeded they soon took over the Democratic party appara-
tus and the new thrust of the party organizations in various communities made the need for continuance of the clubs unnecessary. They
served as a valuable tool for change.

A year after I became president, the clubs had a convention, and
through the assistance of Eleanor Roosevelt's oldest granddaughter, also
named Eleanor but called Ellie, and her husband Van Seagraves, I
extended the invitation to the former First Lady to speak to our convention and asked former Governor and presidential candidate Adlai
Stevenson to introduce her at our dinner. I was awed by Eleanor
Roosevelt, but she immediately made me feel at ease, asking pertinent
questions. Her total lack of pretension impressed me. The next day she
flew to the Netherlands. She told me she traveled with two dresses, one
of which she wore. "Travel light," she advised me, an admonition I have
followed since, with the exception of books and papers I take with me. At
that point in her life she had hearing aids in her glasses. As the banquet
wore on with more speeches than I should have scheduled, she leaned
over to me and said, "I'm going to take my glasses off and reflect a little.
If someone says something you believe I should hear, please nudge me."

Jeanne, not yet my wife, appeared on a television program in her
first legislative campaign with Eleanor Roosevelt, and greatly appreciated how the world's most famous woman went out of her way to
put her at ease.

I saw Mrs. Roosevelt briefly on a few other occasions, and she
remains one of the most impressive political figures I have met
because of her graciousness, her quiet courage in the face of political
hostility, and her compassion for those in need.


In the mid-1950s, scandal erupted in Illinois when Republican State
Auditor Orville Hodge stole approximately $2.5 million. A popular fig-
ure and a favorite of the *Chicago Tribune*, he seemed destined to become
the Governor of Illinois. Candidate for State Auditor Michael Howlett,
a Democrat, came to me and said he had information that Hodge maintained a double payroll, one he made public and the other the real one.
The charge resonated with me because Hodge's appropriations passed
the House 129-2 and 127-2. I cast one of two votes against them because
of the huge increases in his appropriations, caused he said by the need
for new bookkeeping equipment. I had my doubts. The week after that

vote Hodge, a Republican, came to me on the floor of the House with the Democratic leader, Rep. Paul Powell, and explained that the vote was hurting me in my county of Madison, also his home. "People are baffled by why you voted against me," Hodge said. "Even the publisher of the *Alton Evening Telegraph* [the largest newspaper in the county] asked me about it." Powell added that he could arrange to have my vote quietly changed, in order to smooth things out back home. I declined his offer. Hodge's appropriations had not yet cleared the state senate, and Hodge obviously hoped to tell the senators that there had been no votes against him in the House. Partially because of this vote, and partially because of my ties to the newspaper world, Mike Howlett asked me to relay the information about the double payroll to a newspaper that might do something with it. I contacted two people at the *St. Louis Post-Dispatch* and to my amazement they showed no interest. Whether they believed my story too far-fetched to be likely, or they were simply lazy, I do not know. When they failed to do anything, I suggested that Howlett go to Basil "Stuffy" Walters, the editor of the *Chicago Daily News*. Walters assigned George Thiem, a hard-working, quiet but persistent reporter, to the investigation. Thiem discovered not only a double payroll, but a series of checks endorsed by a typewriter — the same typewriter. Hodge, whose office wrote the state's checks, simply wrote checks to various names and then endorsed them to himself on a typewriter. Thiem and the Daily News won a Pulitzer prize, and Hodge went to prison. Politically all of this developed into a huge plus for Democratic candidates in Illinois.

Shortly after these revelations made national news, a friend in the newspaper business, Elmer Fedder, and I drove to Kansas City. While in Kansas City we decided to stop at the office of former President Harry Truman, on the possibility that we might see him. We went to the building where he maintained a few small, modest rooms. We introduced ourselves to his secretary, and soon she ushered us into his office. No Secret Service. No security of any kind. He was cordial, and I am sure we did not stay more than five minutes. What I do recall is bringing up the Hodge scandal. Because of his reputation as a strongly partisan Democrat, I thought he might be elated. Instead he told us, "The word 'politician' should be among the most revered words in our language. What has happened in Illinois tarnishes all of us in politics and discourages people from entering what should be a highly respected profession." My already high respect for Truman rose.

The next time I met him occurred purely by accident. Walking down Michigan Avenue I spotted Frank McNaughton, former reporter for *Time* and the author of the first biography of Truman.

"I'm on my way to see Harry Truman," he told me. "Do you want to come along?" I quickly postponed my next appointment and went to the presidential suite of the Blackstone Hotel with Frank. They chatted for about an hour; I sat there largely as a fascinated observer. I do recall Truman's having a few choice words about the *Chicago Tribune*, which had run its famous headline about Thomas E. Dewey winning. When Mrs. Truman left the room for a few minutes, he leaned over quietly and said, "While she's away I want to tell you what I told a *Tribune* representative when I met one shortly after that election." He then repeated language which someone growing up on a farm in Missouri would use, but which his wife obviously did not favor.

Three months after Jeanne and I married we drove to Los Angeles for the Democratic convention that nominated John F. Kennedy. Because primaries then did not dominate the selection process as they do today, Kennedy appeared to be in the lead with committed delegates, but did not have it locked up. Among the other active candidates still pursuing the nomination were Governor Averill Harriman of New York and Senator Stuart Symington of Missouri. Truman had publically endorsed Harriman. On the way to Los Angeles Jeanne and I drove through Kansas City and visited the Truman library, where the former President now maintained his office. He welcomed us cordially, and we had a fine visit. He made clear his dislike of John Kennedy's father, Joe Kennedy, and the religious issue concerned him. It is hard for young people today to believe that the dominant issue of the 1960 election was whether the United States could survive as a democracy if we elected a Roman Catholic as President. Truman, both a Baptist and a Mason, had an understanding of the strong feeling in both those groups.

I had the opportunity to be with the former president several times after that, the most memorable in our small town of Troy, population then 1,200. In 1962, I read that Truman would speak near St. Louis, and Troy — only twenty miles from St. Louis — would have its annual festival, called a Homecoming, that same night. I called and asked if he could come to Troy before his evening banquet address and ride in our Homecoming parade. He agreed to do it. And when word spread, the thousand or so expected to come to that event swelled to 10,000. Congressman Sidney Yates, a superior public servant by any gauge, then was running against Senator Everett Dirksen unsuccessfully. Yates rode in the convertible with us, as did Illinois Governor Otto Kerner. Truman fit into a small town like a hand in a glove. I had never before been at a public occasion with a former president, and the number of people who shouted, "Hi, Harry!" astounded me. They obviously said this with affection, but I would never have called a former President by his first name. On the parade route, the car stopped in front of our home momentarily where President Truman greeted Jeanne and had his picture taken with my one-year-old daughter Sheila. But the warmth of the crowd greeting him was overwhelming. I particularly recall the local funeral director, Jewel Edwards, who thought Social Security was communistic, standing on his front lawn shouting at the top of his lungs, "Hi, Harry!" We drove in the open convertible to Truman's speaking engagement. Congressman Yates said, "Maybe we should put the top up for the President." Truman, with a smile, responded, "No, keep going. Sidney is just worried about his hair blowing around." As we drove, we discussed U. S. relations with the Soviet Union. We passed an enclosure of cattle, and Truman said, "I don't trust the Soviets any further than I can throw those livestock."

Months prior to the 1960 Democratic convention, Sargent Shriver, brother-in-law of John F. Kennedy, asked Jeanne and me if we would help Kennedy, whom I had met only once briefly some years earlier, but for whom I had a high regard. Both Jeanne and I knew Shriver, had worked with him, and liked him. However, we felt an obligation to Adlai Stevenson, if he should become a candidate. I talked to Adlai and explained the request I had from the Kennedy people. The former governor assured me that he would not become a candidate, and Jeanne and I committed ourselves to helping Kennedy.

The convention produced its moment of awkwardness. At the last minute Stevenson became a candidate, supported by Eleanor Roosevelt and by a sizable number of others — our friends — how many we could not tell. In addition, Adlai had his zealots. At the convention hotel, a pale, bearded young man walked around the lobby carrying a home-made sign: STEVENSON OR ATOMIC DEATH! Adlai took the unprecedented step of walking into the convention before the vote, an action never before taken by a candidate. This man who had been our nominee for the two previous elections evoked a warm ovation.

Jeanne and I, seated with the Illinois delegation which by then had committed to Kennedy, rose and joined in the standing applause for Adlai while most of our Illinois colleagues sat uncomfortably. But the applause did not translate into votes. Kennedy received the nomination. After Kennedy's election, he named Stevenson Ambassador to the United Nations. Adlai contributed to the nation in many ways, among them by stimulating young people to get active in politics. I did not serve in the legislature during the Stevenson gubernatorial years, but one of the veterans of that period, Rep Lloyd "Curly" Harris, told me one day, "You know, Paul, after I talk with Governor Stevenson I come away feeling a little cleaner."

While on the campaign trail prior to the 1960 nomination, Kennedy spoke at a dinner at the Orlando Hotel in Decatur, Illinois. I received word that the Senator wanted to see me in his room. He asked a few questions concerning the downstate political scene, and then about former Illinois Governor John Stelle and Paul Powell. Both Stelle and Powell supported Symington for the nomination. "They're both crooks, aren't they?" he asked. Startled at the directness of someone I hoped would become President, I confirmed his information. Powell, to his credit, campaigned as hard for Kennedy as anyone did after the Massachusetts Senator became the nominee. Whether Powell's motive was protecting his own political hide, or he liked the impressive way Kennedy handled himself in strongly anti-Catholic regions in downstate Illinois, Powell played a role in securing the bare majority Kennedy received in Illinois.

Sargent Shriver asked me to join Max Schrayer, a leader in the Jewish community, in heading the efforts to deal with the religious issue in Illinois. Lutherans, Baptists, and others used their pulpits to denounce the idea of a Roman Catholic becoming president. I had debates on the issue all over the state. In small communities like Steeleville (population 2,059) people packed the local school gymnasium to listen to the discussion of this issue. At Wheaton College's jammed auditorium I sensed that the only two people in the audience on my side in the debate were my wife and my mother. My opponent in the debate said that he had nothing against Senator Kennedy personally, but that "sooner or later he [will be] taken over by the hierarchy of the Roman Catholic Church."[1] I noted that the only colony that initially gave religious freedom to Roman Catholics was Rhode Island, headed by Roger Williams, a Baptist. I added, "I wish more Baptists would follow his example these days." Anti-Catholicism played a significant part in the culture of the early history of our nation, and the 1960 campaign produced the last gasp of the virulent form of anti-Catholicism. Years of indoctrination of fear and hatred collided with reality in 1960.

I became involved because a conference of Lutheran ministers in Wausau, Wisconsin asked me to address them on the question of Roman Catholics and politics. I submitted my address to the *Cresset*, a Lutheran journal of thought published by Valparaiso University in Indiana. Several Protestant and Catholic journals reprinted the article. Sarge Shriver distributed my article widely. When I encountered Eunice Kennedy Shriver, sister of the presidential candidate, at a meeting she said, "We have piles of your article all over our house!" Senator Kennedy had a widely publicized press conference in

Houston in which he dealt deftly with the religious issue, and a less widely publicized but excellent address to the American Society of Newspaper Editors before he had secured the nomination. I mention it here because part of it illustrates how dominant the religious issue became. Kennedy noted:

> I spoke in Wisconsin, for example, on farm legislation, foreign policy, defense and civil rights and several dozen other issues. The people of Wisconsin seemed genuinely interested in these addresses. But I rarely found them reported in the press — except when they were occasionally sandwiched in between descriptions of my hand-shaking, my theme-song, family haircut and, inevitably, my religion.
>
> At almost every stop in Wisconsin I invited questions — and the questions came — on price supports, labor unions, disengagement, taxes and inflation. But these sessions were rarely reported in the press except when one topic was discussed: religion. One article, for example, supposedly summing the primary up in advance, mentioned the word Catholic 20 times in 15 paragraphs — not mentioning even once dairy farms, disarmament, labor legislation or any other issue. And on the Sunday before the primary, the *Milwaukee Journal* featured a map of the state, listing county by county the relative strength of three types of votes — Democrats, Republicans and Catholics.
>
> In West Virginia, it is the same story. As reported in yesterday's *Washington Post*, the great bulk of West Virginians paid very little attention to my religion — until they read repeatedly in the nation's press that this was the decisive issue in West Virginia. There are many serious problems in that state — problems big enough to dominate any campaign — but religion is not one of them.[2]

There is always an idiotic fringe with anti-Catholic, anti-Jewish, and other fierce prejudices, but never in my lifetime have we had a public surfacing of religious bigotry as we did in 1960. I received letters like this one:

> I have been a life-long Democrat but I don't intend to crucify my Christ, my country and my Bible, do you? . . . I am not a fanatic, a klansman, a bigot. I am a Christian, American and a Democrat in that order, are you? Are you a Truman Democrat or a Christ-first Democrat? Is it God, country and party or just party?[3]

That type of letter I expected. But I didn't expect a sermon against Kennedy in the First Presbyterian Church of Peoria, widely distributed, with the general theme that Protestants respect freedom and Catholics do not. While Dr. Franklin Clark Fry, president of the largest group of Lutherans, said he found no difficulty in voting for a Roman Catholic for President, anti-Kennedy articles found their way into official Lutheran publications. One editor wrote in a *Lutheran Witness* supplement: "I would vote for a Jew or for a Mormon if I thought he was better qualified for the position than his Lutheran opponent. But I would vote against a practicing Catholic . . . because being a Catholic he stands for certain principles which are un-American and because he is subject to certain strong pressures which would endanger our American liberties."[4] A publication called *Protestant Journal Magazine*, which I never heard of before or since, arrived just before election day with a full-page inside article headed, "President Lincoln's Warning to America." Lincoln is quoted as saying: "I see a very dark cloud on our horizon, and that dark cloud is coming from Rome. . . . If the American people would learn what I know of the fierce hatred of the generality of the priests of Rome against our institutions, our schools, our so dearly bought liberties, they would drive them away, tomorrow, from among us."[5] A powerful statement! Only Lincoln never said any such thing. He said just the opposite of the people of prejudice of his day, the Know Nothings. Even a publication like *U. S. News and World Report* had a big eight-page feature article: "Both Sides of the Catholic Issue."

In the discouraging flood of prejudiced material, I received a letter from George Lindbeck, professor of historic theology at Yale and a Lutheran theologian: "Political leaders are often able to view Roman Catholicism more objectively and understandingly than are Protestant religious leaders. We, because we are in a sense competitors, are inclined to focus our attention on what is wrong with the Roman Church and not notice its more positive aspects. Also, we are so familiar with the faults of various Protestant groups that we are not shocked by them, as we are by the more unfamiliar defects of Romanism. . . . The layman who is well-informed can do much to help clarify the problems of Roman Catholic-Protestant coexistence in our American Society."[6]

Our neighbor across the street, Dr. H. H. Glenn, believed that if Kennedy were elected president, the Pope would run the United States. His attitude changed dramatically because of Kennedy and also because of Pope John XXIII who assembled Vatican Council II. Shortly after Kennedy became President, the U. S. Catholic bishops issued a statement calling for federal aid to parochial schools. When asked at a press conference about this, President Kennedy said simply, "I disagree with the bishops." Our neighbor, Dr. Glenn, was astounded. That simple statement ended his fears and virtually eliminated the political issue of Catholicism in our nation.

In addition to dealing with the religious issue, we did everything we could in downstate Illinois for the Kennedy candidacy. Eunice Shriver, Kennedy's sister, visited our home for a meeting with women leaders. And Jeanne and I put in campaign appearances in every corner of the state. Kennedy, like Bill Clinton some years later, arrived late at every campaign appearance. On one trip to Illinois it became even worse than usual, and because I had become semi-prominent in his effort in our state, I suddenly got an emergency call to abandon meeting Kennedy and traveling with him, but instead to go to Venice, Illinois, "and hold the crowd for two hours." The crowd stayed, but not because of my presence. I introduced every candidate and city official for miles around, asking for a few words. Candidates for county treasurer, for example, had never addressed such an assemblage. I'm pleased their remarks and mine were not recorded for posterity.

On November 22, 1963, I had lunch in the Sherman Hotel in Chicago with my friend, State Representative Anthony Scariano. Someone came over to us and said, "Did you hear that the President's been shot?" We both thought for a moment he was joking, but it quickly became clear something terrible had happened. We abandoned our lunch and went to a nearby television set, hoping and praying for the best. I knew that the meeting I had driven to Chicago to attend would be canceled, and I started driving the 250 miles to my home in Southern Illinois immediately. Within minutes of leaving, I heard the words on the car radio I dreaded, that the President had died.

In a magazine article I wrote immediately after his death I noted one of the keys to his success as President: "He was never particularly impressed by his own wealth or anyone else's. He admired the person who had a good idea, who could turn a phrase with ease, or who had unusual abilities."[7]

His presidency lifted our vision. He gave us the Peace Corps and pointed the way on civil rights and other issues that his successor would achieve. But he offered more than that. He spoke with an eloquence unmatched by any president since Abraham Lincoln. Words can captivate a nation, bringing out the noble in us.

I had only slight contact with Lyndon Johnson. I first spoke with him in 1956. Larry Irvin, former aide to Governor Adlai Stevenson, and I had charge of Adlai's suite in the Stockyards Inn in Chicago during the

1956 Democratic national convention. After the delegates nominated Stevenson for President, Adlai called a meeting of Speaker Sam Rayburn, Democratic National Chairman Paul Butler, Mayor David Lawrence of Pittsburgh, Governor Paul Dever of Massachusetts, and a few others. They met in a room across the hallway from his suite. In that meeting — unknown to Larry and me — he told the leaders he would toss the vice presidential nomination open to the convention, a dramatic move designed to spark further interest in the campaign. While the group met, the phone rang in Adlai's suite. The voice on the other end said, "This is Senator Lyndon Johnson. I'd like to speak to the Governor." I opened the door to cross the six feet in the hallway and faced an unbelievable jam of cameras and reporters. I had no chance of making that six feet. When I explained the situation to Lyndon Johnson, he let out a string of expletives that did not redound to my credit.

But for the tragedy of Vietnam, Johnson would be judged by history as one of our finer presidents. His accomplishments in civil rights and education and dealing with poverty and other social issues are most impressive. But the escalating war in Vietnam, and the growing public resistance to it, caused him to leave the presidency on a note of bitterness, and he went into virtual isolation for some period.

His first major public appearance after his presidency was for the annual Cook County Democratic Dinner, a fund-raising event that traditionally attracted thousands, some voluntarily, while many who held jobs felt compelled to attend. Johnson had a good relationship with Mayor Richard J. Daley, and Daley persuaded him to come to Chicago. When Johnson arrived, much to the amazement of all of us, he had a head of sweeping long hair. I sat next to Daley at the dinner, who told me, "When Johnson walked into the private suite we had for him, he asked me what I thought about his hair." Daley, who obviously did not like it, said, "I stumbled around for a moment to figure out what to say. I finally told him, 'If long hair was good enough for Jesus Christ, it's good enough for you.'"


One of the finest people I have known in my years of public life became the Democratic nominee for president in 1968, Vice President Hubert Humphrey. I had known him for some time before he became Vice President and strongly favored his nomination in 1968. But the Democratic convention turned out to be a disaster. Senator Eugene McCarthy also sought the nomination, and the convention — like the nation — had deep and emotional divisions on the Vietnam War. At that point I was the Democratic nominee for lieutenant governor.

Jeanne and our children stayed in Troy during the convention, and I intended to use an apartment we leased near Lincoln Park in Chicago for the campaign. I flew to Chicago and took a cab to our apartment, but approximately six blocks from the building, I saw a huge crowd coming down the street, with a Communist flag leading the way. An anti-war rally had been held in Lincoln Park, and the police made the mistake of kicking the protestors out. This mass of humanity, heading in the direction of our taxi, looked like 10,000 people to me; the newspapers the next day reported 5,000. I could see the anger, and hear the shouts. I told the taxi driver to turn around, and I went to a downtown hotel where I stayed for the duration of the convention.

In the midst of the chaos and acrimony on the streets and in the hall on that first day of the convention, police or rioters killed no one, and I thought things would calm down. The first convention fight came over "the peace plank" to the platform. While it did not differ dramatically from the platform presented for consideration, Lyndon Johnson regarded it as a slap at his policy and wanted it defeated. I voted for the peace plank, though the vote from the Illinois delegation overwhelmingly opposed it. Hubert Humphrey, caught between loyalty to Johnson and a desire for a good convention, quietly put out word to a few friends to support it. But Johnson prevailed, and turmoil erupted again on the streets. It looked worse on television than on the streets, because television broadcast only the most extreme conduct. I first knew something serious had happened when I received an urgent call from a politically active high school student in Decatur, Penny Severns, later a state senator, who saw the television scenes and cried as she told me, "Someone has to do something. Dozens of people are being killed." Those reports fortunately turned out to be inaccurate. Part of the difficulty came from the FBI reports to Mayor Daley and, I assume, the Secret Service reports that exaggerated the threat to the convention. In response to their dire forecasts, he had an overwhelming police presence and the police overreacted. Daley did not have the ability — as Mayor John Lindsay of New York had, for example — to stand before the convention and to say in a calm, reassuring voice, "Let me tell you why we have so many police and what we are doing to protect everyone."

When Senator Abraham Ribicoff of Connecticut made a speech in which he denounced Daley's handling of the convention, Daley and those around him stood up and in a famous picture are shown shouting what lip readers said are obscenities at Ribicoff. You can see a young man in a bow tie sitting near Daley, visibly silent as this took place. The only time I had any influence at the convention came when someone nominated Julian Bond, then a young civil rights activist, for vice president. The parliamentarian for the convention, Congressman John Murphy, came down and shouted across me to Daley, "Make the point of order that Bond is not 35 and not eligible to be vice president." That would have added gasoline to the flames! I turned to Daley, seated in back of me, and said, "You don't want to do that!" He hesitated a moment, and then turned to Murphy and said no. Murphy has since denied this happened, but it did.

Conventions in that day were not geared to television to nearly the degree they are today. Now virtually all decisions are known before the delegates assemble, and speeches are timed to get maximum television exposure. Then, conventions frequently went into the wee morning hours; the night the convention nominated Humphrey dragged on and on. Suddenly someone came to me and said that former Senator Paul Douglas was underneath the platform and ill and wanted to talk to me. I rushed there and found a pale Paul Douglas who told me, "I think I've had a heart attack." I told him I would get a doctor immediately, that we should take him to a hospital. Douglas insisted he wanted to stay until Hubert secured the nomination. I found a physician immediately, who said that Paul had not had a heart attack, that he had some abnormal indications but nothing life-threatening. I stayed close to him until after the vote that he insisted on making. "I may die but I'm going to try to vote for Humphrey," he told me with a wan smile, half-believing what he said. In a few days he appeared to be doing well, but not too long after that he suffered the first of several strokes. My non-medical opinion is that he may have suffered a small-stroke that night.

No political figure meant as much to me as Paul Douglas. He towered physically, morally, and politically. We rarely discussed religion, but he had an undefined sense that a person can commune with those who have died. Once when walking in Washington with him we passed St. John's Episcopal Church near the White House, sometimes called "the Church of the Presidents." At his suggestion we went in, sat there in silence for perhaps ten minutes and then walked out. He made no comment about it. On another occasion when both of us attended a Democratic dinner in Springfield, he asked me to join him for a midnight walk in New Salem, Abraham Lincoln's recreated home town. I had to speak at a breakfast meeting about sixty miles from Springfield the next morning so I declined, and I have regretted that many times since. After his defeat for reelection to the Senate in 1966, he would occasionally talk about death being near, and that added strength to his 1968 commitment to Hubert Humphrey and other causes in which he believed. He wanted to serve while he had breath.

Humphrey, tagged with the stigmas of the unpopularity of President Johnson, a chaotic convention, and an unpopular war, started far behind in the polls in his campaign against the Republican nominee Richard Nixon. Many who called themselves liberals refused to campaign for Humphrey, saying there was no difference between Nixon and Humphrey, a terrible miscalculation.

As a candidate for lieutenant governor, I occasionally accompanied the presidential candidate when he came to Illinois. Early in the campaign, when the poll numbers looked miserable, riding on the campaign plane with Humphrey I said, "Maybe this is not our year." Humphrey responded vigorously, "Just remember this, Paul. The good Lord won't let Richard Nixon become President of the United States." He believed it. And it almost didn't happen. Nixon barely won.

Humphrey returned to the Senate a few years later where he once again performed superbly. All of the senators — no exceptions — liked and respected Humphrey.

In 1976 the Democratic presidential nomination had no clear favorites. Humphrey, recovered from a bout with cancer, appeared to be doing well physically. The two leading candidates were a former Georgia governor whom few knew, Jimmy Carter, and a House member highly regarded but viewed by many as unelectable, Morris Udall.

Some of us felt that Humphrey should be our nominee. He didn't say he wouldn't, nor would he declare his candidacy. A few people met and started a Draft Humphrey movement. Every poll showed he would be our most popular candidate, and some of us — unfairly we later learned — had misgivings about nominating a southerner because of our uncertainties on the vital issue of race. Carter said the right things, but did he really mean them? The Draft Humphrey movement had a small group of respected national leaders, and they asked Congressman Bob Bergland — later Secretary of Agriculture under Carter — and me to head the effort. It finally came down to the New Jersey primary filing date. If Humphrey would agree to run there, we felt we could secure the nomination for him. The afternoon before that decision day I ran into Humphrey and he told me that he probably would not be a candidate. Early the next morning he called and said he and his wife Muriel talked until 2 A.M. in the morning and he had decided to become a candidate. Could I get some House members and the press to attend an afternoon press conference? I assured him I would. We worked the phones and then David Gartner, his chief of staff, called saying there had been a change in plans. He asked me to come to the Humphrey office about an hour before the press conference. There a few of us gathered, including Senator Walter

Mondale, who would become vice president under Carter. Humphrey said he just did not want to do it. He had talked to a few people on the phone — Democratic leader Bob Strauss and Congressman Peter Rodino among them — and evidently received enough negative feedback that the early morning eagerness had diminished. The press conference turned out to be much different than we expected. On those kind of close calls, history is made.

One of the more bizarre experiences I had during this period came when I heard that Mayor Frank Rizzo of Philadelphia, whom I had never met, liked the idea of a Humphrey candidacy. I went to Philadelphia and walked into his office where he sat with an aide. He was livid. I didn't know what had happened to cause his torrent of abusive language, but I was not the object of it. Sitting in stunned silence, I gradually learned that nationally syndicated columnist Jack Anderson that morning had written that Rizzo was having an affair with burlesque queen Blaze Starr, not a great public relations plus for a mayor of Philadelphia. "It's absolutely not true. It's a dirty, rotten lie," he assured me in somewhat more picturesque language. "All I did was get up on the stage with her and play with her breasts a little." Not often am I at a loss for words, but I stumbled through the rest of our largely one-sided conversation.

Humphrey's antipathy toward Jimmy Carter made him seriously consider the race. "I don't trust him," he would occasionally say. And because in political circles these things become known, we learned that Jimmy Carter also had no fondness for Humphrey. But after the nomination, and particularly after Jimmy Carter's election, the new president went out of his way to be good to Humphrey and a warm feeling became mutual. In the last weeks of Hubert's life, Jimmy Carter did the gracious small things, like giving him a lift in Air Force One. In life, yesterday's enemies can become today's friends. It is true for individuals and true of nations.

Humphrey's cancer returned not long after Jimmy Carter's election as president. Hubert once told me that if his cancer returned he would not go through chemotherapy again; he did not react well to the treatment. But faced with life or death, he changed his mind. However, it soon became obvious to everyone that he did not have long to live. I still served in the House then. He called one day in October, 1977 and said, "Your House colleagues are stopping by, and it's getting kind of maudlin. They end up crying and so do I. Why don't you have a farewell party for me in the Rayburn Room [a visitor's room off the floor of the House] and make it a light-hearted event." I agreed to do it, but the more I thought about it, a farewell party didn't seem the appropriate thing to do. I went to Speaker Thomas P. "Tip" O'Neill, and asked him what he thought of the possibility of Humphrey addressing the House. "Tip" said that there is a strong House tradition that Senators should never address the House. However, he liked the idea, but he doubted that the Republican leader, Rep. John Rhodes, would agree to it, and he felt he could not do it without John's approval. I went to Rhodes and he enthusiastically approved the idea.

The House floor and galleries were jammed. I asked Mo Udall, Jim Wright, and Don Fraser, all House members, to say a few light words. Then I introduced Humphrey and he went up on my arm to the spot in the House where the president delivers his State of the Union address. Humphrey leaned so heavily on me as we stepped up, I wondered whether he could make the speech. Politicians and actors will understand what happened next. Sometimes when a politician feels completely exhausted and walks into a hall where cheers erupt, they react immediately, the adrenalin flows and they are eager to take on the crowd. Humphrey cautiously worked his way to the podium on my arm, but the tremendous cheers of the crowd buoyed him and he quickly became the old Hubert Humphrey, eloquent, vigorous, a little long-winded, and full of compassion and wisdom. No one there came away with dry eyes; no one there will ever forget it. Two months later he died.

At the Humphrey memorial service, making his first public appearance after national disgrace was Richard Nixon. I respected him for performing that act of courage, and several years later I learned that in his last days Humphrey — who always wanted to be on good terms with everyone — called Nixon and asked him to be at the memorial service. During that tribute Vice President Mondale spoke these simple but moving and accurate words about the fallen Humphrey, "He taught us how to live and how to die."

In 1972, after my unsuccessful race for the Democratic nomination for Governor, Jeanne, Sheila and Martin, and I left Springfield in our old Chevrolet for Alaska. We did not attend the Democratic convention, but listened to it in Illinois before we left. Because I still served as lieutenant governor of Illinois, we made a few reservations along the way, so people could contact us in an emergency. When we reached Banff in Canada, the clerk at the motel said "a Senator Tom Eagleton is trying to reach you." Tom had been nominated for vice president, with Senator George McGovern heading the ticket. I called Eagleton, whom I had known from before his Senate days; he wanted me to help run his vice presidential campaign. I told him that

I had promised my family a trip to Alaska and I had to complete that, and I would contact him immediately afterwards. By the time I reached Alaska, Tom no longer was on the ticket, having withdrawn after disclosure that he once underwent psychiatric treatment. Sargent Shriver replaced him.

I knew McGovern from the days before his service in the House. We were on a panel together at his alma mater, Northwestern University, immediately after his first election to the House but before he had been sworn in. Not so incidentally, at that meeting I met for the first time a newly elected state representative from that area, Jeanne Hurley, who later became my wife. After the 1972 convention, McGovern called and asked me to head his Illinois campaign. I told him that since I had been defeated by Dan Walker in the Democratic gubernatorial primary, he should clear it with Walker who did not think highly of me. McGovern replied, "I'll talk to him, but I spotted him as a phony from the first time I met him. I want you whether he wants you or not." Walker did not object. McGovern's campaign engendered enthusiasm but not numbers. He carried only Massachusetts. Particularly helpful in Illinois, despite all the odds, were Marge Benton, Bernard Weissbourd, and Joe Antonow.

The media and the Republicans portrayed McGovern as a radical, an extremist, in the same way Democrats had unfairly portrayed Senator Barry Goldwater in his race against Lyndon Johnson. McGovern, the son of a Methodist minister and loaded with common sense, did attract some fringe elements with his anti-Vietnam War stance and that frightened many Americans. But they did not control McGovern and would not have played a role in his administration had he been elected President.

I knew Barry Goldwater only slightly before my election to the Senate. One day, waiting for a procedural motion, we chatted aimlessly on the floor and he suddenly asked, "Do you know where Bowen, Illinois is?" I told him I thought I knew every small town in the state but I could not place Bowen. He said his mother came from Bowen. I looked it up and found the town of 539 people located near Quincy. I had the Illinois Highway Department make a sign: WELCOME TO BOWEN, THE HOME OF JOSEPHINE WILLIAMS, THE MOTHER OF SENATOR BARRY GOLDWATER. I presented it to the mayor, had our picture taken, and then gave the picture to Barry on the floor of the Senate. He burst into tears. "I have to go to Bowen," he told me about two hours later. One

Saturday we did. We drove in a parade, all six blocks of Bowen, and then he spoke to a gathering of about 300 people in the little town square telling them how much Bowen had meant to his mother. We visited the property where his mother's home had been. About three years later Barry's first wife died, and shortly after that he said, "I'm going to sell one of our homes and keep the place in Phoenix. But the house I want to sell has all our books. I think I'll give them to the library in Bowen." I told him that I didn't know if they had a library in Bowen, but I checked and they did. Today in that small library in an Illinois community of 539 people, many of the books are a gift of a Senator from Arizona.

Goldwater played a decisive role in telling Richard Nixon that he should step down from the presidency. The Nixon story is in many ways a tragic one. A gifted politician, he would be given marks as an above average president, but for Watergate and its aftermath. I knew him slightly, corresponded with him a little, and found his observations in international matters often penetrating, after his presidential service.

His appointment of Gerald Ford as Vice President, after Spiro Agnew resigned, ultimately gave the nation a needed calm voice. Ford did not serve long enough to be categorized as a great president, but he provided the nation something it needed badly after the Nixon years: confidence in government. We trusted him. I found him to be an above average president in knowledge of government details, and superb in working with Congress. He regularly would have different members of both parties to the White House for consultation. A great service he performed, and one that probably cost him the White House, came with his pardoning of Richard Nixon. Without that, the nation would have been deeply and emotionally divided on the proper way to handle the former president. I did not applaud Ford's action at the time, but in retrospect I believe he acted responsibly.

Hardly anyone thought Jimmy Carter had a chance to become the Democratic nominee. An ex-governor with almost no national name recognition, he pursued what appeared to be a quixotic quest with an impressive singleness of purpose. Early in that quest, Congressman Andy Young — later U. N. Ambassador — called me and asked a favor. His schedule called for lunch with Jimmy Carter, but he had to be in committee for a key vote. Could I have lunch with Carter? Reluctantly I agreed, certain that at best Carter might be an outside shot at the vice presidency. He fooled many of us.

It is exceedingly difficult to emerge from the governorship of Georgia (or Arkansas) and suddenly be thrust into a role as leader of the world as well as of this nation. Carter started by surrounding himself with people he could trust from Georgia, not bad people, but without the broad experience his presidency required. On some things he served superbly, the Middle East mediation as an example. His forthright stand on human rights met with cynicism in the State Department's professional ranks, but he literally helped to change the world for the better. Too often on domestic issues he floundered. One evening he invited Jeanne and me to sit in the presidential box at a concert at the Kennedy Center with Rosalynn and himself, the Japanese ambassador and his wife, and Senator and Mrs. John Culver of Iowa. During the concert's intermission, we went into a small room behind the President's box and had a glass of wine and light conversation. Because of the presence of the Japanese ambassador, we didn't have the chance to talk politics. To make conversation, I observed, "I see, Mr. President, you're going to tell us what to do about inflation Tuesday night on national television." He responded, "I hate to tell you, but there's not much the President can do about inflation." I could hardly believe what I heard! If Hubert Humphrey had been President he would have had a litany of twenty-five things to do. When the economy sputtered, later in Carter's term, he called several meetings at Camp David. I attended one. Among those present were Michael Blumenthal, the Secretary of the Treasury; Vice President Walter Mondale; Bill Miller, chairman of the Federal Reserve Board; Congressman Bob Giaimo, chairman of the House Budget Committee; and Senator Ed Muskie, chairman of the Senate Budget Committee. The discussion wandered everywhere, and I didn't sense the President had a good handle on what to do. I particularly remember Ed Muskie talking to the President in a tough way, rougher than I have ever heard anyone address a President, urging Carter to get control of things. I sat next to Rosalynn Carter, and when Ed spoke I saw her throat muscles bulging. I knew he angered her. (It surprised me then some months later that when Cyrus Vance resigned as Secretary of State Carter appointed Muskie.) I went home from that evening at Camp David despondent. I doubted the President would provide the leadership we needed. Many members of the Senate and House felt the same way, and when Senator Edward "Ted" Kennedy said he would become a candidate, I told Ted I would be for him. I felt in fairness I should let the Carter people know what I planned. I told Vice President "Fritz" Mondale, who relayed it to the President. Carter called and asked Jeanne and me to join Rosalynn and himself at Camp David for dinner. I said I would talk with Jeanne. I called back and told him that I should not waste his time, that I had made a commitment. That was the only time I ever turned down that kind of an invitation from a President. Ted Kennedy's campaign did not do well, and Carter trounced Kennedy in my own congressional district. Ted was disheartened at the negatives that came from his personal life when he wanted to focus on issues. The struggle between the two of them left scars that hurt Carter's vote, but not enough to make the difference.

My evaluation of the Carter presidency is that he was an above average President, but not a great President. However, he is by far the greatest ex-president the nation has ever had, making huge contributions to peace and stability and humanitarian efforts all over the world. The only ex-president to come close is John Quincy Adams, who served the anti-slavery cause in the U. S. House of Representatives after leaving the presidency. Ironically, with the vast experience Carter now has, if he could go back to the White House as president, he would be not an above average president, but probably a great president. He understands the world and this nation much better than when he served as president.

One of the mistakes Bill Clinton has made as president is not to consult or use Jimmy Carter. My sense is that Clinton — like many in politics — does not like to share the limelight and credit. It grows out of personal insecurity. Jimmy Carter found that Presidents Reagan and Bush used him more and helped him more than did the Clinton administration. Part of Clinton's lack of response may come from Secretary of State Warren Christopher's unhappiness with Carter. When Cyrus Vance resigned as Secretary of State, Christopher as Deputy Secretary of State felt entitled to the position and did not accept happily Carter's appointment of Muskie.

I had less to do with President Ronald Reagan than any President during my twenty-two years in Congress. He simply did not feel comfortable discussing details of issues with members of Congress. The only good conversations I ever had with him were about the Chicago Cubs or Eureka College, the Illinois school he attended. Reagan did have a strong sense of direction, and while I did not applaud much of what he did, he had natural talent as a leader and the American people appreciated that.

The Democratic candidate for President in 1984, Walter "Fritz" Mondale, knew government thoroughly from his days in the Senate and as Vice President and would have made an excellent President, had he been given the chance. He had the misfortune of facing the matinee idol, Ronald Reagan, who had superb communication skills.

Some wrongly assert that Mondale blew his chances when he told the Democratic convention: "I mean business. By the end of my first term, I will reduce the Reagan budget deficit by two-thirds. Let's tell the truth. It must be done. Mr. Reagan will raise taxes and so will I.

He won't tell you. I just did."[8] His stand so concerned many Democratic leaders that Mondale shifted away from it, a political mistake. The reality is that the highest point he achieved in the polls came immediately after that statement. It showed candor, courage, and leadership. I suggested to audiences, when in question periods someone said that statement was the reason he lost, that they imagine Reagan taking that stand and Mondale the opposite; I then asked, "How many of you think that Mondale would have won?" Hardly ever did anyone raise a hand. His later service as Ambassador to Japan received high marks.

George Bush came as well prepared for the presidency, in terms of a résumé, as any modern president. Generally in foreign affairs he did well, with the exception of the Western European and U. S. failure to respond quickly to Serb aggression against Bosnia. His action in Somalia (See Chapter 19) was his finest hour, not as dramatic as Desert Storm, but an act of genuine statesmanship. His domestic record is less stellar, but that in part reflects my philosophical differences with him. He wanted to be president but he did not have the same intensity of direction that Reagan had. He appointed Clarence Thomas to the Supreme Court, a weak nomination, but he also appointed David Souter, who turned out to be a stronger Justice than any of us calculated. Bush's courageous action in 1990, calling for slight tax increases to reduce the deficit, cost him a few votes in 1992 but aided the economy.

We are still too close to the Clinton presidency to make an evaluation. I hope it will end on a stronger note as he exits, but I am not optimistic. Bill Clinton's instincts on national policy are good. His greatest problem is that he likes to please people too much. That leads him to say things like telling an audience of wealthy people that he regretted having asked for the tax hike of 1993, a tax hike which, when combined with George Bush's similar action, lowered the deficit and lowered interest rates, giving the nation unprecedented investment and a long period with a basically healthy economy. Clinton does not have the Harry Truman backbone. He polls endlessly and loves to discuss them. He is unwilling to risk temporary popularity for needed but unpopular programs.

That propensity to do the popular is likely to be increased as a result of the personal missteps and difficulties that have plagued him. When the Senate voted to have a special committee investigate the Whitewater matter, I cast one of three votes against creating it. I felt that with the independent counsel already spending large sums on an investigation, and with the Senate and House Banking Committees doing the same, we had no need to spend additional time and money on this. My "reward" for casting that vote was to be named to the Committee. After much publicity and staff work, we ended with nothing. But the White

House often produced documents only when pressed. Lawyers generally advise clients to provide only whatever information they have to — good advice for the average client but bad advice for a president or senator or someone in high office. The reluctant response created an unnecessary cloud over the Clintons. It took on the appearance of a coverup. On the Monica Lewinsky matter, candor should have been the response, but was not. The President's four-minute speech after testifying for Independent Counsel Kenneth Starr added fuel to the fire. Perfection is not expected in high public officials; candor is. The attempted coverup of tawdry — but not illegal — action could result in the President's resignation or impeachment, but that does not seem probable. If the President were to ask my counsel, I would suggest that he ask three historians — David McCullough, Arthur Schlesinger Jr., and Daniel Boorstin — to meet with him to offer suggestions on redeeming his presidency. Listen to them and then don't take any polls or follow those taken by others. Look to the needs of the nation and the judgment of history. Build on your strengths.

The Starr Report is devastating. All but the most zealous supporters have to admit that perjury has been proven. The case on obstruction of justice is not as strong. The dust will settle and Congress will have to decide. A cab driver told me, "He's been a bad husband, and a good president. We shouldn't kick him when he's down." There is substantial sentiment in that direction, but my fear is that his presidency will be so hampered that Clinton's weaknesses will be compounded rather than his strengths. In the midst of all of this rising tumult the media hardly noticed that a House committee turned down the requested guarantee funds for the International Monetary Fund, when those funds are desperately needed to shore up economies in Asia and in Russia — and we will suffer if they are not shored up. But a wounded President so ensnarled in these charges probably made no phone calls to get the measure passed, and would be less effective if he had made them. It is easy to order missile strikes into two nations with few friends, Afghanistan and Sudan, asserting that we hit terrorist targets. But can the President respond to less clearly popular needs, such as dealing with the Kosovo situation? Can a weakened President call upon us to sacrifice to save the Social Security Retirement Fund?

For me the most devastating blow in the Starr Report was that, when the Monica Lewinsky matter first surfaced, Clinton called his friend and pollster Dick Morris and asked him to take a poll on whether the President should tell the truth. The Morris report recommended not telling the truth, and the President followed that advice. I have serious concerns with anyone who takes a poll on whether or not to tell the truth.

It is probable that the House of Representatives will adopt a resolution asking the Senate to try the President. I hope the nation doesn't have to go through that and that some less painful exit can be found.

That less painful exit must be bipartisan. A near party-line vote in the House on whether to try the President and then in the Senate on impeachment would divide the nation, weaken the presidency, and accomplish nothing. Either a small group of respected leaders of both political parties must put together an alternative, or achieve it with a few people like former Senators Howard Baker, Alan Simpson, John Danforth, and Bob Dole on the Republican side and former Senator Sam Nunn and former President Jimmy Carter on the Democratic side. They could recommend a combination of censure, a fine, and a pledge never to seek elected public office again. Other options can be considered.

The President and Congress must think of the institution of the presidency, and how we can conduct ourselves in such a way as not to weaken it. All options should be on the table, and for the President that must include the option of resigning, though that appears unlikely.

Richard Nixon committed a crime and started down the wrong path by trying to cover things up. Bill Clinton did not commit a crime but distasteful acts, and tried to cover them up. That does not work.

More presidential apologies will wear thin. Clinton needs to take decisive remedial action — like bringing in three historians and avoiding polls — and then he might save himself, and contribute significantly to the nation.

The important thing about "washing dirty linen" in public, and we've done that, is not that the public is watching — but that the linen gets cleaned.

Clinton's strong identification with people is no small contribution. He can campaign comfortably everywhere, including African American areas where he communicates well, something many well-intentioned white political leaders cannot do. In a nation struggling with racial tensions, that is important.

No President in our history has had that same ability to communicate naturally and easily with African Americans. It is no accident that after the Starr report emerged, almost the only congressional voices heard strongly in the President's behalf came from African Americans.

Where Clinton really absorbs the issues, as in education, his leadership is solid.

One night Jeanne and I expected a late call from our daughter, and when the telephone rang at 11:30, I put on the speaker phone so that Jeanne could hear it also. Only it turned out to be from President Clinton, calling from Jakarta, Indonesia. So Jeanne heard the entire twenty-minute conversation. He said that after I had discussed the proposal for a balanced budget amendment to the constitution with him, he ran into "Mack" McClarty, his chief of staff, and told him "Paul Simon really makes sense on this." Then a senior senator, whom he did not identify, came and talked him out of it. That senior senator almost certainly was Senator Robert Byrd, chairman of the Appropriations Committee. But, Clinton told me, "I'll try to be with you this time." I said I would work with him to fashion a way of supporting it without appearing to reverse himself. A few weeks later at a press conference a reporter asked Clinton about the amendment and he said he still did not like the idea but would not work against it this time. That did not please me and did not please Robert Byrd. Something this important should either have been vigorously supported or opposed.

Hillary Clinton has backbone and ability. She is not as good a politician as her husband, but I have been tremendously impressed by the way she conducts herself, both in private meetings with legislators and in public. Somewhat like Eleanor Roosevelt, she has her detractors and her fans. I belong in the latter category. Among the criticisms hurled at her is the defeat of the Clinton health care proposal. I attended a number of meetings different senators had with Hillary, and we all came away impressed by her grasp of the issues, and her good intent, whether we agreed with her conclusions or not. The reality is that when more than $400 million is spent to kill a bill (which *Newsweek* reported), it is almost impossible to overcome that pressure. From my perspective, the only criticism that should be made on this issue is that the President and the White House staff and his supporters should have fought back after defeat, taking the issue directly to the American public. Had they done that, my instinct is that the 1994 Republican takeover of the Congress would not have occurred.

Two third-party candidates I have known vary more widely in personality than in beliefs. John Anderson, a member of the House from Illinois, sought the Republican nomination for President in 1980 but was too moderate to get enough votes in a Republican primary. He eventually became a third-party candidate. John Anderson raised issues that the cautious traditional party candidates would not raise. He is a person of great ability and now, in addition to teaching, is head of the

World Federalists, an organization that promotes greater cooperation among nations. The organization is fortunate to have his leadership.

Ross Perot I do not know as well as John. He has a more mercurial personality than John Anderson, but on a surprising number of issues they are similar: both have called for a sizable increase in the gasoline tax to reduce air pollution; both have talked frankly about our deficit problems. In 1992 Ross Perot's discussion of the deficit unquestionably forced to the foreground an issue that both George Bush and Bill Clinton did not emphasize, some would say ducked. In the three-way debates, Ross was the star of the show. He had quick made-for-television responses and a down-home style people liked. But his in-out-in-out approach to the presidential campaign lent an appearance of instability.

When the dollar plummeted, most Americans had no idea what that meant in their lives unless they planned a trip to another country. I decided to make a speech on the subject, knowing no one would cover it or pay attention to it, but in ten years perhaps some historian in going through the *Congressional Record* would say, "Someone did understand what was happening." I sent a copy of my speech to several people, including Ross Perot. A few days later Ross called me, talking in his usual clipped style, "Say, that was a great speech you made on the dollar, Paul. We are going to have a convention in Dallas and I'd like you to come down and talk about the dollar." I assured him I would put them to sleep if I did. "No, it's important that they hear this." I went to Dallas as did Rev. Jesse Jackson, Bob Dole, Chris Dodd, Senator Sam Nunn of Georgia, and a number of others. About two weeks after that he called and said, "Paul, you and I ought to write a paperback book about the dollar. You're a good writer and I'm a good promoter." We agreed that I would send him the outline of a book, though I was cautious. I thought his appearance of unpredictability might make him difficult to work with. But I sent him an outline. He made a few changes and then we proceeded. To my pleasant surprise, he turned out to be easy to work with. He made decisions quickly and did not get bogged down in minutia. The book appeared, and he mentioned it on several television shows. Then he called and asked me to be his running mate for vice president. I appreciated the compliment but I declined. That ended the book promotion.


I did not know Dwight Eisenhower. I tend to give him higher marks than most historians with a Democratic tilt because as the first Republican President since 1932 he accepted the social reforms of the

Democratic years and built on them. His campaign rhetoric sounded more harsh than the record he produced. He also played an important role in civil liberties by quietly assisting in the efforts to demolish the specter of Joe McCarthyism, the loose habit of questioning the patriotism of people when there is no basis for the charges.

Michael Dukakis and Bob Dole were competent people who would have made strong presidents. I knew Mike slightly before the 1988 presidential race, and Bob I have known since my first days in the House. Both are people of substance, but both ran against nominees who had a greater gift of campaigning than they had. While I probably would not have liked Bob Dole's appointments to the United States Supreme Court, and I did the right thing to support Clinton, Bob is tough, and he would not have ducked the difficult fiscal and social issues the nation faces. In order to get the Republican nomination he tried to portray himself as more conservative than he is. It worked for the nomination, but hurt him in the fall.

Mike Dukakis would have stretched our imagination and called upon us to do much more in education, for example. And my instinct is that he would have drawn on some unconventional sources for his key appointments, people who would have lifted our vision for the nation and the world.

We usually judge a nation by the leaders it produces. We have also developed outstanding leaders who did not achieve the pinnacle of the presidency.


The nation has also had some superb business and labor leaders.

A business leader I came to know through his son Howard's literacy leadership is Warren Buffett, whom the magazine and newspapers identify as successful by the wealth he has accumulated, but what impresses me more than that is his broad interest in the nation's and the world's problems. Here is one of the two wealthiest people in the nation — Bill Gates is the other — who says we must pay more attention to the problems of the nation's poor. We have moved, he says, from "the survival of the fittest" to "the survival of the fattest." Frequently those at the very top of major industries are the most sensitive — not uniformly so — and those at lower levels are less likely to be enlightened.

Example can be powerful. When Dick De Schutter, chief executive officer of Searle, the pharmaceutical company, started giving lifesaving drugs to those certified by physicians as needing them but not able to afford them, soon almost every pharmaceutical company in the nation followed the Searle example and did the same.

Illinois has had strong labor leaders, including State Presidents of the state AFL-CIO Rube Soderstrom, Stanley Johnson, Bob Gibson and Don Johnson. One of the local labor leaders who has national potential is Ed Smith with the Laborers' Union. The national union has faced allegations of corruption and securing the leadership of someone like Ed Smith would be good for them and a contribution to the national labor movement. Don Johnston of my staff effectively handled liaison work with labor leaders.

The most impressive labor leader I have ever met — impressive perhaps in part because of my youth — was Walter Reuther, president of the United Auto Workers, who combined battling for his union members with understanding the problems of business and the nation. The most colorful was John L. Lewis, head of the United Mine Workers.

John Sweeney, the new president of the AFL-CIO, is a much above average leader, but so is the man he defeated, Tom Donohue, caught in the battle between the old guard and the rebels for control of the union leadership.

Many business and labor leaders have not reached the level of visibility of those I have named, but serve our nation well. To the extent that the two camps can work together reasonably, the nation is well served — and so are their constituencies.

---

[1] William Scrivo, "Simon, Pro; Taylor, Con," *Wheaton Daily Journal*, 30 September 1960.

[2] Senator John F. Kennedy, address to the American Society of Newspaper Editors.

[3] Jim Drummond to author, 26 October 1960, ISHL.

[4] Rev. H. Earl Miller, *Lutheran Witness*, Eastern District supplement, 23 August 1960.

[5] Harry Hampel, ed., *Protestant Journal Magazine*, October 1960.

[6] George A. Lindbeck to author, 11 December 1959, ISHL.

[7] Paul Simon, "A Man Named Kennedy" *Spirit*, date uncertain.

[8] "Mondale Accepts Presidential Nomination," *Congressional Quarterly Weekly Report*, 21 July 1984.

# Chapter 15

# *International Figures*

The combination of journalism, service in the U. S. House and Senate, and a natural curiosity about foreign affairs has given me the opportunity to have a limited acquaintance with many major players on the world stage, and to learn a little about the international scene.

Humanity being the same everywhere, encountering political leadership in another country is not dissimilar from doing the same here. A number of nations, through their parliamentary systems, develop leadership that is more attuned to the academic community than the leadership our system produces. Dictators like the late President Mobutu Sese Seko of Zaire (now called Congo) would either change their style or not survive long on the U. S. political scene. However, you meet many leaders where instinctively you say to yourself, "He would make a good Senator in the U. S." Or, "She would make a good leader anywhere." And most political type characters you meet in any nation would fit comfortably elsewhere in a democratic setting.

What follows are a few insights, in a scattering of nations and areas. In many nations, Mexico for example, I have met leaders and visited with them but have not been well enough acquainted to make value judgments.

One insight I have discovered: You can judge the extent of democracy in a nation by the number of pictures of "the leader" (whatever the formal title) in evidence everywhere. On my first trip to Spain, Generalissimo Franco even had his picture in my hotel room. That spells dictatorship. The more pictures there are, the less likely that nation has a real democracy. Democratic nations with a monarchy are an exception to that rule. Pictures of their reigning monarch are more akin to our display of the flag. In newly independent Eritrea in Africa, for example, not only did its leader President Assaias Afeworki make the right-sounding statements about a multiparty system and a free press, but no picture displays of him were scattered around the nation. I sensed that Eritrea had started off well. (Eritrea, which peacefully separated from Ethiopia to the credit of both nations, is engaged in a mini-war with Ethiopia over border issues, as I write this. Both nations need every possible resource to help their people. I hope an accommodation can be found quickly.)

David Ben-Gurion, the first prime minister of Israel, was the first international leader of extraordinary vision I met. A modest man, he eventually retired to a kibbutz in the desert. When I met him, he served as Prime Minister and also held the portfolio of Defense Minister. When he left the office where I met him, he drove off in an old automobile. He clearly had a vision of what Israel could become, a vision of Israel eventually working cooperatively with Arab neighbors. I wish he had lived to see even the bumpy peace process that now is unfolding.

Anwar Sadat, president of Egypt, who broke through the rigid Arab wall of resistance to Israel, certainly falls in the category of a visionary. I met with him several times and at one point he talked about visiting "Little Egypt," the southern part of Illinois where we have Cairo, Thebes, Karnak and other communities with Egyptian names. But that "next trip to the United States" did not occur because of his assassination in 1981. I visited President Sadat at his home in the Cairo suburbs shortly after he said he was willing to make a trip to the Knesset, the Israeli parliament, in the pursuit of peace. He made clear he was serious about it. My trip, scheduled long before this news broke, took me to several Arab capitals, and leader after leader said that Sadat would not live to set foot on Israeli soil. They told me that in the Sudan, Saudi Arabia, and my next stop, Syria. Because President Sadat flew into Damascus for a brief visit before going to Jerusalem three days later, the Syrians cancelled my schedule of meetings with officials. As soon as he left, American Ambassador Richard Murphy contacted me while I met with the head of a medieval Jewish ghetto in Damascus, where Jews had to live. The Ambassador said that Foreign Minister Abdulhalim Khaddam wanted to see me, and could the Ambassador come along because President Carter was eager to hear the Syrian response to the Sadat visit. The Foreign Minister, who now is a vice president in Syria, was unbelievable. Just an hour or less earlier he had been meeting with Sadat, a warm, charming

personality. Khaddam denounced Sadat as a traitor, saying he should
be drowned in the Nile. In the midst of his explosive denunciations of
Sadat, someone walked in and handed him a piece of paper. He turned
to me and said, "See, what did I tell you? The Egyptian people will
not tolerate this. The Egyptian Foreign Minister has just resigned." I
feared that he might be accurate. Khaddam's abusive language is also
a clue to the government of Syria. President Assad is bright and cool
and diplomatic, couching language in terms pleasing to visitors. But
in a dictatorship, which Syria is, the foreign minister does not go off
like that ranting against the dictator's wishes. Since that visit to
Damascus I have felt that Syria would join in the peace process only
when it had no other out. I hope we will near that point soon. Former
U. S. Secretary of State Henry Kissinger has accurately described the
situation: "Without Egypt there can be no war; without Syria there
can be no peace." I left Damascus for Amman, Jordan, not in a buoyant mood.

We drove in an embassy car — bulletproof — to the Jordanian
border. The U. S. Ambassador to Jordan, Tom Pickering, who later
served our nation in several key capacities, met me with a Jeep at the
Jordan/Syria border and showed me some of the projects in which the
United States and United Nations worked with Jordan. King
Hussein, whom I had met on previous occasions, was not in Amman,
but that night one of the Jordanian government leaders hosted a dinner for me with perhaps sixteen high government leaders. I shall
never forget that dinner. After an hour or so we all turned to watch
Israeli television showing live the arrival of President Sadat in Israel.
The group gathered around the television set had a massive divide.
Half of them thought Sadat a traitor to the Arab cause and the other
half thought him a hero of unbelievable courage. As Sadat moved
down the receiving line to shake hands he came to Golda Meir, the
former Israeli Prime Minister, and Sadat reached over and kissed her.
The room exploded in groans and cheers. We had a lively discussion
that evening!

The next morning — Sunday morning — I drove to the Allenby
Bridge, the connecting point between Jordan and Israel. The person
meeting me on the Israeli side from the Foreign Ministry said that
Prime Minister Menachem Begin had saved a seat for me in the
Knesset if I wished to attend to listen to the Sadat-Begin exchange. Of
course I accepted. Perhaps as dramatic for me as the scene in the
Knesset was the drive into Jerusalem that morning seeing Israeli and
Egyptian flags flying side by side. I didn't believe I would live to see
that. I sat in the gallery of the Knesset next to Congressman Thad

Cochran of Mississippi, also later a Senator, who happened to be in Israel. Neither Sadat's nor Begin's speech inspired anyone, but their joint appearance did. It changed history.

I had room reservations at the King David Hotel, and because I heard that President Sadat and the Egyptian delegation were staying there, I expected to be moved to another hotel, but I was not. The importance of foreign language study came through in the lobby of the hotel. In the midst of Egyptian generals and officials, Israeli cabinet member (and now Israel's President) Azriel Weizmann moved with ease — partly because of his outgoing personality and his strong commitment to building bridges with Egypt, a position he had long held, but partly because of his fluency in Arabic. It showed a respect for his guests and their culture.

After leaving Israel, President Sadat did something that has received little attention in our media but also helped to change history. Most Arab leaders thought the people of Egypt would be furious at Sadat. He chose to return and drive through the streets of Cairo in an open Cadillac convertible, and millions cheered him. It stunned Arab leaders throughout the region, and changed the climate for the better. The message: You can be for peace with Israel and maintain popular support.

Sadat will be viewed by history as one of the giants of this century.

His successor, President Hosni Mubarak, is a different type of leader, paying much more attention to details than Sadat did, but also showing courage. Visiting with him you sense strong leadership, and that generally has been used for constructive purposes in the Middle East.

Praise must also be given to Prime Minister Begin, a conservative leader who sensed the chance to build peace. He seized the opportunity. I had the pleasure of being at the White House for the signing of the Camp David Accord — a tribute also to President Carter — and to have dinner at the White House that evening with a great mixture of American, Israeli, and Egyptian guests.

Two people of vision in Israel also deserve praise for improving the political climate for peace: Shimon Peres, on two occasions Prime Minister and one of the most impressive world leaders I have met, and Abba Eban, Foreign Minister and foreign policy spokesman, whose clear and eloquent call through the years for reconciliation perhaps prevented him from ever becoming Prime Minister, but who contributed significantly to creating the right atmosphere for peace.

Less of a visionary than Peres or Eban was Prime Minister Yitzhak Rabin, former Defense Minister and professional soldier, who accepted the invitation to quietly negotiate in Oslo with representatives of the Palestinian Liberation Organization, the prelude to the uneasy peace we now have. That took courage for an Israeli leader. A low-key type of personality, he was an unlikely political leader, but Israelis had confidence in his judgment and without his contribution and presence there would have been no Oslo breakthrough. He showed great courage. The tragedy of his assassination should not be multiplied by an even greater tragedy, the failure to achieve a genuine peace. A water engineer before he started his military career, Prime Minister Rabin understood the crucial role that water will play in stabilizing — or destabilizing — the Middle East. He encouraged my legislative efforts to promote research for finding less expensive ways of converting saltwater to freshwater, and asked me to join the water portion of the international talks on the Middle East being held in Madrid. Because of my Senate duties I reluctantly declined.

The White House ceremony on September 28, 1995, featuring President Clinton, Prime Minister Rabin, and Chairman Arafat marked the *chance* to create a new Middle East. Having seen so much hatred and tension in that region, I confess to being a bit misty-eyed as I sat on the lawn and saw these two Middle East leaders shake hands and sign their agreement. President Clinton and Secretary of State Warren Christopher should find great satisfaction in having helped achieve this step forward.

I did not know Prime Minister Benjamin Netanyahu before his election, other than having greeted him a few times. Jeanne and I went to Israel in July 1996, early in his term as Israel's leader. After exchanging greetings in his office, he asked, "Why are you leaving the Senate?" After explaining my reasons, he observed, "I don't want to spend the rest of my life in public office."

"Then think how history will judge you," I suggested.

"History will judge me on the peace process," he responded quickly. "But I have a delicate coalition to hold together while I try to achieve peace."

The night before, Jeanne and I had seen a demonstration, boxes and other items being burned to protest certain streets not being closed on the Sabbath. I told the Prime Minister that I wouldn't vote to close any streets in the United States for religious purposes, but if, to hold his coalition together, he yielded on that rather than things that would be barriers to peace, Israel and the area would benefit. The danger for the Prime Minister and the danger to Israel is that he becomes so preoccupied with the steps necessary to hold his coalition together that the larger purpose for Israel, achieving a stable peace, is not served. It is easy for politicians in Israel or the United States or any nation to fan the flames of excessive nationalism and provincialism. Enlightened leadership must appeal to the noble in us. That's what Sadat did. But Sadat could easily have been provincial, taken no risks, made anti-Israel speeches which would have evoked cheers, and probably lived a few more years. Then he would have been forgotten by history, and his country and the region today would be worse off than they now are.

Let me illustrate with the story of one man, someone I had the chance to meet in Moscow. I pushed and pulled and finally got him and his family out of the Soviet Union. They went to Israel. When I go there, I usually try to meet him. One night we had dinner in an Italian restaurant in Jerusalem and I asked if he had any contact with the Palestinians. "Only in business," he replied. "You can't trust them." The next morning I met with two Palestinians and received almost the identical reply in reverse. Being acquainted with all three, I know that leadership can appeal to their emotions and prejudices and bring out the beast that is in all of us, or leadership can appeal to those three to work together, to build a better Israel and a better Middle East — and it would work. Prime Minister Netanyahu needs to do more of the latter.

The other key figure in that region is Yasser Arafat, who heads the Palestinian authority that will eventually emerge as a Palestinian state; which for all practical purposes it almost is today. I met him only one time. Senator Harry Reid of Nevada, Senator Russ Feingold of Wisconsin, and I, and our wives met with him in Tunis for about forty-five minutes. My sense is that he is deeply committed to helping his people and he knows that can happen only in cooperation with Israel. I also sense he is like a few American political leaders I know: he is impulsive and says and does things on the spur of the moment that sometimes are not helpful to improved relations with Israel and others. The leadership immediately below him, particularly the head of their Parliament, appears to be good. Upon Arafat's peaceful departure as the leader — whenever that might occur — there are sensible people who can emerge. However, if Arafat should be assassinated and extremists within the Palestinian movement take over by force, that will ultimately do great harm to the Palestinian cause and diminish dramatically any real chance for peace. Netanyahu must walk his domestic political tightrope without causing Arafat too many problems among his extremist critics, who believe he should never have signed an agreement with Israel.

I first met King Hussein of Jordan in 1957, seventeen years before my election to Congress. A relatively new monarch then, knowledgeable people told me that he would not last long on the throne. Forty-one years later he still reigns. Like other leaders in the region, he has to perform a delicate balancing act, not aggravating his militant critics within the country as he moves ahead with improved relations with Israel. He knows that is in the best interest of his people and for years he has generally been a constructive but cautious force for good. The Six-Day War cost Jordan and others who attacked Israel in land, personnel, and prestige — and taught him a lesson he wants to avoid repeating. King Hussein and Prime Minister Rabin spoke together to a joint session of Congress, in 1994, a remarkable thing in itself. Afterward there was a small luncheon honoring the two leaders and I walked up to the head table to pay my respects, where Vice President Al Gore Jr. was seated between them. As I approached, the Vice President said, "They've just been lobbying me for your bill on desalination research."

A remarkable couple in Jerusalem whose names few people outside of professional diplomats recognize deserve much credit for the progress that has been made in that region: Terje Larsen and Mona Juul. They suggested to the Norwegian Foreign Minister the possibility of bringing the Israelis and Palestinians together in Oslo, quietly, away from the news media. It worked. Both now are serving with the United Nations in Jerusalem and maintain good relationships with Israeli and Palestinian leaders. Jeanne and I had dinner with them in their apartment and came away with a great sense of gratitude to them. The heroes of peace are not only the big names that we see on the front pages of our newspapers.

I have met with two reigning monarchs in Saudi Arabia and my overall sense is that they try to be a force for stability in the region but their agenda is dominated by the desire for domestic security, and everything they do has a label: caution.

My meetings with top west European officials have been brief but the most impressive have included Margaret Thatcher, former British Prime Minister, simply for her backbone. While she approaches things from a different philosophical perspective than Harry Truman, in many ways she is a Harry Truman in a skirt.

John Hume, a member of the British House of Commons from Northern Ireland, is one of those solid low-key people in whom a person immediately has confidence. He has been a key figure in the reconciliation effort in Northern Ireland. One of the more unusual tributes paid to him occurred when Mary Robinson resigned as President of the Republic of Ireland to take a position as head of the

Office of the High Commissioner for Human Rights for the United Nations. Leaders of the Republic of Ireland informally offered the presidency to someone not even a citizen of the Republic of Ireland, John Hume. It is a largely ceremonial position but Mary Robinson made it a post from which she reached out to the rest of the world for humanitarian purposes, such as in her trip to Somalia during the worst of that nation's ordeals. But John Hume declined that honor, preferring to stay in Northern Ireland to try to bring about peace there. One St. Patrick's Day he found himself in the United States and Jeanne and I invited him and three of his friends and a few of our Irish American friends to dinner that evening. When the doorbell rang, one of John's friends immediately shouted, "Do you have any whiskey?" Jeanne and I drink wine but luckily had a gift bottle of whiskey which we opened promptly. I anticipated an evening with John Hume seriously discussing the future of Northern Ireland, but John's noisy friends wanted a celebration, so we all joined in boisterous singing of Irish songs.

Dominating Europe in recent years has been Chancellor Helmut Kohl, who physically dominates a room as much as he does politically. The absorption of economically weak East Germany into a unified Germany has cost the nation's economy much more than anyone anticipated, and that has hurt Kohl politically, even though the initial move toward unification had immense popularity. Two German leaders of vision who contributed a great deal and whom I instinctively liked are Willie Brandt and Helmut Schmidt. But Germany, starting with Konrad Adenauer, has not had weak leadership, and, to the credit of these governments, they have recognized the gross abuses of the Nazi era and they are determined not only to avoid a repetition but also to be a constructive force in the world.

One of my vivid memories of France is as a journalist when I flew to Paris to conduct a scheduled interview with Prime Minister Guy Mollet, who by the time my plane landed was no longer Prime Minister. A cab driver, when I explained my problem, said: "France gets along better without prime ministers." Not accurate, but he meant it. President de Gaulle changed that system of constantly rotating prime ministers.

I saw two dead Soviet leaders on my first visit to Moscow when I visited the mausoleum where the bodies of Lenin and Stalin were on display. I recall my Intourist guide, who must have been through there hundreds of times, weeping as she walked past the bodies, probably the politically correct thing to do in those days.

On that first visit in 1957 I went to the Bolshoi theatre to attend a ballet performance. The American from Rhode Island seated next to me, Claiborne Pell, later became my colleague in the United States Senate. About one-third of the way through the performance Nikita Khruschev and Nikolay Bulganin, the two leaders of the Soviet Union then known as the B and K team, appeared in a box to watch the performance. During the intermission I thought it would be worth a try to get an interview with them. I proceeded around the magnificent, old, and ornate structure to an area which I guessed might be somewhere close to where they sat. I knocked on a door and immediately Soviet soldiers surrounded me, none of whom could speak English (and I knew no Russian). Soon someone who spoke English arrived and they told me in brusque terms to return to my seat. I did.

In those days Soviets herded visiting Americans together to minimize contact with local citizens. I remember talking to the UPI reporter Roy Essoyan, who began our conversation saying that I should recognize that we were being taped by the KGB. Years later when I went with small congressional delegations to the Soviet Union, we were assigned to a table wherever we ate. We had a little contact with people when we rode on the superb Moscow subway, for example, but the government discouraged it. In one visit our small group ate at a table and a waiter served us who did not communicate at all. From Moscow we went to Kiev in what is now the independent nation of Ukraine but then was one of the Soviet Republics. After checking into our hotel we went to eat in the hotel restaurant — where we found the same waiter serving us! We were more judicious in what we had to say after that. On that same visit to Kiev, which then had few American visitors, I asked the Intourist people if one evening we could go to a restaurant where we could hear local music. They arranged it, but no local citizens were present other than the musicians. Through the U. S. Embassy we did arrange meetings during various visits with Refuseniks, but we always knew the strong likelihood that what we said was being monitored.

The only two top leaders there I ever met were Mikhail Gorbachev and Boris Yeltsin, and both meetings were brief. Gorbachev, not popular in Russia today, nevertheless made a huge contribution to humanity by tearing down the Berlin Wall and the barriers that separated the East and the West. Because of his leadership, the threat of the nuclear annihilation of humanity has dramatically reduced, no small item for historians to note. Things did not materialize as he hoped, and the future of Russia remains cloudy as I write, but my sense is that however flawed the steps to freedom, it will be hard for any "strong man" to completely close the door to freedom. Yeltsin made a stronger impression than I anticipated in our short encounter.

In one of my first trips abroad in 1959 I visited with India's initial prime minister, Jawaharlal Nehru. I had mentioned to Adlai Stevenson that I would be visiting India and he sent a note to the Prime Minister. When I arrived at the Imperial Hotel in New Delhi (a terrible name for a hotel in independent India) I had a note inviting me to the Prime Minister's residence that evening. Before I went, a U. S. Embassy official visited me and said that they would appreciate if I asked the Prime Minister a question. President Eisenhower planned a visit to the Soviet Union, and world leaders had welcomed this gesture, except for the Indian Prime Minister, generally regarded as the leading spokesperson for the developing nations, who remained silent. Eisenhower was eager to get the Prime Minister's reaction, since he thought there would be lavish praise for such a move, rather than silence. Could I get Nehru's reaction? During the course of my visit there — where one of my most vivid memories is of watching a lizard walk up and down the wall while we chatted — I asked him about the Eisenhower visit. He responded that he welcomed this goodwill gesture which could bring the world a little closer to peace, but he thought it strange that no president of the world's leading democracy had ever visited the world's largest democracy, India. He felt that before a United States president visited a dictatorship, recognition should be paid to democracies. I passed that along to the U. S. Embassy. Later, when the Soviets shot down a United States observer plane piloted by Gary Powers, our government at first denied that we had a high-altitude plane spying on the Soviets. When it became clear that we did, Eisenhower scrubbed his visit to the Soviet Union. Shortly after that, he announced he would visit India, where he received a tumultuous welcome. Halfway through our meeting Mrs. Indira Gandhi, the Prime Minister's daughter, joined us. She had been to a small village explaining that they belonged to a country called India. Nehru had to deal with a shortage of food, developing a democracy with a people whose education attainments often were limited, facing China, a neighbor India did not trust and which had taken over Tibet, and precarious relations with Pakistan. I left his residence that evening appreciating his dream of what the world could be, despite the immediate difficulties that pressed upon him, and thinking that if the President of the United States thinks he has problems, he should serve as Prime Minister of India for a short time. Mrs. Gandhi later became Prime Minister, as did her son, Rajiv Gandhi, both of whom I had the chance to know slightly.

On the same trip I visited the leader of Pakistan, General Ayub Khan, also impressive. At that point the up-and-down relationship with India that has always marked the history of these two nations had improved. I asked him why. "It so happens that India and Pakistan are in the same Rotary Club district, and at a meeting in Ceylon [now Sri Lanka] the businessmen got together and said that it didn't make sense for our two nations to be antagonistic, that we should be trading and working together. And we are."

The relationships between the two nations are complicated by the religious division between Hindu India and Moslem Pakistan. It is easy for leaders to stir passions, more difficult to subdue them. The stakes for the world have escalated with the nuclear explosions by both countries. Problems like the status of beautiful Kashmir are soluble, if the nuclear threat can be diminished in these two nations and in China, which India also fears. But all steps forward depend on political leadership that is willing to risk a little and not simply pander to public opinion. That is more likely to happen if the United States pays more attention to the area, not simply when there is a crisis.

I had the opportunity to visit briefly with Generalissimo Chiang Kai-shek and Madame Chiang at their summer residence on the hills overlooking Taipei, Taiwan. Years later as a Senator I received word through a mutual friend that Madame Chiang Kai-shek, who once addressed a joint session of Congress during World War II with a stirring message, would like to make a last visit to Washington. I asked Senator Bob Dole to co-host the event. The demand to attend the event overwhelmed us. Nancy Chen from my staff determined who could attend and who could not. Madame Chiang, at that point around ninety-five — her age being a matter of dispute that I did not enter- — -but sharp and alert. I enlisted my son Martin to take pictures, and when I introduced him to her and she asked, "Are you a good son?" And then asked me, "Are you a good father?" We informed the Embassy of the People's Republic of China about the reception. They voiced no objection. The overwhelming and warm response to her visit had to be gratifying to her.

When the words "vision" and "courage" are used, South Korea's President Kim Dae Jung is a great example. A fighter for democracy in that nation, he had been condemned to death by the repressive governments of both North Korea and South Korea. He fled to the United States where he lived for several years. Early in 1985 he decided to return to South Korea after receiving a signal that he would be tolerated but not welcomed. He asked Congressman Tom

Foglietta, now the U. S. Ambassador to Italy, and me to join him in going back, as a means of conveying to the government there that Kim had official friends in the U. S. I had just been sworn in as a Senator, and was feverishly trying to put my staff together. I felt I could not take time off then, much as I yearned to do so. When he returned to South Korea the police hassled him and life was not pleasant but he continued to push for genuine democracy in his homeland. Gradually it returned. Jeanne and I visited with him and his wife in South Korea in 1995. I admired his courage and felt he had a good influence on the course of his nation, but I did not believe he had a chance of winning his goal of being elected President. But in early 1998 it happened. He became the first South Korean opposition candidate to win the presidency. He invited me to his inauguration, which I could not attend. Since that inauguration he has shown courage on both the domestic economic front and in sending gestures of reconciliation to North Korea. I am proud of this man who is a leader with backbone and compassion and common sense.

Three other Asian leaders I have met should be acknowledged as clearly superior. President Lee Teng-Hui of Taiwan has led his country from being a semi-democracy to becoming a full-blown democracy in every respect. He strikes me as well-informed, practical, and with the personality requirements that a strong leader in a democracy must have. President Fidel Ramos of the Philippines recently stepped down from that post. A little like Prime Minister Rabin in Israel, he is a military man by background and does not exude the political type of personality, but the people of the Philippines had confidence in him. He lifted the Philippine economy significantly. He has made a huge contribution to his country and to that part of Asia. Martin Lee is the leader of the democracy movement in Hong Kong. One word describes him more aptly than any other: courage. He is a zealous believer in democracy and made clear that when China took over Hong Kong he would not flee but stay and fight for democracy. He has shown such great popularity in Hong Kong that it would be difficult for Chinese officials to quiet him either with house arrest or imprisonment.

Tiny Costa Rica in Central America has produced two leaders who have had an influence far beyond their borders. The most recent is President Oscar Arias whose constructive efforts for reconciliation and understanding have gained him international recognition. He came to Washington periodically to quietly and diplomatically play a constructive role in our decision-making. One of his predecessors, President Jose Figueres, advocated democracy when most of Central and South America had dictators. His vision of what that area could become is largely realized, in part because of his determination and courage and in part because of President Jimmy Carter standing up for human rights so clearly and firmly. When our children were five and eight, we drove down the Pan American Highway from Illinois to Costa Rica and visited with President Figueres and his American-born wife in a suburb of their capital. We had practiced with five-year-old Martin to say, "Hello, Mr. President." But when the diminutive and dynamic chief executive swept into his living room to greet us, he grabbed Martin and put him on his lap and Martin had this what-do-I-do-now look about him. I am pleased that both children had the chance to meet this giant in the history of democracy in Latin America.

Speaking of giants, President Nelson Mandela of South Africa has that stature in the freedom movement on his continent (See Chapter 19). The greatest disappointment in leadership in sub-Sahara Africa is Kenya's President Moi. Abundant in resources and talented people, Kenya had an early lead over most African nations in heading toward democracy, but under President Moi's administration that lead has deteriorated. Kenya is not a monolithic dictatorship, but freedom has been restricted. I am not President Moi's favorite person. In meetings with him I have been candid about my disappointment. On one occasion Senator Chuck Robb of Virginia and I visited him at the President's summer residence in Mombasa. He had several members of his cabinet there for his meeting with us. We had just come from Eritrea, and I said, "If you had asked me five years ago who would have a multiparty system and free elections, Eritrea or Kenya, without hesitation I would have said Kenya. But today it is Eritrea." He said a multiparty system with free elections would result in tribal warfare. And after each point he made he would ask a cabinet member whether his statement was right. "The president is right," each would chime, providing background to support Moi. Today international investments in Kenya that should be growing dramatically are not. Uncertainty dominates everything. President Moi could make a brighter place for himself in Kenyan and African history if he were to step aside graciously and help prepare his nation for the twenty-first century. There is a price to be paid for freedom, but there is also a reward. President Moi is denying the people of Kenya that reward.

Closer to home, a Canadian leader, former Prime Minister Brian Mulrooney, repudiated by the Canadian people in an election there, would be a huge success as an American politician. He has all the qualities of leadership we should seek: intelligence, a great personality, interest in everything, and courage. He is the type of personality who would emerge as a leader in any democratic nation. I now serve on a foundation board on which he also serves, and when I see him in action I can't help thinking that if he were a U. S. political figure, he would at least be prominently mentioned as a presidential possibility.


Because of my international interests, I had the chance to know slightly and work with a few of the officials of the United Nations, including Secretary-General Boutros Boutros-Ghali. I came to have an appreciation for the obstacles that a UN secretary-general faces, and I learned to respect Boutros-Ghali. During the 1996 presidential race, Bob Dole, who had a hard time satisfying his right-wing supporters, said in his acceptance speech at the Republican convention, "When I am President every man, and every woman in our armed forces will know the President is Commander in Chief, not B-o-u-t-r-o-s B-o-u-t-r-o-s- G-h-a-l-i [not spelled out, but dragged out]." I don't know what Bob would have done if the Secretary-General's name had been John Smith. But the line got applause and he used it again and again. The always-politically-sensitive Clinton White House responded by indicating that Clinton would oppose the retention of the UN Secretary General, an announcement made without consulting any other nations as far as I can determine. I let the Secretary-General know that I differed with that stated policy and immediately after the election I announced that I would have a press conference on the matter. Madeleine Albright, then our Ambassador to the United Nations, called the night before the scheduled press conference and asked me to call it off. Madeleine and I have known each other for many years and we could speak frankly. I said that I thought we were making a mistake and that unless some major reason of which I was not aware justified our position, I would go ahead with the press conference. She made two points. The first, that Boutros-Ghali did not always do what we wanted. I replied, "I don't want a Secretary-General who does only what we want. That would diminish the constructive role of the United Nations." Then she said, "When he ran for Secretary-General he said he would serve only five years."

"Madeleine," I responded, "I can remember when a Governor of Arkansas ran for reelection and pledged that he would not run for President of the United States." I did not convince her and she did not convince me.

The United States vetoed his reappointment. No other nation on the Security Council voted with us. Secretary of State Warren Christopher, in his first visit to sub-Sahara Africa as Secretary of State, wandered around that continent trying to find support for our position.

Our action seemed particularly inappropriate to other nations when we owe the UN $1.4 billion in arrears. It takes $1.2 billion a year to operate the basic UN operation, not counting peace-keeping. It is like the most powerful person in a community demanding a new president of the Rotary Club to which he belongs: none of the other members agree with him, but they fear him; on top of that he does not pay his club dues.

The action was both inappropriate and badly handled. Fortunately the successor to Boutros-Ghali, Kofi Annan has been effective. But it was amateurish conduct on our part that was unfair to Boutros-Ghali, unfair to the United Nations, and reduced international confidence in how we conduct foreign policy.

# Chapter 16

# *The Media*

The media play an important role in national policy-making, and for the most part it is a constructive role. But improvements are needed.

The media often determine priorities for policymakers. If an issue gets big play it captures the attention of those who determine the course of a community, state, or nation; first, because the issue is in the news, it creates public attention and frequently concern; and second, because those in public life know that the oxygen of political survival is attention from the media, and the seldom expressed but widely understood maxim for officeholders is "If they're covering it, I'll comment on it."

My relationship with the media has been good, in part because of my background in journalism which helps me understand the problems reporters face with deadlines, and that the need to cover many areas with in-depth understanding on any one issue by a reporter is uncommon. I tried to answer phone calls reasonably promptly whether from a student newspaper somewhere or from *Time* or *Newsweek*. Reporters from my state got priority, but journalists from other areas understood that. I would be misquoted occasionally, but rarely out of malice. I confess I always feel more comfortable when a reporter walks into my office with a tape recorder, or asks me on the telephone if it is all right to record our conversation. I not only don't resent it, I appreciate it, because reporters can then go back and double-check something that may be a matter of doubt.

People who were "class" reporters during my state legislative days include Bob Howard of the *Chicago Tribune* and George Thiem of the *Chicago Daily News*. John Dreiske had a column in the *Chicago Sun-Times* that all politicians and reporters read. Others who did a solid job in Springfield, sometimes only coming there occasionally, were Tom Littlewood and Charlie Wheeler of the *Chicago Sun-Times*; Lois Wille, Charlie Nicodemus, Henry Hanson, Charlie Cleveland, Mike Royko and Jack Mabley of the *Chicago Daily News*; Gene Callahan, Jerry Owens, and Al Manning of the *Illinois State Register*; Ken Watson of the *Illinois State Journal*; Mike Lawrence with the Lee newspapers; Ray Serati of the Copley newspapers; Bill O'Connell and Bernardine Martin of the *Peoria Journal-Star*; Ray Coffey, Bill Feurer, and Chris Vlhapolus of the United Press (later UP International); Charlie Whalen, Mike Robinson, and Larry Kramp of the Associated Press; Malden Jones of the *Chicago American*; Taylor Pensoneau of the *St. Louis Post-Dispatch*; Ed Nash of the *Waukegan News-Sun*; "Hap" Lynes of the *St. Louis Globe-Democrat*; Bill Miller and Ben Kiningham with several radio stations; Hugh Hill and Mike Flannery of Chicago television; and Don Chamberlain, who covered the capital for a host of small newspapers and produced mountains of copy. Rumors had it that one reporter from a Chicago newspaper (not mentioned by name in this chapter) could be bought. I have no way of knowing whether that widely held view had validity. But the integrity level of reporters covering the Illinois General Assembly was superior to the integrity level of the state legislators.

Being honest in reporting is not the same as being responsibly aggressive. I use the phrase "responsibly aggressive" because if a reporter is so bent on producing a sensation that facts are twisted, or a portrait is made of a public official that focuses only on a person's warts — and we all have them — then ultimately the media, the public, and truth are not well served. The greater danger is taking it easy, not pushing yourself as a reporter to pursue information doggedly. Look for a reporter who, in addition to his or her assigned work, writes feature articles for small magazines, writes books, or takes extra time to really become knowledgeable on an issue. When you find that reporter, you will see someone who is going to grow in stature and influence.

Some journalists on the Springfield scene emerged as first-class reporters at the national level, including Bob Estill of Copley Press; Bill Lambrecht of the *St. Louis Post Dispatch*; Jerome Watson, Basil Talbott, Lynn Sweet, and Mike Briggs of the *Chicago Sun-Times*; Mitch Locin of the *Chicago Tribune*; Frank Maier of the *Chicago Daily News* went to *Newsweek*. An enterprising reporter who early showed a penchant for hard work, John Zakarian of the Lindsay-Schaub newspapers, later became editorial page editor of the *Hartford Courant* in

Connecticut. Morton Kondracke, a bright young reporter on the Springfield scene, moved to Washington and became a frequent television news commentator and editor of *Roll Call*, a Capitol Hill publication read widely by policymakers. And some superior journalists decided to stay at their home base rather than go national, two good examples being Don Hickman with the NBC television station in Springfield and Betsy Bruce with the CBS outlet in St. Louis.

Two journalistic veterans who don't fit into any easy categories and who are universally liked and respected are Irv "Kup" Kupcinet of the *Chicago Sun-Times* and Jack Brickhouse, former voice for the Chicago Cubs on radio. They both are more than the above descriptions; they are civic icons.

Two reporters who covered my 1984 race for the Senate made a strong impression on me for their hard work and quality reporting: Carol Marin, then with the NBC affiliate in Chicago, and Bruce Dold of the *Chicago Tribune*. Carol, after a courageous and principled battle with local management over the trivialization of the news, advanced to the national television stage and Bruce is now on the editorial staff of the *Tribune* and won a Pulitzer prize.

A maverick journalist who once ran for state-wide office as a Republican, Bill Rentschler, does free-lance articles that often are insightful on societal needs.

While on occasion I would encounter reporters who would be obnoxious, persistent beyond my point of patience, I cannot fault them for that. They worked hard at their jobs. Only one reporter have I refused to grant interviews to after he distorted in a wholesale way an interview for the far-right publication, *The American Spectator.* Not only did David Brock massively and intentionally misquote me, he said I had leaked the information on Anita Hill in the encounter with Clarence Thomas, then later said Jeanne did, before he moved on to other suspects. Neither of us had done it, though my belief is that people should be more concerned with who told the truth between Anita Hill and Clarence Thomas, than with who leaked the information. (A few months ago the *Weekly Standard* said, "Everybody knows it was Ricki Seidman and James Brudney — aides to Ted Kennedy and Howard Metzenbaum [who leaked the information]."[1] Whether "everybody knows" is accurate in their conclusion, I do not know.) Then Brock wrote a book, a work of historical fiction (but not labeled as that) titled, *The Real Anita Hill*, which got undeservedly sizable circulation. In the book, he asserts that a member of the Court of Appeals with Thomas, Judge Patricia Wald, did not like Thomas and because of her "close" relationship to me fed me with anti-Thomas information as she had earlier when Robert Bork and Douglas Ginsburg received nominations to the high court. The only problem with his scenario is that I had never even met Judge Wald. About six months before I left the Senate I testified before a subcommittee, and before I started my comments a woman behind me touched my shoulder and said, "Since you and I are close, I thought I should introduce myself. I'm Judge Patricia Wald." After the Senate confirmed Clarence Thomas, we voted to investigate who leaked the story. Brock asserts in his book that I refused to talk to the investigators. Not only did I talk with them and answer all their questions, but I also provided a written statement of my recollection of events. Inaccuracy is piled upon inaccuracy in the Brock book. Brock, then a young reporter with more ability than judgment, is apparently maturing and, I am told, becoming responsible.

One reporter asked me for a job as press secretary, and after I turned him down to employ someone else, I became the object of several critical stories. Whether he did it consciously, I do not know. It may simply have been that after I did not hire him his esteem for my judgment diminished and these stories followed. Not bad stories, but not good; stories that had a harsh edge to them.

George Tagge, the leading political writer for the *Chicago Tribune*, did not fall into the category of being dishonest, but he combined massively slanted reporting with openly lobbying on the floor of the state legislature for projects of interest to his boss, Col. Robert McCormick. Tagge had ability, but most reporters and legislators felt the combination of lobbying and reporting might be good for his lobbying efforts, but not good for the profession of journalism.

Tagge's principal lobbying work resulted in a good thing for Chicago's economy, McCormick Place, a convention center named for the Tribune's publisher for many years, who had as one of his seven points in a platform for the city: "Build Chicago the Best Convention Hall in America."[2] But Tagge's efforts are not a textbook model for a reporter.

Fortunately he gave a lengthy interview for an oral history project. In it he talks openly about talking to key lawmakers — particularly those who he knew were corrupt — about getting legislation passed. There is no suggestion that he bribed anyone, but he treated bribed legislators kindly in the *Tribune* and found corruption more a joke than something to be pursued as a reporter. For example, he talks about going to State Senator William Connors, considered "one of the honest brokers, or so regarded as an honest middleman or bagman, to whom a very large sum of money could be given with the belief that he wouldn't just keep it all for himself but would distribute [the bribery money] to do the most good. . . . He has the distinction . . . held by no other legislator among the thousands I've known, namely that he actually spent his own money to pass a civic virtue bill."[3] Tagge tells about the *Tribune* crusade against fireworks, and because Connors's daughter strongly favored the bill, Connors spent money on bribes to pass the bill. Connors, according to Tagge, went to members and asked, "How much are the guys on the other side [the fireworks manufacturers] offering you?" Then he told them, "I'll match it."[4] Connors told Tagge about being on the Chicago Sanitary District board before he became an influential legislator, and he had to testify before the grand jury. The prosecuting attorney asked him, "A lot of money has been handed out to members of the legislature to pass bills favorable to the Sanitary District and I want you to tell the grand jury about it." Connors replied, "Who, me? I've always been on the other side."

In this oral history Tagge talks candidly about calling different mayors of Chicago, as well as governors of Illinois, lobbying them on bills.

When he approached the Illinois House minority leader, Rep. James Ryan, about a measure, Ryan told Tagge that he had not heard from Mayor Richard J. Daley as to what to do on the bill. So Tagge got Mayor Daley on the phone and sent a press messenger to bring Ryan to talk with Daley. When Ryan got there Tagge said, "Mr. Mayor, here's Jimmy. Tell him now damn it, whatever it is, but tell him." Ryan listened to the mayor and then said, "I see. Okay, mayor." Then Tagge relates, "This kind of thing went on year after year. Most vexing."[5]

When Tagge had to deal with a governor with whom he did not have a close relationship, Adlai Stevenson, he got major donors to the Stevenson campaign to work on the governor without success, Tagge claims.

Tagge describes working with Rep. Charles Weber, "one of the most unabashed money players in the entire game of politics."[6] The unspoken *quid pro quo* (or perhaps spoken): You help me with this bill, whatever it was, and the *Tribune* won't hurt you.

When McCormick Place moved toward reality, legislators openly called it Tagge's Temple, because he had so energetically lobbied for it.

He recalls handing amendments to key legislators, and praised

Senator Lottie Holman O'Neill, the first woman legislator in Illinois: "She helped me on almost any project in which I sought her help." On another occasion it looked like one of his measures would fall short a few votes, and he whispered to Senator Marshall Korshak, "For God's sake, get me some votes."[7] And he reports that Korshak moved around the floor and got Tagge the votes he needed.

But from Tagge's viewpoint, a terrible bill emerged in the legislature, to require lobbyists to register. But before that became law, and Tagge retired, he managed to get the state treasurer to buy bonds for McCormick Place, and prodded the Chicago mayor and the governor to appoint people whom the *Tribune* wanted on the oversight committee for McCormick Place. But after Col. McCormick's death and the character of the *Tribune* changed, he was "fairly sickened" when the *Tribune* editor told him to stop lobbying against a state income tax.[8]

Tagge had a flexible morality, observing that in the Chicago City Council and the Cook County Board there "are just too many burglars with their hands out all the time."[9] But the same conduct in the legislature seemed to trouble him less.

I maintained a polite but distant relationship with George Tagge. I always sensed that he felt the combination of my intolerance of corruption and my political philosophy, considerably to the left of his far-right approach, marked me as impractical.

However, McCormick Place in Chicago would not be there today but for George Tagge's efforts. He was both an influential journalist and a skilled lobbyist.

Evaluating journalistic figures at the national level is more complicated, in part because of the huge numbers. I will not even start to list the names of really fine reporters. It is trite to say but Washington is a mecca for good journalism.

David Broder probably has as much balance and thoughtfulness as any columnist, and if I were to cite only one columnist as the best, he would receive my accolade. He leaves Washington regularly to rub shoulders with average citizens and listen to them and to maintain connections with people everywhere. I also like his practice of annually mentioning the mistakes he made the previous year. Anthony Lewis also ranks high. George Will is more conservative than I am, but he brings to many of his columns a historical perspective that I like and which marks them as distinctive. In terms of writing style, there is no better column. No columnist works harder than Robert Novak. I differ with him frequently, but I have always found him fair. If he has something in his column about me, he checks it out first, or at least gets my perspective on it. That means extra work but it pays off. No other columnist has as many sources for news scattered around the federal government as Bob Novak. His prose does not ring as George Will's sometimes does, but he has a clear, crisp style. I almost always agree with Carl Rowan, and his words march. You know what Carl Rowan is doing battle for or against and why. Two columnists I also respect who write jointly are Jack Germond and Jules Witcover, but I do not see them regularly. When Mary McGrory is good, she is really good. Like George Will, she has a special talent with words. Roger Simon (no relative) is a thoughtful and entertaining writer. Clarence Page is a skilled wordsmith with penetrating observations about our society. There are others: William Safire, Bob Herbert, Mark Shields, Ellen Goodman, William Raspberry, Thomas Friedman, Cal Thomas, Richard Reeves, Molly Ivins, and many more who add to our understanding.

While they do not primarily cover the national scene, political editors in Illinois keep in touch with members of Congress and play a role in our lives through their stories. They include Tom Hardy of the *Chicago Tribune* (now press secretary to Governor Jim Edgar), Steve Neal of the *Chicago Sun-Times*, and Madelyn Dubek of the *Daily Herald*, which covers much of the Chicago suburbs. Generally they and their predecessors have done a good job.

The field of ethics in journalism as it relates to government is one that needs burnishing, just as it does for legislators. James Warren of the *Chicago Tribune* and James Fallows, until recently editor of *U. S. News*, have made an issue of speaking fees paid to journalistic stars. My instinct is that the answer is disclosure. I frankly think it is a good thing if Cokie Roberts speaks at the University of Illinois, but if she were to draw a sizable fee for speaking to a convention of the tobacco industry — which I am confident she would not do — we should know that so we can make judgments about her coverage of that issue.

A widely listened to TV commentator in Chicago for many years, Len O'Connor, told me about attending a charity race track event when the impresario there, Marge Everett, handed him an envelope and said, "Your horse won."

"But I didn't bet," he said.

"We placed a bet for you," she said as he looked in the envelope stuffed with $100 bills. He gave it back to her. The *Chicago Journalism Review* tells about her operation, which landed Governor Otto Kerner in prison, and enriched many political leaders: "Marge Everett . . . [wooed] them [journalists] not with stock profits but with gift certificates, Christmas presents, sumptuous luncheons, cash payments for participation in promotional events and summer jobs for reporters' children. . . . She made life easy for them however she could, even writing their stories for them. The prose of your favorite turf columnist might have come from a 22-year-old publicity writer. We know, because during the four seasons we worked for Everett, from 1965 to 1968, we personally wrote many columns that appeared under the bylines of well-known Chicago sportswriters. . . . All Everett demanded in return was the reporters' loyalty."[10]

Is it surprising then that the corruption of legislators and other officials by the racetracks emerged only partially and only slowly?

The weakness of the media includes:

- Pandering to public tastes, whether good or bad, wise or unwise.

- Stressing the trivial rather than the substantial.

- Too much cynicism.

- Reduction in the numbers of reporters, resulting in a news loss qualitatively and quantitatively.

- Inattention to international coverage.

On network television's nightly news, the O. J. Simpson trials received more than three times as much coverage as the fall of the Berlin Wall.[11] Which is of greater importance to the future of humanity no one questions. If you add the coverage from Court TV, news features, and coverage in local news programs, the disparity would be much, much worse. When I ask media executives why this imbalance, the answer comes back in one form or another: "We're giving the public what it wants." The same outlets properly criticize office-holders and candidates who slavishly follow the polls. There is an apologetic tone to those who made the media decisions on the Simpson trials. It is not put this bluntly, but the message is: "We know it's irresponsible but we're giving the public what it wants." And politicians who follow the polls will say much the same privately.

During the O. J. Simpson trials, Tim Russert of NBC made the decision that *Meet the Press* would ignore it. ABC saw a ratings opportunity, and temporarily ABC's numbers went up. But shortly after that *Meet the Press* renewed its lead role in viewership — with added prestige.

When former Senator George Mitchell returned to the United States from his successful negotiations of the Northern Ireland crisis, he held a press conference at which almost no one showed up. If it had been a press conference about a woman alleging that the President had approached her to have sex with him, the press conference would have been packed.

As I write this, President Clinton's alleged sexual activities are making the news — daily. It appears that the President is gradually painting himself into a corner by not being candid. But the coverage of this national soap opera has been excessive. It is occasionally hard to tell the difference between the *New York Times* and the *National Enquirer*. There is a legitimate story concerning the president of the United States. But legitimate stories can be overplayed; this one has been.

To those who suggest that pandering is necessary in order to be competitive, my guess is that the *New York Times* makes more money than the *National Enquirer*. *U. S. News and World Report*, which has devoted about one-third as much attention to these allegations as *Time* and *Newsweek*, has gained in stature. If there is a growth in circulation disparity favoring *Time* and *Newsweek* — and I doubt that — it will be a temporary phenomenon. Public officials who have the courage to do the right thing usually — not always — survive and prosper, and my hunch is the same is true for the media. Any short-term loss is more than compensated for in the long run. It is disheartening to read that only 59 percent of adults read daily newspapers, but the downward trend in readership appears to have been arrested in 1997, with nineteen of the thirty largest newspapers gaining in circulation. It is encouraging to read that the *New York Times*, the *Los Angeles Times*, *USA Today*, and the *Boston Globe* are among them, all newspapers that generally do a responsible job.

Pandering is not only the coverage given but the allocation of resources within any one medium. I'm a football fan, but that the *New*

*York Times* has fifty-six writers covering sports and two covering religion strikes me as an imbalance. Each media outlet should be asking itself: what is important?; what will contribute to a better society? I know they will ask what will sell newspapers or attract viewers and listeners. They should. But they should be asking the other two questions also.

My political mentor was Senator Paul Douglas, one of the finest people in or out of public life. A giant in the Senate, he took on a variety of special interests, sometimes winning, more often losing, but educating the nation in the process of the losses. When you take a loan from a bank today, the disclosure statement you receive about the interest to be paid is there because Paul Douglas saw too many people abused. And no one other than Martin Luther King is more responsible than Paul Douglas for the passage of the 1964 Civil Rights Act. (Sharing the honors for this also are President Lyndon Johnson, Senator Hubert Humphrey, and Douglas's Illinois Senate colleague, Everett Dirksen. A late convert to the civil rights cause, Dirksen reaped most of the attention because his conversion played a key role. Douglas recognized the importance of Dirksen's help, but privately and understandably resented the great attention given to Dirksen for his belated assistance, while Douglas, who had labored so long and so hard for the cause, received almost no attention.)

Douglas exercised shrewdness as a politician.

One day in my state legislative years, Paul called and asked me to introduce a resolution that called on him to introduce a resolution in the United States Senate to make the corn tassel the national flower. I agreed to do it. But as the day wore on I became more and more uncomfortable with the idea. I called him that evening and asked, "Are you sure that you want to introduce a resolution on the corn tassel?" The former professor at the University of Chicago laughed and became a teacher once again. "Just remember this, Paul," he said, "the substantial things you do in public life receive very little attention, but the trivial receives attention. You introduce your resolution and then I will introduce it here. Our names will be in every newspaper in the state. It won't pass, but no one will be angry with us, and you will have done something to survive in politics."

I learned a little about politics and journalism that night from a great teacher. I regret to say I have seen the truth of what he told me underscored again and again. We want color in our news, and human interest. I understand why a national CBS radio broadcast a few days ago includes an item about a Kentucky state legislator wanting part of the oath of office for that state's officials to include that they have never engaged in a duel. But too many stories like that confront us, and not enough of the ones with substance.

When I sought the Democratic nomination for President, the *New York Times* sent a letter to each of the Democratic and Republican candidates, asking for our financial records, who our friends were in high school and college, our academic records for high school and college, and our complete health records. While I believe there is legitimacy in asking for our financial records, and people have a right to know our current health status, whether I failed or passed high school chemistry is not a matter of national concern, and if I had an ingrown toenail or hemorrhoids or even a social disease at the age of eighteen, I don't think the nation needs to know. At first I decided not to respond, but in talking to the other candidates, they felt obliged to answer so I did too. But with my response I sent a letter saying that it concerned me that they asked about my high school grades, but not my position on national health care, on urban education, and a host of other vital issues.

In a presidential race, who is losing or gaining three points in the latest polls receives much more coverage than where the candidates stand on poverty or foreign policy. It is easy to cover the trivial. A drop in the polls will receive more attention than an in-depth speech on national health care. The average sound bite on network TV news for the Republican presidential primary of 1996 was 7.2 seconds. Almost half the sound bites were less than five seconds. Try to say something of substance on any issue in 7.2 seconds, or five seconds! The media should be here not simply to make money, but also to serve, and that service can be improved.

When I speak on college campuses there will occasionally be a bright young faculty member who, during the question period after my talk, will stand and tell why the situation in the United States and the world is hopeless and everything is wrong. I respond, "For every reason you give me for cynicism, I can give you ten more. But the cynics aren't going to build a better world. People who recognize there are flaws around us and flaws in ourselves need to muster the courage to dream and to build. Cynicism too often is a pseudosophisticated excuse for inaction, for not being responsible."

As a young reporter and during my early years in the state legislature, whiskey was the great vice of journalists. Today it is cynicism.

Cynicism is contagious, just as enthusiasm is. When reporters who constantly question everyone's motives convey that cynicism in their stories, the public is soon afflicted with the same disease. Reporters should be skeptical, ask questions, dig for the facts, and where appropriate make judgments on motivation. But to assume that no public official ever has any aim other than being reelected is as inaccurate as assuming that it is never a motivating factor.

Where public officials make mistakes — and we all do — we should be taken to task both in articles and in editorials. But painting the political horizon as too bleak discourages citizens from using the tools of democracy to improve our communities and our nation. Cynicism by the media produces cynical citizens.


As a former newspaper publisher, I sympathize with steps taken by media executives to improve the bottom line. They do not operate charitable endeavors.

I follow what many might think is a strange practice in making small stock investments. I look to see what the leaders of companies are doing in terms of good citizenship, and if what I see impresses me I buy a few shares of their stock. I do this on the theory that a business leader who recognizes that in the long term that corporation's future is tied to the community at large will also recognize that short-term payoffs that may help the next quarterly or annual report but will not help the business in the long run should not be sought. This year, in Fort Wayne, Indiana, my host for a talk about Abraham Lincoln was the chief executive of Lincoln National Life Insurance, Ian Rowland. I learned how he helped to integrate the public schools in Fort Wayne, and provided other leadership in that community which did not directly benefit Lincoln National Life Insurance. I bought 100 shares of that stock. It is doing well. By buying in this way I have done better than Standard and Poor's and the Dow Jones averages.

What does this have to do with the media?

Reducing news staff may help a newspaper or magazine, a radio station, or a television network — in the short run. It will look good at the next quarterly meeting of the board of directors and the next annual report. But my strong impression is that it is short-sighted. Over time the news outlet that has a sense of civic responsibility, and does not let the bookkeeper determine how many reporters are employed, will profit more. Certainly society will. In an address to the National Press Club, Walter Cronkite admonished media executives: "Muzzle the auditor! Unchain the editor."[12]

How many media executives are willing to assign a reporter to spend three months looking at how health care benefits affect the lives of people in a community? Most small publications or news outlets cannot afford it, but they could assign someone for a week to do that. The larger publications and broadcast entities could do the three month assignments. If even once a year each small or large provider of information felt the obligation to do one in-depth story or series of stories, the nation would benefit enormously — and so would those who authorize this. The success of "60 Minutes" and its imitators shows that substantial news can sell.

However, the pattern is reduction in news staff at newspapers, in magazines, and at radio and television stations.

If a free flow of ideas is essential for a democracy to flourish, whatever diminishes that free flow of ideas harms us. We're being harmed.

I have criticized the *New York Times* several times in this chapter, but I believe it is the best newspaper in the nation. And in coverage of foreign affairs, nothing comes close to the *New York Times* and the *Los Angeles Times*, with the lone exception of the *Miami Herald's* coverage of Latin America.

Public broadcasting has the best foreign news coverage, but even that can be improved. Radio and television coverage of international affairs can accurately be described as anemic. During the last presidential debate in 1996, the moderator finally asked the panel of questioning reporters, "Doesn't anyone have a question about foreign policy?"

Garrick Utley, a thoughtful journalist who has been the chief foreign correspondent for two major networks, had an article in *Foreign Affairs* in which he observed:

> According to the *Tyndall Report*, total foreign coverage on network nightly news programs had declined precipitously, from 3,733 minutes in 1989 to 1,838 minutes in 1996 at ABC, the leader, and from 3,351 minutes to 1,175 minutes at third-place NBC. . . .
>
> In the half-hour format, [international] reports initially ran a minimum of two-and-a-half minutes, compared to one-and-a-half minutes or even less today. . . .

Reporters become known as "firemen", flying from one international conflagration to the next. In March 1978 I was based in London, working for NBC News. On a Monday morning of a quiet news period, I had no plans to leave the city. By Saturday I had covered South Moluccans seizing hostages in the Netherlands, the Israeli incursion to the Litani River in southern Lebanon, and the kidnapping of Prime Minister Aldo Moro in Rome, and had returned home — three stories in three countries on two continents in five days. Newscasts [have] gained the immediacy of broadcasting "today's news today" at the cost of the more exploratory coverage that had been part of the evening news of earlier years. . . .

Broad viewer interest in world affairs is declining from its modest Cold War heights just as U. S. global influence is reaching new levels. . . . Today more Americans than ever before are working and traveling abroad, from CEOs to sales reps, students, and tourists. International trade is equal to about one-quarter of [our] GDP.

Part of the blame for all of this is in our public schools, where foreign languages reach a small minority of students and exposure to the rest of the world is not in the background of the teachers, who obviously then cannot convey it to their students. Among the twenty-one wealthiest nations the United States has moved from first to dead last in the percentage of national income given to help developing countries. We are also the number one deadbeat — by a country mile — in our arrearages to the United Nations.

The vicious circle of indifference to international problems needs to be broken, and a good place to start would be with media coverage. Even a small newspaper or media outlet could once every two years send a reporter abroad for two weeks to some location and give a report. Would it pay off immediately for the owners in added income? No. Would it pay off for the nation? You bet. Would it pay off in the long run for the media ownership? I believe so.

I would like to see a journalism school somewhere pioneer by requiring foreign language exposure before graduation and at least a small amount of study in another nation. In ways none of us can measure that would help this nation.

For the country that holds international leadership in its hands to be so ill-informed about the rest of the world is not simply a minor flaw, it is a serious deterrent to providing responsible leadership.

Two more media deficiencies should be mentioned.

One is the increasing concentration of ownership. In the case of newspapers, there is little the federal government can do. In the case of radio and television stations, there is much that we could do, but we're moving in the wrong direction. The Telecommunications Act of 1996 passed overwhelmingly. I cast one of six votes against it. The measure contained some good things, but it opened the door wide for concentrated ownership in radio and television. Since its passage there has been a huge shift in radio toward a few large corporations owning all the major outlets. In St. Louis, for example, six of the fourteen stations are now owned by one corporation that has holdings all over the nation. The value of radio stations shot up after the passage of the Telecommunications Act of 1996, and soon the top three corporations in radio ownership had sold everything to one company. I had an amendment on the floor of the Senate to expand radio ownership so that no more than fifty AM stations and fifty FM stations could be owned by one company, a liberal figure compared to that of the Federal Communications Commission rule then in effect, but at least a modest limitation. I would have preferred to stick with the limits of the Federal Communications Commission at twenty AM stations and twenty FM stations, but I knew that was doomed. My amendment, cosponsored by the courageous Senator Paul Wellstone of Minnesota, lost 64-34. Considering that I asked Senators to vote against some of the most powerful people in their states, it is perhaps a small wonder that I received thirty-four votes. But the movement toward concentration of ownership I then predicted has happened and continues happening. Within two weeks of the President's signing of the Telecommunications Act almost $1.4 billion in radio properties changed hands and in a few weeks the total zoomed to $5.2 billion, all of it in the form of greater concentration of ownership.

Can I say that up to this point this has caused any harm? No, but it will.


Television entertainment violence is hurting the nation.

I checked into a motel in LaSalle County, Illinois, turned on my television set, and there in front of me in living color I saw a man being sawed in half by a chainsaw. I knew it was not real but it bothered me that night, and I kept asking myself what happens to a ten-year-old who sees this. I called my office the next morning and said, "Someone has to have done research on this. I'd like to see it." The evidence came in that a great deal of research had been done, all of it showing clearly that we are harming our society with the glorification of violence on entertainment television. There is as much solid research about the harm done by the glorification of violence on our TV screens as that cigarettes do to our physical health. If you have not read a great deal about it, or seen much of the evidence on television, the reasons are in part fairly obvious: those who publish newspapers often own television stations, and television stations are not going to publicize the harm that they do. Few media executives are financially involved in tobacco companies, so there is no restraint in providing the news about cigarettes. But media executives have a powerful financial restraint from telling you the harm that TV violence is doing. People in any business have a tendency to believe that what they do is good for people, and obviously much of what reaches the television screen is good.

After reviewing the research, I called representatives of the TV industry to my office and said, "We need change. In the words of George Bush, I am 'a card-carrying member of the American Civil Liberties Union.' I do not want government censorship. But you have to realize that we have a problem and you ought to voluntarily adopt standards to reduce the violence." The vice president of NBC said, "We've done research that shows that television violence doesn't do any harm." I responded that he sounded like the Tobacco Institute people who come into my office and tell me they have research that cigarettes don't do any harm. The question is not whether harm takes place — that has been proven — but what they would do about it. Then they said that they could not get together to establish standards on violence because it would violate antitrust laws.

I had a bill drafted to make an exception to the antitrust laws so that the industry could establish standards on violence for entertainment television. I specifically did not get into the news side for two reasons. First, the portrayal of violence on the news usually does not glamorize it. Widows mourn. It is grim. Children are much less likely to see it and say, "I want to do that." Second, while I believe there is too much crime coverage on our newscasts — New York City local television being one of the worst places for violation of good sense and good taste on this — I do not favor even voluntary industry-wide standards for news coverage because it too easily approaches censorship.

I am not opposed to all violence on entertainment television. If there is a film about the Civil War, it will contain violence. What we do not want is what researcher George Gerbner of the University of

Pennsylvania calls "happy violence," where the hero or heroine kills several people in ten minutes, with no harm to "the good guy" with whom we identify, and no agony for those killed.

I did not get into the sex or language problems. There is no solid research in these areas, though I believe harm is done. But that is pure instinct and laws usually should be based on more than instinct. It is interesting that in Western Europe frontal nudity is tolerated but not the violence that we accept. Much of our TV violence is combined with sex and directed against women. My sense is that sexual harm comes not from the appearance of a nude body but from soap serials where people are hopping from one bed to another. But our strange moral code is that if children see ten people killed in ten minutes, that is OK, but they cannot be permitted to see a nude body. The degradation of language I abhor. I am old enough to remember how Clark Gable startled the nation when he used the word "damn" in *Gone With the Wind*.

No one suggests that glorified violence on the screen is the sole cause of crime and abuse in our society. Our anemic gun laws and lack of drug treatment and education probably play a more significant role. The cause of crime is a mosaic with many pieces, but to ignore more than 100 studies, at least 85 of them substantial and all pointing in the same direction, is irresponsible. When you look at what children in Jonesboro, Arkansas and West Paducah, Kentucky and Springfield, Oregon have done, we have to ask: Why? At least two of the factors are the ridiculously loose gun laws that we have and the irresponsibility of some in the movie and television industry who glamorize violence. No one who has looked objectively at the research can question that one factor in our society's crime is what the industry gives us on the television screen. We have the most violent television of any nation, with the possible exception of Japan, but there is one huge difference. In Japanese television the "bad guys" are violent, not the people with whom we identify. In the United States it is the opposite. I purposely do not mention programs because I watch television so little. I do not claim expertise, but I have read the evidence compiled by the experts. One children's program that most readers would recognize is produced in two versions, the violent version for the United States and the nonviolent version for other nations. When the *Christian Science Monitor* asked the producer why, she responded that in the United States people expect violence and do not object to it, but they cannot sell it in other countries.

I introduced my antitrust exemption proposal — and the industry opposed it. But coming to my side were legislators as philosophically different as Senator Howard Metzenbaum of Ohio and Senator Jesse Helms of North Carolina. We held hearings and the measure received support from witnesses as varied as Elmer Gertz, one of the great civil libertarians of the nation, to the American Academy of Pediatrics, though the ACLU and the television industry opposed it. President Bush signed it into law.

Reaction came slowly. At first executives of the industry did nothing, though they spent a considerable amount of time talking about it. Then representatives of the television and movie industry called a national meeting of 600 people in Los Angeles to look at the issue, the first major meeting on this issue of top people. I spoke bluntly to them, saying that if the industry did not voluntarily take some action that legislation by my colleagues would come, and added that some senators had limited sensitivity to First Amendment issues. If those gathered expected an apple pie and motherhood talk, I didn't give it to them. *Newsday's* reporter wrote: "The mood had gotten ugly. . . . The antagonism between the TV industry and those who advocate less violence on the airwaves went up a notch. . . . Most of the anger was focused on Sen. Paul Simon."[13] Another wire service report said that my solutions "went over like a bad sitcom rerun."[14] Not all reactions were negative. Jeff Sagansky, program chief for CBS, told the Associated Press: "No matter what you believe about the studies, we have to be part of the solution and in no way part of the problem. As far as CBS is concerned, this is going to have an impact on how we do business."[15]

Many resisted any change, refused to acknowledge a problem despite the mountains of research, most of which they ignored — as the cigarette manufacturers have ignored research. No one wants to believe that what he or she is doing may be harmful to society.

But top executives Howard Stringer of CBS and Tom Murphy of ABC added voices of rationality to the discussion. At one network the officers met and criticized me; when one of them asked the others, "Do you let your children watch our programs?" suddenly the tone of the discussion changed dramatically. The television industry is divided into two camps, broadcast and cable. There is an overlapping, but the two are sometimes hostile, sometimes cooperative. ABC, CBS, Fox, and NBC are all part of broadcast, as are many local stations, though they usually can be found by subscribers to cable television. CNN and HBO are also cable — and they have much company with hundreds of cable outlets springing up, and sometimes disappearing, rapidly. The broadcast side of television adopted a set of television standards, not strong, but at least a nudge in the right direction.

Then cable followed. The broadcast side of television — about 62 percent of the viewership — has at least temporarily improved its product in terms of less violence. The newsletter *Movie Guide* said that 40 percent of the films made in 1996 were "family oriented" compared to 6 percent in 1985. That is in part a tribute to broadcast television, which buys many films. Cable television has improved only slightly. There is no assurance that retrogression will not occur on either front.

There is less cigarette smoking and heavy drinking by the heroes and heroines in today's films, compared to twenty years ago. That has helped to lower our smoking and drinking because we imitate what we see on the screen. A reduction in glorified violence can have the same impact. A *Time* magazine study of the boys who attacked schoolmates in Jonesboro, Arkansas, West Paducah, Kentucky, and Springfield, Oregon, focused primarily on guns but at the end the article noted: "Academics who study such things widely agree that exposure to media violence correlates with aggression, callousness and appetite for aggression."[16] One boy "liked to play two gory video games." And it quotes a study: "These sources bring into homes depictions of graphic violence . . . never available to children and young people in the past."

Those in the industry who deny any relationship between violence in our society and violence on the screen tell advertisers to buy a thirty-second commercial and they can sell soap or cars or perfume. It works. But twenty-five minutes of glorifying violence affects us not at all, they claim.

In my Los Angeles address to the executives of the industry, I asked them to launch studies that look seriously at what is on the screen — not censoring, but reviewing what has taken place. Somewhat reluctantly they agreed to my request. The broadcast industry asked UCLA to do the studies and the cable industry asked the University of California at Santa Barbara, the University of Wisconsin at Madison, the University of Texas at Austin, and the University of North Carolina at Chapel Hill to do a joint study. Some industry leaders perhaps expected to be applauded. To the credit of both broadcast and cable, they spent sizable sums to conduct the studies. The results are not to their liking. The most recent study concludes that 73 percent of entertainment television violence shows no immediate adverse consequences for the person who commits the violence. The clear lesson for children and adults: Violence pays. Only 4 percent of entertainment televison with violence has an antiviolence theme.

A technical development that many see as a big help is the V-chip, which permits parents to program their television sets so that certain shows will not appear. Legislation mandating that was proposed in the Senate, and I voted against it, as did Senator Bob Dole who also is outspoken on this problem. The Senate language ultimately would push government into the field of content, where it does not belong. The industry grabbed onto the V-chip and met with the president, who also has an interest in this, as does Al Gore. The industry leaders met with a few of us in Congress before going to the White House. They are voluntarily rating programs for violence, sex, and language. I have no objection to their doing this, but as I said to them, this is not a substitute for cleaning up their act and having healthier programs. Several things make me less than rapturously enthusiastic about this "solution": 1) The homes that need the V-chip or ratings the most will not use them. 2) In areas of high crime, children watch approximately twice as much television as in other areas, for understandable reasons; parents are afraid to let their children play in the street, and the alternative is television. To many parents, watching "bad" television seems a good alternative, if it keeps young people away from immediate real violence. 3) Children are mechanically adept. When something goes wrong with our VCR, I ask one of our children or their spouses to fix it. Children will find a way around the V-chip. 4) Most homes have more than one television set, making V-chip surveillance more difficult. 5) University of Wisconsin studies show that certain ratings do not retard viewing, but add to viewership, particularly among young males. 6) Even if parents monitor television closely, they are most unusual if, when Johnny or Jane asks to go next door to play at the neighbor's home, the parent says, "OK, but first let me check and see what is on their television set." A ratings system at a theater permits parents some voice in where their children are and what their children see. The television set in the home is much more difficult to supervise.

This battle is not over.

*Inevitably if television industry leaders do not exercise self-restraint, there will be greater government intrusion.*

Over the years I met with most of the major players in the industry. Some have been excellent and responsible. Others much less so. The most dramatic meeting I have had was in my office with a group of cable television executives. Two or three expressed the usual defensive views. Then Ted Turner, who does not fit into anyone's mold, said forcefully, "Let's face it. We have blood on our hands!"

[1] Editorial, *The Weekly Standard*, 20 October 1977.

[2] *George Tagge Memoir*, an oral history project of Sangamon State University (now the University of Illinois at Springfield), 1986, 3.

[3] *Ibid*, 7.

[4] *Ibid*, 8.

[5] *Ibid*, 12.

[6] *Ibid*, 18.

[7] *Ibid*, 23.

[8] *Ibid*, 39.

[9] *Ibid*, 6.

[10] Corman and Swanson, *Chicago Journalism Review*, November 1971.

[11] Andrew Tyndall, "What Gets on the Networks?" *Media Studies Journal*, Winter 1998.

[12] Spring 1998.

[13] Verne Gay, "An Ugly Mood," reprinted in *St. Louis Post-Dispatch*, 8 August 1994.

[14] Lynn Elber, "Networks Shoot Back at Threat of Censoring Violence on TV," *Danville Commercial News*, 10 August 1993.

[15] "Simon Gives Television Industry Two Months to Reduce Violence," *Danville Commercial News*, 10 August 1993.

[16] John Cloud, "Of Arms and the Boy," *Time*, 6 July 1998. Quotation from Sisela Bok, *Mayhem: Violence as Public Entertainment*.

# Chapter 17

# *The Political Process*

We have two major flaws — and a number of minor ones — in our political process: first, our system of financing campaigns, and second, the scientific pandering through polls that has come to dominate decision-making. Others have written about these problems in greater detail, but let me add a few personal experiences.

With only four days left in my last session in the Senate, a House-Senate conference committee attached a "small amendment" that categorized the 35,000 truck drivers that work for Federal Express as pilots for labor-management law. A highly technical amendment, it meant greater difficulty for truck drivers to bargain with Federal Express.

I have nothing against Federal Express. I use it frequently, and its officials simply used the system that we have created for changing the law. How did they use our system? This amendment came in the closing, chaotic days of the session so it received little attention, but the *Washington Post* did note that Federal Express contributed $1.4 million in contributions to incumbent members of Congress in the last two years, plus $100,000 to the Democratic National Committee after a meeting with President Clinton. Would they have been able to get that amendment adopted without having made those contributions? Highly doubtful.

When we learned about it, three of us — Ted Kennedy, Russ Feingold of Wisconsin, and I — opposed the amendment on the floor and tried to get it knocked off. Our colleagues outvoted us badly. At the Democratic caucus — it could as easily have been the Republican caucus — I said that maybe the amendment has merit, but we should hold hearings and do some research on the question; we should not be caving in to special interests. One of my senior colleagues stood up in the caucus and said, "Paul's always talking about special interests, special interests, special interests. We have to pay attention to who's buttering our bread." That's what it's all about.

I could fill this chapter with such illustrations.

Anyone in a major elected public office who tells you that he or she is not influenced by campaign contributions is either living in a dream world or is lying. For my last campaign for reelection I had to raise $8.4 million, and that's not easy with my voting record. The insurance companies, the defense industry, and the oil industry — just to mention three major sources of revenue — do not believe I have a good record. In 1990, on a per vote basis, only two seriously contested incumbent Senate candidates spent less than I did. And of the winning Senate candidates that year, only two spent less than their opponents. Does money always triumph? No. Does it usually triumph? Yes.

I have never promised anyone a thing for a campaign contribution. But when I still served in the Senate and got to my hotel room at midnight, there might be twenty phone calls waiting for me, nineteen from people whose names I did not recognize, the twentieth from someone who gave me a $1,000 campaign contribution or raised money for me. At midnight I'm not going to make twenty phone calls. I might make one. Which one do you think I will make? So will every other incumbent Senator. That means that the financially articulate have inordinate access to policymakers. Access spells influence. The problem permeates our government and too often dictates what we do. Usually it is more subtle than the Federal Express matter, but it is there.

Rush Limbaugh is not my favorite radio commentator, but he does get people interested in public affairs and I sometimes listen to him when I'm driving. Asked by *National Review* if he ever would seek public office, he replied:

> I have no desire [to do it]. Primarily because . . . to be elected to anything, you have to walk around like this — with your hand out. And you have to beg people to put something in it. Somebody always does, and they want repayment. And not with dollars. It's going to be with your soul, it's going to be with a portion of your soul. I don't look at it as fun.[1]

Come join our side on this, Rush!

A *Business Week* survey shows 77 percent of business executives freely admit to contributing to campaigns to get access and to create goodwill with lawmakers.[2] So did nine-tenths of the remaining 23 percent, but they were less candid.

Senator Paul Douglas again and again quoted an old English poem of unknown origin which tells of a danger in our society and every society:

> The law locks up both man and woman,
> Who steals the goose from off the Common.
> But lets the greater felon loose,
> Who steals the Common from the goose.

One man who helped me in my last campaign, claiming to have raised more money than I believe he did, told me I owed him an appointment to a federal judgeship. Even if he had been on the top of the list prior to that conversation, he immediately would have dropped to dead last. But it indicates how people think the process works — and too often they are right. Even Ronald Reagan, no friend of campaign finance reform, said, "I thought politics to be the second-oldest profession. I have come to realize that it bears a very close relationship to the first."[3]

In an earlier chapter I told of an Illinois Secretary of State, a Democrat, who left $800,000 in shoe boxes, much of that money probably from people who gave him cash for his campaign. A few years later a Republican — our Illinois Attorney General, the top state law-enforcement official — got into a domestic spat with his wife. She went to their safety deposit boxes and found $48,900 in cash, to her surprise. Probably abused campaign funds, again. Most states do not require payment by check, as the federal government does for amounts over $100. When I campaigned, occasionally someone would try to hand me $1,000 or $500 in cash, and I said I would like a check. Often the response was: "Well _____ likes it in cash."

One of the nation's most thoughtful citizens, Bill Moyers, made a remarkable speech in San Francisco in December 1997 outlining in great detail the campaign finance abuses by both Democrats and Republicans and how these abuses ultimately threaten our free system. In his speech he quotes Barry Goldwater: "To be successful, representative government assumes that elections will be controlled by the citizenry at large, not by those who give the most money. Electors must believe their votes count. Elected officials must owe their allegiance to the people, not to their own wealth or to the wealth of interest groups who speak only for the selfish fringes of the whole community."[4]

Any reasonably objective person looking at our society has to conclude that poverty is a major problem. We have 21 percent of our children living in poverty, a far higher percentage than any other industrialized Western nation. France — which does not do as well as some other nations of Western Europe — starts with 26 percent of its children living in poverty, precisely the same percentage that we do. But through government programs France reduces that number to 6.5 percent, while we reduce it to 21 percent. William Finnegan wrote in the *New York Times*: "Nationally, our child poverty rate rose by 26 percent from 1970 to 1996. It is today the highest in the industrialized world by a large margin. This mortifying prominence is not a matter of scarcity — the United States is, after all, the wealthiest nation in history. It is, rather, a matter of priorities."[5] When I was a young man visiting New Orleans, I saw two city workers pick up an elderly black man who had died on the street. One grabbed his arms, the other his legs, and they threw him onto the back of a truck as they might throw a bushel of flour. Even in my first visit to impoverished Calcutta, India, or in Somalia, I have never seen death so casually treated. Today that would not happen anywhere in our nation. But much worse, we are insensitive to many of the living who need food, shelter, health care, and other basic necessities. Being impoverished is a major cause of crime. Because the poor are frequently illiterate or close to it, they do not add to our productivity as they could. The list of reasons for paying attention to poverty — excluding the humanitarian reason — is lengthy. But we do not focus on the problems of the poor. We passed legislation — which I opposed — with the label "welfare reform" which is anything but that. Unless modifications are made, many of the poor will face overwhelming problems at the end of the five-year deadline for getting off welfare. Poverty at home and abroad should bother us much more than it does. The Christian-Jewish portion of the world comprises less than 20 percent of the world's population, yet has about 75 percent of the world's wealth. There should be a sense of moral obligation that goes with that good fortune, not just pride. Great Britain in the 1830s had more wealth than any nation in the world and the worst slums of any modern nation. Historians ask why they could not see this inconsistency. Historians are likely to ask the same of us.

Why don't we pay more attention to the poor and find *real* answers to their problems? The poor are not big campaign contributors. Why don't we pay more attention to the 41 million Americans without health insurance? They are not big campaign contributors, while those who profit from the present system are. The list of ways we twist democracy because of campaign money goes on and on and on. It is one reason — not the only one — that so few people turn out at our elections. The public believes that public office is for sale. The situation is not as bad as the public perception of it, but it is bad.

Remember when you were in grade school, and you learned of the philosophical battle between Alexander Hamilton and Thomas Jefferson over the rights of citizens? Hamilton believed that citizens of wealth and property should be given more voice in government while Jefferson believed that all citizens (our constitution exempted women, African Americans, and Native Americans) should be treated equally. How proud you were in the fourth grade to learn that Jefferson prevailed! But now through our present system of campaign financing Hamilton has prevailed.

Achieving change at the federal level will be difficult. My preference for the Senate is a system of public financing, through voluntary check-offs on an income tax form. In order to qualify for aid in a primary, a specified number of $5 contributions would be required, so that people could not just walk off the street and be eligible for assistance. For those nominated in a state like Illinois, instead of spending $8 or $10 million for a Senate race, perhaps $2 million would be spent — and no private contributions could be accepted. Free television and radio time would be mandated, not for thirty-second commercials but for five-minute segments in which the candidates themselves would have to be on camera. We would have more substantial discussion of the issues, and would be much less likely to have so many negative commercials which fuel the widespread cynicism toward government that already exists.

Because federal action is unlikely, states will be the immediate battleground. Maine and Vermont have passed sweeping legislation, and many other states have made improvements, including — finally — my state of Illinois. When enough states move toward genuine reforms the pressure will grow for the federal government to act and finally it will.

One word of warning: Every reform ultimately needs to be reformed. My observation is that reforms in any field last about twelve years, then either conditions change or people find ways around the law. That does not suggest the reforms are not worthwhile. They are.

A look at other democracies in the world suggests that we have much to learn from them about campaign financing. It will take real effort to achieve change. Early in this century a university president named Woodrow Wilson wrote: "Social reform is a matter of cooperation, and, if it be of a novel kind, requires an infinite deal of converting to bring [people] to believe in it and support it."[6]

Nothing discouraged me in my years in Congress as much as seeing polling play a larger and larger role in determining public policy decisions. One newspaper reported that Bill Clinton received $5.6 million worth of polling from the Democratic National Committee during his first term in office. Bill Clinton's instincts are sound, and he would go down in history as a stronger President if he had never seen a poll.

The world recently celebrated the fiftieth anniversary of the Marshall Plan, one of the finest actions in the history of our country or any nation. But after General Marshall and President Truman announced the plan, the first Gallup Poll showed only 14 percent of the American public supported it. But Harry Truman forged ahead, and had to deal with a Republican Congress. The spokesperson for the GOP on foreign affairs, Senator Arthur Vandenberg of Michigan, said that he knew the proposal was not popular but it would serve the nation well and he pledged to do everything he could to get it passed.

I cannot imagine an administration of either political party today proposing something without first taking a poll, and, then, if the poll turned out to be overwhelmingly unfavorable, going ahead with the proposal anyway. That's what Harry Truman did and the world is better because of his courage and conviction. And if an administration proposed something overwhelmingly unpopular, I cannot imagine an opposition party — either one — not trying to take advantage of that today.

Today's political leaders should bear in mind that Harry Truman did not score highly in the political polls of his day, but Calvin Coolidge and Warren Harding did. History regards Truman highly and Coolidge and Harding much less favorably. In the Bible, Jesus is quoted as saying, "Woe to you when all men speak well of you, for that is how their fathers treated the false prophets."[7]

The late Senator J. William Fulbright wrote:

> Our elected representatives . . . study and analyze public attitudes by sophisticated new techniques, but their purpose has little to do with leadership. . . . Their purpose, it seems, is to discover what people want and fear and dislike, and then to identify themselves with those sentiments. They seek to discover which issues can be safely emphasized and which are more prudently avoided. This approach to politics is the opposite of leadership; it is followership, for purposes of self-advancement. . . . [8]

**Sun-Times**

WARMER
artly cloudy tonight, a
ow in the 40s. Page 2
TV listings: P. 80

CHICAGO, WEDNESDAY, NOVEMBER 7, 1984   25¢ CITY, SUBURBS 35¢ ELSEWHERE

Red Streak
Final Markets
Page 83

# SIMON WINS

## *Percy beaten by 60,000 votes*

By Mark Brown
and Lynn Sweet

Rep. Paul Simon
claimed victory and
Sen. Charles H. Percy
bowed out of public
office after 18 years
today with a hopeful
prediction that "may-
be the best is yet to
come."

With 98 percent of the
state's 11,632 precincts reporting, Simon had 2,334,580
votes, or 50 percent, to
Percy's 2,273,243 votes, or 49
percent. Libertarian Party
candidate Steven L. Givot
grabbed the final 1 percent
with 59,120 votes.

Percy reached Simon by
phone at 8:26 a.m. to con-
cede his U.S. Senate seat and
offer his congratulations to
the 10-year veteran of the
House of Representatives.

The front page of the *Chicago Sun-Times*, Wednesday, November 7, 1984, after I won the senatorial seat that Charles H. Percy held for 18 years.

*Photograph courtesy of the* New York Times

The *New Haven Register*, in its November 7, 1984 edition, shows me sharing my senatorial victory with Chicago's Democratic Mayor Harold Washington.

In Malawi, southern Africa, in the late 1980s, visiting refugees from the Mozambique civil wa

Here I am with Fred Koramatsu, the Japanese American who challenged FDR's order to take 120,000 Japanese Americans from the West Coast in February 1942. In the famous — and terrible — Supreme Court Koramatsu decision, the Court ruled 6-3 that FDR acted legally, a decision that ultimately everyone recognized as an injustice. I was thirteen when my father opposed this denial of basic civil liberties.

Israeli Prime Minister Rabin on his first visit to Washington, in 1993, after becoming prime minister. A water engineer before he entered the military, he took a great interest in my bill for desalination research and invited me to join the multilateral talks on water taking place in Madrid.

At a dinner with Nelson Mandela, soon to become president of South Africa.

With Rabbi Jacob Rubenstein, president of the Rabbinical Council of America, at a 1998 gathering of religious leaders at the Public Policy Institute at Southern Illinois University to look at the role of the faith community in resolving the problem of poverty in our nation.

Hillary Clinton straightens my tie before the three of us walk on stage at a political fundraiser in Chicago in 1997.

A few days before the end of the 1997 session Senators Connie Mack (R-Fl) and David Pryor (D-Ark) arranged for the members to wear bow ties for a vote that would bring all the senators to the floor. My staff delayed me by asking me to sign "important" documents. And when I walked on the floor I had a real surprise. *Chicago Tribune* photographer Ernie Cox, Jr. grabbed some of us as we were leaving the floor. In this picture are left to right: Senators Carl Levin of Michigan, Dan Coats of Indiana, Jeff Bingaman of New Mexico, Chuck Robb of Virginia, Joe Lieberman of Connecticut, myself, Bennett Johnston of Louisiana, Barbara Boxer of California, John Kerry of Massachusetts, and John Breaux of Louisiana.

A 1988 cartoon following my attempt at the presidency.

Jeanne Simon, 1997.

*Photograph by Martin Simon*

Our family in Rehoboth, Delaware in 1996: I'm holding our grandson Nick, Jeanne is holding Brennan. Between us is Reilly. Standing, left to right: Perry Knop, Sheila Simon, "CJ," being held by Julie Simon, and Martin Simon.

*Photograph by Martin Simon*

At my old typewriter, teaching a future journalist, my granddaughter "CJ," who is enjoying herself.

In an article of tribute to Senator Paul Douglas, I wrote in the *Chicago Tribune Magazine*:

> Douglas sought public office not to satisfy an emotional need, not to be honored as a solon, but because what he hoped to accomplish had to be done through public office. While others were testing public opinion to determine which way to go on issues, Paul Douglas *led* public opinion. The platformless, convictionless mediocrities who too often emerge in both political parties are leaders in name but not in fact. Long on public relations but short on substance, they seek and hold public office without knowing why.[9]

One of the nation's most thoughtful and gutsy political leaders, former New York Governor Mario Cuomo, noted in a speech: "Poll-watching politicians respond with Pavlovian sureness. They touch every button, satisfy every rabid craving with swift passage of draconian and regressive measures. They serve up a binge of new death penalty statutes as though there had suddenly been discovered proof that the death penalty can save lives." Who are the victims of this policy-making by polls? Cuomo says: "The immigrant, the prisoner, the poor, children, people who can't vote or don't vote. Offered up to assuage the discomfort and anger of an unhappy majority."[10]

There is nothing immoral, from my perspective, in taking polls in a campaign to see in what regions you are weak and where you are strong. Any political leader in his or her commercials will stress the popular stands taken, not the unpopular. I did not make any commercials boasting about my stand in opposition to capital punishment, for example. But I have never taken a poll to decide how to vote on an issue. For a public official to support an issue because it happens to be popular even though he or she believes it is not in the public interest *is* immoral. And it is a growing immorality, defended by saying, "I'm doing what the people want." That is the same argument that producers of sleazy movies and television shows use.

Politics should not be about pandering. It should be about leadership.

A public official ought to ask himself or herself, "What have I done that is bold?" If there is not an easy answer to that, then I suggest a more uncomfortable question, "Why am I in politics?"

Not at the same level of importance as the first two points is the degeneration of a bipartisan spirit on many issues that face our government. We have excessive partisanship in many ways, and ironically we sometimes do not have a sense of partisan responsibility.

When I first went to the House of Representatives, the two political parties had their fights, but generally we worked together. I am a partisan Democrat, proud of my party affiliation, but I also recognize that most problems are "nuts and bolts" problems that require people to sit down and work together for reasonable solutions. Occasionally a question of political philosophy surfaces, but not too frequently.

When the Democrats had the majority in the Senate, I chaired three subcommittees. I don't recall our subcommittees ever having a party line vote on any question. Sometimes we had division, and on occasion I gave more than I wanted on an issue, and sometimes my friends gave more than they wanted, but the net result of our work was good for the nation, and, ironically, good for the two political parties. The public didn't see us playing games for partisan advantage. The general perception of Congress today is that the two political parties are playing games to gain a few votes, and unfortunately there is much truth to that perception. Such posturing serves no one well.

Yet, there is too often bipartisan ducking of tough issues. Which political party is willing to stand up and tell us the truth about the Social Security Retirement Fund? I don't know the answer. The job of a political party is not simply to play it safe, to amass the most votes possible in the House or the Senate or a presidential race. It is also to lead. My instinct is that a party — like a public official — that is willing to lead by taking some responsible but unpopular stands will do well in the long run. My personal experience bears that out, and so does the experience of others — but not too many are willing to take risks.

When I give my "Chamber of Commerce speech" in communities, I tell them they need to do three things to move ahead economically: work hard; be creative; take risks. The same applies to individuals and the same applies to political parties. Unless they are willing to do all three, including taking risks, the nation will not be served well — and they will not serve themselves well.

---

[1] James Bowman, quoted in "The Leader of the Opposition," *National Review*, 6 September 1993.

[2] Scotty Baesler, quoted in "After Distortions, Time to De-Bunk Kentucky Anti-Reform Myths," *Roll Call*, 15 June 1998.

[3] George W. Hunt, quoted in "Of Many Things," *America*, 7 November 1992.

[4] Quoted by William Moyers, San Francisco, 3 December 1997, available from Public Campaign, Washington, D.C.

[5] William Finnegan, "Prosperous Times, Except for the Young," *New York Times*, 12 June 1998.

[6] Woodrow Wilson, *When a Man Comes to Himself* (New York, Harper and Brothers, 1901), 24.

[7] Luke 6:26.

[8] From *Foreign Affairs*, quoted in Paul Simon, *Once and Future Democrats*, (New York: Continuum, 1982), 7-8.

[9] Paul Simon, "Source, teacher, senator, friend," *Chicago Tribune Magazine*, 14 October 1973.

[10] Speech to College of Trial Lawyers, Boca Raton, Florida, 21 March 1997.

# Chapter 18

# *The Emotional Issues*

There are a few "hot button" issues that people experienced in politics know are volatile. They will vary from election to election, and region to region, but there are four to which most people have instinctive responses, and frequently the less they know about the issue the more rigid and determined they are in their positions. Those issues are abortion, gun control, gays in the military, and affirmative action.

The last item, affirmative action, is largely misunderstood. It is not quotas; it is not hiring people who are unqualified or admitting people to schools who fail to meet the standards. It is about opportunity. It is significant that in all the complaints we hear about affirmative action, business executives are not complaining. They have tried it and it works. I did it on my staff and by any measure had a superior staff, in part because we had diversity. Not just for minorities and women, but also geographically. I made sure we had people from the southern part of the state as well as the central and northern areas. We didn't designate certain positions as belonging to one region or another, but we consciously built diversity in geography without sacrificing quality. Did this hurt anyone in Illinois? It helped them and helped me. I had no quota, and I did not have certain spots designated for African Americans, or Latinos, or other groups, but my staff and I consciously strove for both quality and diversity. Carrie Tamashiro Scott, who is deaf, brought a buoyant personality to us, but also an understanding of certain problems no one else could. Because we represented diversity, our reaching out to help others seemed natural. No one expressed surprise when I asked Imam Wallace Mohammed to be the first Muslim to lead the Senate in prayer, co-hosted by Senator

Orrin Hatch of Utah and my Illinois colleague Alan Dixon. We had a base of understanding within our staff that aided us in effectively serving others. When we did the same for minorities, did this hurt anyone in Illinois? It helped them and helped me. Affirmative action — like religion or education or any other good thing — can be abused, but it has been a positive influence on our society. Before this thrust, a working woman made 59¢ compared to the dollar that a male in the same position made. That is now up to 76¢, not good enough but a big improvement. Affirmative action has not eliminated discrimination, but it is helping. At the college level it has given white Americans and African Americans who generally went to virtually all white or all black high schools a chance to get to know each other, to reduce prejudice. One reason white males complain is that employers don't want to tell a person to his face that someone else got a job because he or she had more qualifications; it is easier to say something like, "We had to get a woman on the job." Or a black, or a Latino, or a disabled person, or a member of some other minority group. Getting to know one another and work with one another reduces animosities and builds a better society. One of the ironies in affirmative action at the college level — now threatened by a bad decision (Hopwood) by the Fifth District Appellate Court — is that people don't object to affirmative action for a football player so a school can have a good football team, but when the purpose is improving education, reducing prejudice, and building a better society, suddenly there is objection. When a person has poison in his or her body, sometimes it takes a little pain at the physician's office to get rid of it. And occasionally with the poison of prejudice and discrimination a little pain is necessary to get rid of it. But we are much better off with the slight pain and the great reduction in the poison. I hope that some day we will have a society in which we will not need affirmative action, but we are not there yet.

The gays in the military issue has temporarily died down, but it will arise again because the federal government has taken a fundamentally unsound position. "Don't tell" and you're fine.

When I served in the military we had homosexuals, but we did not clear them for classified material — a reasonable position then, though some differ with me on that, as gays could be threatened with "outing" if they did not turn over military secrets.

Starting in 1993, the issue came up regularly at town meetings. Usually part of the question would include some reference to the

Bible. I answered that the Bible has approximately forty times more condemnations of adultery than any reference to homosexuality — including one of the Ten Commandments — and added, "If we were to remove adulterers from the armed forces, my experience in the Army suggests that our ranks would be substantially thinned." That usually brought a chuckle, particularly from those who had served in the military. Then I posed a question to the audience. "Suppose we have a national emergency and have a draft again. If we say that no one who is gay will be drafted, won't we have a huge number of gays in the country?" The no-gays-in-the-military policy is a relatively new phenomenon and the only other major nation that has such a policy is Great Britain. Senator Barry Goldwater said the question for the military should not be whether or not you are straight but whether or not you can shoot straight.

The underlying concern by those who attack the military on this question is not the status of the military but the whole question of people in our society whose sexual orientation differs from the majority of us. I grew up in a family sensitive to discrimination, but this issue simply didn't come up for discussion, probably because it was generally hidden. My father never took me aside and said, "Paul you ought to get interested in girls." He had to give me other warnings. While I have always opposed discrimination, I am still learning in this field. When we had a bill on the floor to prohibit discrimination in employment on the basis of sexual orientation, I supported it using the phrase "sexual preference" in my remarks, and the leaders of the community carefully explained to me it is orientation and not preference. At one point psychiatrists and others had the theory that this orientation grew out of an unsatisfactory relationship with a parent. Now the scientific evidence is clear that in males there is a genetic factor, and many assume that further scientific research will show the same for females. A college classmate visited me in Washington and told the difficulty his family went through when their daughter told them that she is a lesbian. When he asked her why she chose that lifestyle, she responded, "Dad, you don't think I *chose* this do you?" When we held hearings on this discrimination problem, a woman testified who worked in the kitchen of a Cracker Barrel restaurant and lost her job when the administration of that chain announced that anyone who is openly gay would be fired. When she appeared before us, she worked part-time chopping firewood, having a real struggle. I said at the hearing that I would not go into a Cracker Barrel restaurant again until I receive a report that they have altered their discriminatory policy.

We should judge people by their conduct not by their genes.

Issues rise and fall in public attention. Records from my state government years at the Illinois State Historical Library archives show correspondence on 336 principal issues from 1954 through 1972, and neither guns nor abortion made the top 336. That has changed!

We passed a bill for an identification card for gun owners in Illinois, denying guns to convicted felons and people with a history of mental illness. It caused a little controversy, but not much.

I am not sure what made the gun issue suddenly erupt on the national scene. It could be that the rise in the crime rate caused people to look at our gun laws, and then the relatively quiet National Rifle Association became more militant. During my years in the legislature I do not remember the NRA playing much of a role, though the Illinois Rifle Association did, and the gun owner's identification card legislation was worked out with them. At that point they had moderate leadership, willing to look at problems honestly.

I quickly crossed paths with the National Rifle Association when I went to Congress. Taking the position that almost any restrictions on gun use could cause guns to be taken away from all citizens, they opposed virtually everything, and persuaded a small hard-core group of followers that those of us who favored sensible changes in gun laws were out to take away all their weapons.

My House district in deep southern Illinois is rural, hilly, with lots of trees, and has the large Shawnee National Forest — and thousands of deer and thousands of hunters. They also shoot wild turkeys and rabbits and other animals, but the big thing for hunters is deer. While I am not a hunter myself I know that it is essential for the survival of deer that a number of them are killed each year, otherwise their population growth would outrun the resources for food and they would die off in large numbers. So I'm not opposed to hunting, and I'm around hunters all the time. But I've never seen a hunter with an Uzi, or an AK-47, and rarely a pistol. I've seen more with bows and arrows than with pistols. But when I supported national legislation to require something similar to our Illinois gun owner's identification card, which we had worked out with the Illinois Rifle Association, suddenly I became a threat to the Second Amendment ("the right to bear arms") and to hunters, part of what extremists still believe is some plot by government to foist Communism on them — and now that that beast is dying, some equally horrendous cause that their imagination creates.

I became one of thirteen targeted House members in the nation. The NRA sent out fund-raising letters with my picture and a target imposed over it. I found their positions so extreme that when I went after them directly in my hunter-filled district, not only did a large majority of voters agree with me, the large majority of hunters agreed with me. Legislators who shake in fright at the wishes of the NRA and vote that organization's bidding do not understand their own strength.

Sometimes the NRA people are obnoxious. In Godfrey, Illinois, the NRA members stacked a town meeting. I could tell that when I drove in and saw their cars and pickups with NRA stickers on them. Many wore their NRA hats during the meeting. One woman rose and said her daughter had been killed by teenagers with guns in St. Louis. "We ought to take those guns away from teenagers," she pleaded. The NRA members booed her. Then one jumped up and shouted, "They could have killed her with a baseball bat." I could hardly believe their crudeness. Give me a choice of someone coming at me with a baseball bat or a gun and I can make the choice easily!

A comparison between two large metropolitan areas, Los Angeles and Sydney, Australia, is revealing. Both have relatively similar crime rates per 100,000 citizens, though Sydney has a slightly higher burglary rate, for example. But one crime is dramatically different: murder. Sydney has 7 percent of the number of murders per 100,000 citizens Los Angeles does. That is because of gun laws. Australia has a twenty-eight-day waiting period compared to our five days, and recently the Australian government, with one-fourteenth as many people as we have, spent $267 million buying back guns from citizens. On a population basis, a U. S. resident is four times more likely to be murdered than a citizen in Canada, 150 times more likely than a citizen of Great Britain, and 1,200 times more likely than a citizen of Japan.[1] London has proportionately 66 percent more thefts and 57 percent more burglaries than New York City, but the latter city has eleven times as many murders. New York journalist Pete Hamill writes: "Throughout the 1950s, New York averaged 300 murders a year; by 1994, the city fathers were ecstatic when the number of homicides dropped to 1,600 after years of hovering around the 2,000 mark."[2] More than half the deaths by guns in the U. S. are not classified as murders. A few other statistics of interest:

- Guns kept in the home for self-protection are 43 times more likely to kill someone you know than to kill in self-defense.[3]

- The risk of suicide is 5.8 times greater in households with guns.[4]

- In 1995 there were 179 justifiable handgun homicides and 11,198 handgun murders in the United States.[5]

- In 1994 sixteen children under the age of nineteen were killed each day in our country.[6]

Thanks to the leadership of Senator Dianne Feinstein of California, we outlawed a small number of semiautomatic assault weapons, one of them the Tec-9, used, for example, by a man who entered a San Francisco law office and killed several people. The Tec-9 advertised in *Guns and Ammo* and other gun magazines that it is "resistant to fingerprints." Why does a responsible citizen want a gun that is fingerprint proof?

We passed the Brady bill, named for Jim Brady, the former press secretary to President Reagan who received paralyzing wounds in the assassination attempt on the President. Jim and his wife Sarah have made a crusade for national legislation similar to our Illinois law, requiring that hand gun owners be checked for a felony record or mental illness. The chief sponsor of the measure, Senator Howard Metzenbaum, happily referred to it as the Brady Bill but the usual protocol in the Senate would have been to call it the Metzenbaum bill, which also would have been appropriate because of his efforts to pass it. In addition to checking prospective gun owners, the measure also has a five-day waiting period to purchase a gun, a "cooling off period." If you and your spouse have a fight and you rush to the store to buy a gun, waiting a few days before you can buy a gun may be in your best interest as well as your spouse's. In 1997 the Brady Law for handguns caused 69,000 people to be denied the right to purchase them, out of 2,574,000 who applied. Can anyone believe we would be better off if these 69,000 convicted or indicted felons — the large majority of denials — had been sold guns?

I discovered that to get a federal gun dealer's license cost $10 a year, less than a driver's license in most states, and that three-fourths of the gun dealers did not have stores but sold guns in the kitchens or basements of their homes, or from the trunks of their cars. We had far more gun dealers than service stations. Illinois had 369 McDonald's restaurants and 11,056 gun dealers. Nationally we had 284,100 gun dealers, and 240 people to inspect them. The Bureau of Alcohol, Tobacco and Firearms (BATF), which grants the licenses, grants them almost automatically. CBS Television applied for a dealer license for a dog and got it. Through amendments I gradually raised the fee so that the BATF had enough money to do more background checks, first raising it to $200 for three years ($67 a year) and — equally important — requiring fingerprints and a picture. The portion of my bill that became law that really had an impact was the fingerprinting; people previously used false names, or used their middle names and went undetected. We also mandated that they abide by state and local laws, and that the police be notified of who receives a dealer's license. Police found some dealers operating near schools, and BATF also received complaints from local police about people who had been given licenses. But the gun crowd denounced my action. "Will destroying more than 100,000 small businesses make American safer? . . . If Simon really wants to fight gun crime, he should be working to lower — not raise — the cost of protective gun ownership," one Op-Ed said.[7] By the end of 1997 we had 106,417 gun dealers — a drop of 176,776. The old law, the *U. S. News and World Report* noted, "allowed a small minority of unsavory licensees to score profits by selling hundreds of guns to criminals while attracting little scrutiny from an overworked group of ATF inspectors."[8] The National Rifle Association said the move is "part of a pattern of government harassment." We passed a bill through the Senate to raise the fee to $600 a year, which BATF said would allow more careful screening. It passed with the support of Secretary of the Treasury Lloyd Bentsen, who lauded my efforts, but we lost in the House.

What has caused the small drop in the crime rate in the nation? Several things, I am sure. More police on the streets, more money invested in drug education and treatment, and the removal of shady operators from the gun dealing business.

We also discovered that in one revision of the gun laws, the NRA got a provision put into the statute that convicted felons denied the right to have a gun could have their case automatically reviewed by BATF and get their guns back, again a substantial drain of taxpayer's money for an unworthy cause. Senator Frank Lautenberg of New Jersey and I put a temporary stop to that by killing the appropriations to carry this out.

Like many others, my position on abortion evolved slowly. I never favored the constitutional amendment that many advocate to overturn the Roe v. Wade decision of the Supreme Court. I have always felt it an inappropriate and awkward policy instrument for the Constitution. When I first came to Congress I did vote to bar funds for abortions for people on welfare. Then I gradually became aware of two things: There is no evidence that my votes to deny legal abortions to poor women reduced the rate of abortions; it only denied safe abortions to poor women. Second, as I studied the issue in this country and in other nations, it became clear that the rate of abortions has little to do with the status of the law, and much more to do with the status of the culture. England, Scotland, and Wales, as examples, had more liberal abortion laws prior to the 1973 Supreme Court decision than we did, but had a lower rate of abortions.

I also came face to face with real people and real problems and it gradually occurred to me that these difficult human situations don't fit into neat packages. An illustration I will use because he has talked publicly about it: Tom Braden, a Washington journalist, and his wife suddenly faced a horrible situation. Their daughter had been gang-raped after a Fourth of July ceremony in Washington, D.C. She became pregnant. Tom and his wife and their daughter decided she would have an abortion. I am grateful our family did not have to make that decision, but the question I face as a lawmaker: Should we declare Tom Braden and his wife and his daughter and their physician criminals? Or is this a decision they have to make and that government should not make? A Roman Catholic nun in Guatemala, brutalized in the worst possible way, became pregnant and emotionally was unable to face the prospect of a child from that assault. She had an abortion. Should government deal with her harshly?

This is an area where anyone trying to bridge the gap between the widely opposing camps gets into trouble. It is an issue that deeply divides the religious community, where both sides are convinced they have truth and justice with them. In general, when the religious community is deeply divided on an issue, government should tread with great caution. The late Cardinal Bernardin, Roman Catholic prelate of the Chicago archdiocese, and I would have breakfast together occasionally — just the two of us — where we could talk frankly. At one point he suggested that since people of good will are so sharply divided on this, they should get together on things on which they can agree. Both sides believe abortions should be discouraged, and we know that teenage pregnancies have a much higher rate of abortion than other pregnancies, and that high school dropouts are more likely to become pregnant. Therefore, the two sides could get together to work on the dropout problem, and on having homes for teenagers who are willing to have their babies. I thought the Cardinal's idea an excellent one, but people from both sides shot it down. At one point I introduced a bill to require the signature of two physicians to have an abortion, something required in a few Western European countries. It is a way of saying there is a qualitative difference between an abortion and an appendectomy. But both sides in the abortion question attacked my proposal.

Having said that, the rigidity and the piousness and the unwillingness to face fundamental facts by some of the pro-life people offends me. If our aim is to stop abortions, then we should be encouraging family planning and sex education, both of which reduce the abortion rate, but many in their ranks oppose these measures. They say that sex education in the public schools will require that certain moral judgments have to be made in the process, and even teaching about this as a mechanistic amoral process involves making moral choices. There is truth to that, so are their churches providing sex education classes? With rare exceptions the answer is no.

Jeanne and I once made our home available for a teenager so that she could carry a baby to term, and a family in California then adopted the baby. How many of the pro-life zealots have done something practical like that, something more difficult than carrying signs and booing those with whom you disagree?

The IUD is a contraceptive device used by many American women that aborts the fertilized egg within hours. Have the ministers and priests who want me to pass laws to ban all types of abortions preached against this? I confess the IUD does not bother my perhaps inadequately tuned conscience because life at that stage is so primitive.

Then what about "partial-birth abortions?" When feisty and courageous Senator Barbara Boxer of California offered an amendment that would have banned late-term abortions unless there is a serious health risk to the mother — a measure that would have been signed by President Clinton — the pro-life people opposed it. Would they sooner have a few more dead children and a political issue than sully their hands with political compromise? While only a relatively small number of abortions are late-term abortions, the law needs to be flexible, to give women and their physicians the ability to make decisions in complex cases the law cannot envision. Let me give you the practical case of a woman who testified before our committee. Already a mother, she went to her physician for one of her regular prenatal checkups. He asked how she was doing. She replied that she had an unusually healthy baby because it was kicking much more than her previous child. After doing a sonogram the physician told her the baby was having seizures, that two-thirds of its brain was outside its skull, that the baby would either be born dead or would live at the most for twenty-four hours, and that if she carried the baby to term she would harm her health and could ruin any chances she might have of becoming a mother again. The president of the council of her local Roman Catholic Church, she consulted with her priest and then had an abortion. Should the law declare her a criminal? Should the law declare her physician a criminal? Her priest? I oppose abortions when the fetus is viable except for extreme circumstances, but the law must be flexible in allowing for these extreme circumstances. In the Roe v. Wade decision the Supreme Court legalized abortions during the first two trimesters. From that point on the states may regulate "except where it is necessary, in appropriate medical judgment, for the preservation of the life or health of the mother." That seems sound. In a more recent case, Justices O'Connor, Kennedy and Souter in writing for the majority of the Court, confirmed the state's ability to restrict abortions after fetal viability "if the law contains exceptions for pregnancies which endanger a woman's life or health."[9]

The abortion issue surfaced frequently throughout my years in the U. S. House and Senate. During my House years, it became a major issue in every election. In 1982, after my close reelection contest of 1980, the Illinois Federation for Right to Life placed a large ad in the paper circulated in the Belleville Diocese of the Roman Catholic Church stating "A Vote for Simon Is a Vote to Continue Abortion on Demand."[10] In the previous week's issue I bought an ad with a letter from Father Robert Cornell, a priest who teaches at St. Norbert's College in Green Bay, Wisconsin, with whom I served in the House four years. Father Cornell wrote: "While Paul and I did not agree on every single issue, we usually voted similarly and often cosponsored legislation. Above all, I am firmly convinced that we badly need people like Paul in Congress because of his honesty, ability, dedication, compassion and good sense. . . . Back in 1975 the Catholic bishops of the United States said they 'hope that voters will examine the positions of candidates on the full range of issues as well as the person's integrity, philosophy and performance'. . . . If the voters of the 22nd district use such a basis, Paul will be overwhelmingly reelected."[11]

Periodically someone suggests that I should leave the Missouri Synod of the Lutheran Church because of my abortion stance. They are righteously indignant that our church can be broad enough to include people with views like mine. One congregation in Indiana even petitioned the church body to remove my local congregation from the synod because it tolerates me. The Lutheran church in the nation is roughly equivalent to the religious situation in our country. One-third of Lutherandom, the Missouri Synod, takes the "right to life" position, and the other two-thirds take the position that while abortion is undesirable, rigid laws are unlikely to change conduct and cannot deal with the complicated situations that people face. Within the nation, about one-third of the religious community takes the rigid stand, two-thirds take the more flexible position — both sides claiming to have the moral high ground. I am troubled when some of those who are so vocal in opposing abortion also oppose family planning — not abortions — to developing nations, and are noticeably silent about economic assistance to desperate, hungry people.

My guess is that most people who take the rigid stand have not studied the statistics that show that nations that outlaw all abortions, like the Phillippines and Bangladesh, have higher rates of abortion than does the United States. In the Phillippines, 80,000 women are admitted to hospitals each year with complications from botched abortions. In Ethiopia, 55 percent of maternal deaths stem from illegal abortions. A physician in the Ivory Coast of Africa reported, "Forty percent of the women who come to Trecheville hospital come because of traditional or back-alley abortions. Between 16 and 18 percent of these women die without leaving the hospital."[12]

Logic rarely prevails on these emotional issues. It is always easier to be strong and dogmatic if you stick to beliefs that are based on a selected slice of the evidence.

[1] Peter Ellingsen, "UK: Arm Bobbies or Curb Guns," *Sydney Morning Herald*, 6 July 1996.

[2] Pete Hamill, *Piece Work* (Boston: Little, Brown, 1996), 12.

[3] Arthur Kellermann and Donald Reay, "Protection or Peril? An Analysis of Firearm-Related Deaths in the Home," *New England Journal of Medicine* 24:1986.

[4] Arthur Kellermann, "Suicide in the Home in Relationship to Gun Ownership," *New England Journal of Medicine* 7:1992.

[5] FBI Uniform Crime Reports, released October 1996.

[6] National Center for Health Statistics, 1996.

[7] Dave Kopel, "Raising Gun Dealer Fees Is a Worthless Proposal," *Chicago Sun-Times*, 19 February 1994.

[8] "Gun Dealers: 'Weeding Out the Trash,'" 27 February 1995.

[9] *Planned Parenthood of Southeastern Pennsylvania v. Casey*, 505 U. S. 833 (1992).

[10] *The Messenger*, 29 October 1982.

[11] *The Messenger*, 22 October 1982.

[12] Howard French, "In Africa's Back-Street Clinics, Illicit Abortions Take Heavy Toll," *New York Times*, 3 June 1998.

# Chapter 19

# *Foreign Policy*

Despite United States dominance of the world economically and militarily, our leadership is shrinking. It is easy to lay that at the foot of the presidency, and that is partially correct, but the failure also rests with Congress and with the American people. We have turned inward.

The first President with whom I worked, Gerald Ford, had a fairly solid background in the international arena as the House Republican leader. Henry Kissinger served as his Secretary of State. Ford did not have the same interest in international affairs as Richard Nixon, but the Ford-Kissinger team did reasonably well. Kissinger is a master of details and can outline sweeping scenarios for the future. From my perspective, he had a touch too much cynicism and was more willing to work with dictators than I liked. But he led, and led strongly.

President Jimmy Carter did not have a rich background in international matters but displayed a keen interest, and two people under his administration who sometimes became rivals served him well, Cyrus Vance as Secretary of State and Zbigniew Brzezinski as his National Security Advisor. Vance, highly respected by everyone, played the role of the smooth diplomat. Brzezinski the goad, the questioner, paid less attention to diplomatic niceties. President Carter's great triumph, the Camp David Accord, would not have happened but for this team.

President Ronald Reagan set a direction, a tone in both domestic and foreign policy, but did not pretend to master details. He turned international policy over to a real leader, George Schultz. As Secretary of State he had a great combination of firmness and tactfulness. The climax to their foreign policy came at the meeting in

Iceland with Soviet Premier Gorbachev, where both agreed on reducing the nuclear weapons of the superpowers.

President George Bush had the best foreign policy résumé of any recent President. He also put together a good team, with James Baker as Secretary of State and Brent Scowcroft as his National Security Adviser. Baker, closer to the President than anyone in the Cabinet, moved on things quickly, and had a good relationship with those of us in Congress.

It is difficult to be the Governor of Arkansas and overnight become the most powerful figure in the world in foreign policy. That problem is compounded when interest in the international arena is very secondary. I have seen President Clinton grow as a foreign policy leader, but the first months were awkward.


My first significant involvement in international policy occurred when President Carter appointed me as one of two U. S. House delegates to the 1978 Special UN Session on Disarmament. Secretary of State Cy Vance headed our delegation, and did so when we visited with the Soviet delegation, chaired by Foreign Minister Andrei Gromyko. One clear memory of that meeting: No one in our delegation spoke Russian, and I am reasonably sure all of their delegation spoke at least some English, most of them fluently. We went through the process of translating everything anyway — giving them the chance to reflect on their answers for a few seconds or minutes before replying to whatever we said. I would love to get into a debate on the floor of the Senate where I had that kind of an advantage over my opponent! This is another illustration of the need for Americans to become more proficient in foreign languages.

While at the United Nations I tried to meet with delegates from countries I would not ordinarily have a chance to see in Washington because of our strained relationships. Unsuccessfully I tried to have lunch with the Albanian delegation and the Libyan delegation. I asked the Vietnamese delegation to have lunch with me. I handed them the invitation in writing, personally delivering it on the floor of the Assembly. They told me they would have to check with Hanoi. Soon the word came that they could join me. I asked Congressman William Lehman of Florida, who happened to be in New York City that day to join us, as well as a State Department staff member. The Vietnamese indicated they were eager to have diplomatic relations with us, that they felt they had a promise from President Nixon for $3 billion in reparations but they were willing to forget that. I asked if they would come to Washington to discuss it with a few more key people. They said they would again have to check with Hanoi, and then told me that under the United States rules, they could not travel more than twenty-five miles from the United Nations buildings. Not even aware of the latter restriction, which we applied to several "unfriendly" nations, I told them that they should check with Hanoi and I would see what I could do about the twenty-five-mile rule. We worked it out, and they came to Washington and met for dinner in our home in suburban Maryland with a few Republican and Democratic members of the House and Senate and two representatives of the State Department. The Vietnamese were candid. They said the Soviets wanted to take over the Cam Ranh Bay naval base that we had built, and play a more prominent role in Vietnamese affairs. They preferred to be more independent and if we mutually extended diplomatic recognition to each other, that would help. Sheila, then seventeen, watched and listened to the conversation from our staircase just off the living room where she could see and hear everything. After they left she observed, "It's hard to believe we were fighting them three years ago."

The Americans at the dinner recommended to the White House that diplomatic ties be extended. We recognized that it might not be popular — somewhat similar to Harry Truman's wise but unpopular decision to help Japan and Germany after World War II — but we all felt our national interest would be served by doing it. The White House did not look favorably upon the idea. At that point we were "playing the China card," doing everything we could to keep the Chinese independent of the Soviets, a policy with which I agreed. But I doubt that this move would have made any difference, even though China and Vietnam historically had not been friendly. We could accurately have portrayed it to the Chinese as a way of restraining the Soviets. I eventually conveyed the White House decision to the Vietnamese. Some time later UN Ambassador Andrew Young related to me a conversation he had with the Vietnamese Ambassador to the UN, in which the Vietnamese official hinted that they might not have invaded Cambodia if we had recognized them, that they were under pressure from the Soviets to invade Cambodia. But would that have meant the continued dominance of Pol Pot's ruthless forces in Cambodia? The situation was complex. What is clear is that if we had recognized Vietnam much earlier we could have played a more constructive role in the region.

International policy decisions should be made on the basis of national interest, not national passion. If we had shown Truman-like courage on Vietnam the United States would have recognized that government much sooner. Too often we fail to act — or act — because of domestic politics. Backbone is a valuable commodity both in domestic and international politics.

Another illustration of this same point is our policy toward Cuba, as irrational as any international policy we have, all dictated because of fear of what might happen to Florida's electoral votes, and really the votes in one county there. Dade County (Miami) dictates national policy toward Cuba! Today we are pressing to improve relations with China, and I favor that. But if you ask me who has a better civil liberties record, China or Cuba, the answer is Cuba, although the Cuban performance is not good. Yet we shun Cuba, ninety miles from our shore, and embrace China. If Castro and the Soviet leaders had held a meeting three decades ago and discussed how they could influence U. S. policy to make sure Castro stays in power and does not give his people freedom, they could not have devised a better policy than we have followed. We had trade and exchanges with the Soviets and that helped to bring about change there. With Cuba we do the opposite, and there has been no change. We are in the preposterous position of not another nation on the face of the globe agreeing with our policy on trade isolation. Only two nations forbid their citizens to travel to Cuba: North Korea and the United States. On top of that, President Clinton knuckled under and signed the Helms-Burton act which provides secondary boycotts to corporate officers in friendly nations like Canada, Israel, and other countries who violate what we say is good conduct toward Cuba. The president has regularly waived these provisions that are an embarrassment to us, but he never should have signed the bill. I spoke against it and so did Senator Chris Dodd of Connecticut, who at that time headed the Democratic National Committee, a courageous stand on his part.

One of the frustrations in foreign policy is sometimes to see development assistance being used too much for consulting fees, or things that are not bad but do too little to help those in desperate need in a recipient nation. The Soviets used foreign assistance to developing nations to build show places, visible marks of their aid, and sometimes we succumb to the same temptation. Over State Department objection, and with the support of Bread for the World, a religious-based lobbying group, I offered an amendment in the House that said that at least 50 percent of all non-military international assistance given to a nation must serve the poorest citizens. The argument against my amendment, which has limited validity, is that often it is difficult to know who is being helped, for example, by a new road. But the amendment would rule out some showy projects and at least provide a measuring stick for our officials. The House accepted my amendment, and the House-Senate conference reduced the figure to 40 percent, which did not please me but at least provided a standard. In reviewing the law in one of my last months in the Senate I discovered that at some point even the 40 percent standard quietly had been dropped. A 50 percent standard should be reimposed. Every legislative battle won is not permanently won.

South Africa's cruel apartheid system was headed for two results if it had not changed peacefully: a terrible, bloody civil war and racial tensions in that country that would spread around the world. In my first visit to South Africa I thought a civil war of massive destruction could not be avoided. With the exception of a handful of members of Parliament, all the key players in the government (all whites) seemed set in stone against change. One, Foreign Minister "Pik" Botha (not related to the former president, P. W. Botha), privately admitted that change would have to come but he wanted to become President and would not breathe publicly what he told others and me privately. But in their government he occupied a spot of lonely isolation even to privately express such views.

While economic sanctions carried on by one nation do not assist any cause, they can be effective when nations act in concert. Malcom Fraser, former Prime Minister of Australia, headed a British Commonwealth committee pushing sanctions, favored by all except a few of the commonwealth nations. He read of my work for the imposition of sanctions and stopped by my office to give encouragement. West Europeans, headed by the Dutch who had a historic role in South Africa, were moving toward sanctions. But the head of the largest economic power, Ronald Reagan, opposed sanctions, as did Margaret Thatcher, Great Britain's prime minister. They both said talking to South Africa would have more effect, and sanctions would hurt the poorest people there. The difficulty with jawboning is that it did not convey the seriousness with which the rest of the world viewed this oppression. Also, I had serious questions about the depth of Ronald Reagan's concern on this issue. He sent all the wrong signals. The poor I talked to in South Africa wanted sanctions. A middle-aged man in Soweto township responded, when I posed the sanctions question, "I have two daughters. I have lived without freedom all my life. If I can suffer a little more and give them freedom, I want to suffer." The U. S. House somewhat unexpectedly passed a strong sanctions measure. The head of Reagan's National Security Council, Admiral John Poindexter, had written the House leadership: "This will erode our capacity to promote negotiations in South Africa."[1] The administration said they favored "constructive engagement." We felt we were receiving lip service and nothing more. While the House considered this, I drafted a letter that fourteen of my colleagues in the Senate also signed, urging Senator Richard Lugar of Indiana, chairman of the Senate Foreign Relations Committee, to pass a sanctions bill. Dick Lugar, former Mayor of Indianapolis, is conservative but not rigid, and a man with a conscience. He decided an economic boycott of South Africa made sense, and his move turned out to be crucial. The Senate passed it, the President vetoed it, and the House and Senate overrode the veto. That would not have happened without Dick Lugar's leadership. Some of us have received awards for our work on behalf of freedom in South Africa, but an almost unsung hero is Dick Lugar. The man who emerged as "a caretaker" President in South Africa, F. W. de Klerk, acknowledges the role that sanctions played in moving him and his country to abandon apartheid. But it would not have happened without Senator Richard Lugar, a quiet, competent, solid legislator.

While serving in both the House and Senate, I spoke in opposition to the apartheid regime, and when I emerged as chair of the Subcommittee on Africa of the Senate Foreign Relations Committee I had a greater opportunity to lead. When in South Africa in the pre-Mandela era, I held press conferences denouncing the system, appealing to people of moderation to change it. At one point an Afrikaner (white of Dutch background) approached me, denounced my "fanning the flames of fanaticism" and called me "the most hated American in South Africa," a compliment I'm afraid was not accurate. What is encouraging today is that Nelson Mandela rates high in all the public opinion polls there, almost as high among whites as blacks. What is particularly stunning about this is that under the old regime, the press was under strict limits in handling any reference to Mandela. I particularly recall buying *Newsweek* one day, which had a story about Mandela. The story did not meet objections from the censors, but it included a picture of Nelson Mandela. Government censors had carefully cut out the picture of Mandela from every copy of *Newsweek* circulated in South Africa.

The religious community of South Africa played a key role, particularly the Dutch Reformed, Anglicans, and Roman Catholics, with strong assistance from the Jewish community. De Klerk's brother, a theologian who opposed apartheid, probably played a role, almost overlooked when de Klerk became president. Not many politicians voluntarily give up power — particularly if they face harsh criticism for doing so. Yet that is what de Klerk did. In freeing Nelson Mandela, he brought forward a reconciler. Imprisoned for twenty-six years, Mandela came out of incarceration without a touch of bitterness that I or my friends have detected. I have been with him on perhaps twenty public or private occasions and his lack of bitterness and positive attitude can be described as Lincolnesque. One small insight into the man came at his inauguration in Pretoria. In our VIP section, at his invitation, three of those present were his former prison guards. South Africa has problems but generally is moving in a solid direction. As a former Senator I have far more plaques and awards than I deserve, but one I keep in our home is the Archbishop Desmond Tutu award, presented to me in behalf of the people of South Africa and my friend the Archbishop, for my work for freedom for that country. I cannot say I merit the award, but I prize it.

The best debate we had during my years in Washington was on the question of authorizing Desert Storm. Members participated with the knowledge that lives hung in the balance. While I have generally favored a fast response to military aggression — faster than we have been doing it — I thought in this case a severe economic boycott was worth a try first, and then if the government of Iraq did not change and withdraw from Kuwait, we could act militarily. The weakness of that position was that the Iraqis could get better entrenched, but our abilities so outclassed theirs in both weapons and personnel that I thought it worth the risk. The day before the vote, Dwayne Andreas, chief executive officer of ADM which has major international interests, called and said it was his judgment that if we acted militarily we would make a hero out of Saddam Hussein within Iraq, entrench him in office, and ultimately make change in Iraq more difficult to achieve. That was my instinct too. I joined Senator George Mitchell and two other colleagues in visiting the troops in the area before the vote and I knew they were well prepared and ready to act. The decision by

President Bush resulted in far fewer casualties than I thought we would have. We took the Iraqi troops out of Kuwait, but Saddam Hussein remains solidly in power.

After the 1992 election, in which Clinton defeated Bush, Senator Howard Metzenbaum and I visited Somalia, where we had heard things were grim. They were worse than that. I remember talking to a young mother at a food center who had a little boy four years old with her, skinny except for his extended stomach, but smaller than my granddaughter Reilly then two-and one-half. I asked her how she happened to come to the station, and she said she lived about fifteen miles away but heard that they had food and water here, and she and her three children walked toward the food center in the hot desert sun, two of the children dying along the way. I doubt that that little boy is alive today. Here is part of what I wrote upon my return:

> At this place [the name I don't recall] with about 25,000 people, there were massive numbers of flies — not thousands of them, millions of them, literally. Whether attracted by food or bodies or disease or a total lack of sanitation, I do not know. But they were smothering everything like I have never seen in my life. I write about the flies because of the children. Flies get into the corners of their eyes and the children were too weak to wave them away. . . .

> There was an old man, begging. But the Red Cross and the United Nations people said that if we gave him anything we would be overwhelmed by hundreds of people. Even worse, if we were to give him anything of any value, he probably would be hurt or killed by someone who would take it away.

> The "hospital" was one small tent with a few bottles of pills for an area with 25,000 people. . . .

> There is no government. That means no schools, no police, none of the things that give society stability. . . .

> We flew in on a C-130 that carried nine tons of food — flew in on a dirt runway on which our armed forces' personnel are not accustomed to landing an aircraft. For security reasons they had to

keep the engines running while they unloaded the food and us and then took off right away.[2]

At that point untold thousands had already died and the UN estimated *at least* an additional 250,000 would die in the next sixty days. Small boys wandered around with long rifles. The nation had no government through which aid could be channeled. We saw the Red Cross, a group called Doctors Without Borders, and an Irish relief organization helping. They all did good work, but the task demanded infinitely more than they could provide.

The tragedy did not happen overnight. On January 22, 1991 — twenty months before I visited Somalia — eight of us in the Senate sent a letter to Jim Baker, then Secretary of State, urging action. Three weeks prior to that letter Senator Nancy Kassebaum and I had an Op-Ed piece in *The New York Times* urging UN and U. S. action. Congressmen Tony Hall of Ohio and Bill Emerson of Missouri, who both headed a Hunger Task Force in the House, sent a letter to the warring factions in Somalia urging them to halt their fighting so people could be fed. The letters continued. In June 1992 a *Washington Post* editorial stated: "The indifference must give way to a concerted international response."[3] That same month Ambassador Mohammed Sahnoun, former Algerian Ambassador to the United States who had been asked by Secretary General Boutros Boutros-Ghali to examine and report on the situation, came to my office and told me that 5,000 children under the age of five were dying each day in Somalia. In October 1992 I held hearings on Somalia again. However, most of our efforts to try to help Somalia came during the 1992 U. S. election campaign, with news coverage on polls and Gennifer Flowers and other things which preoccupied the American people and our media. President Bush hesitated to take decisive action during an election campaign, knowing that many would criticize such action as a political ploy — and it would probably not be popular politically.

Senator Howard Metzenbaum and I went there shortly after the election. We returned on a Sunday night. Monday morning the two of us had a conference call with UN Secretary General Boutros-Ghali. At that point he had been authorized to send 3,500 troops to Somalia to help the situation, but only 500 Pakistani troops were there, holed up at the airport at Mogadishu, doing no good for anyone. I urged him to get the balance of the troops there quickly, and — picking a figure out of the air — to get 10,000 additional troops. Boutros-Ghali responded that he hoped to get an additional 3,000 Pakistani troops to Somalia by ship.

"By ship!" I responded. "Thousands of people will die while they travel there slowly." Howard Metzenbaum underscored that.

"But your country charges us too much to get the troops there by plane," he responded.

"Could we get them there by plane and then take it off of our back UN dues?"

"Yes," he replied quickly.

I called Larry Eagleburger who had taken Jim Baker's place as Secretary of State, an old pro in foreign affairs I had known many years, explaining the situation to him, and asked that he call the UN Secretary General immediately. I also said that I would try reaching President Bush but knew that that day was the funeral for his mother, and asked Larry to convey the urgency of the situation to the President and urge immediate action. This all happened on Monday. On Thursday, as I recall, the President called a meeting that included the Secretaries of Defense and State, General Colin Powell, Vice President Dan Quayle, and a few others, including four of us from the House and Senate. The President made a decision to act, and in my opinion it was George Bush's finest hour. He saved hundreds of thousands of lives. I read occasionally where some ill informed columnist or editorial writer refers to "the Somalia disaster" or "the Somalia debacle," but I don't view it that way, nor will history.

Our troops met no resistance, but after being there for a short time, a retired U. S. Admiral, acting on behalf of the United Nations, made a decision that probably sounded right from a military point of view, but did not consider the complicated political scene there. He did not consult with Ambassador Bob Oakley, the skilled U. S. diplomat, nor with U. S. General Anthony Zinni, who knew the situation and handled himself well. Nineteen American service personnel lost their lives. One of them had his body dragged through the streets and we saw it on national television. The American people and Congress were understandably outraged. Senators began demanding that we pull our troops out immediately.

By this time Bill Clinton had just taken over as President. We had a two-hour meeting on the Somalia situation at the White House with the new President and his new cabinet members, Secretary of State Warren Christopher and Secretary of Defense Les Aspin. No one looked good. Clinton, feeling his way in new territory, did not lead. Warren Christopher, an extremely competent person but cautious, did not say a word during the entire two hours, perhaps because he did not agree with the tenor of things. I opposed a pull-out but I clearly was in the minority, and the compromise developed: to pull our troops out in March. I didn't like it but it was better than doing it immediately and so I reluctantly went along. If the President had been in office longer and become more familiar with foreign policy issues, he could have gone on national television and explained the situation and at least a sizable segment of the American public would have supported him. The situation required presidential leadership and the President did not yet feel comfortable providing it.

Shortly after this meeting, President Mubarak of Egypt visited Washington, staying in Blair House, the official guest residence across the street from the White House. Minutes before I went to pay my respects to him, I received a call from the White House suggesting that I ask President Mubarak to keep his troops there after March. I said that with embarrassment I would do it. When I made this request to him, it is fair to say that he was unimpressed that the wealthy and powerful United States of America would pull its troops out but ask a small and poverty-ridden nation like Egypt to stay there.

One of the lessons we should learn from this is that we cannot send a message to terrorists around the world that if they just kill a few American troops somewhere, then Americans will run. It is a policy that invites abuse of our personnel. While the needless death of nineteen American servicemen is a tragedy, unless we are willing to take some risks we cannot provide effective leadership. People who enlist in the armed forces know that they are taking special risks, just as people who enlist in the Chicago Police Department know that. If the Chicago Police Department found a pocket of drug dealers who killed two of the police, the Mayor of Chicago would not announce that in view of the risks he would pull the police out of that territory. To do that would invite terrorism to prevail, and that holds true whether it is Chicago or a far corner of the globe.

To be more effective we should also be willing to have at least a token number of American troops present when the UN sends personnel to Angola or Cyprus or any other spot. We rarely do that. We transport others to places of risk and help pay for them. Our unwillingness to share dangers is almost analogous to the Civil War practice of people with means hiring others to go into the military for them. This practice is resented by other nations, and rightly so.

If the UN is to be more effective in keeping peace it needs to be able to move troops much more quickly. Senator James Jeffords of Vermont and I sponsored a bill to have a force of 3,000 from within our armed forces who would volunteer to be available on 24-hour notice not only to be a part of a UN peacekeeping force, but a peacemaking force if the need arose. They would perform this special duty only if the Security Council of the UN acted and the President of the United States approved. Canada has pushed such an idea. If the United States were to lead on this, other nations would be willing to do the same. What happens now is that after the UN Security Council acts the Secretary General has to get on the phone and start begging countries to provide troops, a slow process when speed is sometimes essential. Senator John Warner of Virginia said he would hold a hearing on our proposal, but in the rush of other activity it did not happen. What interests me is that when I have explored this with some of my most conservative colleagues, they like the idea, with the understanding that these would be volunteers from within our already-volunteer armed force. A small stipend should be given the volunteers who would be taking extra risks.

However, sending troops is not enough. We should be paying our UN dues. It is a matter of national embarrassment that we now owe more than a year's cost of operating the UN, excluding peacekeeping. This is a symbol of our national affliction of withdrawal. The symptoms of this disease are everywhere. Of the twenty-one wealthy nations in the world, we are now dead last in the percentage of our income that goes to help the poor beyond our borders. Denmark, Norway, the Netherlands, and Saudi Arabia all give at least seven times as much as we do as a percentage of income. The nation that provided the most generous act in the history of nations, the Marshall Plan, which salvaged many countries economically and also saved them politically from Communism, a country which once devoted more than 2 percent of our national income to helping the poor beyond our borders, now devotes less than one-seventh of 1 percent of our national income to this cause. Has our income gone down? After adjusting for inflation our per capita income is about two-and-one-half times our earnings when we helped with the Marshall Plan. Are there fewer poor around the world? While the average world income has risen, there is no drop in the numbers of the impoverished. What is different is that under the Marshall Plan your senators and your House members could come back home and tell the Schmidts, "I'm helping your relatives in Germany." The Zaganellis would hear, "I'm helping your relatives in Italy." The Thompsons would hear, "I'm helping your relatives in Great Britain." And other examples. Today the people who need help live in places like Bangladesh, and when your legislators return home there are few relatives from Bangladesh pleading for help. Just desperate, hungry people.

At a high school or college assembly or at a service club meeting someone frequently will ask, "Why do we send all this money overseas when we have these needs here at home?" I ask the audience to guess what percentage of our federal budget goes for foreign economic assistance. The guesses range between 15 percent and 30 percent, when the correct answer is less than 1 percent.

While there are foreign policy deficiencies that can be placed at the foot of the presidency, the failure to give President Clinton the authority to negotiate trade agreements, which his predecessors had, rests with Congress and an indifferent American public. The inexcusable failure of the House to pass International Monetary Fund guarantees, which up to now have not cost the United States one penny — when Asia and Russia are experiencing severe difficulties — is a failure to recognize that when there are severe difficulties elsewhere in the world, they will affect us. When Asia's financial problems suddenly emerged, just as suddenly the orders for Caterpillar products built in Peoria started to fall off, as do orders for a host of other U. S. products. On occasion, myopia is widespread in Congress.

During the Carter presidency I visited in Algeria, and went with U. S. Ambassador Ulrich St. Clair Haynes Jr. to visit Foreign Minister Abdelaziz Bouterlika, who unfortunately died in an airplane crash a few years later. During the course of our conversation he expressed a strong desire to improve relations with the United States, which I agreed would help both of our countries. When he asked what they might do to change the climate, I mentioned that our fifty-two hostages held in Iran deeply troubled our nation. Since Algeria has diplomatic ties with Iran, I said if they could play the role of mediator and get this resolved, I knew we would be grateful. They did precisely that, and when Iran freed the hostages shortly after Ronald Reagan became President, hardly anyone said a word to thank the Algerian government, and soon we forgot their role. I am sure at least a few Algerian leaders resented that, but more important, their service could have caused a warmer relationship between our two nations if we had followed through, and maybe — only maybe — Algeria would not have its serious problems today if we had taken a more constructive role. We muffed an opportunity, and we have muffed too many.

During debates on the Senate and House floor on defense appropriations, members argue that in order to be respected around the world we must maintain a high level of arms capability. That is true. But what other nations question is not our technical ability but our backbone.

In August 1992 Bill Clinton the candidate made a speech criticizing the Bush Administration for not acting in Bosnia. Clinton's criticism had merit, not only of the Bush Administration but of the NATO countries which did nothing while they wished the whole mess would somehow disappear. Then Bill Clinton became President and other things took priority, and still there was no action. We made threats but we didn't act. Finally, on the 500th day of the siege of Sarajevo, NATO, with U. S. blessing, told the Serbs that the shelling had to stop or the Serb artillery positions would be bombed. It stopped. That should have happened on the second day or the fifth day, not the 500th. Then, belatedly we sent in troops to calm the situation at least temporarily, and make an uneasy peace possible — an uneasy peace being better than no peace. In the meantime, Serbs and Croats and Muslims who have had relatives and close friends killed by "the enemy" want revenge, and unless there is strong local leadership encouraged by us, eventually that revenge will take place, and revenge will cause further revenge. When these fires start burning they should be put out quickly, and if the United States does not lead, too often other nations will not act. Leadership requires courage and we have not shown that in abundance.

When reports came out of Rwanda in April 1994 about ethnic killings on a large scale, Senator James Jeffords and I introduced a resolution calling on the United Nations and the United States to do what could be done to stop the slaughter. We had six cosponsors of our resolution, members who had demonstrated an interest in Africa. The situation worsened and our resolution seemed inadequate. In May, Senator Jeffords and I phoned General Romeo Dallaire, the Canadian general in charge of a small contingent of 500 UN troops in Kigali, the capital city. He told us that if he could get 5,000 to 8,000 troops quickly he could stop the killings. Jim and I hastily drafted a letter that we had hand-delivered that same day to the White House and State Department urging immediate action through the United Nations to get troops there to stop the genocide. Nothing happened. Perhaps ten days later I called the White House to see if consideration could be given to quick action. The response: "We don't feel there is a base of public support for taking any action in Africa." That is technically accurate, but if there is no base for public support, the President can get on television and explain our reasons for responding and build a base. Even then, if public support still is not strong, leadership demands action in this type of situation. Jim Jeffords and I sent that letter in May. A month or so later the Secretary General of the Organization for African Unity, Salim Salim, visited my office and appealed for help. He said he could get troops from Senegal, Mali, Tunisia, Ghana, and Ethiopia but he had no means to get them there or to assure supplying them once they got there. He could not believe the world would simply stand by and see this slaughter. Finally in October — after hundreds of thousands had been killed — the UN Security Council authorized action by member nations to stop the killing. France immediately sent 2,000 troops to one part of Rwanda. No one else did anything, other than a few troops we sent to secure the airport in Kigali. (Tom Friedman, in a column in *The New York Times* said that France acts like a great power but does not have the resources; the United States has the resources but does not act like a great power.) The killings continued and spread to Burundi and Zaire, since renamed Congo. The current estimate is that more than 900,000 people died in this ethnic strife — needlessly. Because of what the survivors have been through, many have scarred memories and will seek retaliation. It becomes more and more difficult to stop this killing cycle.

In August of that year I wrote in an Op-Ed for the *St. Louis Post-Dispatch*: "Our political leadership must make a case to the American people that deterring these situations is a cause worth our involvement — sometimes with our troops, sometimes without. We owe it to a future General Dallaire — and to the hundreds of thousands of Rwandans who might have been saved."[4] General Dallaire commented later: "The belligerent parties had signed a peace agreement. Some of them may have signed under duress, but there was still a will for peace. . . . Where there was once a peace agreement in one country, there is now instability in an entire region."[5] He noted that during one four-month period more people were killed in Rwanda than during four years of the civil war in the former Yugoslavia. In February 1998 General Dallaire testified before the United Nations Criminal Tribunal investigating the mass killings. He said that in April 1994 they could easily have created a force to stop the killings "but there was a lack of political will." The defense lawyer commented, "It seems to me that you regret that, Major General." Dallaire responded, "You cannot even imagine."[6]

When President Clinton made his first trip to Africa in the spring of 1998 he stopped briefly in Kigali and apologized to the people of Rwanda for the community of nations not having intervened. If we can follow the apology with action the next time something like this occurs anywhere, then the apology becomes real and meaningful. Otherwise it is an empty gesture.


The Clinton foreign policy has had successes. The peace agreement in Northern Ireland is a sizable step forward, and former Senator George Mitchell deserves much of the credit for what happened. That was an easy one for the President. It required his attention and some late night phone calls, but no risk of political capital.

In the Middle East we have played a constructive role, slowly pushing both sides toward peace. Here greater ground could be gained if the President were willing to risk a little political capital. Secretary of State Madeleine Albright from time to time has sounded tough, and then has had to reverse field because of a lack of White House backing. Despite that, I feel that eventually a better situation will emerge in the Middle East.


What should our relationship be to dictators?

We should have exchanges with students and others in their countries, continue to trade with them, make clear to their people our stand for human rights, and permit few weapons or instruments of military potential to get to these nations from the United States.

In practical terms, what does that mean? Take China as an example. Trade? Yes. Exchange of students? Yes. But we have sold them weapons we should not have. We have waffled on our human rights stand, and when the freely elected vice president of Taiwan, Liem Chan, an alumnus of the University of Chicago, is elected to that school's governing board, we tell the Taiwanese government not to ask for a visa for him to come to meetings of the board in the United States because we would have to turn him down. Giving him the visa might offend mainland China. That gains us respect from no one, including the Chinese government. It also sends mixed signals to the Chinese and others about our commitment to freedom and to helping defend Taiwan should China decide to invade. Taiwan's status is an emotional issue in Beijing and the danger is that a Chinese leader who is weak will buttress his power by creating a national crusade to invade Taiwan. Unfortunately, as historians Will and Ariel Durant have written, "Nothing so strengthens a government as a declaration of war."[7] That would be a disastrous policy for China and for Taiwan.

We should be clear that a military "solution" to this issue is not tolerable, and our weak-kneed knuckling under to China on things like the University of Chicago matter sends the wrong signals.

Our policy toward China should follow the pattern that Bill Clinton showed as he conducted himself superbly in his visit there — friendly, but not backing off our commitment to human rights. That the exchange between the two Presidents was broadcast live in China is a hopeful sign. The President and Mrs. Clinton's attendance at a church service in Beijing — even though not covered by the Chinese media — was important. Hillary Clinton's visit to the former synagogue in Shanghai also sent a quiet but solid message. It is possible that a genuine democracy could emerge in China in the next decade, though it probably will take longer, and in a dictatorship reversal is also possible, particularly as the nation faces serious economic problems or serious water shortages. But a combination of friendliness and firmness on human rights is the policy that is needed, and sometimes is lacking.

While no two issues are completely analogous, we recognized both East Germany and West Germany, to the displeasure of both sides. But that recognition did not prevent the two sides from eventually merging *peacefully*. There will be no peaceful merger in Asia unless China accepts democracy as Taiwan has. The longer China puts that off, the more unlikely it is that Taiwan will fall under the flag of the People's Republic of China. Foreign policy should be built on realities, not myths. It is a myth that Taiwan is part of China today. Mexico has more historic claims to Texas than China does to Taiwan.

Because of the differing histories of the German and Chinese situation, it would be a mistake for us to suddenly announce recognition of Taiwan. But we can do things that fall short of that while making clear to China that we will not turn our back on a nation that has a free press, a multiparty system, freedom of religion, and other freedoms that the citizens on the mainland do not have. Taiwan could contribute significantly to some of the UN agencies without being formally seated in the United Nations, though I hope we might gradually move toward formal seating. Taiwan has more population than two-thirds of the members of the UN and more economic power than nine-tenths of the members of the UN. We should help build a bridge between China and Taiwan, but playing a game of Make Believe with China while we turn our back on Taiwan does not help anyone.

As a consistent international policy develops, it should include that democracies are given special treatment where choices have to be made. I favored Bill Clinton going to China, but it would have fit our ideology better if prior to that he had made a visit to the world's largest democracy, India. That not only meshes with our ideology, it also fits our security needs. Stable democracies do not attack each other. The threat to world peace with rare exceptions will come from dictatorships. While I regret the nuclear explosions of India and Pakistan — the Hindu nuclear weapon and the Muslim nuclear weapon following the Christian, Atheist, and Jewish bombs, as some note — more attention to India and Pakistan earlier might have prevented this, and developing a sounder relationship can help in the future.

I hope that China has no expansionist plans in Taiwan or elsewhere. However, China's neighbor to the north, Mongolia, has serious concerns when they see maps printed in China that include Mongolia as part of China. Dictatorships often have visions of grandeur and military conquest. We must recognize that possibility with China or any other dictatorship, and conduct our international policy in ways that make that less likely.

This requires firmness and friendship, but also a strategy that looks at fundamentals. It is nice to have the presidents of China and the United States announce that nuclear warheads are no longer aimed at each other; in the event of an accident that could be significant. But in ten minutes nuclear warheads can be redirected. Today the U. S. nuclear stockpile of weapons is large but declining. China's is much smaller but growing. Pressure by the United States and other nations to stop all nuclear testing, and to not stockpile more nuclear weapons should be our declared and clear aim. Smiles at joint press conferences are better than frowns, but they are not a substitute for fundamental strategy.

Vacuums do not exist long in domestic or foreign politics. Someone moves in. On foreign policy, we have not left a total vacuum, but timorous leadership leaves at least a partial void. Threats which other nations know we will not act upon do not fill a void. We talked tough and talked tough and talked tough on Bosnia and then finally, belatedly inched ahead. "Speak softly but carry a big stick," was Theodore Roosevelt's famous line. Our motto seems to be, "Speak loudly, carry a big stick, but rarely use it." As I write this, military tensions are high in the Serb province of Kosovo, where 90 percent of the people are of Albanian background. We have threatened the Serb leader several times; we have had military maneuvers near the bitterly contested territory; but my guess is that Milosovic believes we are all bluff and no action. Former Secretary of Defense Frank Carlucci, critical of both the Bush and Clinton administrations for waffling, observes with accuracy: "The erosion of the credibility of the U. S. threat of force has created the unstable security environment that Milosevic exploits today."[8] I don't know what the right answer is to that complex situation. I know the wrong answer is to bark and bark and not bite. That kind of dog doesn't even frighten a postal carrier.

Worse than providing no leadership is to attempt to retard constructive efforts by other nations. On the proposal to outlaw the production and deployment of land mines we have been dragging our feet — even though a sizable segment of our military leadership supports it. Our excuse is that land mines retard the North Korean forces. What retards North Korea are not a few land mines on the border but the overwhelmingly superior South Korean forces, plus the presence of 120,000 U. S. troops. Those who don't want to outlaw land mines should visit Angola and see so many men, women, and children with limbs missing because of land mines, many of which are built in the U. S. or financed by us. Equally egregious and indefensible, the United States joined seven other nations — out of 148 — in opposing an international criminal court to deal with genocide. A temporary court exists in the capital of the Netherlands. We should have applauded its permanent creation instead of being an obstruction to justice.

Economic sanctions should be a rarely used tool of diplomacy, utilized only when we know that most developed nations will join in them, and only when we believe they can be effective. Isolated sanctions by one nation are not effective if the desired aim is to change the course of a government. It can hurt a nation economically, but otherwise simply reinforces the grip of the leadership we ostensibly want to change. In South Africa sanctions worked because we were dealing with a semi-free government where people could criticize usually without fear of imprisonment, and because developed and developing nations joined in the effort almost without exception.

Senator Richard Lugar of Indiana and his Indiana House colleague, Rep. Lee Hamilton, have introduced a Sanctions Reform Act that would require an annual review of sanctions. I have not seen the language of the bill but the concept is sound.

Part of sanctions is telling U. S. citizens that they cannot travel to certain countries. Unless there is physical danger to American citizens in traveling to a particular nation, we should be *encouraging* them to travel to areas of difficulties, not discouraging them. If we had 10,000 more Americans traveling to Cuba, Iraq, and Iran each year, we would have a greater base of knowledge of what is happening in these countries, and it is at least possible the influence of these visitors might help to modify the conduct of these governments. Denying Americans the right to travel when there is no physical risk is a denial of our rights to free speech, for free speech assumes the freedom to find out facts in order to discuss policy rationally.

Sanctions and travel tend to be emotional issues in foreign policy, and another is trade. The North American Free Trade Agreement (NAFTA) became a hot issue, one where I differed with my friends in organized labor, as did some of their other traditional supporters in the Senate like Ted Kennedy and Tom Harkin. In announcing my decision on NAFTA I said: "The unspoken premise of some opponents is that there are only so many riches to spread around this region of the world, and if we permit our neighbors to the south to have more, we will have less. It is the same false assumption of those who wrote about population two centuries ago: There are only so many goods to be divided, and if you increase the population, gradually everyone will become poorer. The average person in the world today has a much higher standard of living than in those days, and our population has grown tenfold."[9]

I gave a series of Illinois illustrations on the issue. Gatorade, for example, is made by Quaker Oats, headquartered in Chicago. Mexico charged an 18 percent tariff on Gatorade. Quaker Oaks said that if NAFTA were approved, they would be able to sell more Gatorade in Mexico with U. S. jobs, but that if NAFTA lost, they would have no choice but to build a plant in Mexico.

After the approval of NAFTA, the United States sold more of our cars there in the first three months of 1994 than in all of 1993. The dire predictions of a huge growth in unemployment and lowering of our standard of living have both proven false — despite a serious Peso problem in Mexico. Since the signing of NAFTA, 13 million more jobs have been created in the United States, our unemployment rate has gone down, and our average income has risen slightly. NAFTA did not cause most of this, but NAFTA was not the drag on our economy many predicted. According to the Commerce Department, in 1996 exports to Canada supported 1.6 million jobs and exports to Mexico 750,000 jobs. Most of these existed prior to the passage of NAFTA, but NAFTA has helped.

The experience of less wealthy Spain, Portugal, Ireland and Greece in joining the European Community is instructive. After joining, their standards of living grew faster than in the other European Community nations, but the standard of living also increased in France, Germany, and the other welcoming partners. And migration from the new partners to the other nations declined.

Columnist Carl Rowan wrote in the midst of the heated debate: "When fear is at war with promises and hopes, fear almost always triumphs. And NAFTA is being assailed by some very potent peddlers of fear. . . . Twelve Nobel Prize-winning economists have endorsed this free trade agreement. . . . I don't believe anyone will suffer in the long run from a trade pact that makes Mexico a more prosperous country and offers reasons for its citizens to stay home."[10]

I also spoke out for programs for the employees and employers in those businesses that were harmed, saying that we should have transition programs for them.

After the passage of NAFTA, the combination of labor opposition to further trade agreements, plus the Pat Buchanan crowd making the same speeches, plus excessively partisan Republicans who wanted to limit Bill Clinton in any way that they could, caused Congress to block giving Clinton the same authority his predecessors had to negotiate "fast track" trade agreements. The failure to give the President that authority may be emotionally satisfying but it is economically self-defeating.

One of the last trips abroad I made as a Senator was to North Korea with Jeanne and Senator Frank Murkowski of Alaska and his wife Nancy. We landed in the first American plane to enter that nation since the Korean War ended. We stayed in their official guest houses, with no contact with the people of North Korea, except for the contact scripted by them. One of our weirdest experiences came with a concert presented at a beautiful concert hall in Pyongyang. Our small group, the four of us and a few staff people, sat alone in the huge auditorium while they performed for us, including a chorus singing "Old Black Joe" in Korean-accented English. We met with the top North Korean officials, with one notable exception: Kim Jong Il, the son of Kim Il Sung, the dictator in the nation for decades. The father died six months before we arrived, but they told us we could not see the son because he was still in mourning. The father had his pictures and statues everywhere, including a huge statue dominating the parliamentary hall. Even dictators today feel compelled to maintain the fiction of democracy through rubber-stamp parliaments. People referred to Kim Il Sung, the father, as "the great leader" whenever mentioning his name. They followed that prudent policy also during his life. Any radios sold in North Korea had but one station that could be reached, which gave them the official government line. Television had the same monolithic approach. But when people are told over and over and over that someone is "the great leader," eventually they believe that. Now the son, who rarely sees anyone, has assumed the title of "the great leader."

These titles have great significance in North Korea, and significance for relationships between the two Koreas. When Kim Il Sung died, President Clinton issued a perfunctory, and what would ordinarily be meaningless, message of sympathy to the people of North Korea upon losing their leader. But in South Korea, the leadership used the occasion to castigate him as a ruthless murderer who had caused untold misery to the people of both nations — all of which is accurate, but North Koreans, most of whom had never known any other leadership and who genuinely appeared to revere him as "the great leader," were stunned by the South Korean reaction — stunned and angry. It could be that display of anger was entirely well-scripted and phoney, but I doubt it. It seemed to be general and genuine.

Whether our plane could fly us from North Korea's capital Pyongyang to South Korea's capital Seoul took endless pre-trip negotiation, the final compromise being that we would fly in to Pyongyang and then drive the roughly seventy-five miles from Pyongyang to Seoul. We drove on the four-lane road in North Korea for the seventy-five miles and during the entire trip saw exactly two trucks on the road — no other traffic — both coming our way. Even the capital city of Pyongyang had few cars and almost no bicycles, the favorite mode of transportation in many developing nations. When we neared the Demilitarized Zone (DMZ), the North Korean military leaders took us to the actual foot-wide concrete line that marks the boundary between the two nations. They instructed us to stay on the North Korean side until told to cross over. We walked up to the line and then the military personnel on both sides exchanged formal greetings and orders, and then told us we could walk into South Korea.

In South Korea we met with all the top leadership who were eager to get our impressions from the North because communication between the two sides is almost nonexistent. When I told them as diplomatically as I could that South Korea's reaction to the death of Kim Il Sung did not help in reconciliation, suggesting that they soften any future comments, I obviously hit upon a nerve, and I detected no eagerness to accept my suggestion. The North Korean dictator had invaded their country, caused the deaths of hundreds of thousands of South Koreans, and families not to have even minimal communication with each other, many South Koreans having no idea whether their closest relatives are alive or dead. For South Korea's leadership, softening their stance would be like the leaders of our country expressing sympathy to the German people on the death of Hitler. That bridge in South-North relationships is still to be crossed, a small one in many ways but an emotionally charged one on both sides. But with South Korea's new president, progress is more likely to occur.

In both North Korea and South Korea I talked to leaders about bringing a small group of parliamentarians from both sides together for discussions in the United States, frankly trying to do it here because it would be helpful for the North Koreans to see how our process works. Both sides agreed to the idea, but in following through to try to make it happen, conditions from both sides so far have prevented it. With changes that have taken place on both sides, I may explore the possibility of bringing them together at Southern Illinois University.

In 1989 Poland became the first Warsaw Pact nation to throw off Communism and embrace democracy. A number of factors made that possible, including the role of the Roman Catholic church with Polish Pope John Paul II, and a charismatic shipyard worker who became a leader, Lech Walesa. President Bush went to Poland in 1989 and received a warm welcome, and when he returned he suggested that the United States provide $100 million in aid over three years to Poland, $10 million the first year. In view of the dramatic break the Poles had made, this seem woefully inadequate in a $15 billion foreign aid budget. The Polish leaders — including Roman Catholic Cardinal Glemp — openly criticized the inadequacy of our response. I went to Poland three weeks after Bush, and after meeting with the Prime Minister Mazowiecki, Lech Walesa, Finance Minister Leszek Balcerowicz, Cardinal Glemp, and others, I borrowed a typewriter from U. S. Ambassador John Davis Jr., with whom Jeanne and I stayed, and at midnight wrote a bill for $1 billion in aid for three years. The U. S. designed most of our $300 billion defense budget to contain a Soviet threat, and here we had an opportunity to dismantle slowly and contain that threat peacefully. Spending only a fraction of 1 percent of the defense budget to do that seemed conservative. We finally worked out a compromise between the Bush proposal for $100 million and mine for $1 billion at $938 million, including a small amount for Hungary. A good compromise!

Lech Walesa appealed to me to get a branch of an American bank in Poland. He said it would symbolize confidence in Poland. It seemed reasonable and when I returned to Chicago I called the heads of the two big Chicago banks asking them to look at it, thinking it would be a natural in view of Chicago's large Polish population. Both had burned their fingers in Latin American loans and declined. I called John Reed, head of Citibank in New York City, who immediately took to the idea and said they would do something. Two days later he called back and said that Poland had no laws about signing notes and not paying them, no laws on mortgages, no laws on many things that are part of our culture, but not part of the culture of a nation ruled until then by Communists. He had to decline.

I am pleased to report that Poland today is doing well, remarkably well.

In domestic politics I tend to fight for the underdog, and I have the same inclination in international politics. Nate Shapiro is a name few would recognize in the Jewish community of Chicago, his hometown, but Nate made a crusade to save the Ethiopian Jews, most of whom could not read and write but for centuries had followed Jewish traditions. A small minority in Ethiopia, they experienced occasional persecution and rarely acceptance by the larger population. Thanks to help from Israel and Jews outside of Israel, several hundred were rescued and it created a fascinating new diversity in Israel, but problems for the government in Ethiopia with its largely Muslim population which tended to be anti-Israel. Then an agreement was worked out to transport the remainder who wanted to emigrate, with no public announcement to be made. That worked for a short period until an Israeli official leaked the information in a radio interview and the Ethiopian government halted the humanitarian effort. Nate Shapiro heard that I would soon leave for Ethiopia and asked if I would talk to the new President, Meles Zenawi, about renewing the exodus. The President explained his political dilemma. I asked if he would be willing to do it with the understanding that it would be done quietly, and all Israeli officials would be contacted to keep quiet the matter. He agreed, and so far as we know, all Ethiopian Jews who wanted to leave now have had that opportunity. The children of those who fled are blending into the Israeli culture well, though their parents, like new immigrants to any nation, sometimes still have difficulties.

The Jews in the old Soviet Union faced great difficulties and whenever I went there I met with those who either wanted to emigrate or who wanted greater freedom and said so publicly. They received the label "refuseniks," though that title also embraced some non-Jews. The saddest story concerns two little-known people, Ina and Naum Meiman, who wanted to emigrate to Israel. Ina taught English and authored a widely used textbook in the Soviet Union. Naum had been a physicist but many years earlier had been denied access to anything classified, probably because of being Jewish. The technical reason for denying them the right to emigrate is that he might reveal state secrets as a physicist, a fraudulent excuse but one of many the Soviets found for not letting people emigrate. I took our daughter Sheila to Moscow on one trip — at my expense, I hasten to add — and visited the Meiman's in their small apartment, lined with books. We had a heart-warming evening with them, and when we started to leave, Ina took a brooch she was wearing and handed it to Sheila and said, "Here, I want you to have this in case something happens to me." It was a touching moment. A few days after we visited them the KGB ransacked their apartment, pulling books off shelves, taking a few of Naum's old papers, not doing much damage but causing needless agony for them. Shortly after that physicians diagnosed Ina with cancer, but she could not get adequate treatment because of the limited medical skills in this field in Moscow, and perhaps also because of who she was. I appealed to the Soviet Embassy to let her come to the United States for treatment and made speeches on the floor of the Senate about it. Finally, after months of delay they let her leave. I met her at Dulles Airport outside of Washington and saw immediately her situation had deteriorated. She went almost directly to a hospital, and while her spirits were fine there, she missed Naum. The Soviets would not let him come with her, but he insisted that she go. Upon her death I desperately tried to get the Soviets to permit Naum to come here, but again to no avail. Years later Naum did get to leave and went to Israel. He stopped to visit with me when he made a short trip to the United States. I have not heard from him for several years. If he is alive, he is an old man today, made older by the unnecessary harshness of the Soviet regime.

Abe Stolar's story has a happier ending. One day in Moscow a man walked up to me speaking perfect English, sounding like a Chicago native. And he was. His father, a dedicated Communist, thought the Soviet Union would be "the worker's paradise," and brought his family to Moscow. Abe was nineteen at the time. During the Stalin purges his parents disappeared. Abe married and had a son, but he wanted to leave the Soviet Union. They would let him go but not his family. I appealed to the Soviets to no avail. Before Ronald Reagan made his trip to Moscow I talked to Secretary of State George Schultz and urged him to make sure the President met Abe. I turned on television one evening and saw the President meeting with Refuseniks and, sitting next to the President, Abe Stolar. I thought surely he would be permitted to leave. But no luck. Months later I received a phone call from Vienna. Abe and his family were on their way to Israel, free. Within a year Abe visited Chicago. Before he came I asked what he really wanted to do in Chicago after all these years. He said he always dreamed of staying overnight in the Stevens Hotel — it has been named the Conrad Hilton for decades — and wanted to see a Cubs game. Bill Smith, the manager of the Conrad Hilton, arranged for him to stay in a plush suite at the hotel and when I took him to Wrigley Field people recognized him from his story on television and cheered him and waved to him. Abe could not have been happier. He and his family are living in Jerusalem and doing well.

The Armenians have been persecuted and scattered, their story much like the story of the Jews. I have tried to help Armenia, both with its relationships to neighboring Azerbaijan, with economic assistance to the government of Armenia, and with small help to the American University in Armenia in the capital city of Yerevan. Key to a stable economic and political future for Armenia is a gradual improvement in their relationship with Azerbaijan and Turkey. Armenia's dispute with Azerbaijan over the Nagorno-Karabakh region is the emotional and political barrier to that happening. It is a little like the Israeli-Arab situation, with the logic of cooperation overwhelming, benefitting both sides, but hard-liners in both camps making the necessary political compromise difficult. At one point I had dinner with the ambassadors of both countries to see if informally we could explore options for a process of more creative negotiation, but I made no headway.

"The shrinking globe" is an overworked phrase, but it conveys the reality. We are more and more involved with everyone, and living politically in Fortress America is to invite an impaired future for our children. History will not be kind to us if we do not strive more effectively to build a safe and stable world. Whenever we turn our backs to brutalities in nations *when we could prevent them* we cloud the future unnecessarily. There are those who take the cynical attitude that "small wars" are inevitable and we should be realistic and tolerate them. Small wars can erupt into much bigger wars. Not too many years ago cynics and many religious leaders said that slavery has always existed and will always be part of humanity's history and it is folly to pretend otherwise. Somehow we moved away from slavery. Key leaders and a small number of dedicated citizens asked us to do better.

Violence unchecked invites more violence. Listen to the response of one war veteran to a question about his war experience: "Not only did I learn to kill with a noose of piano wire put around somebody's neck from behind, but I learned to enjoy the prospect of killing that way."[11]

Resolving problems without resort to violence will not be easy for the United States or the community of nations. George Will had a thoughtful column pointing to the dangers of nations being splintered because of ethnic or economic reasons.[12] The threat of nuclear war has largely been supplanted by the threat of instability. Creating 100 new nations is not in anyone's best interest, but how does the United States, working with other world leaders, deal with the problems of the Kurds? Of the division in Sudan? Of Kosovo? Of Nagorno-Karabakh? Of many similar situations? The answers will not come easily, but the simplest and politically attractive answer — and the wrong answer — is for the United States to be a spectator, pretending violence will not spread, or assuming that another nation will fill a vacuum of leadership.

The United States has the opportunity to improve the lot of humanity, to appeal to humanity's nobler instincts. Whether we will have leadership that will move us in that direction is unclear. Whether many of us will demand that kind of leadership is also unclear. In a world with no shortage of potentially explosive confrontations, we are responding without much zeal, without much creativity and without much courage.

When Sheila was eight and Martin five our family drove down the Pan American Highway to Costa Rica. El Salvador and Honduras had just battled in what became known as "the Soccer War," a brief conflict that erupted after a soccer game between the two nations. Because bombs had destroyed bridges, on two occasions we had to drive our Chevrolet down embankments and across creek beds to continue our journey. Martin asked, "Why do countries fight each other?" I told him that within two hours I could probably tell him. About forty-five minutes later Sheila and Martin were fighting in the back seat over some trivial matter. I said, "Now I'll tell you why nations fight each other."

[1] "Sanctions Jolt," *Chicago Sun-Times*, 13 June 1986.

[2] Paul Simon, "Haunting Scenes from Somalia," *Murphysboro American*, 3 December 1992.

[3] Editorial, *Washington Post*, 19 June 1992.

[4] "U. S. Should Work to Prevent Tragedy," *St. Louis Post-Dispatch*, 28 August 1994.

[5] Romeo Dallaire, "United Nations Assistance Mission for Rwanda," published lectures by Army War College, Fort McNair, Washington, DC.

[6] James C. McKingley Jr., "General Tells Rwanda Court Massacre Was Preventable," *The New York Times*, 28 February 1998.

[7] Will and Ariel Durant, *The Age of Voltaire* (New York: Simon and Schuster, 1965).

[8] Frank Carlucci, "Foreign Policy 101: Conflict Prevention in Kosovo," *Chicago Tribune*, 25 June 1998.

[9] Paul Simon speech, Brookings Institution, 20 October 1993.

[10] *Chicago Sun-Times*, 19 September 1993.

[11] Sheldon Hackney, Interview with Paul Fussell, *Humanities*, November-December 1996.

[12] George Will, "Separatist Movements Tear at the World," *Chicago Sun-Times*, 27 June 1998.

# Chapter 20

# *Fiscal Problems*

The public impression of the two major political parties is that the Republicans show no sympathy for the poor, and the Democrats are fiscally imprudent.

There is some truth to both impressions.

Spending more than you take in is an addiction that is not easily broken by either a government or an individual. It is politically convenient for government to spend more than we take in and let future officeholders worry about the consequences.

Thanks to a more robust economy, temporarily the budget figures look better than anticipated. In addition to congressional and presidential action to achieve this, part of the credit goes to Alan Greenspan, chairman of the Federal Reserve Board, and to Treasury Secretary Robert Rubin, the most widely respected member of the Clinton cabinet. But speeches by leaders of both parties that the budget is balanced is, to put it charitably, a slight exaggeration. The "balance" does not acknowledge that in the fiscal year in which I write, 1998, people will pay into the Social Security Retirement Fund $100 to $105 billion more than we will pay out. If you do not count the retirement funds — which we should not — then the deficit remains. And we are heading toward serious problems, even assuming that the economy does not experience a substantial dip, which sooner or later it will. Former Budget Director Robert Reischauer, now at the Brookings Institution, says, "The future still looks terrible, but the day of reckoning has been postponed by a decade or more."[1]

The difficulty in getting Democrats to face fiscal realities goes back to the FDR days, when we had and needed deficits. Republicans, in knee-jerk response, criticized Roosevelt for creating deficits that the nation needed to respond to the depression. Democrats, responding to the unjust GOP attacks started a knee-jerk reaction to any claims that deficits are unwise. It is true that the champion deficit-creator of all time was Ronald Reagan, a Republican, but he had Democratic and Republican congresses that worked with him to create the deficits.

The *gross* interest expenditure for Fiscal Year 1998, $356 billion, compares to $10 billion for Fiscal Year 1963, the last year John F. Kennedy served as President. That is almost $1 billion a day in Fiscal Year 1998 for interest. Another measure: Ten times as much is spent on interest as on all the federal education programs combined. No other part of the budget has grown as rapidly in percentage terms as interest, for which the American people get nothing other than higher interest rates. Administrations like to use the *net* interest rate figure ($245 billion for Fiscal Year 1998) because it looks better. That subtracts the interest paid by the Social Security Retirement Fund and other funds from the totals paid out. It would be like taking the Department of Justice budget and subtracting the amounts collected in fines to get the *net* cost of the operation of the Department of Justice. It is a miserable way to budget, except for political reasons.

Thomas Jefferson could not be at the Constitutional Convention of 1787 because of service to our nation in France, but when he returned he stated that if he could add one amendment to the Constitution it would be to require a balanced budget. He wrote that one generation should no more be willing to pay the debts of a previous generation than to pay the debts of another nation. We applaud those who founded our nation on most things (slavery and women's suffrage being exceptions), but their advice on fiscal policy we ignore. George Washington's Farewell Address warned the nation about piling up debts. Alexander Hamilton called growing debt "the natural disease of all governments."[2] Many more early American heroes could be quoted, all with similar warnings. When Andrew Jackson became President, he declared he would rid the nation of its debt, and by 1834 he had done that. Starting in 1866, we had twenty-eight successive years of budget surpluses. The debt problem jumped up suddenly. By today's standards, FDR, Harry Truman, John F. Kennedy, and Lyndon Johnson were fiscal conservatives. Even during two of the years of the Korean War, Harry Truman balanced the budget. In his first presidential debate with Richard Nixon, John F. Kennedy said, "I believe in the balanced budget, and the only conditions under which I would unbalance the budget would be if there was a grave national emergency or a serious recession."[3] During the early years of the

Reagan presidency things started to get out of control, because of policies supported by Democrats and Republicans in Congress. From George Washington through Jimmy Carter, the nation built up a debt total of $1 trillion. It is now $5.5 trillion. In seventeen short years the debt has moved from one-third of our national income (GDP) to five-sevenths of it.

While the debates on fiscal policy have added a temporary element of restraint, we still need constitutional restraint, not as rigid as Thomas Jefferson's proposal to prohibit all indebtedness, but the proposal that we developed in the Senate requires a 60 percent majority of both houses before we can have a deficit. That would make it possible in years of recession or other national emergency to have a deficit, but not year after year after year.

Here is the language I worked out, primarily with Senators Strom Thurmond of South Carolina and Orrin Hatch of Utah — both of whom provided excellent leadership — and their staffs:

Section 1. Total outlays of the United States for any fiscal year shall not exceed total receipts to the United States for that year, unless Congress approves a specific excess of outlays over receipts by three-fifths of the whole number of each House on a rollcall vote.

Section 2. Prior to each fiscal year, the President shall transmit to the Congress a proposed budget for the United States Government for that year in which total outlays do not exceed total receipts.

Section 3. Any bill to increase revenue shall become law only if approved by a majority of the whole number of each House by a rollcall vote, unless such bill is approved by unanimous consent.

Section 4. The Congress may waive the provisions of this article for any fiscal year in which a declaration of war is in effect. The provisions of this article may be waived for any fiscal year in which the United States is engaged in military conflict which causes an imminent and serious military threat to national security and is so declared by a joint resolution, adopted by a majority of the whole number of each House of Congress, which becomes law.

Section 5. Total receipts shall include all receipts of the United States except those derived from borrowing. Total outlays shall include all outlays of the United States except those for repayment of debt principal.

Section 6. This article shall take effect beginning with the second fiscal year beginning after its ratification.

Balanced budgets result in lower interest rates. Bill Clinton's 1993 tax package that brought down deficits and interest rates, together with George Bush's 1990 move in the same direction, have created investment and jobs that have been a huge help to the nation. Politicians who produce "tax cuts" that result in higher deficits and higher interest rates are in fact increasing taxes for citizens and businesses through those higher interest rates.

I did not always favor a constitutional amendment to require a balanced budget, though I favored balanced budgets. I visited with Senator Paul Douglas, not only a distinguished former Senator but also a distinguished economist, former president of the American Association of Economists. In discussing the deficits, Paul said he felt we were headed into trouble, and that he may have made a mistake in opposing a constitutional amendment requiring a balanced budget. I am sure he never dreamed we would be this far in debt.

My chief antagonist in the Senate on this issue, a colleague I respect, Senator Robert Byrd, headed the Senate Appropriations Committee. If we had received the same percentage of votes for the amendment from Democratic members of the Senate Appropriations Committee as from the rest of the Democrats in the Senate, the amendment would have passed. In 1994, for example, of Democratic Senators not on the Appropriations Committee we lost by less than a 2-1 margin. Of Democratic Senators on the Appropriations Committee we lost by a 5-1 margin. I do not suggest that all of them consciously opposed it because it would restrict the power of the Appropriations Committee, which it would, but in politics as in life it is easy to confuse our self-interest with the best interest of others. For example, people of wealth too often easily conclude that whatever is in their best interest is in the best interest of the nation. Sometimes it is, but sometimes it is not. When it is not, it is difficult to convince them. It is also not easy to convince members of the Appropriations Committee that anything that might restrict their power would be in the best interest of the nation. To a lesser extent that holds true for all members of Congress.

I am particularly grateful to my Democratic colleagues who voted for the balanced budget constitutional amendment, despite great pressure. Those who played a key role over the years included Senator Deconcini of Arizona, who took a strong stand despite being on the Appropriations Committee, Senator Dick Bryan of Nevada, Senator

Chuck Robb of Virginia, and Senator Bob Graham of Florida. Other Democratic senators who voted with us in 1995 were Howell Heflin of Alabama, Tom Harkin of Iowa, John Breaux of Louisiana, James Exon of Nebraska, Joe Biden of Delaware, Sam Nunn of Georgia, Carol Moseley-Braun of Illinois, Herb Kohl of Wisconsin, and Ben Nighthorse Campbell of Colorado, who since has switched to the Republican party.

The late Senator Paul Tsongas testified in subcommittee hearings I held. (Senator Byrd had hearings on this at the same time, he and I battling each other even at the committee hearing level.) Paul, a humanitarian but also a pragmatic person, said: "If you ask yourself why are these deficits always voted, the answer is very simple . . . There are a lot of votes in deficit spending. There are no votes in fiscal discipline. What you have here is a sad case of pursuit of self as opposed to pursuit of what is in the national interest. The balanced budget amendment is simply a recognition of that human behavior."[4]

Jonathan Rauch, in his book *Demosclerosis*, writes:

> Children don't organize and lobby. . . . One way to take from the young is to reduce spending on them [but] another way is to pile up debts that they'll have to pay. Imagine yourself in the shoes of a politician facing demands from a swarm of noisy lobbies. Every time you hand out a subsidy check or a tax break, some group says, "Thank you," and rewards you with votes or campaign contributions or both. To pay for the subsidy you can raise taxes, but that's politically risky. Why not put it on credit? No group screams if you do that, because many of the people who will pay don't exist. . . . What does a budget deficit mean? Not economic collapse or calamity. Rather, incremental but inexorable diminution of future wealth.[5]

Former Colorado Governor Richard Lamm, a Democrat, and former Republican Senator Hank Brown, also of Colorado, coauthored an article on our debt and concluded: "Never in history has a generation so pre-spent its children's money."[6]

Nobel prize-winning economist James Buchanan observes: "It is difficult to construct a plausible argument against a constitutional rule for budget balance once the elementary facts of the matter are acknowledged."[7]

The two major traditional arguments against the constitutional amendment are, first, that the Constitution should not be trivialized by unnecessary amendments and detailed prescriptions; and, two, that the amendment would hurt poor people. The *real* argument against it is that it would restrain the Appropriations Committee and Congress somewhat, but that argument is rarely used publicly. Additional reasons for opposition that surface occasionally are that it would force the courts into legislative details, that balancing the budget would devastate the economy, that we made it either too easy or too hard to have deficits with the 60 percent provision, and that if families and corporations and states have deficits, why shouldn't the federal government do it?

The arguments do not stand up under serious examination. Let me take them one by one:

*"We should not trivialize the constitution."*

Of course not. Is getting hold of our fiscal situation a major need for the nation?

It obviously is. We have demonstrated that it is simply too easy for members to vote appropriations and not revenue — and make great speeches defending both. We have done that now for thirty years in a row. After my first election to the state legislature I received a letter from a man in Roxana, Illinois, that had thirteen points. The first twelve were increased services he wanted from government, and the thirteenth was to cut taxes. We have adopted his program. We should be facing the long-term problems of Social Security retirement now, before the fund is depleted, but it is too easy to coast. If not faced soon, when the Social Security crisis is upon us then a future Congress and administration will have three choices: cut Social Security retirement dramatically; increase taxes dramatically; or print more money. The worst of the three options is the last, but it is the easiest politically. Even with the fiscal problems we had a few years ago, we had at least one senator who privately said we should print more money, have some inflation, and diminish our indebtedness in that way. There is at least the strong possibility that Adam Smith's commentary about the course of nations applies to us. In his classic *Wealth of Nations* he wrote that the history of all nations is that when they pile up debts they eventually debase the coin. In his day they had no paper money or credit cards so nations simply put less and less gold or silver into the coins, and they became less and less valuable, and governments reduced their debt in that way. Adam Smith wrote that he knows of no nations that have piled up debt that have escaped that fate. More recently Oxford University Press published a book by Michael Veseth, *Mountains of Debt*, a historical study of national debt starting with the Italian city-state of Florence, and his conclusions are much the same as Adam Smith's. It is possible we will avoid that destiny — but not probable — without a constitutional amendment.

*"The amendment would hurt senior citizens and poor people."*

If you look only short-term, this argument may have limited validity — though very limited — but any long-term look shows that these are the people hurt the most. Bob Myers, chief actuary for Social Security for many years, is a strong supporter of the constitutional amendment, arguing that is the only way to avoid monetizing our debt, printing more money to devalue the debt. While that would solve our debt problem, it would devastate the Social Security Retirement Fund. With large deficits you have higher interest rates, a tax primarily on working men and women in two ways: first, the interest they have to pay on home mortgages and car loans and credit cards, and second, higher interest rates from higher deficits reduce jobs and increase the numbers on welfare. After the drop in interest rates following the Clinton tax package of 1993, the number of jobs to mid-1998 increased by 15 million and the numbers on welfare fell by 5.4 million.

In June 1994 the General Accounting Office reported that unless we face our deficit problem a gradually declining portion of our federal budget will go for education, health care and other national needs, and an increasing percentage will continue to go for interest. Neither political party would adopt a platform that indicates we should devote more and more of our budget each year for interest — yet that is what each has done.

The reality is that neither balanced budgets nor deficits automatically hurt or help poor people. During the Reagan years of big deficits, programs for poor people were cut, while during the years of near balance under Truman and Kennedy those programs expanded. These are legislative decisions. I strongly favor a national health care program, for example, while others do not. We should differ and have our debates on this. Where we should not differ is that if we have national health care it should be on a pay-as-you-go basis. We should not have health care today by borrowing from our grandchildren. That's what deficits are. I had the experience a few years ago of sponsoring a health measure for those requiring long-term care, to be paid by a one-half cent increase in Social Security. Two of my Senate colleagues said they would like to cosponsor my bill if I would just drop the tax that pays for it. That is politically attractive, but wrong, and should not be possible.

While I differ with Phyllis Schlafly, the conservative political leader, on many issues, she makes more sense in opposing the constitutional amendment than her liberal counterparts. She argued in the *St. Louis Post-Dispatch* that an amendment would lead to lower interest rates and probably some tax increases which would result in more opportunity for the federal government to spend money on health care, education, and other social programs. There is validity to that position. All econometric studies show that such an amendment would result in lower interest rates, and for each one percent that interest rates are lowered for the federal government, an additional $55 billion is ultimately available. But Congress and an administration would determine whether it is for programs or tax cuts — or even lowering the total debt a little. To give you an idea of what $55 billion could do, that is almost twice what the federal government now spends on all its education programs. All econometric forecasts project a lowering of interest rates of *more than one percent* with the adoption of a balanced budget constitutional amendment.

People who are advocates for the poor and seniors will not automatically have either an easier or a harder time with a constitutional amendment in place. But any long-term projection suggests that those who are advocates for these causes ought to adjust their thinking. However, it will mean that if they advocate major new programs, like health care, they will also have to advocate the taxes to pay for them. That is the way it should be. Social programs or highway programs or defense programs "on the cheap" would become a thing of the past.

*"The amendment would force courts into legislative details."*

It is highly unlikely because both future congresses and future courts would want to avoid this. Unlike many constitutional amendments where somewhat vague principles are involved, here the measurements are precise and Congress can meet the constitutional requirement, either by balancing the budget or a 60 percent vote not to balance it. Members of Congress take only one oath, to uphold the Constitution. We take that seriously. Even under a fiscal tool like the Gramm-Rudman-Hollings bill, when it became a little awkward, no one suggested that we should ignore the law. We simply changed the law to get out of our awkward spot. The advantage — or disadvantage — of a constitutional amendment is that the Constitution cannot be quickly changed. There is no absolute guarantee that members will abide by the Constitution, but it would be contrary to the traditions of the Senate and the House were we to ignore it.

Proponents made clear in debate that the intent is to balance the budget, but if we come within 3 percent that would fall within the intent of those of us who framed this amendment, with up to 3 percent then to be made up in the next fiscal year. One of the nation's finest economists, Fred Bergsten, Assistant Secretary of the Treasury under President Carter, is a convert to the desirability of a constitutional amendment. He suggests that a small surplus be built each year so that if there is an economic dip, congress and an administration can act quickly to stimulate the economy, perhaps under some formula. What we do now when there is a recession is talk and talk and talk, and then act. It takes so long that most economists believe we do little if anything to ameliorate the situation.

*"Balancing the budget would devastate the economy."*

Our coming this close to balancing the budget shows that argument never had substance to it. Rather than harming the economy, balancing the budget consistently will lower interest rates and give us a real economic boost. Keeping on the path of more and more debt is what will devastate — and ultimately ruin — the economy. When we have had economic downturns, Congress has consistently — with one exception — voted an extension of unemployment compensation benefits, as one example, with more than a 60 percent vote.

*"It will be too hard to have deficits when needed."* Or *"It will be too easy to have deficits."*

Neither is accurate. A 60 percent vote in Congress is not easy to get on something controversial, but it can be done. It should not be easy. It should not be extremely difficult. We need both flexibility and restraint. This amendment provides both.

*"If families and corporations and school boards and states borrow money, why shouldn't the federal government?"*

Families have to do it in order to buy a house. Companies often do it to expand their productivity and profits. School boards generally have no choice if they're building a new school. States sometimes have to do it, though most state borrowing is politically comfortable rather than economically wise. But ordinarily there is no necessity for the federal government to do it. To waste money on interest, forcing interest rates up, in addition to imprudent spending, is unwise public policy. But in unusual circumstances it simply takes a 60 percent majority in both houses, plus the signature of the President to create debt.

The reality is that balancing the budget requires unpopular actions, either in spending or in taxation, or both. With the confidence that either action would result in something concrete happening, members are more likely to show courage. And they could have political cover. "I hated to cast that vote but under the mandate of the Constitution, I really had no choice," is the speech that will be made. Let me give you a practical example. Senator Larry Craig of Idaho, a conservative Republican who was of immense help as we worked on this amendment, said on *Meet the Press* that while he did not favor tax increases, if the amendment were to be adopted and the only practical way of balancing the budget would be through a tax increase, he would support it. Throughout the debates I have been candid in saying that I believe that slight tax increases will eventually be necessary to balance the budget.

In 1995 the constitutional amendment fell two votes short of getting the required two-thirds majority. One of those who switched from opposition to support, Senator Bill Cohen of Maine, now Secretary of Defense, called deficit spending "fiscal child abuse," an appropriate analogy. While some voted for it for political reasons — four Democrats supporting it when they faced reelection, and then opposing it after getting reelected — other Senators told me they wished they could be with me but they had projects before the Appropriations Committee and feared the consequences if they offended the chairman, Senator Byrd, though I am certain he never threatened reprisal. But we all knew he has a long memory. The only Republican voting against it, Senator Mark Hatfield of Oregon, a respected member and chairman of the Appropriations Committee.

The international implications of this should not be forgotten. In 1956, shortly before the presidential election, Israel, France, and Great Britain invaded Egypt. They acted because President Nasser of Egypt had taken over the Suez Canal, considered an international resource. Without firing a shot, President Eisenhower threatened to dump our holdings of the pound sterling, the British currency, and the three nations withdrew. They were — and are — our friends and they felt that that friendship, plus the pending U. S. election, would bar any action on our part. But a weak currency caused the retreat, not any powerful weapon. Without a drop of blood being shed, powerful armies retreated. With more than one-third of our debt now in foreign hands, we are not in a good situation to demand action from nations that are our bankers.


Social Security Retirement is the 800-pound gorilla that lingers in the shadows of all fiscal debates. A few — very few — economists say that there is nothing to worry about. Some predict disaster in less than two decades. The position of the trustees of the system is that if there is no action by the year 2032, at the latest, the system will run out of money. That is caused by a combination of more people retiring and fewer people working. In 1955 there were 8.6 workers for each Social Security beneficiary. It is now 3.2, and by the year 2040 it is projected to be 2.0. That spells danger on the road ahead. If the projections of a few demographers about our expanding length of life are accurate, then those with the more pessimistic view of the fiscal future will be accurate because the system will have to support even more of us.

Members of Congress are aware of the need for change, but as with balancing the budget there are no popular answers, so both political parties avoid doing anything, even though in the long run it jeopardizes the chances for Social Security retirement funds for our children and grandchildren. Because over a trillion — yes a trillion — dollars will soon be at stake, what we do has immense importance to our economy, and immense importance to individual retirees. Thanks largely to Social Security, seniors living in poverty have dropped from 35 percent of our population to 11 percent. The system is not perfect, but it works. It is a steady source of income to the seniors and to the economy, reducing the harsher impacts that otherwise would be felt by all citizens during an economic downturn.

While in theory the Social Security payments should supplement other retirement income, in fact it is the sole source of income for millions of retirees. So when we play political games with Social Security, we are playing with the fiscal future of the nation and with the lives of many people.

At the request of three Senators, I invited three former Senators and the Chief Deputy Actuary for Social Security to convene under the auspices of the Public Policy Institute I now head at Southern Illinois University in Carbondale. Those who joined me were Senator Alan Simpson of Wyoming and Senator John Danforth of Missouri, both Republicans, and Senator David Pryor of Arkansas, a Democrat. The theory is that if four of us who will never seek public office again — two Republicans and two Democrats — could agree on a program, then maybe we could take some of the partisan edge off finding a solution. We recommended two fair and controversial changes: first, that the Consumer Price Index, the way we measure inflation, be corrected; second, that citizens should pay Social Security Retirement tax on all income, not just the first $68,400.

The first suggestion, correcting the Consumer Price Index, is opposed by senior groups. As we now measure inflation, we do not consider substitution; if the price of beef goes up, people shift to chicken, as one example. We do not consider the large discount stores; the reality is that chains like Wal-Mart have changed our buying habits and given us many products at less cost. We do not consider generic drugs. I take two pills each day for high blood pressure, and they work, I'm pleased to say. I pay $12 for the generic drugs but would pay $74 for the original. Making corrections like these will reduce slightly the increase senior citizens receive each year, but it is fair.

The suggestion that we should pay taxes on our full income is also fair. Why should a low wage earner who makes perhaps $10,000 a year have to pay Social Security on every penny earned, while a person who makes $1 million a year pays Social Security on only the first $68,400 earned? The person making a million dollars would have to pay an additional $58,000 a year. I make well over $68,000 a year. If by paying a little more I can secure Social Security Retirement for my four grandchildren, it is a small price to pay. This change would affect only 6 percent of our population, but would account for a majority of the funds needed to keep Social Security sound.

These two small changes would protect Social Security retirement for the next seventy-five years.

All of us will have to sacrifice. And the American people are ahead of political leaders on this. An NBC-*National Journal* poll in October 1997 showed that 83 percent of the American public believe that it "will be necessary to make major changes in the way that the Social Security system operates in order to guarantee the future stability of the system."[8]

Congress and the administration are inching slowly toward facing the reality that we ought to make adjustments.

Some of our friends on Wall Street see this as a bonanza for the stock market. They want to privatize part of Social Security so that greater returns are received by beneficiaries. It sounds plausible at first blush, and it has the added appeal of pleasing generous contributors who have ties to Wall Street. *But with increased income comes increased risk.* Do we want to risk the future of these seniors? And if we permit each person to determine what stocks are purchased, some will make out well, and some will not, but the administrative expenses of Social Security, now less than one percent will soar — and so will the broker's fees! Small wonder that the *New York Times* has a story headed, "Interest Groups Prepare for Huge Fight on Social Security" with a subhead, "Wall Street Is Eager."[9] Another suggestion that would reduce overhead is to have those who operate Social Security determine where to invest the money. But do you really want the U. S. government to be the principal stockholder in General Motors and a host of other corporations, ultimately controlling their destiny?

The one part of this argument that has merit is that the savings rate of the United States is low, far lower than is healthy. We now compensate for that by borrowing from other nations. That, compounded by our federal government deficit, sends international interest rates higher, and the poor nations that struggle with heavy debts suffer because of the fiscal imprudence of the United States. International economist David Calleo calls it "obscene that the world's richest country should also be its biggest borrower."[10] A New York Federal Reserve Board study concluded that a lack of savings in our nation reduced the growth of our economy by 5 percent in the decade of the 1980s.

Because of our low savings rate compared to other industrial nations, we would be wise to act both to increase savings and to strengthen the retirement of seniors. Of the twenty-two wealthiest nations, we are seventh from the bottom in our savings rate. Nations that save more than three times as much as we do as a percentage of income are Spain, Hungary, Japan, France, Belgium, and South Korea. If we were to require that all income above $15,000 a year should have a one percent investment tax, paid three-fourths by the employee and one-fourth by the employer to be placed in savings accounts, mutual funds or stocks, at the discretion of the employee with no more than one-fourth of the amount over a four-year period going into any one place, our economy would be lifted and so would the future of many retirees. It should be saved strictly for retirement, or an estate. Neil Howe, the chief economist for the National Taxpayers Union, a conservative group, comments accurately, "If you really want a large increase in genuine net savings, you need a mandatory program."[11] My guess is that it would result in savings of much more than one percent when people saw the benefits of savings and investment. But if the worst happened to some, and these savings and/or investments were all lost, they would still have the protection of Social Security.

Sound fiscal policy also should try to avoid the extremes of poverty and wealth. The trend in the United States for two decades has been for the income of the bottom one-fifth to rise slightly, but the income of the top one-fifth to rise dramatically. That may be temporarily satisfying to the top one-fifth, but over time, if not corrected, it is social dynamite. That is why the suggestion of Senators Simpson, Danforth, Pryor, and myself to pay a Social Security tax on all income has the double benefit of reducing that disparity slightly, while it buttresses our economy by helping the Social Security Retirement Fund. The disparity in income is another reason to avoid deficits. Those who pay the interest are primarily people of limited means. Those who collect the interest are the economically more fortunate. The biggest income transfer program by the federal government, by far, is not taking from those who are more fortunate to help welfare recipients, but our interest expenditure, which accomplishes the reverse. That might be a wee bit — but only a wee bit — defensible if the money stayed within our nation, but more than one-third of the interest payments now go to the wealthy beyond our borders. Foreign aid for the rich is many times our foreign aid expenditures for the poor.

---

[1] Peter Passell, "Not so Fast: Here Comes the Budget Crunch," *New York Times*, 11 January 1998.

[2] Thomas K. McCaw, "Hamilton the Hero," *New York Times*, 2 May 1993.

[3] Carried by all networks, September 26, 1960.

[4] Paul Tsongas, testimony, Senate Subcommittee on the Constitution, 15 February 1994.

[5] New York Times Books, 1994, 153.

[6] Richard Lamm and Hank Brown, "The Best of Legislation, the Worst of Legislation," *Christian Century*, 3 December 1997.

[7] James Buchanan, "Constitutional Imperatives for the 1990s," *Thinking About America* (Stanford: Hoover Press, 1988), 257-258.

[8] *National Journal*, 1 October 1997.

[9] *New York Times*, 30 December 1996.

[10] David Calleo, *Beyond American Hegemony* (New York: Basic Books, 1987), 102.

[11] Julie Kosterlitz, "Savings Time," *National Journal*, 21 September 1996.

# Chapter 21

# *Professor, Journalist, and Volunteer*

After making my announcement that I would not seek reelection, job offers and feelers started to trickle in. Jeanne and I were not certain what we would do, though I felt I would get offers to become a lobbyist, which I didn't want to do. One such offer was more than five times the salary I receive from the position I finally accepted. I wanted something where I could make a difference, where I could still have an impact on public policy. I also did not want to work for the Clinton Administration, not because of philosophical differences, but because I felt a more clear-cut break would be good for us. They did talk to me about one possibility, and I declined. A few months after I left the Senate the White House called with another offer which I also declined.

One possibility did intrigue me, though it never came close to becoming a reality. A former United States Senator came to my office and told me that the President of the World Bank, dying of cancer, was not expected to live more than a few months. Some of those interested in international issues had discussed the possibility of my becoming the President of the World Bank, which is not a bank in the traditional mold, but a fiscal tool to help developing nations. I had watched Bob McNamara's performance there with admiration, where he brought his considerable administrative skills and sensitivity. As my visitor pointed out, my former colleague on the House Budget Committee, Rep. Barber Conable of New York, became the World Bank president and did an effective job, but did not have as much international background as I have. I would have had to resign from the Senate. My visitor did not pretend to speak for the White House, and this position is traditionally named by the President of the United States, subject to ratification by other nations. I told the former Senator that the idea did intrigue me but I could not consider it unless the Republican governor of Illinois, Jim Edgar, would appoint a Democrat to take my seat, which I doubted that he would do. I said he could do it with the understanding that the person appointed would not run in the next election, but in a Senate where the Republicans already had a small majority, I would not feel comfortable turning my seat over to a Republican. I told him that he and his friends would have to sound out Jim Edgar. They did, and told me he felt he could not do that. I completely understood. Shortly after this a White House staff person asked if I was interested, but I told him that door had been closed. The person named, James Wolfensohn, is doing an excellent job, both reaching out with more hands-on oversight of World Bank projects and in shaping up the administration of the organization.

I sensed that I should work either with a foundation or with a university. Several universities sounded me out about assuming a presidency, but I did not want to get into that because it would enmesh me in administrative details and not leave me free to speak on public policy. Teaching position opportunities flowed in from schools as scattered as Brandeis, UCLA, and the University of Texas, all of them attractive — approximately thirty in all. No foundations contacted me. But we had more generous offers in other fields than I deserved. Among those in the academic arena we weighed carefully were the University of Illinois in Chicago, where the position would give me the opportunity to work on problems of urban poverty, and the University of Illinois at Springfield, where I had once taught. In both cases I like the chancellors, James Stukel at Chicago (now President of the University of Illinois) and Naomi Lynn at Springfield. Leadership in a school is an important consideration for anyone looking at a position.

The offer I accepted, from Southern Illinois University at Carbondale, offered me the least amount of money of any of those who made concrete offers. The two faculty members largely responsible for initiating this for SIU are John Jackson, now the Provost, and Joe Foote, dean of the College of Mass Communication and Media Arts. I had worked with both men long before they assumed their present positions and have great respect for both. I knew the President of SIU, Ted Sanders, when he served as Illinois Superintendent of

Education for our elementary and secondary schools and as Under Secretary of Education in the Bush cabinet. I like his understated style. The University offered me a chance to teach and to head a Public Policy Institute which I founded. Governor Jim Edgar came to Carbondale for the announcement that I would accept the SIU offer, a gracious gesture on his part. While we differ politically, I have always had great respect for him. SIU offered me $140,000 a year, and I called Ted Sanders and told him I would accept the offer, but to make it $120,000 a year instead. As I looked at various salaries at SIU I felt the larger figure a little out of balance compared to some other salaries. Jeanne took part in my decision-making and applauded even the salary move.

The attractions to SIU in Carbondale include having two of our four grandchildren living in this area; having a home we had built on eleven acres out in the country that we had never really lived in other than during Christmas recess and occasional weekends; and two even more significant factors for me. One is that a high percentage of SIUC students are first generation college students. A second is that SIUC has a surprisingly high percentage of minority students, surprising in that Carbondale is located in the foothills of southern Illinois, a region with only a small percentage of African Americans and Latinos. SIUC is twelfth in the nation among state universities in minority enrollment. SIUC is second in the nation in giving baccalaureate degrees in education to African Americans, third in the nation in engineering-related degrees to African Americans, and sixteenth in the nation in giving health profession degrees to African Americans. Both first generation students and minority students — often the same — are people with much potential who often need a little encouragement, and I hope I am helping a little on that.

The Public Policy Institute at the University I head has a bottom line that makes it somewhat different from most such institutes. That bottom line: Is there a possibility of something concrete happening as a result of looking at an issue? I am not interested in simply having a fine intellectual discussion. I do not suggest that universities who do that are not contributing; they are, but I want an action-oriented Institute. When we brought Senators Simpson, Danforth, and Pryor to Carbondale and they recommended changes in Social Security that elevated the issue in a bipartisan way with concrete recommendations. We sent those recommendations to members of the House and

Senate and to the White House. I've responded to questions from members of the House and Senate on this, but I'm not getting into the lobbying business. It is too early to say if anything will come as a result of our recommendations.

We brought together a unique gathering of religious leaders to look at the issue of poverty. As a young man I participated in the civil rights movement. Faith groups of every variety came together and said this is a moral issue. Not all of them, but enough so that they prodded our conscience. Poverty is also a moral issue. An unusual, small group gathered, from Imam Wallace Mohammed, the Muslim leader, to radio/television-evangelist Dr. Pat Robertson; from Dr. John Buehrens, president of the Unitarian-Universalist Association to Bishop Marshall Meadors of the United Methodist Church; from Rabbi Jacob Rubenstein, president of the Rabbinical Council of America, to Elder Jose Rojas of the Seventh-Day Adventists.[1] In a two-day session they produced a surprisingly eloquent statement on what government should do and an inventory of what individual congregations should do. The "Statement of Commitment" received only a little attention when it occurred, but it is starting to have repercussions in the far corners of our nation. Rabbi Rubinstein and Dr. Daniel Weiss, General Secretary of the American Baptist Churches, both commented that they had been in gatherings where a diverse group is brought together for public relations purposes, but this was the first time they could remember such a diverse group of leaders actually working together. That in itself is good.

By the time this book is published we will have brought together some key people from around the nation to look at the question of alternative sentencing for non-violent criminals, and community follow-up for those who are released from prison.

That gives you a tenor of what we are doing. In addition to the major symposiums, we also have Idea Exchange lunches, where we invite smaller numbers of experts to brainstorm on an issue of significance. Students are welcome to observe. The Idea Exchange can lead to the larger symposium.

When the University contacted me about heading a public policy institute, they wanted to name the Institute for me. I asked them to defer that honor until and unless we have an endowment of at least $10 million so that the Institute can be genuinely independent. I don't want some anemic entity named for me. I do not want a state legislator, unhappy that we entered some controversial area — alternative sentencing is an example — threatening to cut off funds for the Institute. After I am no longer around, I want the Institute to be independent and effective, fully free to explore the most controversial of issues. Also, if we should find some generous donor who would put up a good portion of the needed money, I want to name the Institute for the person he or she designates. We also are encouraging people to keep us in mind in their estate plans. The first person to do so is Robert Luken of Alton, Illinois. May his tribe increase!

One of the difficult areas that I mentioned in Chapter 17 is campaign financing. Working with Mike Lawrence, former press secretary to our Republican Governor Jim Edgar and now Associate Director of our Institute, I asked the Republican and Democratic leaders of the Illinois House and Senate to each designate a legislator to negotiate a campaign finance reform package. The four — Senator Kirk Dillard, Senator Barack Obama, Rep. Jack Kubik, and Rep. Gary Hannig — worked at it dilligently, with Mike Lawrence lending assistance where needed. Most observers thought we were wasting our time, and I didn't harbor great optimism that it would happen, but I thought it worthy of a try. The result: On the last day of the legislative session the biggest step forward in Illinois in this field in twenty-four years. Until the passage of this legislation it has been legal to use campaign funds to buy your spouse a fur coat, buy a sports car, pay your children's college tuition, or buy a house — all actual examples. That is now changed, along with a number of other restrictions that will give Illinois the opportunity for better government. Credit must go to the four legislators who negotiated this mine field, and to the legislative leaders: Senator Pate Phillips, Senator Emil Jones, Speaker Mike Madigan, and Rep. Lee Daniels. Pate Phillips and Mike Madigan played particularly crucial roles. So did Mike Lawrence and the Joyce Foundation, which made possible the limited funds needed to launch this. Mike played a critical role throughout this endeavor and is a great asset to our Institute. Is the bill that passed everything I would like to see in such a measure? No. Is it a big step forward for our state? Yes. And it illustrates the catalytic role of the Institute for successful policy initiatives.

Not being tied down to a Senate schedule means I can now volunteer. I am on several boards, including three that actually pay me money, something I could not do in the Senate. I'm accepting speaking engagements where I believe I might make a difference, not just entertain people who want to see and hear an ex-senator, like seeing and hearing a two-headed calf.

A speaking engagement I enjoyed came at the invitation of Texas A&M University and former President George Bush to be one of two speakers for the dedication of the George Bush School of Public Service. Dick Cheney, former House member and once Secretary of Defense, was the other speaker. I served as the token Democrat for the occasion. The line that drew the loudest applause came when I suggested that it should have been named the George *and Barbara* Bush School of Public Service. It was great to see many long-time friends, including Dick Cheney who had his office next to mine when we were House members. He has served the nation superbly in several capacities. He now heads the Halliburton Corporation.

U. S. Ambassador to Croatia Peter Galbraith called and asked if I were requested by the Organization for Security and Cooperation in Europe (OSCE) to head a group monitoring the presidential election in Croatia, would I do it? With my affirmative reply, soon the chair of the OSCE, the Foreign Minister of Denmark, extended the invitation and I headed to Zagreb. Croatia, once part of Yugoslavia, is in a region torn deeply by ethnic strife. Too few leaders in the area are appealing to people's nobler instincts. Appealing to fears and prejudice is easy, ignoble politics. We had 113 volunteer observers from twenty-six nations. I met with the two leading presidential candidates, including the incumbent, President Franjo Tudjman. After gathering observations on election night from our team scattered around the nation, I held a press conference in which I called the elections free but not fair, and urged Croatia — which yearns to be part of Western Europe — to move to fully free and fair elections and to get rid of their deep ethnic divisions, both easy for an outsider to say, much less easy to accomplish. Candidates had the freedom to say anything without being jailed or intimidated. But the law permitted campaigning only for sixteen days, a big advantage to an incumbent president who had posters of himself all over the country for purposes ostensibly non-political. On the state television evening news for the first week of that sixteen-day period, President Tudjman received 1,100 seconds of coverage and his principal opponent 16 seconds of coverage. Having an Ambassador there like Peter Galbraith, a non-career diplomat, served our nation well and served the people of Croatia well, even though he was not high on the popularity list of President Tudjman. Peter, an old friend, spoke bluntly about deficiencies there, when a more seasoned career diplomat might have danced around the subject, not wanting to offend anyone. While generally I support naming career diplomats to these posts, at times there are advantages to having an Ambassador who is not worried about his résumé.

I had returned from Croatia only a few days when former President Jimmy Carter asked if I would co-chair monitoring the presidential election in Liberia with him and with former President Sogolo of Togo. I had been to Liberia twice during their civil war and I accepted. Jeanne joined me on this trip, as did Rosalyn Carter. The scars of the civil war are everywhere. Monrovia, the capital city, has no system of electricity or water or sewers. Liberia, founded by ex-slaves from the United States, has more historic ties to our country than any nation in Africa, but we have paid scant attention to their needs. When Samuel Doe overthrew the government and became the dictator, we worked with him as long as our Voice of America facilities remained unmolested. Our disinterest in the people of sub-Sahara Africa has been appalling, nowhere more than in Liberia. The Carter Center has had a small office there for several years, doing good work under difficult circumstances. In contrast to the election in Croatia, in Liberia the election was both free and fair. Military forces from other West African countries have been enforcing the cease fire and maintained order the day of election, and there were no incidents. Polls opened at 7 A.M. About 6:45 that morning President and Mrs. Carter and Jeanne and I drove through the streets of Monrovia, and at every polling place there were 200 to 300 people lined up waiting to vote. They did not have cars or bicycles, but they had motivation. When I asked why they were voting the answers varied, but again and again I heard, "I want peace" or "I'm doing this for my children." Because of the lack of electricity, the polls closed at four in the afternoon. After visiting a number of precincts, we stayed at one to watch them count the ballots. Representatives of the various candidates watched the counting, as they did for the balloting during the day. When I went from polling place to polling place during the voting and saw the judges I would ask, half in jest, "You're not fighting each other are you?" They always laughed and said they were not, yet not long ago they were. When the sun went down they lit candles as they counted the votes. The judges would show each ballot to all the observers. Liberians elected Charles Taylor. We met with him and the other candidates before the election. There were complaints about an imbalance of resources among the candidates for the election, and we assured them we knew another nation that had the same problem! But none of the candidates charged fraud. President Carter, President Sogolo, and I met with the President-elect again when the result became clear, urging him to be inclusive in his government, and to deal forcefully with the problem of corruption that permeates almost any nation that goes through a bitter civil war. One of every eight

Liberians died in the war. President Carter has returned to Liberia one time since the election. Progress is slow. The United States and volunteer agencies need to follow the Liberian scene closely, helping where we can either with economic assistance or investment or simply a guiding hand.

Frequently people ask, "Do you miss Washington?" I miss my friends, though we stay in contact with many of them. Occasionally, as on the tobacco debate, I'd like to be on the floor of the Senate to make a speech. I miss seeing Martin and Julie and my two grandchildren there. We do not see them as often as we formerly did.

But I like being able to tell Jeanne I'll be home for dinner and I know that I can do it. Trent Lott or Tom Daschle or Saddam Hussein or a flood in the Midwest will not alter that. And a change is good.

I'm still writing. Even though I started my career as a journalist, I had no idea I would ever write a book. After my election to the legislature I went to the Illinois State Historical Library and asked for a book about Lincoln's years as a state legislator, the public office he held longer than any other. They told me that no such book exists. I wrote to the two major living Lincoln scholars, Carl Sandburg and Allen Nevins, suggesting that they write a book about Lincoln's legislative service, and they both wrote back saying that I should write such a book. So I did. And I've written seventeen other books, counting three I coauthored. My coauthors were Ross Perot (Chapter 14), my brother Art, *The Politics of World Hunger*; and Jeanne, *Protestant-Catholic Marriages Can Succeed*, written in the pre-Vatican II era.

In addition to writing books, I teach two courses a semester and I do a bi-weekly commentary on the ten NPR stations in Illinois, one of which won an Associated Press prize for commentary. I also write once a month for an Internet magazine called *Intellectual Capital* launched by Pete du Pont, my former House colleague and former Governor of Delaware. I am still somewhat in a fog in the whole world of computers and e-mail and Internet, but the staff tolerates me graciously. And I write op-ed pieces and magazine articles when requested, or when I feel moved on a subject.

The last book I wrote, *Tapped Out: The Coming World Crisis in Water and What We Can Do About It*, is causing a small stir even before its formal appearance. I hope it can help lead us to face this problem, before a series of international crises are upon us. Senator Harry Reid of Nevada is now heading efforts in the Senate to face this issue that

I formerly championed. A capable legislator and leader who understands the water problem, I hope he can generate the support the nation and the world need.

I am sometimes asked which of the books I have written is my favorite. That is like asking which of my children is my favorite. I like them all! But the least read of my books is probably the most fascinating, a biography of Elijah Lovejoy, the Abolitionist killed by a mob in Illinois. Titled *Freedom's Champion, Elijah Lovejoy*, it has received great reviews but limited readership because virtually no one has ever heard of Lovejoy.

I have other requests to do books, and like my speeches I do them where I hope to do some good, not simply entertain.

Jeanne and I are both in good health, play tennis regularly, and sometimes combine work with pleasure. For example, when asked to speak at the annual Santa Fe United Way fund-raiser, I accepted. Jeanne went with me and we spent a few days traveling around that fascinating and stimulating area. A month from now as I type this (yes, type), I will be lecturing in Innsbruck, Austria, for the University of New Orleans, and Jeanne and I will rent a car and take a few extra days in that beautiful area. Last year the old legislative roommates from Springfield days, Abner Mikva, and Tony Scariano and I, along with Zoe Mikva, Leah Scariano, and Jeanne took a week off and traveled to Sicily, meeting no officials, just enjoying the culture and food and each other's company.

Reading a great variety of nonfiction is one of life's pleasures for me. When Jeanne and I get together with our children a vigorous game of Canasta gets my mind away from whatever book or project on which I am working.

However, I remain a workaholic, most satisfied when I am busy. I see so many things that need to be done where I want to contribute. "Time is the most valuable gift any of us has been given, other than good health," I tell my students. "Use it not to watch television 3.9 hours a day as the average American does, but to help others." I try to do that.

I am grateful to you as a reader for taking your valuable time to follow this personal journey, which continues. I wish you well in your journey.

<hr>

[1] Those drafting this statement were Dr. Victor L. Brown Jr., Welfare Services, the Church of Jesus Christ of Latter-Day Saints; Dr. John Buehrens, President, Unitarian-Universalist Association; Reverend Barrett Duke, Director of Denominational Relations, Conferences and Seminars, The Ethics and Religious Liberty Commission, Southern Baptist Convention; Reverend Dr. Richard L. Hamm, General Minister and President, Christian Church; Bishop Leroy C. Hodapp, United Methodist Church (Retired); Reverend Dr. Isaac I. Ihiasota, Rector, Episcopal Church of St. Andrew; Reverend Dana C. Jones, Pastor, Maxwell Street Presbyterian Church; Reverend Yeprem Kelegian, St. Mesrob Armenian Church; Reverend Herbert Martin, Progressive Community Church; Bishop Marshall L. Meadors Jr., Resident Bishop, United Methodist Church, Mississippi area; Imam Wallace D. Mohammed, International Spokesman for the Muslim American Society; Reverend John D. Paarlberg, Office of Social Witness and Worship, Reformed Church in America; Mr. Howard A. Peters III, Secretary, Illinois Department of Human Services; Reverend E. Roy Riley Jr., Bishop, New Jersey Synod, Evangelical Lutheran Church in America; Dr. Pat Robertson, Chancellor, Regent University; Elder Jose V. Rojas, Seventh-Day Adventist Church; Rabbi Jacob Rubenstein, President, Rabbinical Council of America; Ms. Maureen Shea, Office of Public Liaison, White House; Mr. James W. Skillen, Executive Director, The Center for Public Justice; Mr. James M. Wall, Editor, Ecumenical, The Christian Century; Reverend Dr. Daniel E. Weiss, General Secretary, American Baptist Churches; Professor William Julius Wilson, JFK School of Government, Harvard University. Unfortunately, because of committee meetings of the Roman Catholic bishops, none of the Roman Catholic bishops was able to be present, but Roman Catholic leaders have since praised the statement.

# Index

Hayes, Charlie, 179
Haynes, Ulrich St. Clair, Jr., 339
Hayward, John and Muriel, 131
Hazzard, Les, 34
Healey, Joe, 41
health care, 178
Heflin, Howell, 189, 359
Heinemann, Ben, 125
Heinz, John, 143
Helms, Jesse, 182, 202, 207
Helsinki Accord, 148-9
Herbert, Bob, 289
Hickman, Don, 285
*Highland News-Leader*, 80
Hill, Anita, 190-1, 285
Hill, Hugh, 284
*Hill, The*, 195
Hitler, Adolph, 54
Hochberg, Larry, 156
Ho Chi Minh City, 83
Hodge, Orville, 242-3
Hofeld, Al, 202
Hoffman, Russ, 80
Holden, John, 133
Hollings, "Fritz", 73, 205
Holloway, Jim, 127, 128
Hoops, Walter, 60
Hoover, J. Edgar, 21
Horn, Mr. and Mrs. Paul, 56
Howard, Bob, 283
Howe, Neil, 367
Howlett, Michael, 87, 90, 98, 108, 110, 242-3
Hudson, Keith, 191
Hume, John, 273-4
Humphrey, Hubert, 83, 133, 250-5, 258
Hurley, Bill, 70
Hurley, Bob, 70
Hurley, Ira, 70
Hurley, Margaret Reilly, 70
Hussein, King of Jordan, 269, 272-3
Hussein, Saddam, 333-4
Hyde, Henry, 154
Hynes, Tom, 237

Icen, Richard, 90
Illinois Bar Association, 42-4
Illinois Crime Commission, 65-6
Illinois Racing Commission, 45-7
*Illinois State Journal, The*, 61
*Illinois State Register*, 103
Innouye, Dan, 168
Israel, 155-6
Ivins, Molly, 289

Jackson, Andrew, 356
Jackson, Jesse, 210, 212, 217, 221-3, 264
Jackson, Jesse, Jr., 223
Jackson, John, 128, 372
Jacobs, Col. Arthur, 49
James, Kay, 182
Japanese Americans, 20
Jarrett, Vernon, 199
Jarvis, Ben, 28, 29
Jascula, Rick, 91
Javits, Jacob, 203
Jefferson, Thomas, 356-7
Jeffords, James, 205, 340, 341
Jerkins, Jayne, 189
Joan Marie, Sister, 96
Johnsen, Nancy, 45, 177
Johnsen, Paul, 25
Johnsen, Ray, 25, 31, 35, 45, 49, 74, 91, 143, 177
Johnson, Al, 156
Johnson, Lyndon B., 250-1, 356
Johnson, Stanley, 266
Johnston, Don, 266
Johnston, Robert, 108
John XXIII, Pope, 71, 248
Jones, Emil, 375
Jones, Malden, 284
journalism
    ethics in, 284-6, 289-90
    and lobbyists, 286-8
Joyce, Ed, 110, 156
judiciary, 185-93
Juul, Mona, 273

PAUL SIMON served in the United States House of Representatives for ten years and in the United States Senate for twelve years. Earlier, he served in the Illinois House and Senate and as Lieutenant Governor of Illinois before moving on to national politics. During all of his years as a public official, he was known for exceptional constituent service. He holds forty-seven honorary degrees and has written seventeen books. Simon is currently a professor at Southern Illinois University, where he teaches political science and journalism. He lives in Makanda, Illinois, with his wife, Jeanne. They have two children and four grandchildren.